A Farmer's Son

-|-

Autobiography

by

the Rev. Eugene Andrew Lehrke

Copyright 2020

Preface

My inspiration for this autobiography arose from two books which I read in 2017. The first was actually a series of books resulting from a discussion in literary circles about Laura I Wilder's *Little House on the Prairie* series, which I had never read. The debate was whether they reflected authentic history, or were partly myth. Eventually, and sadly, the extended debate resulted in these books now being proscribed as racist -- supposedly demeaning to native Americans. I thought I was somewhat qualified by my own well remembered childhood experiences to judge them. Besides, being well read in American history, I believed I could make an informed assessment. Further, reading them should be interesting if they did provide genuine history. So I've just now read the whole lot even though they are children's books. And there are indeed a few incidents that appear to be larger than life.

An unintended result was that I said to myself, "You have vivid memories of this sort yourself that may be of interest and enjoyable to others." But did I want to saddle myself with another major project? An autobiography? Egotism? My new significant book of theology is just done, with excitement and relief. Isn't it time at age 87 to finally retire. Well, I'm already bored and needing a worthwhile pastime each morning, and cherish the feeling of having made a contribution at evening rest. I can't understand putting a functioning mind out to pasture as sadly happens with many retired.

Secondly, a friend sent me a digital copy of Thomas Merton's autobiography *The Seven Story Mountain,* which I've recently finished. Merton was an author of assorted books, widely praised, a Trapist monk in KY, who died 1968. This particular book is essentially his story of maturing from an irreligious youth to become a firm advocate of the piety of Roman Catholicism and the peace of Trapist silence. It has always struck me that none, or few such autobiographies, tell the story of a religious person who can't remember an earlier contradiction. Surely there are other pious Christians whose story of faith from birth might be inspiring and worth describing. My story may not inspire, but there is no myth involved!

In this attempt, I'll not try to be funny -- I'm satisfied that a good story needs no comic relief. Neither will I use a dialogue format -- I don't always perfectly remember exact conversation, but the substance is not elusive. Rather, I'll recount impressionable and seemingly significant events and experiences as I remember and now understand them. My apologies in advance to Ma and Pa if not everything from my childhood jibes with their now perfect memory; I trust their forgiveness. My three sisters are also monitoring my honesty from heaven, but much of this will be a new vantage to parallel their own pilgrimage.

Chapter 1 -- Old & New House - 1933 -1939

Out of the blue, one Summer Sunday morning in about 1939 when I would have finished third grade, I announced to Ma that I wasn't going along to church. I had no particular reason. Was I exploring the limits within a well ordered and responsible family? It was pure whimsy, not really a devilish feeling -- intentionally naughty. Such would have been recognized and never actually work. Ma was quietly receptive. Though I was subconsciously testing the discipline I had been meekly accepting, I was actually thoroughly comfortable with and happy to be in church every Sunday. Did I think I'd get away with it? No one else in our family of parents and six kids ever stayed home from church, unless it was a blizzard, or if someone was mighty sick -- nevertheless left behind, perhaps even without a nurse. We were a pious and meek brood. We were frequently late and then not allowed to find a pew after the entrance hymn had already been sung till after the first prayer and the congregation was seated for the scripture lessons; But we were dependably in attendance.

Ma didn't say a word. I couldn't believe it. I was getting away with it? And no one else intervened, either to scold or to protest that it wasn't fair. Pa declined to be fatherly since Ma had already mysteriously decided -- they never contradicted or overruled each other; And yet, how was it that I was to be free?

To avoid the swirl of everyone getting dressed in their best church clothes, I went outside, fooling around near the house in the east side yard, absentmindedly doing nothing that was satisfying. It was already unnerving. I sheepishly watched them get into our 1938 dark green four-door Plymouth and leave. I watched till they disappeared over the hill by Rushmeier's farm, a mile and half to the south. Now, what fun could I have? What did I want to do? I had completely forgotten that when we played, we played together. We had few toys, just each other, but an ample farm yard with many attractions. I was alone and feeling somewhat helpless. I'm sure that by the time my family got

5

to church 2.5 miles away, I was thoroughly ill-at-ease. I probably went to stand on the cistern south of the milkhouse, as I and my brothers did so often to watch the Guernsey cows grazing in the pasture and our draft-horses enjoying their Sabbath rest. I surely didn't go to the chicken yard or the hog barn, well possibly even the pig yard. I might have gone into the cowbarn to look for the kittens, but even that wouldn't have been any fun by myself.

Essentially, I waited for my family to come home, an unconscious admission that I didn't function alone. I was a part of them, not whole, all by myself. I couldn't have explained it, but I felt it. I found myself keeping track of the time till they would return. Besides, when I eventually thought of church being over, I wondered who I then wasn't getting to play with in the front yard of the church on the old horse hitching-pipes along the road that served us young boys like a jungle gym. That was an additional connection I had overlooked in choosing to stay home, and which I was then missing. That was the fun part of our intentional weekly connection to God, likewise overlooked and severed.

I was waiting for them when they came home, somewhat concerned for what any of them would say, but no one said a word. They all went into the house to change out of church-clothes. I timed it to when Ma would be back in the kitchen starting preparations for Sunday dinner. She was fortunately alone when I went in, and I said to her in essence, "I'm never every going to do that again." She gave me a motherly smile and said not a word.

I didn't however immediately make a vow to become a pastor. That would come years later after my own various dreams had evaporated, laying bare once again the critical need for connections to family. The possibility of becoming a pastor might have already been mentioned by Pa, but not seriously considered, dismissed in favor of bigger ideas of my own.

The most such a thought of ministry came to me was but in play. Ma had taught me to stand on a "stage" and say, "Ich bin der Herr Pastor. / Ich predige euch was for./ Und wen Ich nicht mehr predigen kann, dann streiche Ich meine Pfeife an." (I am the lord Pastor. I preach something in front of you. And when I can preach no more, then I'll strike-up my pipe.) I wouldn't dismiss that this was my clever Ma's conscious attempt to impress my vocation. She had the requisite mind and faith.

This whole display in play was like a seed, not simply dormant. Its ectoderm had split, visible in our play. I don't remember any sibling ever saying this, as I often did when climbing over and under everything in sight all around the farm yard as a little boy. When finding myself high up on something, I'd often puff out my chest and boldly proclaim, "Ich bin...." They would laugh, and so would I, not consciously meaning a word of it.

My otherwise earliest memory is from what was apparently the Summer of 1935 when I was two and a half years old. I remember watching Ma washing clothes in a tub outside in front of the old house in which I was born. It was only to the additional extent of it being a warm summer day. She was most likely washing by hand since the house had no running water or electricity. That she would have had a gas-motor wash machine is quite unlikely, given our poverty. I was standing or sitting just about where Ma was then standing to take that photo of my two oldest sisters in their Sunday finest several years earlier, in 1929 or 30.

Our old house had been built about 1880 by my maternal grandmother's sister's family. All my life I've been amazed that it was possible for this house to serve our own family with five children at the time, and eventually a sixth. Yet it had served that Fluegel family of 16 children; Although it then had an additional first floor room, the removal of which is evident in the photo.

On the first floor of that 24x15 house, there was only the one room serving as kitchen and living room. In addition it had a narrow pantry across the north side which extended under the stairway in the NW corner. It had no basement. Our lighting was with kerosene lamps. There was a standard wood cookstove with oven and hot water reservoir standing against the pantry wall. (That stove was moved into the new house.) For heat we apparently had a potbelly wood/coal stove in the center of the room, apparently later moved to the milkhouse, replacing a smaller one long lying on the junk pile behind the chicken barn. There was a passive heat register in the center of the ceiling to warm the upstairs bedrooms. Those bedrooms were divided into two by a wall including the chimney. The north smaller room, where I and Walter slept, included the open stairway, and had to be used by my parents and sisters to go to the larger south room in which I had been born. There likewise had been born all of my siblings except for Bernice, the oldest, born in the hospital in New Ulm. I even have a foggy memory of a doctor coming there for the birth of Leslie in late September 1936, my youngest brother, a month or so before we moved out.

I still remember the house very well since it was not raised till Walter did this after I left for university and seminary. When the new house of 1936 was being built on the same location, it had been briefly moved aside till the new house was finished in late Fall, and then removed near the grove of trees to the north, beyond the orchard and vegetable garden. It stood there on stone blocks, its door often wide open but for a screen door, with skunks often living underneath. The windows for the most part remained. It was an obvious place for us children to play, yet never ghostly to us. Although after dark it might have been spooky. It still had an old worn-out couch in the smaller upstairs bedroom on which Walter and I had probably slept.

My second oldest memory probably is from October of 1936 when I was 3 and a half years old. It was in the late forenoon of the day on which our family moved into our new house. The major stir of that event produced the indelible memory of being put out of the way in the SE corner on the new kitchen floor, with the sun streaming in on a cold day, yet being blessedly warm inside. It was exactly where I was thereafter to sit at the kitchen table which had apparently not yet been moved in. I was playing with remnant bits of 2x4, some of them triangular. They were perfectly good building blocks for me, for want of the toy blocks we couldn't afford.

What a blessed new house that was and still is for Walter. We then had a well-insulated four bedroom brick and stucco home with storm windows and hotwater radiators throughout, warmed by a sizable wood/coal furnace in a poured-wall cement basement. That basement space included a large clothes washing area and big table for butchering or laundry, a separate fruit cellar room for preserves, wine, crocks of sausage preserved under lard, etc. There was also a large potato-beet-apple-onion and carrot cellar room with a sand floor. The main part of the basement was big enough to hang up clothes to dry, should the weather be too miserable outside.

The new house had plumbing with flush toilets on both floors with running water from a cistern of rain water under the back entry, and fresh water from the deep farm well. Although there was as yet no electricity till three years hence when the power lines were extended, we had temporary carbide gas lighting in the kitchen, such as we had in the barn and milkhouse, brought in safely with 1/4" iron pipes.

Ma must have in comparison considered herself and us to be in heaven in that new house. She had survived 12 years since marriage in the un-insulated old house with single-pane windows -- in MN!!!. And Pa??? But how had they managed to build this house in the trailing years of the Great Depression? We have no answers other than that labor and material surely were reasonably affordable. Pa had lived in that old house since 1916, at first as a bachelor, and then a few years with his sister, Lydia, as housekeeper, till she was wed.

In the years before Pa had married he had, at any rate, naturally spent most of his time outside and in the barn and fields. Without help on the 160 acre farm he was surely in the house barely to eat and sleep. It speaks highly of Ma that she didn't demand a better house from the start, or at least sooner; Although the Depression had surely made it impossible . That new house was clearly his special love for Ma and us, for which he had anxiously and painfully struggled through the Depression, finally to see ahead to make us conformable.

The barn we had was on the other hand first rate, large enough for eight horses, 20 milk cows and up to 20 heifers. It had been built in 1916 in coincidence with Pa's brother, Fred, getting married to Ma's sister. Grampa Lehrke had then at the last minute decreed that -- he and grandma planning soon to move to Gibbon -- Fred and Amalia would stay on the homestead kitty-corner to the SW from our farm. He had bought our farm from the Fluegel relatives of Ma, which Pa then took over. On that decision hang years of heartache difficult to be sorted, as we'll try.

So as of early Winter 1936, we Lehrkes all finally had a warm bed in our grand brand new house, though I don't remember any bedroom discomfort from the old house. Nevertheless, though perhaps not a memory from that first night in my bed under the east gable of the new house, I distinctly remember a feeling of comfortable bliss in that "boy's bedroom." There is still the fuzzy remembrance of Ma tucking me into bed with prayers, which had to have been from that early time. Walter would have been simultaneously bedded, since I always slept with him till leaving home. It was an old bed with an iron pipe head and footboard, steel rail sides with spring and steel cable network to support a 4" mattress, plus featherbed in Winter. It's quite likely that it was the hand-me-down bed of my parent from the old house. But they surely didn't yet have the nice full bedroom set of furniture of my earliest memory. It was not till much later that Leslie was given his own bed in the NE corner of our room. He had only been a few months old when we moved into the new house.

My three sisters had the south upstairs bedroom, as large as a master bedroom. It must have seemed to them as heaven. Being older, they would have been more aware of discomfort and inconvenience in the old house. Memory doesn't include where they slept in the old house; Surely likely in the bigger bedroom of my parents. It also had only a closet under the eves sloping from four feet tall down to the floor. How in the world had the family who built the house (my grandmother's sister and their family of sixteen) ever managed in that small house?

Strangely, although those bedtime prayer had to have been in German, I now remember them in English. It's also possible that at that early age this prayer was a repetition of my earliest table prayer. Each member of the family prayed their own prayer in succession around the table before each meal. The youngest praying: "Abba; Lieba; Vater; Amen." (Daddy!; Dearest! Father! Amen) True to German culture, Pa is not remembered ever being in our bedroom, unless in later youth there was a fight or too much fun going on. Not that he didn't have the requisite piety to supervise our bedtime prayer. Rather, let this serve as a spiritual image of Pa: Had the devil himself dared to visibly invade any part of our farm, Pa would have grabbed a ready pitchfork and chased him all the way back to Chicago. He was always spiritual and stern with us, particularly if he sensed any evil in the mix.

Understandably, my recollection of home furnishings in the new house are a conglomeration from the years of my early youth. The fine dining room table and eight chairs, seating up to 12, probably came after a few years. But the Victrola phonograph (trade name: Mellowtone) had probably been an earlier gift to Ma, and would surely have been in the living room in the old house. It had then been moved to the spacious hallway between the three upstairs bedrooms of the new house. (It's cabinet now houses my music system in my condo.) Pa did enjoy good music, except for opera, but it was Ma who cultivate in me a love for the classics.

Until our first radio in the early 40s, that wind-up phonograph provided our music, indelibly to be imprinted on me -- a culture from Ma's side of the family which enjoyed this classical art form. Ma herself didn't play an instrument, as a brother and sister did, but she was a lover of good music. The two of us were enraptured together by it. From as early as I can remember we two never failed to

11

listen on early Sunday afternoon's in Winter to the Longenes Symphonette and then the NY Philharmonic during its season. She had about two dozen 78 12" records, which all of us actually often enjoyed cranking out. Every time I now hear Respighi -- *Ancient Aires & Dances*, I remember that phonograph music from my youth. There was also plenty of Tchaikovsky and Beethoven, but fortunately (to me) no Mozart, nor polkas. One record was pure fun for us kids: *The Whistler and his Dog*. We couldn't wait to hear the dog barking out of the phonograph.

Another interesting memory of "music" is associated with Pa's rocking chair and from pre school days. Walter and I were seated side by side one Winter morning deep in Pa's upholstered rocking chair, rocking away and humming. We weren't singing a tune, but modulated from one pitch to another in a steady hum. It was fun to come from dissonance to harmony and back again. Walter never became a singer, while I was always in a choir, from High School and church, to University and Seminary, and now again here at church in Lake St. Louis.

A grand architectural feature of our living room was apparently a special favor to Ma -- a 12 inch deep south bay window fully ten feet wide, made for dozens of houseplants -- most moved outside in Summer. Gloxinias were in their dormant Summer period on a table in our boy's bedroom by the east windows. She was well taught by Grandma Krueger who I remember also kept houseplants, as did all of Ma' sisters. Ma could likewise not abide sitting still. With all the chores, and large half acre vegetable garden, she still had considerable flower gardens all around the house -- proudly shown off to visitors before Goodbye.

Though Pa certainly knew what a hoe was, he was not inclined to gardening, other than planting potatoes with a one-bottom plow in an annually migrating field garden plot. From very young we kids were recruited to place cut sections of potatoes in the furrow for Pa the cover with the next plowed furrow. Walter and I spent many hours in those field gardens, weeding the sweet corn, peas, beans, etc., and of course, the many potatoes -- just as my two

12

oldest sisters had before us. We would often play a game side-by-side of trying to be the first to get to the end of our row. So in that hurry, there surely were a few casualties. All without a straw hat, for which I, but not Walter, am paying for with dermatology $s. How blessed were the rain showers and thunder storms which gave approved relief from the field garden. We would hang up our hoes in the machine shed, and watch the rain off the roof, flooding past the big open door, knowing we were free from the hoeing till another day. Fortunately, I had sisters to help Ma hoe the home garden.

I remember the old house quite well standing forlorn beyond the apple orchard. It stood there like a haunted house till long after I left for university, without even a door and with more than a few broken window panes. We children wouldn't have taken up a dare to enter it after dark, although we played in it regularly by day.

I've often wondered how we did Winter in our uninsulated old house. By 1936 there were five of us children with a sixth on the way in a house that measured about 15 x 24. I can't exaggerate this poverty since my children saw and explored that old house, and I know by my own experience that it had no insulation and built to naturally result in cold floors. The side wall cavity was open to the space between the floors -- called balloon construction, since the thin inside wall with floor boards and ceiling resembled a balloon.

That balloon construction later brought a blessing. When I was about 10, WWII sugar rationing inspired my Pa to try keeping honeybees. However bee culture was in its infancy and so they swarmed without producing a harvest. Fortunately, the swarm found a home in the front wall of our abandoned old house via a small hole five feet up next to the front door. That particular Winter I noticed honey combs under the upstairs bedroom floor by peaking through a hole in the floor that had been the passive air register in the center of the room used to bring heat from the livingroom below with its potbellied stove. Looking

13

sideways through that opening towards the side wall were honey combs, the bees having retreated to cluster back down into the side wall when it got cold.

Without permission I sawed off each floorboard between these two floor joist till I got to the honey comb. And then having a round 30" washpan ready, I cut each remaining floorboard with the combs attached underneath. I filled the washpan to the delight of my parents, forgiving without comment my destruction of the old bedroom floor, as well as any sawdust on the combs. It was beautiful white honey, a full 8" tall and reaching the rest of the 3' length to the side wall.

Our living in the cold MN winters in that house, you must know the relief and thanksgiving we all often felt after 1936 with fully insulated house and a basement coal furnace with hotwater radiators throughout. We kept using feather beds out of habit for a few more years but really didn't any longer need them.

Chapter 2 -- Pa and Ma

My mother, Anna Frieda Krueger, was born on January 20, 1896 in Wykoff MN. Soon thereafter, her family moved to a farm in Moltke Township, Sibley County MN next door to the west of the farm Grampa Lehrke had homesteaded some 25 years earlier. The two families went to the same church, St. Peter's Lutheran, two miles directly south, but apparently were never close neighbors. I believe that they simply didn't share the same philosophy, nor were even of the same piety. (We'll address that in chapter three. For now let's simply note that the Lehrkes were Prussian in spirit while the Kruegers were low Germans. That difference between my parents would become my gift toward moderation.) What brought Pa and Ma together was apparently the romance and marriage of Pa's brother and Ma's sister almost a decade earlier.

What a catch Anna was for my father. Apparently, it was that she was already 28 years old that she chose not to wear white for their wedding on June 9, 1924, but she was nevertheless lovely. I take it that it wasn't because my father wasn't particularly handsome, nor that she felt unloved. It might seem as though Pa took his time to look around, considering that he was already nearly 33 years old. More likely it was that he was a Lehrke, and much too busy on his 160 acre farm where he was hard at work. Perhaps for a while he also felt no need to hurry since his younger sister was keeping house for him; But when Lydia had left the year before, herself to get married, he dared to set aside his plainness, trusted his worth, recognized Anna's potential as reflected in her sister successfully married to his brother, and so he finally thrust caution aside and asked my still lovely mother to be his mate.

Yes, what a catch she turned out to be for him! After three daughters over the first nine years, one might guess that he may have been slightly disappointed for lack of sons to become farm hands, but how could he have complained since his Anna was quite ready always to help as needed in the barn and fields? I wasn't there to witness, but later saw her unstinting cooperation. Not only had Anna been well trained as a cook, gardener and housekeeper, but there was no fault in how she cared for us children, including the supervision of our school homework in which she was quite a taskmaster. She wasn't occupied with her loveliness while it lasted, nor worked desperately to prolong it. Instead she gilded it with a life of contented marital partnership.

I was blessed with being quite close to her, and never sensed a figment of unhappiness for her marriage -- other than the occasional presence in our home of her fatherinlaw, such as during the harvest. He had to be there as the master of the thrashing machine. Besides, though I never witnessed even one public display of her affection for Pa, there was never the slightest suggestion of disharmony in all the years they had together. She never spoke to us of their relationship, but it was telling to note in the odds and ends of memorabilia she left behind, a valentine-like card from Pa which she had pasted into a scrap book. Long after her mate was in the grave, she placed that on the inside back cover, even though several final pages are empty. Doesn't that already tell the real story? It was easy for her to find for meditation. Anyway, they slept together in the same bed to the last.

Pa was always up first in the morning, calling up the stairs to us boys to get going before he left to start the morning farm chores. But Ma was quickly making noise in the kitchen with the stove, doing the part of a snooze alarm till Walter and I got going and followed Pa to the barn. Pa was completely helpless in the kitchen as a result of Ma's being so comfortably in control.. Rainy or wintery days were my frequent occasion to watch and keep her company with her kitchen work -- I noticed and learned without intent. When I became a breakfast cook in my university dorm cafeteria, all I needed to do was visualize how Ma did things in her kitchen.

She was in complete charge of the poultry, other than grinding or buying feed. I suspect that the building of the large chicken barn was her idea for joint venture once they had been married. She cared for 1100 chicks every Spring, 800+ of which were sold live as fryers by mid-July, with 200+ becoming her laying hens. Besides she tended two dozen ducks, herself incubating them under clucks from the chicken barn, and oft times geese, and for a few years even dozens of turkeys. She was in the chicken barn gathering eggs almost as soon as we were out feeding the dairy cows and horses. And then she joined us to milk her 3-4 cows by hand -- the more difficult ones -- until we eventually had milking machines about the time I was in High school. At noon and again in late afternoon she gathered around 200 eggs, deftly extracting them from under a currently sitting hen, without getting pecked, something I never managed. It was like they knew and trusted her.

After the milking was done the cream was separated in the milkhouse to be taken to the neighborhood cream depot at the crossroad east of the church. And the skim milk was carted to the hog barn to be mixed with ground oats as pig feed. Walter and I soon took over in the milkhouse running the cream separator while Pa went to get other things ready for the day. By then Ma and my sisters had breakfast ready so we wouldn't be late to school.

A special experience I'll always remember are the many days Ma and I spent together several years, shocking oats as Pa ran the tractor and grainbinder by himself. Because it was usually hot and the work very hard, we bonded all the more. She never groaned or grumbled, was obviously a long practiced expert with that work, and never with a get-it-done any old way. Clearly she had been at home in the field for years before I came along, demonstrating and working at this with my oldest sisters as well. But she didn't do pigs or horses, only because there was no need, or she might have.

I was blessed both by her example of a responsible work

17

ethic as the best form of loving others, and by her warm spiritual companionship, particularly as that extended into her 80s in a nursing home. And June loved her as much as I. Our regular trips to visit her in Gaylord were consistently a gift to the three of us.

Pa , Andrew Arthur Lehrke (1892-1957), was definitely the son of Friedrich William Lehrke (1861-1946) and Grandma Bertha nee Bulau (1864-1937). The kind of love, discipline and care he dispensed to me and my siblings was quite surely an imitation of that which he experienced with his parents -- Prussian. He took himself seriously, always in control of emotions. Pa regarded us kids with an invisible love, but it was love. I don't remember ever sitting on his lap, or he ever playing any sort of game with us. He was altogether focused on being the best farmer he knew how. Conservation of energy? And he was observably quite good at all he had to do. Aside from that, he guarded his time for rest. He related to us as a teacher of what he knew, and as quickly as he thought possible, or when it became necessary, put us in the harness. Fortunately, I usually caught on rapidly and was rewarded with simple but virtually invisible approval. If criticism was called for, it was usually biting -- When I'd be using a hammer and not holding it by the end, he'd offer to cut the end off to make it shorter, since I wasn't using the whole of it anyway. He quickly turned me loose to proceed, and went to do his own work. There would never be a review with me unless the work was sufficiently unsatisfactory. If there was pride for us, he kept it to himself, probably not even sharing with Ma. In quiet and subtle ways he encouraged me, daring to recognize my potential.

In certain respects, my father was an enigma, i.e., not easily read, and many surely misunderstood him on account of his quiet ways, often simply dismissing him as of no account. I heard it from his own mouth several times, and it may be proper to say that it encapsulated his basic philosophy: "Speech is like silver, silence is like gold." It wasn't that he didn't easily and properly say what was needed for order in

18

our family, and order there was. And there was no problem in my understanding what his opinions were on ordinary issues, yet he didn't occupy himself with thing too great for him -- Psalm 131:1. He knew himself, his limited education and experience, but he was satisfied that he knew what he needed for who he was -- he had no inferiority complex.

Pa was not ready with a word or wisdom, not a conversationalist, no more than small talk with my uncles or neighbors. He had only a 9th grade education, of which he wasn't embarrassed. Diligent service under his father taught him what he thought he most needed to know. I would judge him to have been of average intelligence. It was telling that he valued and considered my views, often boldly offered. I honestly felt loved and approved; nonetheless I was often spanked in anger when I was still young and naughty; I had it coming, but for the anger.

Many times he would, after the fact, and in our quiet retreat toward home, in a few words brush off as pompous what had been said by others in a company -- not analyzing, nor wishing he had said this or that. He regularly had problems, though quietly endured, with outspoken uncles, preferring the company of more gentle ones, like Uncle Martin. So it was also with my mother, his words were few, and that was likely true in their bedroom as well. He read the daily newspaper, yet I couldn't say how thoroughly. He was never by me observed to be reading a book, not even the Bible, and of course there was no TV.

He worked very hard -- no one would have ever called him lazy. He was highly organized, kept things neat in yard and field, appreciated good things in the house, loved my mother for all she was to him and us, and very proud of our new 1936 home. He loved to show off his fields in their prime to frequent Sunday visitors. There was some detectable frustration in not becoming more prosperous like his father had been, or some neighbors; But in humility he would have said that he was content with who and what he was. And he was proud of his children, treating us with hope, mostly impartially with a few pardonable exceptions.

I benefited from special expectations; He genuinely believed in me, even often asked for and trusted my understanding.

His spirituality might have been hard to read on account of his quiet nature, but I sensed it readily, and particularly in retrospect. Of note, and admittedly indirect, was a very open early wish for me to become a pastor. I was quite soon said not thought to belong on a farm -- explained and justified by my hayfever. He himself had hayfever and sympathized with mine. Without saying it, there was brother Walter, who was also strong and dutiful, he was to be the farmer.

His gentle nudging continued when it would have been time for me to go to prep-school with its pre-ministerial curriculum at Concordia, St. Paul MN. That instead of public high school, but I declined. He was also quiet when I elected the UofMN and premed. Pa faked some satisfaction, but when premed inorganic chemistry did me in for lack of proper high school science and math, he was quietly ecstatic when I announced that I had been accepted for enrollment at seminary.

He beamed those 600 miles to Springfield IL, and to admission professors at seminary when presenting me. We even stopped to visit a cousin in route to show me off as his offering to the church. I was his gift of thanksgiving to his Lord. Again when I was ready for internship, though he had heart trouble all summer, he and Ma took me to my plumb assignment in a west suburb of Chicago -- also with the sense of offering. And still again on completion of internship, Pa and Ma came to hear my final exhibition of proficiency; So fortunate since he then at least got to meet my fiancée. He strung life out into that Fall. Hospitalized, I not knowing that he was near death, he died early in the morning, 10-3-1957. He mysteriously came to me postmortem. As was typical of him, he blessed me wordlessly in a vivid dream of presence which was interrupted by the dean at my seminary dormitory door with the news. I've always cherished that dream as the golden silence of his love. That all may seem to be more about me than Pa, but it speaks more concretely about him than other generalities I could offer. I'm at peace about my father because there never was a question of his vital spirituality.

Andrew was his name, and quite appropriate, since it fit with his strong masculinity; The name basically means, man -- the Greek form of the Hebrew Adam, also meaning, man. Unfortunately I know little of the terms, conditions and experiences of his childhood and his relations with his siblings. What I know quite well is the relationship he had with his father, who was around till I was 13. He was frequently at our farm, particularly late Sunday afternoons. Pa always expressed a ready deference to my Grampa. (He lived for a short time with our family after Grandma died -- soon after our moving into the new house. Consequently, we regarded the west bedroom as his. Ma however frequently grumbled about Grampa in general terms and was known to thoroughly dislike him, yet never to my observance openly hostile with him.) My father never spoke an ill word or like emotion of Grampa in our presence. It's unlikely, however, that he defended him with Mom in their privacy. It really was a similar kind of Prussian relationship which he had with Grampa that I later had with Pa, and which I anticipate that I would have had with him had he lived beyond my mid 20s -- obedience and open respect.

The significant difference was that Grampa was intellectually superior to Pa, while I had this as an advantage with Pa, and he generally respected me for it. Which is not to deny Pa's incredible common sense and apparent ability to profit from Grampa's teaching. Unfortunately, although Pa understood old-style farming better than most, and was not lazy at it, he never did make the transition to modern agriculture. He did come to use tractors when I was still quite young, but his spirit was with his Belgian and Percheron draft horses. This was the mode of farming that his father taught him.

21

In portraying Pa's spirituality, it's naturally in relation to myself. He was a Prussian in upbringing, so matters of his own faith were not freely discussed. Still faith was virtually transparent to us, and dependable signified with a humility which directly belied hypocrisy. I remember only one brief theological discussion, and this from my teen years. He objected to the words, "we glorify you [O God]" as it was phrased in the Gloria in the new English hymnal. He couldn't understand how we had any power by mere words to add glory to God who already has all the glory. That's as much as he said, and I was left to defend the hymnal and the traditional liturgy. I tried, not knowing if my explanation was accepted, not being followed with discussion.

On Sunday morning Pa sat in the west part of the balcony with the other older men. Confirmed boys and unmarried young men sat in the east balcony, separated by the choir pews in front of the pipe organ. Downstairs, the women sat on the west side with young girls at the very front where their conduct was monitored by all and addressed later at home. Other younger men sat on the east side with their wives, with the unconfirmed boys up in front where they dared not act-up lest they be reprimanded on the spot, even by the pastor. Also at times reinforced with the mother taking a seat in a usually empty pew directly behind, after a pinch of the ear. (Is this the tradition behind the now empty front pews?)

Pa was generally quite satisfied with my work ethic but owing to my serious hayfever condition, and then particularly after my confirmation, he gently suggested my becoming a pastor. It indirectly showed his deep spirituality to give up his first son -- although he did have two more to become farmers. I brushed this encouragement aside, but I can be sure that he prayed about it consistently. He was possibly proud of my announced intention in late high school to become a doctor, yet I was never accompanied by him to the U of MN for enrollment and attendance. I went by bus on my own.

22

Pa's emotions were plain though quiet when I announced that I was accepted at the Springfield seminary. My grades, especially chemistry, were obviously not good enough to be admitted into medical school -- straight A provided the only chance. I had decided on applying to seminary on the basis of a supernatural vision which I decided wasn't advisedly and humbly to be shared, leaving my family generally mystified. At first my siblings were decidedly unsupportive. But my father was unquestioning and immediately made plans to escort me to the seminary. It was with the solemnity of making an offering that he accompanied me to IL, with Walter to help drive back home.

Throughout seminary years, we never discussed my studies. His ninth grade education didn't allow him to do so, and our Prussian emotions also didn't allow for it. But when I was to begin my internship at Glen Ellyn IL, Pa and Ma took me in spite of his not yet being fully recovered from a serious heart condition. Again it was an act of offering, proud of what they had brought. And so again, on the last Sunday of my internship, they were present to savor the moment even though I was not going home with them, remaining to work at Kraft Foods, Chicago, for that Summer. There was the additional attraction of meeting my fiancée.

Pa's sense of discipline, reflects both on him, and was in turn reflected on us six children. He was mostly a no-nonsense Pa. Once on a nice Summer day when older sisters had prepared for us to eat our noon lunch outside, he stubbornly took his plate back to the kitchen table, this even though a "picnic" lunch was often served at work out in the field to save time. He was all work, his diversion was resting. Sunday afternoon visiting with relatives was however done in a completely relaxed mood.

I mostly avoided his ire by being dutiful and busy enough to satisfy him with my chores, or field work. Sister Jan had a problem with that, as she admitted. When I left for university, she decided to leave as well for Minneapolis for

23

a job with Ma Bell. She was done with being an unpaid hired hand. Fortunately I was strong and didn't easily tire; already by high school I was fully grown and a fit 190 lbs. That meant that I was as big as he, and early on no longer subject to corporal punishment. But it was my safety that I was never prone to sass my parents, as sister Jan admitted she had. But I have one painful memory as an early teen of goofing off when he had gone to town. He came home to find the big drive belt that had been used to run the burr-mill for grinding feed not yet rolled up and put away. Possibly it was because he had been to the bank regarding financial problems; He was in a bad mood and my goofing off resulted in a nasty spanking. Thankfully such punishments were usually reasonable, never otherwise arbitrary.

As a young boy, spankings were quite routine as a lesson, also by Ma. One benefit was that lack of honesty was early on impressed on me as being a stupid tactic. I soon learned that my lies were always found out and resulted in greater punishment; Having apologetic honesty, was then often rewarded with a mere reprimand.

Pa always wanted things nice, and we did have a farm to show -- the weed-free and healthy crops, the neat and prosperous looking well-painted farmyard of outbuildings etc., were his pride and joy. He radiated when we had visitors, with grand tours of the whole farm. Perhaps living in that dreadful old small house till 1936, gave birth to a hunger for more class. He had somehow learned that quality was a better buy, but it also was his undoing in countless later instances. That grand 1936 two-story brick four-bedroom home was genuinely appreciated, but was far more quality than any neighbor had, or was even found in town. I have no idea how he financed this with six kids at the tail end of the Great Depression -- theft wasn't a possibility. Then there was also the 1948 Buick Roadmaster with fluid-drive -- a poor choice of excessive quality when a Plymouth had served well, and others drove Chevys. Likewise, he had to have an expensive wire-tie

John Deer bailer, when cheep custom bailing was the way most still did things. At the end of his time as a farmer, he passed on a burdensome mortgage on the farm to son, Walter, the result of small income and the heavy cost of transition from horse machinery to mechanization in the boom times after WWII. (150+/- eggs/day?, cream from the milk of 20 cows?, but no cash crops? Only a few dozen feeder pigs or steers per year.) He had been in a subsistence mode of farming most of his years, and done things the old hard way long enough. Grampa was no longer looking over his shoulder, he was physically wearing out from hard work, wanting some "quality" in his ending years. He died at only 68, but he had already outlived his age. Eternal rest grant him O Lord!

As I have said, Pa was all work and no play; and I say this in the best sense of the word, even though I might have enjoyed more play. I imagine therefrom having "richer" memories. He understood his lordship over the cows, chickens, horses, hogs, etc. These couldn't fend for themselves, and mercy demanded obedience to this given, not chosen, work. From morning to night, he was the model of diligence.

Yet, he accepted the understanding that he didn't run his own world, in that he obeyed the Sabbath, for him transferred to Sunday in Christian fashion. Animal chores of course began and ended that day as well, but the between time was for him a time of worship and rest. Not even in harvest time was this violated. The only exception in memory was one time when we hauled hay on Sunday morning and all afternoon, never even went to church. For that, we all slunk, wishing we could be invisible, like self-condemned sinners, hoping that no cars would drive by to see us distrusting God on account of the predicted bad weather.

After Sunday dinner around noon, he would nap in his big rocking chair if visiting relatives wasn't on the agenda. Otherwise, the afternoon might include the play of wandering through the yard and fields, not really to take

25

stock, or setting an agenda for the week, but to wonder and marvel, worshiping for what had been given into his hand and the strength to do. I know this from delightedly tagging along on the inspection / show accorded to Sunday visitors. Not that there was any God-talk, we were all good Prussians, after all -- perhaps still are. I could simply feel the deference to the divine operation in which he felt privileged to share. It was a silent faith, but golden.

Laziness or an industrious spirit doesn't I believe come to us in the genes. If I can claim that I'm not lazy by nature, then it most likely was taught by example; And I had the good fortune of faithful parents. My father was by the time I was old enough to notice, already more than half worn-out. By age 14, when he was only 55, I seemed twice as strong as he. Still, though easily tired, he never let up till supper time, other than a half hour rest after dinner at noon. An image of him, the strength and significance of which will never fade, dates from when I was home from seminary the Summer before my internship. Though other animal chores had been passed to others, he had relieved Ma from her customary evening chicken chores. The ground feed grain was still carried in five gallon pails from the granary, two at and time. I can still see him sitting down to rest on top of a pail, not more than 100' from the granary. He probably rested once more at the chicken fence gate by the barn, half the remaining distance he still had to carry the feed.

It was industriousness that most likely had Pa become a mixed farmer, raising some of all the common crops as well as keeping all the ordinary farm animals. He didn't have peacocks or goats, nor raised wheat for sale, but did raise nearly everything else. Most everything he grew was as feed for his animals. The mix of it all made it interesting as well as always providing something to do. There was never a dull moment, which is how he wanted it, even when he was tired.

I too found such mixed farming a constantly interesting way to live, though I would have been happier if we hadn't

26

raised chickens. They were nice as chicks, but once they were chickens, I could do without. Every Spring an order for 1100 chicks was place with Raeder's Hatchery in Sleepy Eye MN; and usually they unbelievably came by the mail. It was high excitement to get home from school and quietly sneak into the brooder house so as not to frighten the cute 2-3 day old chicks. They were sheltered by a 5'x5' metal brooder hood with side curtains almost touching the straw on the floor, with light bulbs for warmth. That was encircled by the 12" wide drive belt on edge, ordinarily used to grind feed, used as a fence to prevent the chicks from getting chilled far from the brooder.

Eventually the young chicken were allowed to run free in their eastern part of the fenced farm yard. This made for an endless vigil and chasing chickens out of the house yard and gardens when they somehow got out. I fortunately escaped chicken chores except for the weekly barn cleaning and manure hauling. Once they had wings to flap and raise dandruff and manure dust, they were too unpleasant. There was nothing I hated more than to clean the chicken barn every Saturday morning through the Winter. I would rather have had to muck the cow gutters for twice as long, or be forever tending the draft horses -- my primary assignment.

A nightly ritual in Summer, once it was nearly dark, was to shake the young chickens out of the trees where some would fly to roost. It was not considered safe till all chickens had been herded into their brooder house and the door carefully locked. Foxes were legendary but rare; skunks were always around but the chickens were not their prey; mink and weasels were more of a proper concern but they too were not that common and they wouldn't have caught chickens roosting in a tree. But I was an obedient kid, though I had older sisters who delighted in frightening me about boogie-men out there in the semi-dark with the roosting chickens.

With such a farm background I was amazed in my first parish after ordination in Sask.. For whatever reason, few of those farmer members any longer kept any animals. I worked a six day schedule, but those members seemed to have heavy duty only for a few weeks in Spring to sow their 1000+ acre fields and then again for a month of so in the late Fall to combine the wheat. Otherwise, they went to have coffee in town, played games like curling, watched their kids playing hockey at the arena in town, or went to Mexico for the whole Winter. That to me didn't compute. I wonder if things are even worse now with their oil wells? Not that I really envied them, unless I was tired.

Pa was a patriarchal Prussian. We six children "bowed", and my mother was his grateful wife. Their relationship would have made a modern feminist scream. But by my firsthand observation and years of consideration, I have concluded that God judged them to have been deeply in love and satisfied -- what else is desired? I see them now holding hands every day, marveling to each other what by God they helped each other to do and endure for the realized glory of their family.

At table I sat immediately to Pa's left, directly across from Ma, no better place to witness their wordless conversation and relationship. Till I left for university, I never saw a cross glance between them, nor heard a disrespectful word in either direction. A few years after I left home Ma had a heart attack from the emotion of being asked to cosign for a large mortgage on the farm, obviously due to Pa's poor dealings. But her emotion was not, I trust, directed against Pa, rather for shock of seeing their true financial state, having lived in the bliss of assumed family prosperity.

Pa and Ma's visible love was all about each one of them doing a fair and fitting part in raising our family. It was mostly wordless cooperation schooled by years of dedication and devotion. Such was the routine of their love. It varied by the season of the year, such as Pa taking time to plow the garden before going to his field work, and Ma then raking the clods and planting the seeds, or later hoeing. She didn't by my time directly help with thrashing or making hay or filling silo, since that was with multifamily cooperation, with Pa's machine and tractor.

She had plenty to do making meals for the workers. But she had her own well-worn denim jacket hung proudly alongside of Pa's outside-clothes by the back door. They lived comfortably together for each other, and for us, the fruit of their love. They hardly needed to bother with valentines.

I have a sense that my own spirit is an amalgamation of those of my parents. Theirs in turn were quite different of each other. Each reflected the dominant spirit of one of their parents, not a noticeably amalgamation. I fortunately had sufficient personal experience with these elders to make that judgment. Pa had parents of which Grampa was so dominant that one saw in Pa virtually nothing of Grandma's personality. She was apparently so passive that Pa reflected Grampa. And what I saw in that father and son, I have come to loosely label as Prussian. By this I mean an authoritarian attitude, highly self confidant, almost arrogant. My mother, on the other hand, derived her spirit primarily from her mother who was incredibly humble and kind. And her father was much in the same spirit, but apparently stood in Grandma's shadow according to the spirit. We will come back to that maternal family shortly.

Regarding Grampa Frederick Lehrke, perhaps you will be able to discern after reading the following, and then also my next chapter about Great Grampa, how Grampa was a unique and even stronger spirit compared to his father. His father, Gottlieb, had nonetheless courageously struck out from home, crossing an ocean with a new wife, brother, half-sister and neighbors to live with friends and relatives in a new land. However, Frederick, his son, went essentially alone into Indian country in 1882 in western MN to claim 160 acres of farm land by planting ten acres of trees on a desolate largely swampy prairie. After having built a house with lumber brought from 75 miles back home by horse cart, he returned home two years later to be married and to bring a wife with him to the edge of civilization. There were only a dozen others living in sod huts or shacks in all of Moltke township, Sibley County, at the time. I judge him to have been brave, but significantly also of above average intelligence. And in particular, he was exceptionally self confident. And it was that success, far beyond that of his father, which afforded his proud, not particularly humble bearing.

Grampa Lehrke was not easy for me to come to know for reason of that spirit. He found it difficult by my time to relate to children and teens, such as I was by the time he died. His success in his vocation of farming is well recorded. He didn't write to tell about it, other than via a regional newspaper interview championing him as a notable pioneer, in which interview Grampa seemed to strut. After only twenty years on the prairie, he had managed to come to own 400 acres -- two full sized farms according to those times. He then retired after 35 years, moving to town where he built a large house. Those years had also been far from kind. He had lost three of his eight children in the prime of youth -- Emma, his first, to diphtheria at four, Albert to diabetes at eight, Adolph to ruptured appendix at 23 -- being the oldest son and primary farmer heir. And Grandma Bertha had long been an invalid from diabetes, dying ten years after they moved to Gibbon MN.

All that aside, with his Prussian spirit, he unfortunately had no interest nor felt any responsibility toward us and me. It was as if he considered us kids to be of no significance to himself. With Pa being by that time his apparent closest and dearest kin, why were we never loved or favored? We considered him mean because of his coldness. (During one extended Summer visit, I leaned a nail against a tire of his green Plymouth coup out of spite. He must have backed up first.) And then there is the sad matter of his son Fred, who was buying the homestead from him after he and grandma moved to town, but Fred then dying from TB and diabetes at 35, leaving a family of five. That family was unsympathetically abandoned by him with the debt intact, left for others to help redeem. Grampa was at the time clearly proud of Pa, who had gotten our farm (either as a gift or loan) -- although having served without other reward. So why were we apparently "nothing" to him? For example, I unforgettably remember him from when I was possibly six, gruffly scolding Walter and me, as he typically did, for wrecking our shoes by playfully and loudly clomping around on the hard ground of the chicken yard north of the barn. We had fastened empty lye cans by stepping on them, crimping them to the instep.

Grampa lived a while with us in the new house after Gramma died in 1937, when I was four, a funeral I remember, even meeting her the previous Summer -- Pa had taken me and Walter along to town and then stopped in briefly to see Gramma. Grampa used our west guest bedroom in the new house. (It suggested that he had possibly given a loan towards the house construction.) These visits were a great ordeal for Ma who couldn't tolerate his harsh coldness to her -- possibly related to his disregard of the Krueger family for their more moderate means and ambitions? I remember Ma's moodiness when he was visiting, muttering to herself in agitation. It came to irk her, for simple example, that Grampa required a separate portion of potato salad, without onions. (Such was our typical Sunday supper, often served with cold ring bologna, or our own summer sausage. For these suppers I was bumped from my seat at the table to Pa's left.)

He was always on hand during oat thrashing time, also when he later lived in Stewart -- with his widowed sister. He was the indisputable chief engineer of our old wooden thrashing machine -- one he had probably himself used all his life. He meticulously tuned and repaired that machine with its many belts and gears for a week or more of preparation. I once was called on by him to crawl inside of it to make some adjustment. At least I consented and succeeded. We thrashed together with a neighbor at the time, but never with Aunt Molly. To these expeditions I begged to go along when still quite young, offering to level out the grain in the receiving wagon. "Why should they need to feed a little child besides?" But Pa was willing, so I got to go -- a rare difference of opinion between them.

Strangely, Grampa didn't help with the farm chores when he visited, also when on extended stay. Particularly, never with the milking, which was Pa's main effort; Apparently he wasn't into dairy. He however considered himself a master of horses. After I had started school and was in

32

charge of the horse barn, I was at times pleased for his brief day visits, he having already done my evening horse barn chores of mucking out the stalls, etc. Yet, I never recognized this as being done as a favor to me. It was never mentioned. I wish he could have loved us so that we could have believed it.

Regarding Grampa Franz Krueger, of which Ma later on at times spoke and wrote to me as the one to whom she was entrusting those memories, let's just call him plain. He had been born somewhere in WI but then grew up in Wykoff MN. He had only briefly attended school -- Ma said, only half of a year -- as a result of his father's debilitating alcoholism. He and his mother Caroline took over the work of farming, forming a compatible partnership, over against the disinterest of other siblings. She was highly talented in all the arts of pioneer life in house, barn and field. She was the local saint in any time of neighborhood need. She then died when Grampa was a teen and his father married a widow with some children. Eventually, Grampa Krueger married my saintly Grandma Marie Emilie from the large and hardy Erdman family; And after having four children, including Ma, they moved to Moltke Township, Sibley County, next door to the west of the Lehrkes. They did well enough for themselves on that farm. It had better soil than SE MN, but not the best of Moltke since it was lower wetter land. This is obvious from the fact that the county ditch eventually ran through their farm.. That neighborhood was apparently chosen by them since the family of Grandma's sister, Helen Fluegel, already before then owned what eventually became Pa's farm; This farm, Grampa Lehrke bought when the Fluegel family's mother, my great-aunt, died and the father, August Fluegel, wanted to move back to Wykoff.

Ma was embarrassed to tell me of her grandfather's alcoholism, but found it possible by reason of her pride in how her father had nevertheless responsibly matured, overcoming that significant handicap. So in a letter, she briefly related how her grandfather, F.W., had become

33

addicted: He was in the German army, in a special division of the Kaiser where the drinking began. He was wounded in a war, and when it ended, he declined the Kaiser's special request to stay. He rather immigrated to America. Where he found his saintly wife had been forgotten. He first tried farming in the St. Joseph MO area, but the soil was stony and poor, and he had no aptitude for farming. The family soon moved to WI, and then to Wykoff MN. A better farm didn't solve the lack of aptitude, and addiction progressed.

I didn't really get to know my Grampa Franz Krueger very well; he is from first memory a frail and already worn-out farmer, nearly blind, though only in his early 70s. I never saw him walking, always only quietly sitting, holding a cane. They lived less than a mile away, so Grandma often walked to our home for the day. I remember her as kind and saintly. Grampa would then come to bring her home with their car in late afternoon, once driving into the ditch on the way home by reason of poor eyesight -- I still remember exactly where it supposedly happened. I on occasion walked to their house and was generously received, during which I remember her baking bread and Grampa sitting by himself in a dark room. We had inconsequential brief conversations in German. I once went to visit him with a cousin when the extended family gathering was at our home, and he had stayed home alone. By then he was totally blind and ask who was there. I replied in German, "It's me." But he failed to recognize my voice He died when I was 14, while Gramma lived to meet my three children. After I left home she migrated a month at a time between her children's family homes including mine. She unbelievably attended my wedding in far off Chicago. By then she was already almost 90. I took that as affection, as well as an expression of piety, holy pride that I was soon to be ordained.

What had brought my Lehrke and Krueger parents together to precipitate my family was not simply that they were next door neighbors, as mentioned in the previous chapter.

34

Rather, it was that Pa's brother, Fred, had married a
Krueger daughter, Molly. With that relationship in place,
Pa met Ma, a sister of his new sisterinlaw. Eight years later
Ma and Pa were married to link these families a second
time. However, that linkage never resulted in a warmer
fellowship between my two grandparent families.
Eventually this carried down into the next generation.
There was an unfortunate and poorly understood
estrangement that arose between my family and the family
of Pa's brother and Ma's sister, apparently involving the
probate of Grampa Krueger's estate, but also the old matter
of Grampa Lehrke's two farms.

Besides Grampa Lehrke's original 160 acre tree claim
homestead, he had a few years later added an 80 acre parcel
to the north -- railroad land, purchased at $8 per acre (a
government grant indirectly to finance railroad
construction.) Then soon after the death of my Great Aunt,
Carolyn Fluegel, at the birth of her 16th child in 1904,
Grampa Lehrke bought that farm at $40 an acre from
August Fluegel who wished to return to Filmore County. It
was kitty-corner to the NE across the Moltke - Grafton
County line, the farm on which I grew up.

The estrangement began and then grew over the next 25
years in the wake of Fred and Molly's marriage in 1916.
The story is that Fred and Molly came home from their
honeymoon to find that they were not, as expected, to live
on the Fluegel farm, but on the homestead; And Pa had
moved to the Fluegel farm. Grandpa had apparently made a
unilateral decision which did actually make some sense. Pa
and Fred and Grampa had been farming the entire 400 acres
together. Now Grampa was planning to retire to town
where he did build a house into which he moved the
following year. The two farms were to be divided between
Fred and Pa. Meanwhile, he and Gramma were to stay in
the house on the homestead along with Fred and Molly,
possible even the younger sister Lydia. It was a big house
that Grampa had built there some years after the first
homestead house. It could be divided with Fred and Molly

in one part and Grampa and Gramma in the other. And there was a barn -- now older but well built and still serviceable.

The Fluegel farm to which Pa had moved apparently had no barn at all, and the house was old and tiny, uninsulated and without basement. Perhaps Grampa considered bachelor Pa up to the privation in that house. It was probably unexplained compassion to have the newly weds in a decent house. (We're not sure if Pa was asked to pay for his farm -- probably so; But Fred definitely was required to pay for the homestead. Grandpa had no other pension plan. Perhaps Pa managed to quickly pay his farm off since he was single, worked hard and saved. This, while Fred soon was handicapped with his TB and diabetes, along with the expenses of a growing family.)

What surely heated emotions from the start was that Pa (with Grampa's help?) then in 1916 built a beautiful modern dairy and horse barn on the Fluegel farm that same Summer after Fred and Molly's wedding. It was according to the latest style: a hip-roof for a larger haymow with a center hay carrier. The dairy part had concrete floors and gutters, and modern stanchions for 20 cows, even watering cups plumbed from the farm well. The horse barn was large enough for four teams. There were few better barns around.

At the same time there was something inexplicable about Grampa's relationship with his son Fred and my Aunt Molly. (Was it long term antipathy toward the Krueger's or was he dissatisfied with Fred's work or attitude?) Other than selling them a farm and home on presumably generous terms, there is no indication that he held his son and wife dear. And then tragedy slowly descended with the erosion of Fred's health. When he died twelve years later in 1928 of TB and diabetes, as the Great Depression began, Grampa Lehrke's empathy for this family apparently died as well. Uncle Fred left five children aged ten and under. Without support from the extended Krueger side of the family, they wouldn't have survived. Apparently, the childless Uncle Martin and Aunt Ida, Molly's sister, redeemed the mortgage, or gave a loan to make payments. Besides, Grampa and Gramma Krueger, by their nature brought spiritual and physical support as their moderate means allowed.

Can we excuse Pa and Ma for apparently doing no more than renting Molly's excess acreage? They did have their own significant struggles, living in our old miserable house compared to the far better house that Molly and cousins called home. And our family wasn't unscathed by the Depression.

This all is witness that my widowed Aunt Molly and five cousins living on the Lehrke homestead were in a closer relationship with my Krueger grandparents. And these cousins, since they were somewhat older, got to know Grampa Krueger far better than did I and my siblings. That's because he had in a sense adopted that family in their virtual abandonment. He apparently sympathized, having had the same handicap -- poverty for lack of a father to lead and care. Apparently Grampa Krueger assisted them even with the business and finances for this daughter and her children.

When Ma's brother Emil took over the Krueger farm, Grampa and Gramma moved in with Aunt Molly since it was a large house -- built by Grampa Lehrke some years after he had homesteaded. He had built the first smaller house I still remember standing alongside. They each had their own section of that fairly new house. That arrangement surely was to help this daughter's family in their poverty. Several large Krueger family celebrations are remembered to have been held there, including their 50th wedding anniversary. (Years later, that house again served two families when Sigmund and family lived there separately from Aunt Molly.)

Wilmar, the youngest of that family, related to me an incident he witnessed, illustrating that relationship: This being from the depth of the Great Depression. Pa was renting the 80 acres of that farm which was directly across

37

the road to the west from our farm, it being too much for that family to care for -- having no adult male farmers. At grain thrashing time, Grampa Krueger and Aunt Molly's boys showed up with a wagon to haul home the equivalent of the rent that was owed for those 80 acres. Wilmar tells it as if this was a forcing of the issue regarding an injustice, also including back rent. This happened before I was born, and true enough, the Depression lingered long for all farmers. But that Pa -- knowing his spirit as well as I did -- would have intentionally withheld rent even because of his own poverty, is totally unthinkable.

Nonetheless, this had to have been a bold confrontation with my Grandfather Lehrke who had abandoned this family and was now running that thrashing machine. Furthermore, it witnesses to the desperation of Aunt Molly's family in their poverty, to have been so forward. Picture it: Pa, who was ultimately in charge of the harvest, allowed this confiscation to proceed on the principle of rights, however irregular, with Grampa Lehrke obliged to stand aside. Pa's ordinary deference to his father had the limits of his own integrity. However, it also shows Grampa Krueger's strength.

Consequently, until I was a teen, there was no commerce or fellowship between my family and Aunt Molly's. The only very strange exception was that Cordula, Molly's oldest, became a godmother for brother Leslie at his baptism in 1936. Our family was never invited to the procession of weddings in that family until that of Wilmar, the youngest. I still remember being at home and hearing the festivities of Cordula's wedding reception from afar. And Sigmund, the oldest, wasn't respected as a farmer by Pa, who actually only observed his work by driving past.

Finally the ice was broken one Sunday after church. I, at about the age of 10-12, was already in the car when I saw Ma and Aunt Molly in conversation; They were standing directly in front of our car by the east side of the church. I was mystified and hopeful, watching these sisters finally acting as sisters, but hearing nothing and not later daring to ask. Thereafter, there was at least limited intercourse. I never at the time understood what had been the issue. Pa then eventually began hiring Marina's husband, who had built and lived on the 80 acre parcel across the road from us, to bale hay and straw for us. Later from the time of being in High School, Sigmund regularly picked me up for weekly Men's Choir rehearsal at church. He found it impossible to be anything but cheerful.

After one rehearsal, Sigmund needed to go to town to pick up something, even though the roads were treacherous. On our return from town, at the curve by the Kramer farm, Sigmund couldn't hold with the curve and was pulled or slid into the ditch. He never let up on the accelerator. He just drove furiously for a short way in a ditch with several inches of snow and back up onto the road. Then he laughed boisterously with me for the good fortune. He had a bit of the Krueger spirit; And he didn't regard his 16 year advantage over me to matter. How blessed I'd have been by more of this cousin.

I do remember Aunt Molly well. Understandably, her life of loss and privation created a sober personality. There is no smile on her face of my remembrance. To crown her life, her daughter Marina and husband were both killed together in an auto accident, leaving three small children. These my aunt took in and raised in her portion of that large house Grampa Lehrke had built; Sigmund and family were living in the other part. She outlived Ma; Was even at Ma's funeral on the near backside of an early Winter storm which could have been her excuse, as it sadly was for many.

Wilmar is also the source of an awesome incident involving his family and Grampa Krueger one Christmass Eve about 1930. Knowing horses well, it is to me fully believable and beautiful. He and Gramma had come to take this family to church with a horse drawn farmer's work sleigh on which a grain box was customarily fixed for Winter travel. In it straw had been loaded as a mattress; Hot bricks warmed on the kitchen stove were wrapped, and many horse blankets had them bundled together in the sleigh box. They got to church just fine, and the horses were possibly sheltered in stalls in the barn north of the church. (Some of these were still there when I went to school in the 1940s. We often played in them, much favored for hide&seek.) But by the time the worship had ended, the area had been engulfed in a raging blizzard. Grampa bundled his extended family into the sleigh, started the horses on their way, tied up the reins, and himself crawled under the blankets with the family. When the horses came to a stop, they had faultlessly traveled the two miles into the teeth of the storm and were standing by Grampa's K's barn door.

Our horses did something similar one Summer evening, with me at the reins, during oats thrashing at our neighbor's farm. After a day of work and supper for our whole crew, I was to drive the team home with the wagon. The team paid no attention to my will. They trotted at full speed for home, turning into our driveway on their own, actually cutting the corner so short that the wagon clipped the ditch. They didn't slow or stop till we arrived at the gate by the horse barn. There I unhitched the wagon, drove them to the watering tank in the cow yard, then back to the horse barn door. There I disconnected their reins, allowing them to find their own stall, to be unharnessed for the night.

Chapter 4 -- Great Grampa Gottlieb Lehrke

The west upstairs bedroom in our 1936 new house became
the family library in the sense of a place for dictionary,
encyclopedia, atlas, photo albums, etc. I spent a surprising
amount of leisure time there beginning at an early age,
accompanied at first by my older sisters. The room
included a large roll top desk, curtesy of Grafton Township,
since Pa was clerk of the town board and justice of the
peace. For me, the most hallowed item in that room was
Gramma Lehrke's photo album. It was hallowed by me
because it included a professional photograph of great-
grandfather Gottlieb. I was fascinated by his being dressed
in what I was told was his Civil War uniform and what
looked like a medal. There was talk of his having been
wounded, but his military records I later retrieved didn't
support that. I also eventually determined that it was rather
his veterans uniform and related lapel ID, but no matter. I
was impressed and took proud ownership of Gottlieb from
before I started school. I never spied that album in our
library play without looking up that photograph in
particular.

With that adulation I was also soon advanced to find there
and study a book he had presented to Grampa: *Minnesota
in the Civil War and Indian War 1861-1865.*(I now have
this oversized 844 page volume in my library.) The book is
in English, but Gottlieb's autograph on the presentation
page is in German, translated as follows: "Friedrig Lehrke -
- a gift from your father Gottlieb Lehrke -- Waconia Minn.
1899." The book had been published in 1891 by the MN
Legislature. I was much impressed with his German
penmanship and signature. The book included the MN
regimental histories from the Civil War and their complete
rosters. In the roster of the second MN regiment there is a
marked entry: "Lenkey, Gottlieb, age 44, mustered in Sept.
22 '64, mustered out July 11 '65, Drafted". I was perturbed
that they had misspelled our family name, but many years
later, having retrieved his military records, I saw that
Lehrke had been misspelled in a half dozen ways in the

41

muster records. (In Spring 2002, using that regimental history, Addie and I physically traced his march under General Sherman by car from Atlanta to Savannah and on to Washington DC at war's end.)

Thus you sense how intimately I feel attached to Gottlieb, and therefore am minded to introduce him into my own biography. Once one learns of one's roots, one can feel being an extension, even inseparable, as it has become for me with Gottlieb. Once pastoral ministry took me back to MN in the mid 60s, I had the opportunity to visit Trinity Lutheran church in Waconia MN where Gottlieb and Henrietta had membership. The pastor showed me his burial record with its attached note indicating his place of birth, Neu Palseshken, West Prussia. Also noted was that he had served nine months in the Civil War. With that I began years of research, using the Mormon Genealogical library which fortunately had the church records from Neu Palseshken (in German). I also studied the history of West Prussia (now part of northern Poland), aided with maps etc. of that time and area, recovered by cousin, Paul Gaboriault, a librarian.

Slowly I gathered the early vital statistic history of Gottlieb and Henrietta in West Prussia and their probable reasons for immigrating to MN. Facetiously, but also realistically, we could now say that they came to the US because of the potato -- that is, they and too many other were alive because of potatoes. The Spaniards had brought them back to Europe from western South America. In a surprisingly short time potatoes spread across all of Europe, alleviating hunger, poor nutrition, and childhood mortality. At the same time, by the mid 18th century the almost perpetual warfare in Europe in the aftermath of the Protestant Reformation began to subside, giving way to a century of relative peace. The result of this and the potato was a population "explosion". The birth records of Neu Paleschken in particular from the latter half of the 1700s and early 1800s clearly reflect this reality. The result was that in their largely agricultural society, the more numerous youth were finding it hard to find a place to farm and establish a family. Some began to look at other trades for lack of places to be farmers as their fathers had been. But many like Gottlieb had farming "in their blood." Also related was the social and political instability that Europe experienced in the mid 1800s which created a yearning for a better freer life, even elsewhere.

At the same time our US was becoming known to have great potential, promising prosperity and as an inviting place to live, even with peace, plus religious freedom. Besides, the US government also openly invited Europeans to help settle the large open spaces of the mid-continent. The Louisiana Purchase in the early 1800s had made available a safe and free territory with fertile farmland whose potential was widely discussed in the more conflicted and constricted societies and countries of Europe. Already before this, there had been a significant migration of Germans to PA, OH, IN and IL, all of which also had a climate not unlike West Prussia. Significantly, the new citizens in these constantly westward shifting frontiers were well enough educated to write back to neighbors and relatives of the *lebensraum*-- refreshing breathing space -- in these United States.

We may think of Gottlieb and Henrietta as brave pioneers, which they certainly were by our standards, but they had been preceded by many of their own kind and place. We must remember that the frontier had by their time already moved west through WI and well into MN. By 25 years after their arrival it was to shift into ND and SD, providing an attractive new agricultural homeland for countless north Europeans. Certainly Gottlieb and Henrietta had exchanged letter with relatives and neighbors who had proceeded them precisely to Waconia MN; And then they eventually wrote to those left behind in West Prussia to help the frontier move westward. No wonder that the formerly large Lutheran church in Neu Palseshken completely flickered out by the very early 1900s, with the Roman Catholic church taking over the vacated building.

We now know exactly when and how Gottlieb and Henrietta emigrated to the United States. Immigration records are now available in the form of their ship's register. This reveals that they arrived on a German ship named *Julius* at New Orleans on January 2, 1858 from Bremen, Germany. I was also fortunate to have many conversations in the 1970s with Esther Arndt, who was Gottlieb's granddaughter. Esther was a credible source of much information, having grown up with Gottlieb in her home and being already 13 years old when he died. She told me the family's story that Gottlieb and Henrietta had been at sea for 13 weeks. And that the ship had gotten lost in a storm, most likely a hurricane -- considering the season of the year. As a result, the ship eventually changed course and made port at New Orleans instead of New York as originally planned. Furthermore, they were said to have had a child who was stillborn and buried at sea. Considering their oldest child, Augusta's birth date of about four months before setting sail, that would, if true, have been a miscarriage possibly caused by the stormy sea voyage.

The manifest of passengers on the ship, *Julius*, for that voyage, signed by J.C. Meyer, master, totaled 144. Included were 8 single persons and 53 families; Besides there were 11 babies not otherwise counted -- obviously including Augusta Lehrke. Of the total, 2 were a pastor and his wife, E.A. & Emmy Kretschmar, from Prussia, who occupied Cabin I, with a destination of New Orleans. Cabin II listed 13 individuals. All the others are listed as "Between deck". Of these persons, 29 indicated that they were farmers, besides several such as a tailor, merchant, miller, tinsmith, shoemaker, saddler, carpenter, blacksmith, waiter, laborer and painter. Nine persons are listed as having the native county of Danzig -- the major city of West Prussia about 40 miles NE of Neu Palseshken. This included the Lehrkes, brother Johann, 4 of the Carl and Rahel Klug family, a teacher, Julius Kautz, a farmer and Gottlieb Wacholtz, a blacksmith. All of these 9 (10 with Augusta) indicated a destination of "Jova" (??). No MN destinations were listed even though that's where a few of their relatives and friends already lived.. Possibly Jova was Iowa, but ???.

Esther also told me a most intriguing story of that voyage. According to this, Gottlieb left West Prussia a relatively rich man, having the sum of $800 in gold coin which he carried in a small wooden chest. (This chest is rumored to still be in existence among the descendants of Gottlieb's second oldest, Amalia Kieker.) Perhaps, we shouldn't consider this sum surprising since Gottlieb was already almost 38 years old; and it certainly represented a liquidation of nearly all of his property, possibly also including family and wedding gifts.

This entire sum of money was reportedly stolen from him on board ship or on the Mississippi River boat and never recovered. To add insult to injury, the leading suspect of the theft was whispered to have become a neighbor of Gottlieb. The only eventual neighbor on board ship with them was brother Johann, and Carl Klug, whose wife, Rachel, was Gottlieb's half-sister. Both came to live next door to the south and north. Any specific identification by name of who took Gottlieb's money would probably never have been mentioned out loud for young Esther to hear. And she was not one to pass along suspicions to me if she had any. She and some others concluded that the thief "borrowed" and lost it by gambling on the Mississippi River boat they apparently took to come up from New Orleans. But that is also a guess.

When Gottlieb then eventually landed in Minnesota, without a penny to his name, he is said to have had to borrow an ax to fell trees with which to build a home. All this could have been far more serious had it not been for the fact that there were others who had and would emigrate from the same area of West Prussia, in fact from the same parish. These had settled in this area near Waconia. With a sawmill in Waconia, the ax was apparently used to prepare logs to be sawn as opposed to constructing a log cabin.

We must exercise our imagination when wondering how it went for them on arriving in MN. Apparently, they eventually took a river steamboat to Carver, which at that time was the landing place for immigrants bound for east-central MN. It was the primary business center for the whole area and the place where these pioneers would afterwards come to trade in those days before railroads. Their eventual destination was to be Waconia, about 12 crow-flight miles NE from Carver. Waconia already had both a flourmill and a sawmill. It is more than likely that they had relatives there unidentified to us. Our imagination needs to factor in the great difficulty of major "suitcase" living, because they would have brought along as many possessions as possible, since there would be no going home. And all this with a daughter less than a year old.

There is another suggested possibility. Edward Lehrke's interesting journal which suggests that the men of these Waconia families had come earlier than 1858 to establish homes before returning to bring their families to MN -- his memories from late in life are however not always supported by known facts, and thus far, this possibility is considered unlikely.

Secondly, in 2009 we found an English language newspaper obituary for Gottlieb which made the claim that he had at first come to Chicago before "deciding to go west". That obit included the brand new incredulous information, that Gottlieb was survived at death in 1915 by a half-sister, a Mrs. Klug. Using the newly found immigration record which listed a Rachel Klug, we returned to the Mormon History Center where, using her birth date from the US Census, we discovered from the church records of Neu Paleschken that Christlieb Rachel Klug was indeed a half-sister of Gottlieb and Johann.

The third possibility, which I will for now accept as credible, is information from a German language obituary for Gottlieb. It was written by someone who rather obviously was well aquatinted with Gottlieb, rather than a newspaper reporter. It also states that Gottlieb had at first lived in Chicago, stating that it was for six months. Then it speaks of their living for three years in Carver MN before purchasing a farm in Waconia Township. In the mean time, we probably need to imagine Gottlieb working as a farm-hand to support his family in view of his being robbed of his money. It furthermore confirms the English obituary that Gottlieb and Henrietta had ten children, two of which had already died by Gottlieb's death in 1915. We knew of Gustav's death just 1 ½ months earlier, but the other child in not likely the suggested miscarriage on the sea in route to America, since it speaks of "a girl who died in infancy." The German obituary is here following translated slavishly, preserving the German style:

"Plato, Minn., 18 Jan. -- Gottlieb Lehrke died on 24 December, 1915. Lord Lehrke was born on 19 February, 1819 in Neu Poleschke, government center Danzig, county Berndt, province of West Prussia. Here Lord Lehrke went to school and was also confirmed. Lord Lehrke married himself with Henrietta nee Lenz in the year 1852. In year 1857 he moved with wife and child to America where they lived six months in Chicago; thereafter they came to Carver, Carver County, Minn., where they lived for three years, and after three years Lord Lehrke bought a farm in Township Waconia. In year 1864 he was called under the colors/flag and served nine months in the Civil War.

His wife died on 18 June, 1901, and on 17 August, Lord Lehrke settled into the home of his youngest daughter, Lady W F Leistiko in Stewart, Minn., where he lived for six years, and then they moved to Brownton, Minn.; here Lord Lehrke lived five years and then moved to Plato, Minn., where he lived till his death. Lord Lehrke was bedridden only 1 ½ days.

He reached an age of 96 years, 10 months, and 5 days. Born to him and his wife were ten children of which one was bedded in the grave before the mother, and two went ahead of the father. There survive the deceased eight children: F. Lehrke from Gibbon, Lady Julius Bulau from Stewart, Lady Albert Kicker from Fairfax, Lady Ch. Thiem from Stewart, Lady Adolph Tester from Waconia, Rudolph Lehrke from Waconia, Lady Hermann Pretzel from Glencoe and Lady W. Leistiko from Plato, Minn., so also 39 grandchildren and 27 great-grandchildren.

Lord Lehrke was bedded to his last rest in Waconia on 27 December next to his wife."

This German obit of Gottlieb, claiming a six month delayed MN arrival, makes sense in one important respect, and at the same time raises significant new questions. Did the whole group of nine from Neu Paleschken detour to Chicago? And was it on account of their two month delayed arrival due to the storm at sea? Knowing about the prospects of a MN Winter from having lived in northern Poland would have made all of them naturally concerned about arriving and getting settled in midwinter in MN, assuming that this had been their original intent. Furthermore, though Winter river travel to Chicago was then possible, the Mississippi would have been too frozen in January or February to be able to navigate all the way to St. Paul, and certainly not on the Minnesota River to Carver, the limit of navigation. At the same time, train travel from New Orleans seems like a questionable possibility even to Chicago, let alone St. Paul, given the state of railroad development in those early days. Another matter to imagine is how they managed to live in Chicago for six months? Having only farming skills, Gottlieb would likely have had only unskilled manual labor as a possibility. Without doubt, we must consider them brave and, above all, disciplined and faithful.

So if this emigrant party then did travel from Chicago to Carver MN in the Summer of 1858, apparently by rail, and live there for three years, what we must think of is life in a subdued but nevertheless busy, rough, dirty, expensive frontier town. They were old enough to be careful and obviously industrious enough to be willing to work. The three year stay in Carver makes sense even though they had friends already living in Waconia where it would have likely been even more expensive for them. Again, what gainful employment might they have found? Johann was a tailor, and Carl was a teacher who however probably spoke only German -- not a problem in a Germans community. But Gottlieb was a farmer. Yet should one imagine unemployment to have been a real problem in that determined and lively time of expansion of population and economics?

One can rightly imagine that Gottlieb knew beforehand something of what was required to acquire land for farming. There was as yet no Federal Government land program such as the Homestead Act of 1862. Apparently, he would have been aware of the 1820 Cash Entry Act by which a settler paid no less than $1.25 per acre for Federal land, provided that it had been surveyed and still not staked or purchased by another person. Probably, the area around Waconia was already largely claimed. At any rate, Gottlieb purchased 40 acres -- Twp. 116, range 25, sec. 29, SW ¼ of the SW ¼ -- on May 21, 1862 from August Filbrant, for which he paid $60. This would have been a year after he supposedly moved to Waconia from Carver. Carver County land records showed us that Filbrant was already at least the third owner. This same parcel was purchased again in 1879 for $200 -- apparently after a mortgage was defaulted and somehow redeemed. In 1870 he already had purchased a kitty-corner 40 acre parcel to the SE in section 32 for $200.

That Gottlieb's brother, Johann, purchased a neighboring parcel of land to the NE of Gottlieb's original purchase, suggests that any ill between them, if there was such from a theft, had been put behind so as to focus on the significant challenge of establishing a homestead. There was a lot to be done before farming was possible since the area was forested. Trees were a blessing as a resource for building

49

and fuel, but also a major initial handicap for one intending to farm. More than likely their very first efforts when they eventually received title, were more in the nature of gardening and farming between tree stumps.

Johann's first purchase was for 32.3 acres also in section 29, described as lot 4 -- irregular in size because of fronting on the SE shore of Lake Patterson -- from Maria Volkenant for $80 in 1866. He then likely had had other employment for those previous eight years, most likely as a tailor, as he had declared himself to be on the immigrant ship manifest. This was a trade he apparently had learned in the German Army as mentioned in Edward's journal. Incidentally, he had in the mean time gotten married in 1861 and a daughter was born in 1862. In 1873, Johann purchase another adjacent 48.8 acres for $244 directly north of Gottlieb's first farmland, and then a neighboring 80 acres in 1878, for $1500 which was directly east of Gottlieb's home.

Gottlieb gradually prospered in Minnesota, but not without hardship and great risk. The Carver County Register of Deeds lists numerous mortgages, apparently for seed money to be paid back at harvest -- a decidedly predatory banking practice. In 1898 he retired from farming and moved into Waconia with Henrietta where they lived until she died in 1901. The last years of Gottlieb's life were then spent in Esther Arndt's childhood homes. Her mother, Paulina, was Gottlieb's youngest daughter. They were reportedly basically very happy years. First, they lived for a while in Stewart MN, then in Brownton and finally in Plato MN. Esther's father was a lumberyard man and apparently a mater carpenter. Besides, he was a master woodworker, cabinet maker. She remembers especially that Gottlieb was fond of children and was affectionately greeted by the children of the town when he would go for a walk. He was Santa Claus to many of them, apparently on account of his handsome white beard. Esther's brother, Harvey Leistiko, remembers often playing a card game with Gottlieb called "Totes Leben" [Death Life]. He clearly pictured the scene of a chair as a card table between the two of them. Harvey told me that he never heard his grandfather speak English, and they were always admonished to speak German to him. On one occasion he did hear Gottlieb try to speak in English, but upon stumbling over the words he broke out into loud laughter.

His birthday was always remembered with a keg of beer, at which time his children and their families would come for a visit, except for Rudolph and family who had taken over Gottlieb's homestead. (???) In a letter to me in 1982, Harvey Leistiko, Esther's brother, added the following in reference to Gottlieb's birthday parties: "Those were the days of the Model T Ford. Uncle Friederich [my grandfather] always came in his big car, an Overland, most always with the top down. He would like to tell what a joy it was to drive through the country at night in bright moonlight without the headlights on. They were Presto Lights then and not as illuminating as modern auto lights. Your letter mentions that you have his chair [and I still do]. When he lived with us he always had a captains chair right along side his bed and on it he kept his Bible and prayer book [Stark's -- which I also have]. I understand this chair was given to him by two of my mother's sisters; I think it was Aunt Emma and Aunt Gustie." Harvey also wrote that he had acquired this captains chair and would eventually give it to his son, Bill, who recently wrote that he has and treasures it. Esther remembers Gottlieb as having been kind and not temperamental. (I have another chair of Gottlieb's as pictured in an outdoor picture of Gottlieb and four children including Esther.)

Harvey remembers that he was sick in bed with the flu when his grandfather, Gottlieb, died on that Christmass Eve. He remembers his father bringing him downstairs for a few minutes before they took Gottlieb away for the funeral service. But Esther remembers being in the room with Gottlieb when he died. She was watching by his bedside while her mother was preparing supper. Then she had to quickly run to the lumberyard to fetch her dad. For a 13 year old such a memory would obviously be cast for life, especially since she had never known home without him. Esther's father paid for the funeral expenses by himself. Gottlieb died essentially penniless. He was almost 96, a full life for sure, always apparently in good health. He had been sick (with the flu?) only 5 days, and in bed for only a day and a half.

Chapter 5 -- Early Memories

One week in 2017, I was on retreat with a dozen area Lutheran pastors of my religious order; I was visiting with another retired pastor during our free time. We were asking each other what we were "up to." I replied that I had finished a book of theology and was now working on finishing the bare basement of our condo. He was intrigued that I had the necessary skills, so I briefly explained my boyhood. I compared myself to musicians in many familiar stories who came to excel on the foundation of very early and consistent opportunities to practice. (Often I've wished I'd have had the chance to take piano lessons as a child. My early attraction to music might well have carried me to some success.)

I was fortunate to have had a father who kindled in me a broad set of manual skills. When I was three, my parents managed to build a desperately needed new house. The collateral result was that there were many lumber scraps given to me as toys by which to arrange something. I have a vivid memory of the day of moving in, sitting on the kitchen floor that sunny day, playing with assorted lumber scraps much like with the familiar children's building blocks of that time. Pa, not being in position nor temperament to let a possibly useful item go to waste or be discarded, saved many odds and ends of that building project and others.

Possibly seeing an economical opportunity to develop some useful skills in me and my brothers, Pa rigged up a "carpentry shop" for Walter and me. It was an old wooden truck cab; Our very own building. It was only about six feet square and possibly five feet' tall; And of course it had no floor. It stood through my childhood just south of the machine shed. Where the dashboard had been, Pa made a simple tool bench for us with a shelf beneath. Here we gathered such lumber scraps as Pa donated. Side by side we sawed and nailed odd bits of wood, perhaps the original inspiration for both of us now eventually having and enjoying a well appointed woodworking shop.

Probably as Christmass gifts we each had our own set of basic tools: small hammer, hand saw, pliers, etc. (I still have and occasionally use my coping saw) as well as a supply of nails. It was a great place to play with these tools and scraps, particularly on a rainy day. The windshield was intact, so we had a broad view of the hog yard and fields beyond and with plenty of light. I even remember that Walter's place was to my left. From the age of 4 and up we practiced basic carpentry skills in this shop.

As we progressed, we were welcome to Pa's tool bench in the machine shed, along with its tools and pails of used nails, screws etc. . We were on our own with no one to kiss a banged, slivered or cut finger. That prepared us for later assorted carpentry project on the farm which Pa supervised. Not that Pa couldn't cut a square end with a hand saw, but I was commonly handed the saw or hammer We practiced and practiced, and got to be trusted, and silently applauded? By the Summer before my junior high school year, we were fully ready to help renovate our cow and horse barn. The piano keyboard is still largely a mystery to me, but not the hammer, saw, etc.

As mentioned in an earlier chapter, Ma had from marriage helped with many of the farm chores. And my two oldest sisters were likewise recruited from as young as possible to help with daily farm work, and also in the field, particularly in harvest time. This was because Pa had always struggled to have enough help. I suspect that through the years he periodically had had a number of temporary hired hands. One year in the late 1930s I remember his having a hired man for the whole Summer. His small family lived in our abandoned old house behind the orchard.

During the 1940s, being the time of WWII, there was a German prisoner of war camp at New Ulm MN. In need of help on the farm, and grampa not able or willing, I remember Pa discussing the idea of applying for a prisoner of war to help him, particularly in the grain harvest. This was being done by others, but it seems that Pa lost his nerve, and nothing came of that.

A coincidence then saved the day for a number of years till I and my brothers came of age. Help mysteriously arrived in the person of a hobo named Julius Zarbuck. Exactly how this came about isn't remembered. But Pa must have met him in Gibbon looking for work, dared to think well of him, and brought him home. He was passing his Summers "riding the rails", working at odd jobs he found here and there only when needing money. He never spoke of any family, and told me that in Winter he lived in the St. Andrew's Hotel in Minneapolis MN, which I remember from university days as being along the tracks close on the north side of downtown.

He was about Pa's age, possibly a bit older since I remember him as compatible and friendly with Grampa Lehrke. Grampa seemed to envy Julius for his free life style in contrast with his own discipline. He was a stereotypical hobo, having little more than the clothes on his back and a pipe in which he smoked Peerless tobacco. (I was attracted to and begged his tinfoil tobacco wrappers. Eventually, beginning at university, I also for a number of years smoked a pipe, using at first Peerless tobacco.)

He was a good sized man near six feet, had dark disheveled hair, always without a hat, and he wore bib overalls. He was very humble and friendly with us kids -- like the grandfather we wished we had. We hung around him in leisure time, also when he visited with Grampa who seemed to wish us boys to leave them alone. He refused to sleep in the house, never ever came further in than the kitchen, and only for meals. Ma also found him pleasant and approved. After Sunday's dinner he would stay to listen with our whole family to the Lutheran Hour on the kitchen or living room radio, but going no further than the doorway into the living room, sitting on a kitchen chair.

55

He refused to go to church with us for what now seems an understandable reason. What would they have said or thought in Moltke of a hobo in mean clothing in their church on Sunday morning when farmers also dressed up? He explained his need to stay back to wash his clothes and take a bath. This he did with the hand pump on top of the cistern south of the milk house. I don't remember his being offered soap or towel, nor any way to heat the water. He must have put his washed clothes back on still wet. He probably used the big pan from the milkhouse used for washing milk pails and cream separator parts. When we got home from church, he was all primed and ready for Sunday dinner. He slept in the hayloft by choice.

He wasn't remarkably strong but quite able, with an easy going spirit. When the sun was hot he tended to drink too much water, upsetting Ma, who of course worked alongside shocking the bundles of oats which Pa was cutting with the grain binder. She thought he would do better by sticking with coffee, as she and Pa did. Drinking excess water, he would at times get "sick" and then poop out for a few hours till he cooled down. But over all, he did his share of shocking bundles of oats and occasionally barley. And then at thrashing time a week later, he pitched the bundles onto hay wagons for transport to the machine. There Pa pitched them into the fearsome mouth of the thrashing machine with its slashing sharp blades, the machine being monitored by Grampa who was the general engineer; He also tended the straw blower and grain spout running into a wagon or truck.

I trust Pa paid Julius well enough since he would come back years running for the grain harvest. If he was too early, and the grain not yet sufficiently ripe, he'd loaf around smoking his pipe. I don't remember his helping with any other farm work. For a few years he also came in October at corn picking time to unload the husked cobs into the corncrib. But this was apparently work too strenuous for his liking. I myself eventually found it very hard, working with a scoop shovel, throwing cobs of corn from the wagon through a 2'x2' ports on the insides of the double corncrib with its drive-through, till it was full to that level. After that, it had to be thrown up over the top of the crib three feet above my head. Not till later did we have a grain elevator.

Those were busy Summers and my two oldest sisters had been long before me recruited into the harvest time. I possibly tripped myself into an earlier than expected participation. One day when I was possibly six, with the whole family out in the grain field shocking one morning, I and Walter, possibly even Leslie tagging along, went across the road in our play where Sigmund, our neighbor and cousin, had cut his grain. The bundles were yet lying un-shocked. We thought it would be fun to set up some of the bundles into shocks. "Well then, you can better do this in our field", said Pa when he learned of what we had done that morning. So Ma took me under wing to work with her. She firmly planted two bundles and I would add two more on one side, while she added two on the other. She'd then start the next shock, while I added still another bundle on either end.

Thrashing had for years been done by joining with a neighbor family, though each would cut and shock their own grain. That work was considered an art. Pa and Ma frequently remarked about the artistry or lack thereof in a shocked grain field. Already before I was in high school, that neighbor family bought a combine, leaving us to trash alone. This meant the whole family had to be involved. Ma had taught one after the other of us kids to shock. Once Walter had been taught, she then stayed home to cook. And at thrashing, we kids loaded the bundles on a hay wagon using horses to pull the wagon. They knew where to go without a driver, the reins tied up. We could all load since the horses obeyed voice commands as we made our way down the rows of shocks. When the wagon was full as high as we could pitch the bundles, it was driven to the trashing machine. There, when Pa finished unloading the other wagon, the team re-hitched to it for the next load. There

57

was little stopping for rest. It was unacceptable to let the thrashing machine run empty when the weather was fair. For an hour at noon, and then at mid afternoon lunch time we did stop for fifteen minutes at most. Time was of the essence.

Once in later years, thrashing was delayed well into August by rainy weather, one year in particular. I was home from university that Summer and already working at Green Giant in the night office team for the sweet-corn pack. But I was required to come home to help with the much delayed thrashing during the afternoon. This is when I would run the trash machine myself, including the manipulation of the 20 foot long by 12 inch straw blower pipe and the grain spout. A proper straw-stack had to be carefully constructed so as to shed rain. Staying wide awake on either job with only a morning of sleep was not fun. Pa never did buy a combine, nor resort to hiring one. He was convinced the old wooden thrash machine could best a combine with less waste. It died about the time he did.

Making hay was the other intensely busy time of hard work each Summer. We always had around 20 acres of alfalfa for feeding the cows during the Winter, and a 20 acre slough around which we cut grass for horses. The alfalfa was harvested three times each Summer, with the first and largest cutting in early June. As far back as I can clearly remember, it was already being cut with the Farmall M tractor Pa had bought before the War, though I vaguely remember Pa cutting with a horse drawn sickle. The 7 foot wide sickle mower was mounted directly to the back of the tractor, making that work quite simple and easy. But raking it into rows was work that Pa still did each morning with a team of horses when the weather was fitting, meaning that it was usually quite warm, and the hay would be dusty. Then in the afternoon the team was hitched to the hay wagon, trailed by the hayloader. The two horses straddled the windrow of hay, it passing under the wagon and was picked up by the loader, delivering it to the back end of the hay wagon. Pa stood there distributing the hay around the wagon with a pitchfork, sister Jan drove the horses, being perched on the ladder-like front of the wagon. I would at first only trample down the hay; Eventually I had my own pitch fork to level the hay. A sling of two ropes was first laid front to back, and hay was loaded till it was trampled about 3 feet deep, onto which another sling of ropes was laid and the wagon was topped off to about six feet high.

We had a drive-through barn open to the hayloft on either side -- cows were kept to one side, the horses to the other. Up at the inside peak of the driveway there was a carrier on a track to which the slings of hay were attached by a pulley and long heavy rope, which wound its way back down and outside by other pulleys. That whole affair was hitched to the horses who would pull the sling of hay up and over into either loft. There it would be tripped to spill the hay wherever there was room. From quite young, I took over from Jan the work of driving the horses for lifting the hay to the loft. She, however always drove the team in the field. I never knew if Ma had similarly helped Pa with making hay, for he surely couldn't have done it alone.

This was the time-honored way of making hay till hay bailers became available in the mid 1940s. That was custom or hired work. Pa then sometimes hired various bailers, but finally bought one himself. That left the horses out in the pasture, but for us it was very hard work. Lifting 90 pound bails of alfalfa onto a wagon, again onto an elevator, and again into place in the loft, was not play. It was sweaty dirty work I never regretted leaving behind. My hayfever made it all the worse, not that this was true hayfever, but having a sensitive nose, the inevitable dust and tangy aroma triggered sneezing. This hay-making was always hurry-up work to finish before the weather brought rain. Only eventually, as Winter arrived, was there satisfaction for having done this work for the love of the cows and horses who were thereby well provided. Especially if we had been able to make hay without it getting rained on, it stayed tender, smelled so sweet and was so eagerly accepted that we smiled and sighed a, "Your welcome!"

The final busy hard work each year would then be filling silo in Fall. Pa had one built quite early, made of clay brick in the mid 1920s. This filling couldn't be done till well into September, or else the corn and eventual silage would be too wet. Pa had a corn binder which made bundles that were also stood on the cut ends in shocks till the silo filling could be hired. A distant neighbor had a chopper blower and the pipes to reach the top of the silo. Before I started school this harvest was also a community project and very heavy work. The farmers had long low slung wagons to haul a load of 100 lb. bundles home. This I only got to observe. Soon after I started school there became available a mobile chopper pulled by a tractor which cut a row of standing corn and blew chopped corn stock, leaves and cobs into the top front of a trailing wagon with tall sides and a top. This was also hired work. I was then involved in raking the cut corn out of the wagon and into a hopper that fed it into the blower to send it up the pipe into the top of the silo.

But before all that could be done came what was always proud high excitement to me. Pa being somewhat afraid of heights, very early recruited me to crawl up to the top of the silo using the chute for unloading silage each Winter day. Then I'd walk a 12" plank spanning the 15 foot top edge of the empty silo to reach the window in its roof on the opposite side. I'd be careful not to look into that dark abyss near 40' down. (Walter and I even did this in play, without of course telling.) Once at the window I'd guide the raising of the filler pipe into place and secure it. What parent today would dare to endanger a young child in such work? They would put them in jail. But this was work that needed doing, and Pa had great faith in me, always quite soon considering me able, and I was confident and eager. I and Walter got to do many "dangerous" things like that serving our proud father and family. We grew up fast in that way. Fortunately, I was also already 6' tall and weighed 190 pounds by eighth grade.

Because I grew up quickly there was another bit of heavy farm work that I was delegated to do when still quite young. As soon as my legs could reach the clutch and brake pedal on our Farmall M tractor, I got to cultivate corn. This would have to be done three times each year with our rotating field of more than 40 acres. Each time it would take several full days -- Twice between the first and second cutting of alfalfa and again before grain cutting and thrashing season. That left enough slack time for hoeing potatoes and the field garden. Eventually Pa also bought a Farmall C which was then used to cultivate corn. I was happy with my skill of driving a tractor so as not to destroy any hills of corn. With my hayfever I learned to drive with my knees when tending to my sensitive nose. And I'd sing to my self, including the chanting of the liturgy, particularly the Lord's Prayer, both in German and English.

Speaking of heavy farm work, I'm reminded of a Winter that came early when I was possibly in fifth grade. Pa still had about ten acres of unpicked corn. The snow was too deep to do anything but wait for Spring. However, Pa was then concerned that some of the corn was broken down and would not all be properly picked up by the corn picker. He decided that we should pick the corn by hand with a team of horses and wagon, like in the days of old, with a tall bang-board on the opposite side of the wagon from where we walked and picked. For this we wore a special leather glove on the left hand with a steel hook attached to the palm. With such a glove and hook we husked corn. The cob is then broken free of the stock and pitched into the wagon, banking it off the bang-board. Pa did himself work with Walter and me on this project, the horses driven by voice; But what a disagreeable work it was! The dried out corn leaves were sharp and dusty, making one sorry for ancestor farmers in the days before corn pickers.

Walter and I were still quite young when Pa came home unexpectedly with a 22 caliber rifle for us from a trip

61

to the South St. Paul stock yards after delivering a load of hogs. It was as I now suspect, Ma's idea. At times cotton tail rabbits and various birds wouldn't leave her garden alone. I don't remember how good Walter became with that rifle, but I soon became a first class marksman. I couldn't hit a rabbit running away, but if they sat still for me, they were dead. We wouldn't eat them for supper except in Winter. When we were not hungry for another rabbit supper (they taste like chicken, really!; Well, almost.) the chickens loved them as well as the cats. However feeding rabbits to the half dozen cats we always had was not to Pa's liking, because a hungry cat catches more mice, always a concern on a farm with grain bins. The common sparrow, another parasite on a farm when feeding animals, was our target practice and the kittens loved the treat.

Chapter 6 -- Elementary School

What can I say about my brother Walter? In saying that he was my intimate companion through all the years of our childhood is almost an understatement. We did virtually everything together, both work and play. We were an ideal brotherly match. (Leslie was three and half years younger from me, and was not up to our speed, also ill when younger and thus pampered. He was commonly excused from the work that bound Walter and me together.) Being older and stronger, I was introduced to helping on the farm ahead of Walter, but he quickly followed by choice. My main chores became the care of our horsebarn with our 5 Belgians and Percherons. And quite soon thereafter Walter got the assignment of cleaning the dairybarn with its 20 cows. That kept us busy after school, followed by feeding cows and milking, with which Walter got involved early on as well. Only thereafter came supper.

Even before school age we were both assigned a garden hoe and sent out to the field garden. It was a large full acre garden, rotated from place to place each year (think football field size). This was mostly potatoes, but also sweet corn, popcorn, peas and beans for canning or freezing. Also other vegetables overflowing from the house garden that our sisters and Ma kept up. (It was WWII rationing and economizing time for our family of six kids). Not that we were having fun hoeing potatoes in the sun but we were together, and Walter was no slacker. We often made a game of it. Not saying that we were sad to see a thunder shower coming, sending us home. That was never a retreat into the house, rather a time to sit just inside the machine shed with the big door open to watch the waterfall off the roof, and the ducks having the time of their lives. As soon as the shower was over it was often time for barefoot strolling along the fieldroad with little rivers that we dammed or re-engineered.

We were both expected to help with the farm work as soon as we were able. The periodic cleaning of the calf and bull pens was also a joint assignment as needed with Walter. I was mostly the leader in work or play, good or bad. I was never corrected by him and visa versa, we restrained each other from excessive foolishness where needed by gentle reluctance, like jumping down from too high a perch. We were both trained in honesty and knew we would in a pinch rat on each other, keeping us somewhat in line. I don't remember any disagreements. We trusted each other based of a good track record with each other, and also with Ma and Pa.

We both enjoyed our neighbor kids of our own age, the Schlagel family to the north and the Kirchhoff twins across the field a mile east. Many a Sunday afternoon -- our only extended play time -- was spent with the twins in games at our home or theirs: like cops and robbers -- hiding from each other or being hunted. We each had homemade wooden guns with a spring type clothes pin to shoot rings cut from a tire innertube. A limiting factor with the Kirchoff twins was that Pa saw fit to buy us only one bike to share, which we did, or rode double. In good weather when needing to walk to school, we changed off, morning or evening.

Walter was the right choice to get and stay on the farm. He was slower in school than I, but with his practical engineering skills he had no competition. He took over a farm on the brink of foreclosure when Pa died, turning it into a well managed and profitable living for a large family, even eventually buying the neighboring Lehrke homestead after Sigmund died.

The fortunate bond between Walter and myself has been mutually beneficial. Neither of us became prodigals. We more or less kept each other straight. The two of us were virtually like twins, always together in mischief, play or work. We had few secrets or privacies. We even compatibly slept together in a double bed till I left home for university. Yet in some fundamental ways, Walter and I are unlike. Always a tad smaller, but never excusing himself from anything. Undoubtedly it surely happened, but I can't remember ever being angry with him.

I started school in 1940 in the same schoolhouse that my mother and father had attended at St. Peter's Lutheran Church, Moltke Township, in north rural Gibbon MN. Actually, that building still survives, remodeled into the home of a classmate. It now stands on a farm two miles west of the church.

I have apologetic memories of my schooling of those early years. I didn't hate school, yet first grade in particular is remembered as an ordeal -- there was no kindergarten. It was very difficult for me owing to my lack of fluency in English. We had never spoken it at home. I didn't actually know the language except for the little my older sisters dared at times to use. Sunday worship was then still in German. English was used in school by state requirement. Even so, I had a German grammar class through second grade, after which the start of WWII forced an end. My handicap kept me barely near average throughout my elementary school years, and unfortunately I accepted this as who I was. Considering myself to be ordinary in my studies compromised a daring to excel. By fifth and sixth grade I did begin to get more interested because of having a gifted teacher, Martin Raedeke, but Summer vacation was still a relief to be the farm boy at which I did excel. By Summer's end it was part interest and part relief from the moderation of hard farm work that had me ready to go back to school. Nevertheless, before and after school I relaxed into the comfort of doing farm chores. I have sensed myself to have been at a disadvantage through most of my life compared to what could have been had it not been for a late start with English. At the same time, I appreciate being fluent in German, such as when traveling in Europe and in seminary study and research.

Speaking German exclusively at home would continue for years. I'm unsure that I ever conversed with Pa other than in German, though I eventually must have. Pa and Ma didn't till years later approve of speaking English at home, and we weren't much minded to do so. Nevertheless, I even enjoyed a class in German reading and grammar in high school. Interestingly, grammar in particular is associated with the unhappy struggle remembered from my first grades with homework overseen by Ma, who was apparently determined that I would excel in her preferred language. It still pains me to remember sitting in the highchair with Ma ready to administer the ruler when I got stuck with my recitations of conjugations. German grammar had been very hard for me with its methodical order, even though I had good practical usage in conversation. Then in high school, German grammar was easy.

However, I must have been satisfying my teachers in early elementary school, since I remember being seated in a desk at or near the back of the row in grades three and four. We were appointed desks at the pleasure and wisdom of the teacher who preferred slower students up front to help and monitor. In grade two, I sat in the second from the front, which coincided with getting a red E (serious failure) in arithmetic in one term on my report card. Geography, though, was a favorite subject, and my rapped attention to it resulted in a problem with which I still struggle. We had a complete set of maps for the whole world high up on the front of the room above the blackboards. Unfortunately that was the south wall. Maps are consistently oriented with the top to the north. So when I now attempt to orient myself to a reported current event, say in England, I need to stop and determine this to be toward the east of myself, not to the west.

Those years in the lower four grades were the first years of WW II. Even in our nominally German community there arose a animus against things German. Conversation came to be politically correct even at recess. The coincidence of the war, with food rationing, in those years is connected in my memory with a curious government program of supplying even parochial schools with surplus canned food for supplementing our brought-from-home noon lunch. I remember the canned beans. Because of sitting at a desk at the back of the room, I was delegated to supervise the hot plate on which this food was warmed during late morning.

Nov. 11, 1940, when I was in second grade, is a date of a significant memory, namely, the Armistice Day Storm in the upper Midwest. We all got home before the storm became too furious, but we were out of school for three days, with Ma tutoring us around our dining room table with our studies, possibly more for passing the time. Pa refused to allow anyone else to go outside to help with the chores. This was not only for fear of our safety, but apparently preferring to be busy and out of the house full of kids. We consciously felt completely snug in our new house in contrast to looking out the windows, especially on remembering the old house standing open back in the grove. Our situation was not up to the tales of people getting lost in a storm when going out to tend animals unless they had a clothes line strung to the barn. This was less dangerous for Pa only because we had a well established grove of trees on the west and north of our farm yard. Besides our west grove we even had more than an acre of grove across the road to the west. The result was that the snow banked over the road to a depth of up to 12 feet, particularly at the north end of the grove. And this resulted in days of waiting till a snowplough could reach us. When we looked outside toward the barn during the second day of the storm, we could often see it, but mostly not at all. Pa would come back in the house as our hero, telling of the loud creaking of the barn roof over his head when up in the loft throwing down hay into the inside drive-through for feeding cows and horses. Pa also relieved Ma from her chicken barn chores. That was perhaps in part to have her make sure none of us got outside to have fun.

It was eventually quite some fun to go outside where we then could walk on the deep banks of snow without sinking down, the strong wind having packed them hard. Then finally at school, our recess times had us explore the deep banks all around in the church yard. The church and school

67

also had a grove, but much smaller and thinner, especially to the north behind the parsonage and teacherage. So the highway across the front had been deeply drifted. Thereafter we had giant ridges of ploughed snow on either edge. Perhaps it was with this storm that we first saw the wonder of a rotary snowplough, making a better way on the highway, amazing us one school day with an arch of snow being thrown 50 feet to the side.

There are only a few other memories, though very faint, of those first four years in school. It was a one room school house, but with a second story used for confirmation class for the eighth graders during the first hour every morning. Perhaps it also served for parish meetings and as a space for recess for the lower grades when the weather was bad, but I fail to visualizing this. One special memory has however always remained of those years. On the day after an annual congregational meeting at which Pa was elected to the School Board, Verna, a lovely classmate "congratulated" me on that. That friendship left me speechless, but forever sealed my admiration for her typical grace.

I was perhaps ten years old when it so happened that my January 21st birthday fell on a Sunday, and we were to have open house for family and friends. Its reason was actually more because my mother's birthday was the day before mine. Nevertheless, I begged to be the one to answer the door for this evening gathering since it was my birthday that day. Guest after guest made no comment to me on arrival, rather asking where my mother was so as to greet her with, "Ein Gluckliches Geburtstag!" Not that I minded at that age to live in her shadow, and yet....

St. Peter's Church, built in 1991, stood on the highest part of the church yard on the north side of the highway in rural Moltke Township. It's a traditional white with a stippled bell tower, having two large bells which we sometimes could hear from home, over two miles away as it rang one hour before worship, or to announce a death in the parish. Next toward the east was the one room school house for the four lower grades. The entire church and school yard of about 10 acres was our school playground, particularly when we played hide&seek. The only off-limits were the garden areas behind the parsonage and teacherage. We even trespassed in the wooded overgrown small first cemetery directly behind the church (later restored), neither considering it spooky nor disrespectful.

Next to the east of the school for the lower grades, separated by the main playground area, was the single room school house for the upper four elementary grades, and beyond it were the outhouses. And then there was the cow pasture for the called teacher for the upper school who was the principle and organist. (The teacher for the four lower grades was not called but contracted from year to year and boarded with one of the church families.) He also had a small barn for several cows. This pasture was often later used as a ball field, though not by the school children. Then further to the east and up on a higher hill, is the cemetery.

Further back from the highway, the parsonage was up behind the lower school, and the teacherage behind the upper school. In between these was a woodshed which served all four. During my lower grade years there were also still remaining some open horse sheds with roof behind the church, though then no longer in use. My guess is that these were built by or rented to any who wished to unhitch and shelter their teams during church worship or meetings. Others apparently hitched their teams during church to a long heavy pipe 3' above the shoulder of the highway stretching the width of the front of the church yard. That pipe long remained and was used by children in good weather to play after church while parents visited outside after church. It was our Sunday alternative to the merry-go-round over near the upper grade school.

My first year in the upper grade school, when in fifth grade, school was at least a month late getting started in Fall because of the death of Teacher Dorn during the Summer. Teacher Martin Raedeke eventually accepted the call and

69

came in October to teach the four upper grades. He was apparently restricted by this late arrival from setting up a preferred curriculum until the following year. So I found myself in sixth grade listening in also with the class of fifth graders, essentially taking two grades at a time. This was especially the case with science, about which I became quite fascinated. It would have been elementary by today's standards, but this was for the first time enlarging my view of the world -- that there was more of significance to life than farming. I could then dream of other things. All the other subjects, like geography, were interesting to me as well, except for English grammar, which was hard. I probably by then spoke English plainly enough, but speaking only German at home continued to retard my command of English over the years. In retrospect, it would have served me well had composition been included at that elementary school level.

What was unique, of course, with a parochial church school, was the lifelong advantage it gave me of familiarity with the full range of significant bible stories. Each morning through seventh grade, the first hour of each day in both schools addressed all grades together, a study of one of the major bible story in historic sequence from both Old and New Testament, annually repeated. This totaled near 200 stories -- one per day through the school year. We used a book devoting one page for the text of the story and one with a picture for that story. On this the teacher elaborated according to ability. I've often since asked myself how these stories might have been applied to us children, or if they were focused mostly on the facts of the story. In addition we memorized Bible passages and the chief parts of Luther's Small Catechism.

These bible stories of God's grace did effectively speak to me of God's love and my responsibility to love. This was in fortunate contrast with the heavy emphasis on discipline in my family -- most likely true in the whole community and congregation. This for me stirred up an accumulation of guilt that weighed almost unchecked. It took years for me to successfully address. I distinctly remember, particularly in early adolescent years of fearing a crushing punishment for my sins, like with the collapse of a bridge before I was able to pass over. It was good that I then never encountered a long tunnel, which might have been too terrifying to attempt.

We were well prepared for the pastor teaching our year of confirmation studies in eighth grade during that first hour of school until Palm Sunday. In the upstairs of the lower school the pastor used an expanded catechism. We would already have memorized its chief parts in the lower grades, namely the Ten Commandments, Lord's Prayer, and Apostles' Creed. But then in confirmation class we were required to memorize also Luther's explanation of these, plus his for Baptism and the Lord's Supper. In this connection the pastor led us through the synod's expansion of the catechism via related questions with synod approved answers and bible passages designed to prove these parts of the catechism. We did thereby get a solid exposure to the complete range of dependable Christian doctrine and teaching. Palm Sunday was our oral exam in front of the whole congregation. It was in place of the sermon on that day. Pastor Rohde pointedly asked individual class members random questions of truth and Lutheran doctrine. Sadly, the Palm Sunday gospel story went by the board, never explained in a sermon for which there was no time. I was, however, by these year of instruction way ahead of most of my classmates at seminary. Pastor Rohde was a serious man-of-God, of the old school, not given to fun or humor, nor enterprising ways of getting his teaching points across. Yet, I owe him much. His Sunday sermons were mostly too deep; And they were simply read, he shaking his head whenever he misread his text.

During those years in the upper school I was physically growing up faster than the other boys with the associated adolescent handicap of coordination. This didn't hinder me with my farm chores since the adjustment there was minute and constant. But those same chores also kept me from practicing at home the games we boys played during school recess and lunch hour. I could handle a pitch fork well enough, but a baseball bat was another matter. Consequently my self esteem suffered from doing more poorly on the playground than some of my admired classmates. In choosing up sides, I would typically be left standing till near the end, and also didn't get my choice of playing positions on the ball diamond. When I did, I'd often embarrass myself, further limiting my honor.

Chapter 7 -- Life on the Farm

Life on the Lehrke farm in south-central MN in the rural north of Gibbon, was a happy annual cycle to me, a series of exciting anticipation, effort and reward. That was because it had a holistic, also subsistence character -- we were in control of life. We were only remotely in step with a system of commerce; We were primarily working for ourselves as we happily preferred. Our family, like many others in our area at the time, was largely independent from the world in the sense of being considerably self-sufficient for daily bread, yet also helping as best we could to serve the world as an expression of responsible human community. It strikes me in retrospect as an ideal, almost a vision of heaven. With few exceptions, we ourselves produced whatever was needed. Pa didn't plant cash crops -- an interesting one time exception was buckwheat, although occasionally, soybeans; Even this was with the associated objective of creating bee pasture. We reflected the self-sufficiency taught and enforced by the Great Depression, and then as well, effected by the rationing enacted by our country at war.

Consequently, there was hardly ever any downtime, waiting for a cycle or seasonal effort to generating income. We were living our own life. (So I was quite unsettled by the farming June and I encountered in Saskatchewan in my first parish where farmers chose to have nothing to do all Winter; Even during Summer they were mostly waiting for the harvest to provide income to live. Consequently, as their pastor I never had difficulty finding people at home unannounced. Some did have gardens, as I was expected to, to effect a saving on the salary.)

With my childhood family, even on a day in the depth of Winter, we always experienced usefulness to serve the family: animals to feed for eggs, milk, butchering or market. What was in excess of our needs, was marketed to purchase what we couldn't grow -- tools, coffee, clothes, etc. We had only 160 acres. About 40 of these was planted

73

with corn for silage to feed the diary cows, with the balance
left to ripen. That was picked and cribbed to dry, and then
ground as needed to feed chickens, hogs and to supplement
the silage and hay for cows, bull and calves. (They
noticeably loved it to our delight. We once had a Guernsey
bull who would wait when given his ration of silage until
we topped it with a scoop of ground corn; After this he
used his nose to mix it, and then eat.) Another about 40
acres was planted in oats, fed to supplement hay for the
horses in Winter and when working in Summer, but mostly
ground as needed for chickens, and to mix with skim milk
to fatten hogs. (In Summer, the chickens were given whole
oats on the ground outside. This always produced a happy
scramble to get their share. And for us it was a delight,
making us smile.) About 20 acres was in alfalfa for cow
hay, and 10 or so acres in slow-draining grassland for horse
hay. (As I've said, they loved us for our love.) That left a
grove of trees to supply firewood for heating, and a good
sized pasture for cows and horses to feed themselves from
about May into October. (We knew they loved this grass by
how eagerly they ran, even kicking up their heels, when the
gate from the yard to the pasture was finally opened in
Spring after the ground had become sufficiently firm.)

Many farmers those days did about the same, although a
few raised beef cattle instead of dairy. Very few grew
mainly cash crops. We raised money for taxes, charity, and
clothing by marketing, not milk, but cream in those days
before we could qualify for producing grade A milk.
Possibly that amounted to 3-4 gallons of cream per day.
Other income was realized from: near 200 eggs per day,
picked up weekly; 40-50 annually fattened hogs; 800 spring
chickens; about 200 year-old hens that were being replaced;
a half dozen male veal calves annually; occasionally a few
dozen turkeys. From this we first helped ourselves, and
added as many geese and ducks as we might need. The
latter were all raised by Ma from eggs by goose & gander,
drake and hen, and incubated under chicken clucks.

Much fruit and vegetables was canned, or later after having electricity perhaps frozen. Our cellar room preserved a mound of potatoes from a half acre + plot, plus apples, beets, pumpkins, carrots etc.. The grocer in Gibbon occasionally sold Pa some bananas, sugar and flour, and dry cereal for Sunday breakfast -- since Ma saved time thereby to get us ready for church.

Fall, like all the seasons, was pregnant with anticipation, and produced a heady stream of bounty. The sweet corn would be long gone by September, but there were more tomatoes, cucumbers, cantaloupe, watermelon than we could use, along with cabbage, beets, carrots, etc. What we couldn't use, the chickens enjoyed -- we just threw it over the fence to them. There were onions to braid into bundles to dry in the shelter of the still empty corn crib. There were new potatoes to dig for immediate use -- gauging the eventual harvest -- while leftover old partly shriveled ones were being fed to eager chickens as their supper desert. The old beets had earlier in Spring been likewise used up to spice the feed of the hens still being cooped up.

There were ripe bean vines to pull and dry in the sun on the huge canvas normally used under the head of the trashing machine to catch spilled grain. These beans were threshed by walking on them. The grapes would by September be ready to "steal." Ma would later make a little wine from what was left. We'd have our choice of a half dozen apples from late Summer on, not counting the hard "Winter" apples, later picked and saved in the cellar. There was a small grove of yellow and red plumbs behind the chicken barn which we would shake to get the best ripe and perfect ones, some of which were canned for jelly, leaving the rest for the chickens. And Fall was the high excitement of newborn calves in the pasture to guide home after school.

The latter was more exciting to us than coming home from school to feast on fruit, and certainly preferred to homework which could wait. That fun was a bit touchy since our cows were not exactly friendly pets (only one that I can remember) though all enjoyed having their throat scratched when firmly fastened in their stanchions. A new mother cow could be quite protective. When we got home from school at this time of year, we would stand on the cistern south of the milk house to survey the dairy herd in the pasture to spy a detached cow with a calf. Usually it could already walk, was licked clean and dry, and not afraid of us. We didn't even use a rope to guide it home; There the following mother was put in her stanchion with its calf alongside. Later, as other cows were allowed into the barn for milking, the calf was penned with others till the next nursing time over the following few days.

These Fall occasions commenced the annual milking chores of which we had been relieved for the Summer -- fortunately, for reason of the excess of field work. The first few days after giving birth, the milk couldn't be saved; it was excessively rich, almost like cream, actually yellow with a tinge to orange. (Of course the barn cats got their share, happy to end the Summer fast.) So the baby calf was allowed to nurse as much as it wanted, and the balance was milked by hand and fed to other recently born calves, who had been penned and weaned after about a week. They were slowly taught to drink from a pail of skim milk supplemented with vitamins and minerals for a more complete diet. This was far from easy boy's work -- they had no natural ability to drink, much like a baby. They would butt the udder when nursing for instinctive stimulation. Thus when forcing their head into milk in a pail with a finger in their mouth to suck on, they would slurp and gag on the milk in a pail; There was much spillage from butting till they learned, still long continuing to butt.

For some time, after the cows gave birth ("freshened") in early Fall, they were only let into the barn for milking in morning and evening, then turned out to spend the night or day in the pasture to save on the Winter stores. Then in late Fall they were held in the fenced cow yard, the gate to the pasture closed, and the herd kept in their stanchions over night and much of the day. (During the day we were

76

conveniently in school so as not to monitor this season of breeding with the bull. Eventually, we couldn't help seeing this less than 30 second union, but Pa never did discuss any of this science.)

Keeping the cows then mostly confined, saved the yard from complete contamination. (I'm explaining all this, not to gross you, but to have you understand the great extent of our happy work of loving our animals so they could love and serve us in return.) Behind the back of the cows in their stanchion was an 18" wide gutter by 6" deep, keeping the cows clean and dry, and making easy work of removing manure. This was done daily through the Winter and became Walter's chore after school (first turning the cows out into the yard), while I did the same with the horses. After this I'd help him to renew their straw bed. We both had manure carriers that ran on a track over the walkway and out the door on a cable. It held several bushels and tripped itself to empty via a cleat on the cable over a manure pile on the far side of the yard. This was allowed to "marinate" till after the grain harvest each Summer when it was by tractor front loader and manure spreader used to fertilize the harvested grain fields before being plowed under. With our annual crop rotation the farm was thereby fertilized every three or so years without using any commercial chemical. That was true organic agriculture.

Then came feeding time. But first, Walter or I alternating, had to climb up the chute into the top of the silo and throw down 6-8" of silage from the complete perimeter of its 14 feet diameter. (There were removable doors the whole height of the chute.) Most of the Winter it would already be dark by this chore time. That required taking a kerosene lantern up the chute with a fork. This was often heavy work in January, requiring a pick ax around the perimeter where the silage would be frozen. All through the Winter, each side-by-side paired cows were given a half bushel of silage topped with ground corn. Then the milking began, followed by a generous feeding of alfalfa hay.

We had no milking machines till about my time in high school. So both Pa and Ma, both oldest sisters, Walter and I, each milked 3-4 cows -- we kids getting to milk the easier and more gentle cows. Our pails were emptied into a 5 gallon milk can or directly into the reservoir at the top of the cream separator in the detached milk house (all brick or concrete for easy sanitation), run by electric motor, discharging skim milk and cream from two separate spouts. The cream was run into cans and lowered into a 3x3'x6' deep concrete cistern of cold water in the corner of the milk house. The skim milk was carted in cans to the hog barn where it was mixed in a 55 gallon barrel with ground oats as "slop" for the hogs who fought to get a place at the trough. In that place there was no mercy. A runt sadly got left behind. Pa was hardened to this reality, but we kids had pity as we could. Once, when I was possibly in third grade, there was a runt that Pa predicted would soon die. Walter and I begged to take it out and feed it, essentially making it into a pet; With much reluctance, Pa allowed it, but "Our animals are not pets!" We nursed it back to full health, and it was eventually able to rejoin the herd.

The horse barn was on the north end of the barn, separated by the hay driveway from the cow barn, open into the hay lofts on either side. This horse barn was my bailiwick from as young as I can remember -- before school? Except when Grampa came to visit for a day or season, I alone did the feeding and the cleaning of stalls. (What a precious memory it would be to me if Grampa had taught me about the much he obviously knew about horses.) I was highly favored thereby by Pa and felt honored. In a follow through, Pa always passed on to me money from the sale of horse hair from the trimming of manes and tails, which he still did each Fall after the horses no longer needed to swat flies. This horse barn was in its construction an antique, reflecting pre-tractor farming. No longer was there need of room for eight draft horses. I sense it was designed by Grampa who did farm almost exclusively with horses. Our barn was built by him as Pa took over that farm in 1916. It had four double stalls plus a center work area for harness, halters, etc. and a water cock and basin. Each stall had a full width manger 4' deep -- holding 4 bushels of hay -- with a small grain trough for each of the two horses to either side.

The east stall, next to the door into the yard, belonged to Toppsie and Daisy, black Percheron mares, 5.5' tall at shoulder, 1700-1800 lbs. They were reasonably gentle and lovable. (Although Daisy once kicked me breathless. I was carrying a large fork-full of straw from the straw-stack beyond the yard -- in the early days before baling -- to bed the horses who were loose in the yard. Daisy was in my way and simply expected me to go around her. I thought I held rank in the yard, so I poked her in the butt with the handle end of the fork, and she kicked me flush on the chest, sending fork, straw and me flying. I was otherwise unhurt but did have the wind-kicked-out of me.)

The next stall was for Maggie and Nancy, mother and daughter Belgians -- same in color as Clydesdales, but just a bit shorter in the leg and near 2000 lbs. These were my beloved's. Maggie could actually be approached out loose and free in the open pasture -- unless she sensed that she was to be harnessed. But once she was, and this I soon got to do, she was the most cooperative and hard worker to be imagined. If she was hitched with Toppsie, she never minded Toppsie being lazy. Toppsie would hang back so that the evener locked and had Maggie pulling the whole load. I'd have to slap Toppsie on the butt with the reins to do her part. But Nancy was sadly never broken into a harness. What a pair she'd have been with her mother -- near a matched pair -- beautiful white star on their foreheads. I to this day wished I'd have harnessed her without Pa knowing, and then driven the two for him to see and admire. Maggie would have consoled Nancy as when in the stall together. And knowing Nancy's temperament, that simple breaking-in would have been doable, and a source of lifelong pride.

Then on the west side of the center work area, was the stall for Duke. He also was never broken. The day of horse farming was fading away, and I perhaps more than Pa mourned over it for these beautiful animals who could be loved far far more than a red or green tractor, in fact, in a reciprocal relationship. I did my share of cultivating corn etc. with the Farmall, and might feel a bit different had I had to do that with horses, but still.... Then one day I came home from high school to hear that Pa had traded off both Nancy and Duke for a donkey. I was angry! I honestly don't believe we ever hitch up that donkey. He just helped by eating the Canada thistles in the pasture. (Then whatever happened to Toppsie and Daisy? I don't recall. They must have been sold as a team.) Not long thereafter, we learned that Maggie was sick with encephalitis. It was her second bout, having recovered from it once when she was pregnant with Nancy. But there was no longer an urgent need for horses, and Pa apparently despaired over the extended veterinarian bills; And so we saw Maggie lie down in the yard, never to rise. I still have tears for memory of the sight of the rendering truck who backed into the yard, attached a winch and pulled this magnificent horse up into a half load of dead farm animals. I think I'd have been willing to dig a grave for her, and put up a board reading, "Here lies Maggie, the best and most beautiful and faithful horse we Lehrkes ever had."

A review of Pa and Ma's farming, under which we grew up and were shaped, would be incomplete without mentioning our chickens. The very fact of having a major chicken barn, built in the mid 20s, about the time of Pa and Ma's marriage, indicates chicken farming to have been a significant part of their joint master plan -- it's unlikely that Pa kept chickens before Ma was on board to care for them. It was probably begun as her chosen special project to join in generating income. That barn had two stories, about 40x25' in size, large enough to keep 250 laying hens. The upper story was accessible only by an outside ladder and used for storage of miscellaneous chicken equipment, including a then no longer used sizable egg hatching unit, indicating a serious earlier program of incubation.

Beside this barn, there was a similar aged octagonal brooder house for young chicks about 25' in diameter; And, in my time, a second brooder house appeared that was used to divide up the young pullets when the main brooder house became too small for the rapidly growing 1100 chicks purchased annually. The octagonal shape of the main brooder house was to keep chicks together for warmth in early Spring -- having no real corners.

Those 1100 chicks came early each Spring via US mail from Readers Hatchery in Sleepy Eye MN. They came in multiple cardboard boxes with peep holes all around, and divided into compartments for a dozen chicks each to prevent congestion and suffocation -- chicks need not be fed till about the third day after hatching. It was high excitement for us kids coming home from school to see and hear all those "cute" baby chicks peeping. (And that's about where the fun ended with me and chickens.) Prior to this annual use of the brooder house it had to be scrubbed and sanitized (no longer would chicken farmers use creosote for this as we did). An octagonal metal brooder hood with electric light for warmth and curtains all around the 5" high outer sides stood in the middle with straw bedding. It was then surrounded close by with the big drive belt used for grinding feed and thrashing, standing on edge, used early-on as a fence to keep chicks from straying too far from the brooder when out for feeding, and then possibly getting chilled. Of the 1100, 500 were unsexed chicks -- near half and half male and female -- and the other 600 were sexed roosters intended for sale with the other roosters after we would butcher what we ourselves wanted to freeze. These were sold live as spring chickens to a butchering house which sent their truck at the time of their proper weight. Walter's birthday on July 1st was traditionally celebrated with a meal of the first Spring-roosters.

It was a major chore for us kids at nightfall to make sure all the chickens were in their barns for the night once the weather had turned warm enough to allow all the chickens to range outside during the day. Not that we were ever told of predators like weasels having made a major indiscriminate killing in a chicken barn when a door was left open during the night; But Pa and Ma implied the myth, and we were to be diligent about security. It was spooky for us young kids being out at near-dark, which it would take for the chicken to mostly retire. Older sisters, now relieved of this duty, loved to tease us boys, suggesting that the spooks were out and about. The old laying hens knew their place on their own, but many of the young pullets went to roost in the trees. So we had to shake them down out of their favorite box elder grove nearby. We were glad to be back in the house as quickly as possible. "The spooks didn't get you?"

The day in July, when the rooster were shipped was always pure chaos in the closed up brooder house full of young chickens. The feathers would fly as they fled us who were all recruited to catch and crate the roosters, and free the young hens. (Not fun with much chicken dandruff in the air.) Soon thereafter the truck came back to crate up the old hens still alive, which had been laying for a year. These had by then slowed down or stopped laying eggs. That then left the 250+/- pullets/hens to run loose till Fall. They were then trained with feeders to occupy the main chicken barn with its 25' long metal two story egg laying compartments on either end of the barn. These pullets would soon begin laying an egg per day -- not quite free ranging. They had roosting poles along the back wall.

Once these hens were confined in Fall, the other not-so-fun work began. Ma still mostly took care of the chickens all week -- indicating that this was her agreed farm project from the start. That barn needed "mucking-out" every Saturday morning all through the Winter. After feeding all other animals and milking cows before breakfast, the next regular agenda item was bringing the manure spreader to the far chicken barn door (Walter and I, dragged with negative-excitement. He had a similar dislike of chickens.) The chickens had to be crowded to the other half and kept away from the open door as we forked and scraped the soiled straw manure into the spreader; Then a fresh straw bed was installed, but always with lots of chicken dandruff in the air from much disturbed hens. Next, we moved the manure spreader forward to the first main door, and herded the chickens to the other side on the fresh straw bed. Then things went better since the hens were eager to try to find remaining grain in the straw, and so were more pacified. We would then clean that second area and bring in new straw bedding. It was a relief thereupon to leave the chickens behind and spread the manure out on a field. Both of us then moved on to mucking-out the horse and cow barns, plus the pig barn. All this had to be done before a typical noon dinner of mashed potatoes, pork hocks and sauerkraut. (Finally, in old age, that's again an acceptable menu, even cherished, if the sauerkraut is well cooked.)

This left us, not with a desire for a nap, rather wanting some freedom. That was fortunately our anticipated agenda for Saturday afternoons -- it kept us focused and moving through the morning. Hauling the loads of manure out onto the empty fields was already momentarily relaxing, but it was great to be totally free till the evening chores of feeding and milking. But this was often disappointed by Pa's agenda. About monthly, the afternoon had to be spent shelling cob corn from the corncrib, hauling the cobs to the house cellar via the basement window near the furnace, (to be used for fire-starter) and the shelled corn to the granary. Probably there was even need to grind a new supply of feed.

On top of that, other Saturdays also would often be the time for cutting wood for the milkhouse stove and house furnace. This would mean already having a pile of logs and big branches from the grove, continually gathered over time. For this we had a 30" buzz saw mounted on the front of the Farmall M -- very dangerous, with no shields or guards. Pa and Walter lifted the logs onto the cradle, moving it into the saw; I would hold onto the piece being cut off and then toss it onto a wagon or pile -- a nonstop routine. (We lived with danger all around and learned to respect it.) That firewood too had to be hauled to the furnace room window or to the wood pile.

So what did I do if my Saturday afternoon was free? Though I had already memorized every tree in the three acre + grove, I had no greater pleasure than to stroll through it to make sure it still was as it had and should be. I'd probably eventually, after being 10-12, carry the 22 just in case I saw a fox squirrel. These were hated for the waste of many cobs of corn; If they took only what they could eat from the corncrib, that might have been OK; But they frequently fumbled this overly large item, only to leave it and get another. Particularly in Winter, I enjoyed monitoring the tracks in the snow to see what other life was there. How many pheasants where there? I had a trapper eye and usually had a few traps set baited with shelled corn that needed checking. Cottontail rabbits were a frequent supper at our place, and any excess were much enjoyed raw by the laying hens. Ma had little work with making this into and enjoyable supper since I presented her with a skinned and gutted carcass, only needing to be cut apart.

Or, I'd visit the cow barn, glad to take in the enjoyable clean aroma -- a mixture of silage, hay and cow-scent. This, while not needing to be doing chores. And, of course, I never tired of the horse barn and its aroma. This would be time to enjoy friendship with the horses, rubbing their nose or chin, or currying them. The farm was full of things that were a feast to the heart and eyes, far more than a store or mall was ever to become.

Pa's farm was not large, only ¼ section / 160 acres, but in his earlier time it was still more than he alone could do -- particularly in harvest times -- given the non-mechanized farming of the time. I remember an occasional hired-hand, but it was mostly a family affair with Mom tending a large flock of chickens and ducks, as well as helping to milk a sizable herd of cows. She also still helped with shocking many acres of oats till I was a teen.

My second oldest sister Jan, being healthy and strong, early-on became Pa's unhired-hand, not only in the yard but in the field as well – not always a voluntary role. Eventually, Walter and I relieved her to some extent, but for some time before early mechanization took hold, we three became the crew; and our temperament and spirit allowed this strong still existing bond to develop.

Nothing more I can say illustrates this better than memory of the alfalfa hay harvest, or pitching bundles of oats for thrashing. Apparently this was the first and most typical collaboration of us three. (Before proceeding, we need to remember how a hay rack / wagon is shaped and how we made hay before there were balers. The rack had three foot sides but a six foot tall front and back, with the front including a wide ladder for the utility of getting up or down from the top of a six+ foot load of hay. The wagon was hitched to a team of horses and towed a hay loader behind the wagon, the whole affair straddling a windrow of hay.)

Jan was always the teamster handling the reins while standing on the inside of the front ladder-like rack, eventually buried in hay up to her waist when the load was full. Walter and I were the compactors, crushing/trampling down the dry and brittle hay that Pa distributed from the loader with a pitchfork. Eventually we helped with pitchforks.

Appreciate in particular how dangerous this was to all four of us, especially to Pa, Walter and I, with nothing to hang onto after the load was mostly full. This considering the moving and bouncing wagon on steel wheels; Not that Jan was much more comfortable driving the team standing on a ladder. In this way we managed to haul home and unload with slings and pulleys a wagon load (even yet in the late morning) after Pa would have raked enough hay into windrows. Then two more loads before a mid afternoon lunch and at least another before evening chores and supper.

It was fully as bonding an experience for the three of us as an army foxhole, though we never really thought it through. It was hard work, but the comfort was that it was useful for others, in this case our milk-cows which partially supported us. For me there was likely a deferred sigh of thanksgiving when Winter had set in -- surveying a warm barn full of contented cows munching alfalfa.

This crew of us three worked together on many chores throughout my grade and high school years. After this it terminated, but the bond has remained. I left for university, allergic to alfalfa dust, Jan quickly followed me to Minneapolis to work for Ma Bell. And Walter quit school early to start taking over the farm with Pa's decline.

My default image of Thanksgiving was cast in childhood on the farm, yet it might well serve anyone – hearing a parallel experience can tease new insight. I once preached a complete Thanksgiving Day sermon reflecting the unique exhilaration of a farm family at that time of year, justifying this as gospel since Psalms is replete with summaries of agricultural prosperity for signaling blessedness. The old saints accepted such personal blessings with thanksgiving, yet not for judging an unfortunate neighbor, who was rather their opportunity for multiplying blessedness.

We were poor by the standards of many, it being the waning years of the Great Depression. Yet the onset of Winter brought no anxiety. This, even though there was no new money in the bank – we had not harvested any cash crops. But the hayloft, silo, corncrib and granary were full, as was the fruit and root cellars, along with a fullness of canned goods in the basement pantry. We had a warm house and sufficient food. It was blessedness, represented additionally by plentiful feed for all the farm animals for producing eggs, milk, pork, etc.

Even if the Winter snow was already on the ground by that day, we greeted the morning of Thanksgiving in a relaxed and joyful mood, consciously celebrating prosperity. That day we still had chores with horses, cows, hogs and chickens, but that was an easy routine compared to seed, cultivation and harvest time. With church at 10am, we nevertheless got up in good time to feed and milk.

I entered the barn that morning through the adjoining milk house after starting its woodstove, my first assignment was the horsebarn. Toppsy, Daisy, Maggie, Nancy and Duke would hear me coming and I would sometimes hear them getting up in their stall, not to be caught sleeping -- always proud -- but waiting gratefully for a manger full of hay, and a pail of water. There was no point in being skimpy, and Pa would anyway check later to make sure I had given enough so that the manger was not soon empty. Cleaning the stalls would wait till late afternoon.

Next, I joined Walter in feeding our herd of 20 cows, beside the bull and caves. . We had milking machines later when I was in high school, but until then each of us would milk 3-4 cows, and then separate the cream to be picked up every other day by the creamery truck from town. Next, the skim milk was carted to the hog barn and mixed with ground oats for their feed. It was contentment to share the bounty with our animals who in turn were noticeably content.

I remember going to church, followed by Thanksgiving dinners of duck with family -- sometimes turkey. But the better spiritual part was often the afternoon, contentedly strolling the farm yard alone with a feeling that all was well, more than good enough. Or, as the early church father, Origen, says was the original of Jesus in the Lord's Prayer, now translated as daily: supersubstantial.

Chapter 8 --- High School

I didn't start to surprise myself as a student till high school. In part that was because I quickly became best friends with the best students, Norman, Lucille and Jeanene. (Which came first, the friends or the interest?) It seemed that others were merely enduring high school. The social or sports aspect was the main motivation to be in school for most boys. None but Norman and I had dreams of college with leaving the farm or small town and family. It really wasn't even hard for me to be in the top of my class along with these three friends. I could do school in class and study hall with limited homework.

This was the case even though my high school years involved a radical relocation and context. It would have been much less radical had I been able to attend the high school in Gibbon along with my elementary parochial school mates -- an established and comfortable peer group. They probably were the leading click of their class. Instead I was refused bus transportation to Gibbon, although being in that school district. This happened because the bus was privately owned and elected to refuse to come the extra few miles to our farm. Pa once again gently suggested my going and boarding at Concordia College in St. Paul, which would have put me on track into the MO Synod ministry, but I again demurred. (I wouldn't then have had to learn Latin on my own.) Then the possibility of attending Dr. Martin Luther in New Ulm was briefly considered where sister Caroline studied in their teachers college. This would also have involved boarding, and in turn possibly have directed me toward the Wisconsin Synod ministry.

Somehow, I nevertheless got a ride for the first day of high school at Gibbon; But that evening I became aware by George, my neighbor to the north, of the Buffalo Lake bus being willing to come the extra half mile to pick me up. Their district included the land across the road from our farm, so they only trespassed by turning the bus around in our driveway. (I wonder if the Gibbon district ever paid the

Buffalo Lake school for my education.) In that school I knew no one other than our neighbor boys with whom Walter and I had been playing for many years -- though Ma was not too happy for us associating with these Roman Catholics.

Unfortunately, I was immediately set-upon at high school by a click of three sophomore boys. Being new and without friends, I was their perfect victim for fun. They were self declared jocks, and one was the son of the school superintendent, making them important and bold to bully. The class there had mostly been together since first grade. I was the "new kid on the block." What set it off was that I had shortly before had ruptured appendix surgery and wasn't allowed just yet to participate in the physical-ed class in which the boys of all high school classes were combined. So I was judged to be a big sissy in their eyes. This was all the more so by what happened on the day about a month later when I turned in my doctor's permission slip to join in the phy-ed hour. The coach had been detained, so I had to wait with presenting the slip till other boys were already on their way out to the ball field. Knowing him to be hard on any who were late changing clothes and getting to the field, I was overheard asking the coach if I was nevertheless to change an participate that day, realizing that I'd be late. This was overheard and ridiculed by giving me the nick name, Do-I-Gotta, a derision long to be used. I was thoroughly humiliated shortly thereafter on freshman initiation day, which was the job of the sophomores.

My own classmates were however generally accepting of me, and one, Norman, who rode the same school bus, became my best friend for the duration. He was a closet and celibate gay, different, but respected for getting top grades. We became an odd couple, without girl friends, and especially not part of the town kids and their fornication and parties. Pa kept me tied down on the farm, except for Sunday afternoon, which I then often spent with Norman. We played cards, or just drove around the neighborhood.

89

Pa had bought a 1948 Buick Roadmaster, so the 1938 Plymouth was at my disposal. Later, I would sometimes drive it to school.

I was respected not only by my own class members but especially by all my teachers, always getting the best test grades in subjects like history and the sciences, and near the top in all the others. I sang in the choir, became the first tenor in the school boys quartet and mixed octet -- winning the MN state high school music contest one year in that division. I represented our school in oratory in the regional declamatory contest. Unfortunately a snowstorm had me miss the bus to that event, to which I drove myself. I was allowed to participate even though late, but the awards had already been granted. Yet I was assured by the judges that I'd have won and gone to the state contest.

Because I was trusted by the principal, I was already as a freshman taught to run the movie projector for any school event throughout my four years. High school was mostly a breeze, with little homework required aside from study hall. Yet in retrospect, I never really learned how to study, which was typical of small rural high schools. A few of us had an agenda, but there was no track for us to get there. Sadly, though the school had a science laboratory, it was only for our teachers to use for demonstrations, not for our experimentation. And in math, the curriculum ended with sophomore algebra. Thus, I had additional handicaps beside the division of my life between two languages.

Already as a freshman, I joined the baseball team in Spring, having overcome my clumsiness from the previous few years associated with my rapid growth spurt starting in seventh grade. It was an impossible dream because of the jocks who resented my trying out for a position they claimed as a right. In an early scrimmage game, I hit what was obviously a home run, but I was intentionally tripped rounding first base by the first baseman, one of the sophomore click of three. Was it not observed by the coach? Then, being assigned to play in the outfield, I missed judged a fly ball, and further embarrassed myself with loosing my cap in the process. Playing on the team also meant team practice after school and missing the bus, which Pa was not approving; So I quit the team. I simply didn't fit in anyway with those for whom sports was the way to impress the girls.

I likewise had learned in phy-ed class that I wasn't built for basketball. Besides, I had never played the game, missing out on the years of practice required to excel. But football was a possibility. However, my doctor refused my request by reason of supposed high blood pressure. Staying after school for practice and missing the bus home became more possible by my junior year. The old team doctor in Buffalo Lake said I was fine. Pa then gave-in to allow me to drive to school on game days. I was big enough to compete, but all the others had accumulated seniority with the coach. I made the team as a junior, but it was six-man football at our small school, and the senior class dominated. I did get to play briefly, but not enough to letter. However, in my senior year, my science teacher and principal took over coaching football, and he started having separate defense and offense teams. The three jerks had graduated and other jocks preferred offense. That gave me space on defense. I nailed down the defensive right-end position and had much fun and success. My reward in old age is a left knee too often injured in dragging down a quarterback or halfback with inadequate knee pads.

Walter joined me at Buffalo Lake high school when he was ready, when I was a junior. Whoever was ready first for the 8:30 high school bus watched out the upstairs window through the leafless grove. So the cold was of no account. School was always good fun, having a close classmate friend who rode the same bus and was likewise a good student – the two of us were third and fourth in final class rank. We arrived home from school about 4pm, in time to listen to the radio program: Jack Armstrong – the all American boy, with commercials by Wheaties. I still favor that cereal about once per week. But by 4:15, Ma made sure we were making ready to go out for chores. But first, there often was my trap line in the grove to check with the possibility of catching a cottontail rabbit. When time allowed, I did this also between morning chores and breakfast. I usually had up to five traps baited with corn which kept the cottontails under control.

Walter went directly to clean the cow barn gutters while I did the horse barn. I could usually finish first, so I then normally crawled up into the silo with a kerosene lantern, since by then it was usually dark. I threw silage down the chute to the extent of a depth of about 8" of silage from the 14' diameter – enough for the evening and the next morning feeding of about 30 head of cattle. By then it was again time for feeding silage and the milking routine, followed by supper, school work and bed. And that ended of the day with the pleasure of our warm draft-free bedroom. I remember it being cold in Winter on our MN farm. But we managed, not too much needing to be outside except for a full day of work on Saturdays -- grinding feed, shelling corn, even making firewood. God always seemed to be good enough all around. It was a joy to tend our animals, our friends.

Those Summers during high school, I hardly ever left the farm, particularly the Summer before my senior year. Pa had elected a barn rebuilding project that was all consuming. By then Walter and I were well prepared to be his main crew. Our 40x80' 1916 barn had been built on a poor and shallow foundation, and the wood side walls were by then dry-rotted from animal humidity. A house moving crew was hired to raise up the barn onto trestles of timbers -- one side and half of each end at a time -- the hayloft then empty. We then could cut off the lower side walls and remove the old foundations. These were cracked but still in unmanageable pieces. This was before jackhammers were available to us; So we did it with a chisel and sledge hammer, and then pulling the pieces away with the tractor. I've already noted the unbelievable, that many sections of old foundation, too large to move away, were broken by Pa and me, he holding a large chisel with his hands, without

92

gloves, and me wielding a six pound sledge hammer. I now cringe, both for his trust and my own ability. I remember however, having experienced my adolescent growth spurt earlier than normal, and by then already being 190 pounds of muscles; I was again amazingly coordinated, enough to faultlessly hit the chisel with maximum force. Pa was firm with me, but there is in this retrospect no question of his pride in me.

Once half of the old foundation had been removed, Walter and I dug the trench by hand for a new reinforced poured concrete foundation -- the suspended barn looming overhead. We dug it 12" wide and 6' deep. I stabbed off a shovel full with a tile-spade, and Walter, standing opposite from me in the trench, cleaned up after me. (To our amazement, the black topsoil reached to the bottom of the trench -- and this on a slight hill.) When we had finished one side and half of each end, the concrete and bricklaying crew of Bandow uncle and cousins from town, mixed concrete and poured the trench full. And then a new brick wall was laid by the same crew reaching to the underside of the hay loft. Once this wall was cured, the barn was lowered onto the new wall and the other side raised onto trestles to repeat the process with the second half.

In between that heavy work, we made hay, which all had to be baled and stacked in the field till the barn was done in Fall. Then it was finally hauled home and winched up into the hay loft -- lots of extra handling. This rebuilding didn't reconfigure the calf pens and cow stanchions, but the horse barn was reduced to one stall for two horses, and incorporated into one large barn space. The hayloft driveway was eliminated and an outside door access to the hayloft was made on the top north end. This reconfiguration provided room for a secure bull pen and a large area for feeding steers.

That modern bull pen almost became the death of Pa. A year or so later, one Winter day, he noted that the bull had fleas. So he attempted to shoo him into his corner stanchion where he could be secured. For this Pa stepped into the pen,

93

and then heard the gate click and lock behind himself. The bull with 10" horns immediately attacked, eventually throwing Pa over the 6 foot sides made of large vertical pipes. Fortunately, Pa had only some broken ribs. Needless to say, the veterinary doctor eventually came to remove the horns.

The Summer after high school was a desperate scramble to earn funds to allow for attending university. Pa didn't offer to help, nor apparently had the means. We must have naively thought I could with Summer earnings make it happen. I was blindly determined. The sweet pea harvest was about the only opportunity presenting itself without leaving the farm. There were scattered farmers around the area who chose to make two cash crops on part of their land by raising sweet peas for Libby in Sleepy Eye, then followed by a second crop of soybeans. Libby had an established pea vinery four miles from our farm -- essentially a stationary combine. I successfully applied. We started work at 6am. There were two of these side by side to which pea vines, cut and hauled by truck, were brought and shelled. I was at first one of two who stacked the shelled vines on a pile -- hauled home in Winter by those participating farmers as silage. I also needed to help box the peas for transport to the cannery. Each vinery machine had a series of hoppers on one side of its length. The peas automatically emerged by grade -- from small to large -- from front to rear through holes in its big rotating drum like shape into eight wooden hopper boxes to be kept separately. When these boxes were full, they were stacked to the side for a Libby truck to pick up each day. It was very dirty work, especially at the end of each day to disassemble the vinery drum of six rubber panels with holes. We had to clean the insides of matted pea vine pulp. Depending on the press of the developing pea fields, we occasionally worked all night to stay ahead of any too rapidly maturing peas. We usually didn't get home till near midnight. We were off for an hour at noon during which I dashed home four miles away to eat dinner, and again for supper.

Later during the harvest, for about a week, the peas were maturing far too rapidly; So a portable but stationery vinery was brought to a farmer's field nearby, and I was elected to run that whole affair by myself. I was helped only by one who fed the vines into the machine. I should have, but didn't get a raise for that greater responsibility. The six weeks run of the pea pack netted me just over $500. I had no bank account, so I just kept the checks till I arrived at the U. There I successfully deposited the checks which were already past expiration.

My oldest two sisters had in previous years been working in the Green Giant Corn cannery in nearby Winthrop. This was my next attempt at Summer employment. Jan applied for me. (The corn pack usually followed close on the pea pack, and also normally ran for six weeks.) I expected to work somewhere in the factory, but Jan had told them that I was smart enough to work in the office. Which then was my surprise when I reported. I worked on the night office crew of two who couldn't begin work till the 6pm cutoff for each day, the factory mostly running 24/7. We had to compile and report the weight of each truck that had unloaded during the day with ears of corn, crediting it to the individual framers. But my own vastly harder work was to calculate the bonus incentive for all the factory workers. By factory divisions, the productivity was measured to determine a bonus on their time and wage scale. I was for several days way in over my head, especially in terms of meeting our 6am deadline for the previous day's calculations. A messenger waited to deliver our productivity figures to the main GG office in Le Sueur each morning. Even more demanding were the plant managers, anxious to know how efficiently their divisions were working.

The following Summer, since Winthrop only canned sweet corn, I found a job driving a two ton truck, hauling the pea vines to a large four-vinery station near Le Sueur. I roomed and boarded with a farm family which had two trucks being hired to haul vines. Their hired man drove the other truck.

We took turns driving up and down the pea fields alongside of the vine cutter which had an elevator that spilled the vines into the truck box. Those were commonly long days. One day we were required to work through the following night because the crop was maturing too rapidly. I made it till 5am when I fell asleep at the wheel on a return trip to the field from the vinery. Driving the big truck into the ditch broke the front steering and suspension on one side. The repair cost was deducted from my wages. Had I not been immediately awakened when the front wheel entered the ditch, and then cranked hard on the steering, I might have driven on without anyone knowing of the stolen minute of sleep. Otherwise I did good work, keeping up well with the two-truck partnership. But remembering my office work in the corn pack at Winthrop the previous year, to which I would return each Fall through university and my first three years at seminary, I applied in subsequent years to do night office work in the pea pack.

This office work a Winthrop had readily qualified me to work the night office shift in multiple GG factories in southern MN during the pea pack in the following Summers. How I well remember trying to sleep during the hot Summer days of the June and July pea packs in southern MN, in Montgomery and Blue Earth. It was commonly upstairs close under the roof of a rooming house without AC. We ate all our meals in the plant cafeteria. Nor was it fun to interrupt sleep time to attend Sunday morning worship. And the schedule of 6pm to 6am didn't allow for whatever recreation might have been available in those small towns. Fortunately, it allowed me to nearly meet my educational expenses till the last year in seminary. Jan carried me with an accumulation of small loans till June took over.

Chapter 9 -- University & Seminary

By retrospective meditation of now more than sixty years since high school, I can confidently say, on the strength of an uncommon theological understanding of the divine principle underlying the sixth petition of the Lord's Prayer, that I was by my strong personal desire to become a doctor of medicine being tempted by God in allowing that attempt to get under way. He allowed me to pursue an appetite not properly vetted in prayer and competent counseling. He thought, "Now Eugen will have to learn by the failure of his dream that such is not my plan for him." I had, for just one example, completely dismissed the implied caution of a visiting high school counselor -- unbelievably counseling my class as a whole, instead of individually. He inquired about our respective dreams after graduation. He heard my public announcement to study premed at the University of MN; And he then asked me in front of the whole class if I was the valedictorian -- a veiled caution of pursuing such a dream even for the top scholar in a small rural high school. I was undeterred, and simply expected God to bless me in what I had decided.

It was a "rush" to get started with a heroic effort. In mid Summer, between the pea and sweet corn harvest I packed a suitcase, got a ride to Stewart from Walter, and hopped on a Greyhound bus to Minneapolis to register at the university. They had scheduled a two day orientation for new students, facilitating the registration itself, along with an exposure to book store, dorms, frats, campus layout, etc. When I arrived at the bus depot in downtown Minneapolis, I went to the nearby Drake Hotel to stay overnight prior to the accommodations anticipated at the U. But there were no vacancies on account of a large convention being held at the Raddison Hotel nearby. On a now-what? moment I went to the Raddison and got a room, feeding my excitement at making my way into the world beyond the farm. The next day the U grandly welcomed me, and got us aquatinted, including a registration at Pioneer Hall, a men's dormitory. The U provided no cautionary counseling, nor questioned my high school transcript. There was just the proviso that I lacked a requisite course in geometry. That they advised was no serious problem. Though it would not accumulate on my transcript, I could easily fulfill this in extension night-school. OK, I was all set, and returned to work in the Green Giant sweet corn pack.

In time for classes to begin, I again went by way of the Greyhound bus, bringing with me my un-cashed pay checks from Libby and Green Giant to open an account at a bank near the dorm. By then I realized however that these funds wouldn't suffice. I knew that I'd have to work and study on top of attending classes. There was little point in asking if this was possible. With my Prussian discipline, I proceeded as possible. My first job was setting bowling pins in the Coffman Student Union, a social and recreational facility on campus. It lasted about a week or so (miserable work, setting two allies by hand). By then I had gotten wind of possibly working in the kitchen of Centennial Hall men's dorm, which also served meals for my dorm. I worked there early each morning before classes, running the motorized potato peeler (like a large top loading clothes washing machine), producing mostly-peeled potatoes or carrots for a crew of four older women who would finish off, cutting out the eyes. Thus I had the evening hours for study rather than needing them to earn supplemental funds. That job lasted for several quarters when I instead applied to scrub one of the two dinning hall floors after the evening meal. "I can and must do this!" Finally, during my second year at the U, I was a breakfast line cook, for an hour and half each morning, working on a large grill preparing either fried eggs (two dozen at a time in rotation), French toast, or pancakes. (The cases of eggs came for government storage. Occasionally these including a bad one, which needed to be quickly trashed.)

My classes that first year involved zipping back and forth across the campus, beginning with English Composition at Fowell Hall at 8am, a mile diagonally across the campus from the dorm. (We had been tested in composition at orientation, and by reason of untaught skill, I was assigned to the most basic level.) I then returned to the south edge of the campus for Zoology -- classes had only ten minute intermissions between, barely sufficient with a rapid walk. Then it was on to Chemistry Hall taught by the principal of the department for a class in inorganic chemistry; It was scheduled exclusively for premed and med-tech students. It was intentionally designed toward maximum difficulty. This would eventually help reduce our class of premed students to about half, so as to fit the maximum allowed into med school. Not all but many, including myself, were often snowed under within 15 minutes into class. Thus the light on my dream was beginning to flicker, though it was not quickly abandoned. Besides, there were other classes such as humanities, intended to soften the scientific regimen of premed. On top of this I just had to join the 300 voice university choir, singing concerts of major choral works with the Minneapolis Symphony (later renamed Minnesota), for which we received academic credit.

Life on the farm had allowed chances to rest and breath. But with minimal sleep and relaxation I was getting further and further behind by the day. My high school simply had not conditioned and prepared me for the pace and level of difficulty. I was not equivalent to others in my classes who appeared to be making the grade. Chemistry lab, in particular had me totally in over my head, since in high school it had only been the teacher who demonstrated. Now without experience I had an equipped lab space I hardly knew how to use, to say nothing of the complexity of following the assignment describing the experiment required. It wasn't much different in Zoology lab, dissecting frogs etc. to trace veins and nerves. I, unlike many classmates, had never held a scalpel. A butcher knife is not quite the same. Already before Spring quarter began, I knew; my grades didn't support a continuation of the dream, but I continued the schedule till blissfully free for the Summer. Nonetheless, my normal self confidence was being shaken. I wasn't yet specifically facing it, but I sensed that God had set me adrift, spit me into a tornado of unrecognizable chaos where he was intentionally invisible for effect.

Well, what does a Prussian, who knows not how to give up, do then? At least they allowed me to register for a second year at the U. Therewith I was finally connected to a vocational counselor. But he simply sat back with the required non-directive method: "What do you want to do?" I had no clue at that point, too recently completely disillusioned. They didn't use a test for aptitude. I therefore elected to pursue liberal arts in general, which was slotted within the same college as premed. I took classes in philosophy, logic, even a class in advanced German literature. Besides this I can't recall, having a merciful mind that tries to forget the dreary or joyless day. But the forgetting was not easy for being assigned a dorm mate that second year who, also from a rural area in SW MN, did well in premed. He stayed a friend through life, an accomplished doctor of allergies. (Thus a subtle reminder through life of my own failure.) I pumped myself up often with the conviction that I had sadly missed a coveted chance to be a surgeon for want of an appropriate high school education.

It was in the process of registering for a third year at the U in July or early August when I faintly heard the Spirit echoing my Pa, who had years earlier several times tried to nudge me toward pastoral ministry in the church; But Pa had by then given up on any verbal suggesting. I'm not sure he any more prayed this for me. When again in touch with a U counselor in the process of registering for classes, I let it slip that perhaps I might eventually apply to a seminary. He urged me to go immediately to Concordia in St. Paul where I was graciously received. But I was informed that I was beyond conveniently fitting into the synod's pre-ministry track which had begun at the start of high school. However, they told me that there was another track in the LCMS, namely, Concordia Theological Seminary in Springfield IL. It was constituted to accept and catch up men whose inclination and vision for ministry didn't come till adulthood. They had per-seminary years with classes normally taken already in high school. Well?, ???, but why not? What else was there that made sense to me at the time? Nothing! So they helped me to apply to the seminary.

I was tentatively relieved as I was driving home, single-mindedly intent on working the corn-pack in the office of Green Giant at Winthrop MN. My car radio happened to be broadcasting Beethoven's ninth symphony. During the final Ode to Joy fourth movement which had not previously, nor since greatly enraptured me, I was overcome with an overpowering emotional/ spiritual sensation. And I was also suddenly peacefully resigned and strongly convicted that my seminary application was the divine intention for me. I was for the first time in over a year comfortably at peace about my future.

I was being captured, and blessed with an incredible sense of well-being. I sensed that my desert had come into bloom. I was finally consciously heeding the Spirit of God's directing. Pastor Rohde, a sober man, whom I went to see, was happy for me to have decided to "address the urgent need of the world"; Knowing me from confirmation studies, he gladly supplied the recommendation required by the seminary.

My Prussian spirit however prevented me from sharing my spiritual supernatural encounter, nor my plans for revised study with my family. I had after all as yet no assurance of acceptance at seminary. I was then still at home awaiting the corn-pack when I received a draft notice for induction into the US Army slated for mid-September -- two weeks before the U's Fall quarter would have begun. Routinely, all men had by age been required to take a pre induction physical exam, about which I had completely forgotten as being of no significance. After all, I was a student with a deferral. Diabolically, they knew they had me, were I again to choose to enroll at the U. I was without a student deferment during the Summer when the U was out-of-session.

What was I to say to my family, other than to put them off, eventually simply stating that I wasn't planning to be inducted. That resulted in their incredulity. I was still without a reply from the seminary, anxious, but confident I'd be accepted. To myself I reasoned, "Why should I bow with a two year army delay in a time when our nation was not at war?" (The Korean War was already over.) Yet, I could hardly explain myself to my family. They couldn't believe my nonchalance. I made no preparation for the army, and was unwilling to explain since I was awaiting an uncertain seminary reply.

Meanwhile, I fortunately had the inspiration of contacting the MN adjutant general and was comfortably informed that if I began seminary classes any day prior to the date of the draft notice, I had an automatic divinity deferral. So I waited, and finally by late August the seminary welcomed me to come. On sharing this letter of acceptance I was however greeted with family suspicions that I was draft dodging. A brother-in-law, himself a veteran, bold and angry, called me a draft dodger to my face. Not having been touched by God, this wasn't rational without bold faith. I brushed that insult aside within my certainty of having experienced a divine call which one can hardly dare to ignore.

None of this bothered my Pa. He was delighted, quietly ecstatic that I had accepted God's plan for me, and with great pride for what he saw was his offering. (You have to be a Prussian to know a Prussian and be able to discern their invisible state of euphoria.) His prayers for me had most likely merely been on pause. Ma was also quiet, but simply beamed. Her thoughts were surely already proudly racing ahead to my ordination, about which she also had felt denied. She may even have already thought of sewing a pulpit gown for me, as she soon did -- being quite proficient as a seamstress. (I plan to be buried in it, though I haven't worn that heavy gown for years.)

Now, how was I to get to Springfield some 500 miles away? I don't believe I ever got so far as to consider that

102

before Pa explained his well determined plan. He would personally take me to seminary that September. The farm work could wait for such as this. At any rate, a new season of milking was not yet under way. Leslie was put in charge, and Walter was to go along to drive on the way back home; I of course would do the driving down to IL. I had long before eased Pa out of the drivers seat when I was going anywhere with him.

Pa even planned and had us stop off in Davenport IA to celebrate my seminary decision with his first cousin. No, Pa was not any longer to be denied. He was accompanying me ostensibly to physically present me to the church, his long intended offering. He was not to live to see my ordination, but to him it was already a certainty. His confidence in me was unspoken but real. (He didn't live to see me graduate, but he did mysteriously visit me in an early morning dream after he died during that final year of seminary, I not yet knowing of his death till an hour later. Thus I was provided with another confirming conviction that I was obeying a divine call.)

Seminary life was far from a breeze, but it was humane and possible, given my religious foundation, as well as being affordable. The close spiritual fellowship in dorm, classroom and dining hall was consoling and encouraging - - a healing balm from the all-around harsh experience at the UofMN, where it's admittedly required rigor met up with my unqualified status. There was no tuition at seminary in those days. We were only responsible for room and board, books and personal items. I dared to see my way with little more than my Summer earnings. I did eventually work at odd jobs on Saturday, like lawn care or washing walls for people who called the seminary for help. (I did get a loan from sister Jan to finish the year prior to internship.) I was blissfully free to study, and the studies were engrossing, not such as with which high school had failed to prepare me. Yet English composition would have been a huge assist. Finally the Spirit had me where he wanted me, and was naturally helping with inspirations that were exciting.

103

That first year I essentially completed a bachelor of arts degree, although from a non-accredited school, which didn't matter to me at the time. I had preparatory studies in Greek, German, basic doctrine, biblical introduction, psychology, with physical exercise, etc. All these to get up to full speed for the next year's curriculum of true theological education, which was at a masters degree level -- Master of Divinity. (Again, since the seminary was at the time only on the path toward becoming accredited, that academic work wasn't fully recognized. However, years later, once the seminary became accredited, they awarded me a Bachelor of Divinity degree in partial recognition, as a good will gesture.)

Besides, I applied to sing in the world-class seminary choir with daily rehearsals in preparation for miscellaneous Sunday area church appearances and an annual two-week multi-state Spring concert tour. (This was a clever and subtle PR and fund raising program.) That would also lead to many Lutheran Hour Choir appearances on international radio, alternating with the St. Louis seminary chorus, to which we were preferred. The Summer before my intern/vicar year, we did a two week Lutheran Hour Choir tour through the Midwest with the then current speaker/preacher. There were also European choir tours in which I didn't participate.

That first year I lived in a two room dormitory suite for four men -- separated study and bedroom. I roomed with two classmates plus one who was in a pre-seminary junior class which I had been allowed to skip. The campus was quite old and relatively small, but a new dorm and also classroom had just been constructed. This old seminary was coming of age regardless of its old buildings and poor neighborhood next to a railroad yard. (The seminary eventually relocated to its present site in Fort Wayne on a splendid campus.) There were around 250 students enrolled; my class had about 60 to start, 53 of which eventually graduated in 1958.

104

After a Summer of now familiar work at Green Giant in different plants in southern MN, the real theological education began -- four years, including internship prior to the fourth year. There was no mistaking the rigor. A few in my class did the minimal, but I was on a mission of recovering my self confidence, grateful for the chance of redemption. In general, there were five or six hours of class with a faculty-attended and officiated chapel in midmorning -- ostensibly to demonstrate the preaching of a sermon. There was a heavy concentration on doctrine, and intensive study of the more critical biblical books, with attention to and reading them in the original Greek language. Theory of preaching, followed by assigned sermons with preaching labs within sections of our class, pastoral care and psychology, and much more filled out the curriculum. The aim was to equip us as pastors, yet also to prepare us for postgraduate study if we chose. So even a B report was not a happy grade to me. Recklessly, one could think, "Oh, well. I only want to be a preacher." Slowly I did finally learn how to actually study. But there were also to be some embarrassing less-than-serious diversions from study.

That second year I was in the new dorm in a suite of three rooms for four men -- two study rooms for two, and all four were in a common bedroom. My studymate, Jim, was one who had been a roommates the first year. He had invited me to come to Detroit (hitchhiking) that summer to buy a cheap used car. (When I brought it home to MN, Pa was not pleased. Perhaps he understood my early adult wish for more freedom, but he knew I was cramping my budget, especially with future auto repair with a much used car. "I'll just do it myself", and gas was cheep.) It would come to haunt me shortly. I took the car, a 1948 four-door Hudson sedan, to seminary. We now had transportation to church, an occasional night out for a beer or two with bull sessions, etc. Then at Christmass holiday recess, having my own potential ride home to MN, I loaned my car to four seminarian friends from New England. On the way back to seminary, in Harrisburg PA, the car broke a piston. They put it in a downtown parking garage and took the train back to seminary.

Fortunately my roommate that year, Jim Sattelmeier, was able and willing to help me retrieve my car during semester break the end of January. His amazing resourcefulness, exemplified by this trip, was a gift that inspired me that has been life-defining. Jim, was experienced in auto repair. He must have returned home for tools and his auto repair manual. So we took his suitcase of tools and another with our clothes, and hitchhiked US 40 and the PA Turnpike to Harrisburg, not knowing any more than the address of the parking ramp. Jim called a church of our synod to explain. The Lutheran pastor who served there, a bachelor, graciously gave us accommodations in his apartment, and the next morning we set to work. We found my car in an unheated January-cold parking garage up on the second level. We put the front end up on blocks, lowered the front end suspension on longer bolts brought along per the manual's direction (thereby being able to remove the oil pan). Then we unbolted the straight-eight cast iron head and removed the broken piston. We were fortunate to have an auto supply store a block away where I bought a new piston and rings.

We slapped the engine back together in a total of two days work. But the engine refused to start, the battery now drained. So we pushed the car onto the elevator to return to the first level, then out the door onto a downtown city street which fortunately had a downhill slope. Jim pushed and I got in to steer, alternately releasing the clutch when we reached the necessary speed to turn the engine over. After about a block, the car sputtered to life. We picked up our suitcases and I drove us back to seminary. We drove all night to get back in time, Jim sleeping in the back seat and I fighting sleep through PA, OH, IN and finally IL.

That experience with the assistance of Jim has gone a long way to shape the faith-dependent life I've had, filled with expectations and blessings that almost never fail. Sadly, Jim quit seminary after that year, afraid that his boundless interests would distract him too much from ministry. Furthermore, I've never been able to track him after graduation, not seeing him since those two years of friendship. Yet I frequently remember and treasure his resourcefulness and the faith that he inspired in me.

If I'd have told Pa about all that, he would have said, "Nun besichts du?" -- Are you awake now? By Spring, I was fortunate to sell the car, even with a knock in the engine -- apparently from a complaining main rod bearing. It also had used-up shock absorbers.

I'm unsure how I then got back to MN and to Green Giant the next Summer, likewise then back to seminary for the following year. For this I was back in the old dorm with three underclass men. They were not really disrespectful. But they were typical sophomores, reluctant to quickly buy my doctrinal and biblical explanations over against their unstudied convictions as expressed in dorm bull sessions. Actually, they were glad for the chance to lean on and challenge an upper-class man by the fact that I was well included in their group of friends. It seems as though I had for that year almost neglected friendships with my own classmates except for class time, now that Jim was gone. We had many good bull and beer sessions wherever. One of that extended group of roommates was elated in Spring to learn that my internship assignment was to his home parish in Glenn Ellyn IL where he himself would unofficially help that Summer.

That then seemed to be a very different Summer. I felt I didn't need to have a job for seminary expenses since I would be salaried as an intern through the next school year. However, I should have worked to earn towards another car I'd need on internship. Consequently I signed on for a two week tour with the seminary choir, billed as the Lutheran Hour Choir, daily singing a mini concert at Lutheran Hour Rallies in the Midwest, as previously mentioned. Walter was in the army, Leslie was in charge on the farm, and Pa was in serious decline with miscellaneous heart problems. He wanted to go back to vacation for a spell at his favorite family fishing resort near Brainerd MN. He and Ma and I went together. I was their driver, but did enjoy the fishing and relaxation. However, Pa had a heart attack after a few days and was admitted for about a week at the local hospital. He rallied and we eventually went home.

Chapter 10 -- Internship & My June - 1956

The following recount of my Summer of 1956 may seem too impossibly lucid for belief, given that it recalls events from over 60 years ago. It's however dependable because it follows a script written down years ago. That was done because of the multiple blessed events in a most sacred time in my life, which I was determined to dearly remember.

To begin, I had been assigned by the presidents/bishops of the LCMS, in consultation with the seminary, to a year of internship at Grace Lutheran Church, Glenn Ellyn IL Therewith my self confidence (suffered by the failed effort to become a doctor of medicine) had been largely restored. First, by reaching this significant milestone in my study of theology. Secondly, the church had by that choice appointment confirmed me in that self assessment. The full significance of this appointment was not however at the time apparent to me. Nevertheless, I was considerably reassured from beyond myself. The effect was a recaptured spirit of well-being.

What I didn't know at the time, which might have defeated me with overconfidence, was the import of a meeting at the seminary shortly after my appointment, and before the previous school year had ended. I was summoned to an informal meeting with the dean, Dr. Eggold, and the Rev. Carl Harman, the pastor at Grace Church, who was to be my intern supervisor. Strangely, we met outside, merely engaging in pleasantries. These two apparently knew and respected each other. Harman was a district vice-president (auxiliary bishop). I assumed that he came for a meeting which was coincidental with that convenient time of introduction between myself and Pastor Harman.

What I didn't yet know was that Harman was considering, or had even already accepted a call to a church in AZ, all of which had not been anticipated when Grace had applied for an intern. The two had obviously not met for friendship, but over concern about my needing to serve in a pastoral vacancy in a large parish. Was I up to the demand? Might there be a need for a reassignment? Apparently the dean had full confidence in me, and was introducing the two of us to reassure Harman, without subjecting me to a difficult and worrisome possibility not ready to be made public. Apparently, I made a good impression in that brief meeting, and my appointment was allowed to proceed, effectively adding significant partners in prayer.

All Summer I was blissfully unaware of the escalated challenge, content with beginning a new chapter of my life. I had also thought I had been freed from the urgent need to pursue my usual Summer employment at Green Giant, by reason of anticipating of a salary. Meanwhile, it was hoped that I could help out at the farm where Leslie was taking charge, because Walter had been drafted into the army. Also since Pa was struggling with a heart condition. Farm work seemed like a pleasant change of pace in what was understood and comfortable. (Ma also had had a heart attack the previous Summer -- on the evening before sister's Caroline wedding.)

As already related, they both wished for me to take them that Summer for some relaxation at a resort near Brainerd MN at Wise Lake. There Pa then had a mild heart attack and was briefly hospitalized. By mid August, both were well enough to "take" me to Glenn Ellyn. They were not to be denied their proud moment of presenting me to the church. I was their gift to God, hoped for and prayed about for many years. (Thoughtlessly, Pa was expected and did manage thereafter to drive himself and Ma back to MN, though he must have assumed and expressed his confidence.)

We arrived at Grace in time for a late afternoon meeting with the six deacons of the church and June Radtke, the executive secretary of the congregation. They were covering for Pastor Carl Harman, my intended supervisor, who had accepted a call and left for a parish in AZ earlier that Summer. I was to be serving alone for a while in that

110

600+ communicant member parish in an affluent upper-middle class western suburb of Chicago. The deacons meant to say that they were there to help. I was so consumed with this major new chapter of my life that I gave little thought to June, beyond having the impression that she was a lovely, gracious and a confident church secretary.

The deacons were introducing her to me as my primary contact for orientation and information. They informed me of having secured some Sunday preaching assistance for the near term from an ordained pastor who would preside at monthly Communion. But they expected me to otherwise serve and provide a pastoral presence: leading worship, preaching and visiting the hospitalized and homebound, teaching confirmation classes -- which classes were already scheduled to start, etc.

The meeting with the deacons went well, and the chairman, Mr. Youngbludt, an executive for the Northwestern RR, invited me and my parents to his elegant home for dinner. My parents were to stay there overnight. They were treated with utmost respect regardless of their obvious humble nature. After dinner I was taken to meet an elderly couple, by the name of Bum and Pappy Niles, members of Grace who lived just across the city limits in next door Wheaton. With them I was to room and board as part of my remuneration. Their simple two bedroom home and all-around hospitality was to become a year long gift.

My further orientation over the next week was then in part with Park Fredricks. He was a member of Grace and to be a third year seminarian whom I had met in my dorm during the previous year. He had been retained as an unofficial Summer vicar by Grace to help cover during the pastoral vacancy. Park took me on a complete round of visits with the shutins of the congregation, and introduced me around as the new student pastor. Thereafter, I was on my own, depending on June as my assistant and coworker.

June was undoubtedly an incomparable and heaven-sent gift, whom I was most blessed to meet just at that time and situation. Born in Chicago, then living from junior high school age in Wheaton IL, graduated from Valparasio University IN with a bachelor of arts degree in social service. She had returned home after graduation seven years prior since her father, who had been a senior executive for the IRS, had recently died. Her mother had quickly been offered and taken a significant position in the appellate division of IRS in their downtown Chicago office. To this she was commuting daily by train. At the same time, both of June's aging grandmothers in turn had then come to live at the Radtke home for care. To be nearby these grandmothers, June took the position of the pastor's secretary in her home congregation of Grace, Glenn Ellyn IL. This allowed her mother to provide the more significant primary financial support for the family.

Now seven years later, my inauguration as an intern in this church was a huge moment for me. There were many logistics to be negotiated. One of these was buying a car for which I had no funds. (What was I thinking? I should have earned one that Summer. But that's how thing went in those days without proper counseling.) The church janitor, who was a trustee, a retired and highly regarded member, quickly connected me for that with a friend who gladly loaned me the funds. For such reasons I didn't at first have the luxury to take serious notice of June beyond her being a confident and helpful woman. In fact, it probably wasn't till some time later that I began to appreciate her personal significance: She was an incredibly resourceful person who knew about everything in the church and the community. Without her I would have been truly alone in a situation too large for me. And she was incredibly empathetic, especially of me. All Summer, she had been administratively in charge at Grace, and would largely remain so till the new pastor came in November. She was broadly trusted by the congregation and at ease with all the routine church office work, including the monthly newsletter and the Sunday

112

worship folder. She was effectively the Sunday School superintendent.

Work in a church office had previously only been barely observed by myself. But I began functioning somewhat comfortably those first weeks with June's ready assisting information. In the afternoon I visited parents and teens to organize two catechism classes, each of near two dozen; And then I taught those weekly after-school classes. That along with the regular parish duties of visiting shutins, those hospitalized, and the lapsed Sunday School children's parents in preparation to stage Sunday School Rally Day. June's confidence in me was graciously projected, enabling my pastoral presence in a congregation which was saddened for the loss of a much loved pastor. I don't remember much of the details except that I had the steadying contributions and ready information offered by this lovely woman in the office next to mine. The connecting door was always open. She already had the new Sunday School year with teachers and materials well organized, along with the schedule of guest pastors for the monthly Communion Sundays. All other Sundays I led and preached. Having been the church secretary for seven years, and well trained by a competent pastor; she knew where things were, what was what, and who was who. From the start, we worked well together.

Besides, she subtly showed a ready compassion for me in my overmatched new surroundings and responsibilities. For simple example, I distinctly remember the first time: supper one evening with her and her mother at their new Glenn Ellyn home several weeks later when she expressed mild anxiety, a concern echoed by her mother. They were alarmed for my evening pastime of driving alone through the larger community to get aquatinted with the neighborhood, not appreciating how a farm boy generally has a dependable *local gedechtness* -- not likely to get lost, always conscious of place. I was enjoying this orientation to my new community as well as driving my little car.

113

The special moment for June and me came one night in early November in River Forest at what is now Concordia University about 15 miles away. The new pastor, Emil Hartman, had just arrived in the parish and was on that Friday night unbelievably preoccupied, when at the same time there was a church voters meeting of his new congregation. He had not yet been installed as pastor and so felt no obligation to attend, and considered me to be responsible for the opening devotions. But he had also considered it possible for me to be his errand boy and go first to Concordia to pick up his son, a seminarian at St. Louis, who was getting a ride that far for a weekend at his new home. Hartman was more importantly committed to a dinner engagement with friends from his old church in Chicago.

I went to meet his son in my subcompact Hudson Hornet. But the pastor's son didn't arrived by the time I had to get back for the start of voters meeting. Being in a hurry to avoid being late, I drove my little car just a bit too fast. Consequently it threw a rod bearing, producing a loud knock in the engine. After doing the voters meeting devotions, the only option that came to mind was to drive slowly to June's house and ask her to take me back to Concordia in her mother's car to fetch the pastor's son.

She was, as ever, more than willing to help. We got to Concordia, but still not finding anyone the likes of a seminarian waiting for a ride. So we sat in her car talking the time away while watching for the pastor's son. She was never at a loss of something to say to anyone, a most natural and pleasant conversationalist. I was impressed by her maturity and confidence. Because we had already come to enjoy each others company, the time was far from heavy; There was no end of things to talk about -- the congregation and community which I was eager to understand. At some point I got the nerve to ask her if she would consider dating.

After a brief silence, she humbly responded with a confession: "Are you aware that I'm probably six years

114

older?" (There must have been some calculated interest in me for her to have made that approximate calculation. I was to learn later that she had already resigned herself to the likelihood that she was to remain an old-maid. Eventually, she would look after her widowed mother much as she had gone home after college to care for two dying grandmothers in turn. There was nothing lacking in her confidence, based on a long record of being competent, but she didn't consider herself attractive. That she had never had a boyfriend suggested this to her mind. Her social life involved women friends, most of whom were also still single.)

"Do you realize that I'm probably six years older than you are?" It was clear from the kind way she said this that it was not a put-off. She then immediately offered to introduce me to some eligible girls. I refused her self-deprecation by bluntly telling her, "No! I'm specifically interested in you." She couldn't completely hide her welling emotions. I had been unwilling to accept her modesty. But she was struck by my admission of being attracted to her. I was being boldly forward, reasoning that we were mature adults -- why jockey through extended indirection and traditional games? After a gestating pause, our emotional gears were quickly meshing. I don't remember the specific words that finally followed, but she was clearly consenting with anticipation. I believe we held hands, already to be forever joined. We never looked back thereafter, except to often marvel to each other and celebrate that straightforward unembarrassed conversation at such an opportune/divine coming together (hence I know I'm here reflecting June's state of mind). Our life had been quickly cast together, and we both sensed it. Taking her home later that night is a blur -- too much merged with our ensuing courtship.

Finally, about 10pm, Pastor Hartman drove up alongside with his son already in the car, having eluded us and called home to be picked up. Hartman gave us a preview of the year at hand by berating us for our incompetence, suggesting that we had obviously been too distracted with each other to be on watch. That could just possibly have been partly true. It's interesting how others may sense something about us that we ourselves are just beginning to understand. Imagine his point of view, suspecting the new intern and his secretary getting closer than he considered convenient, or proper? But he never latter addressed it.

Our subsequent first date followed already on the next day. It was a Saturday afternoon of hiking in nearby Mortons Arboretum. This became typical, leading to visiting other places of natural beauty, such as June had come to enjoy, like Garfield Park Conservatory in Chicago, the lakefront with boardwalk and Buckingham fountain, etc.. Shortly thereafter, I was at June's home for Sunday dinner, attended also by her Uncle Adolph and Aunt Catherine. They had come from their home in Chicago to install curtain rods in their brand new home. Uncle Adolph, loved June, and unable to contain his hopes for her, subtly commented on a noticed magnetism between June and I. Besides, there was no mistaking the welcome of June's mom from the very first. (June never told me how it went when she told her mother about me.) Already by Thanksgiving, little more than a month later, at this same aunt and uncle's home in Chicago, overflowing with June's extended family of cousins and nieces, they considered us virtually engaged. Well, I was already part of their family. This, apparently out of a happy excitement that their much loved and respected June might finally have a husband after all. And we might have made pledges to each other by Christmass had it not been for the seminary's prohibition against unmarried seminarians being engaged before the end of internship.

I took a train home to visit my parents the week after Christmass, and explained to my mother and pastor that I had met a woman about whom I was quite serious, who was however six years older than I. Both of them softly counseled me to consider the negatives. Pastor Roth, the recently new pastor at home, even confessed that his wife

116

was older than he, implying a strained relationship. I dared to believe that his experience was not as fortunate as the one I dared to anticipate.

There were not too many evening church meetings in those times; More often than not, I began to spend many of them at June's home, playing canasta, etc., and then holding hands watching TV on their living room couch. We'd then talk till late hours after her mom went up to bed. Bum and Papa Niles were at times upset by my getting home long after they had retired. June was so emotionally starved in her extended old-maid-hood that leave-taking was always long and hard.

My internship year, for its frustration of having a supervisor who had no room for my help in the parish, brought the blessing of making me more self reliant, finding my own chances for ministry. He had no interest nor ability to be my supervisor. Nevertheless, it did then have a redeeming value of finding a woman who could and was excited to share in my calling. Before the new pastor arrived in the parish, I had started two confirmation classes, was regularly visiting a significant number of shut-ins, doing the hospital visits plus leading Sunday worship. Besides I had been calling on families with Sunday School delinquents. Except for the latter, and teaching the junior confirmation class, as well as working with the young people's Walther League, all that dramatically and firmly ended when Hartman took over the parish. I sensed that he couldn't dare to share the respect and possible devotion of parishioners.

I had a frustratingly light load for the balance of my internship, grudgingly allowed to preach once per month for his conviction that he was a superior preacher who needed to solidify his position as the pastor. With the first sermon I preached after he was installed as pastor, and immediately following the first of two services, when meeting him on the stairway, he proceeded to point out my supposed unscholarly understanding of Jacob as a type of Christ; He was convinced that Jacob was rather a first-rate rascal. That was to remain the extent of his evaluations of my sermons.

I did have the use of his desk in the otherwise unoccupied pastor's study, newly acquired by the congregation. He used it only for about five minutes each mid morning to come and give June his secretarial work and her marching orders, while I was completely ignored and briefly banished. Apparently, he preferred to do his desk and study work in the parsonage next door where I was never invited or ever comfortable to trespass. Henceforth, June was considered his secretary, no longer the executive church secretary; He was to be directly contacted at the parsonage for all affairs; He clearly considered June a regrettable holdover from the previous administration to be dispensed with when convenient. She would have quit except for me, so she soon planned to resign when my year was over at the end of the following June, 1957.

Hartman shed no tears over either of us at that parting. My report to the dean on returning to seminary that Fall made a daringly full disclosure of this misfortune; And it was to my knowledge never addressed by the seminary, as it should have been with the bishop. Blessedly, I escaped criticism or extended interrogation. Apparently he trusted and believed me. It's quite possible that Pastor Harman had privately shared my ordeal with the dean. June was at times writing him.

Under modern circumstances, I might have been assigned another year of vicarage. I did feel somewhat cheated. Should I have early-on called the seminary, yet toward what open conflict? The seminary might have transferred me to a different assignment. Nervously I wondered all year how they would view my engagement to the parish secretary in such a conflicted circumstance. Personally, I felt that my vicarage was fruitful enough, since I had gained much confidence under trial, and at least had found a true mate, who also had incomparable experience with parish administration.

Ma and Pa came for my final Sunday at Grace on June 30, 1957 when I preached on Luke 11:5-13, sermon #32. Interestingly it was about prayer, which was to become my ministry long interest and focus, even especially now in retirement. There was a parish picnic in a local park that day following worship at church. I remember that Hartman did not attend. On recently reviewing my sermon files, I found that I had also preached on the first three Sundays that month, with Hartman apparently preaching on the second last one. Obviously he had taken the opportunity for a vacation before I left the parish.

I still vividly remember that last Sunday as being a nice Summer day. I was proud to be introducing my country-simple parents to the congregation, demonstrating some confidence to them in ministry in a social setting so unlike theirs, and especially introducing my fiancee to my parents for the first time. The congregation had also made the picnic a farewell to June, whom they were proudly sending on to become a pastor's wife. They had reasons to be quite confident that she would be a "Mrs. Pastor", as it's occasionally said of an exceptionally competent pastor's wife, as self-effacing as the Blessed Virgin, seeking no personal fulfillment other than private servanthood in happy bond with her spouse.

The rest of that Summer was perhaps the happiest Summer of my life, with the additional reason of feeling free after having completed a difficult vicarage. It left only a supposedly sure-thing last year at seminary before ordination. Particularly, there was the distinct joy of having found a worthy companion for life and ministry. The first thing I did was to give her a ring. She was uncomfortable when I kneeled before her to present a formal petition with the ring. To her, my proposal had long been a done deal to her delight. She gave me an expensive Omega watch. She had long before been rejoicing in this inevitable milestone. She elected not to look for another job till after I returned to seminary. So we first took a weeks vacation together at Uncle Paul's place near Michigan City IN, her mother

119

coming along. From there Paul and June's mom commuted by rail to Chicago each day, he at the main Chicago post office where he was the Chief Postal Inspector, and she at the Appellate Division of the Chicago branch of IRS. For that precious week we were left all day with only the joy of each other, almost but not quite like a honeymoon. I remember now the horrible sunburn I got at the beach on Lake Michigan.

After this vacation, June's Uncle Paul made arrangements for me to meet the man in charge of hiring at the main catalogue distribution center of Sears in Chicago. I was immediately hired and put to work. But it was incredibly menial. I managed to work only that one day. I spoke that evening with a deacon at Grace Church, Ed Kash, who with his wife were leading members. He was a VP at Kraft Foods at their downtown Chicago world headquarters and plant. He had me come there the next day for a job with very good pay on the oleo production line. There I worked till September. Several times, when our schedules coincided, he came to my factory floor to give me a ride home after work in his fine car. I was his snitch, reporting on the gambling in my division of the plant.

So I stayed on at the Niles family home where I had been comfortably boarding all year. I rode the commuter train to work each day, and still had a fair amount of time with my June. I worked a two week rotating shift; But with June not working, my free time could always be spent with her when not mowing their lawn, doing odd household jobs for them. In particular, I rototilled and seeded their back yard which had not yet been established at their year old new house to which they had moved from Wheaton shortly before I came to Glen Ellen.

September 1957 till graduation from seminary in June of 1958 would have been a long and hard nine months had it not been for my decision to spend almost every weekend in Glen Ellen. Fortunately, US Highway 66 from Springfield to Chicago was an expressway with enough traffic to allow for easy hitchhiking when there was no one from the seminary community who was also going up to Chicago for the weekend. I had sold my not-too-dependable little car shortly after throwing another rod bearing on returning from MN from my Pa's funeral in October (to be narrated shortly). There were some harry hitchhiking trips involving unsavory characters, a few of which were Chicago mobsters who apparently felt constrained to do a compensating good deed. The worst of it was waiting for rides, which for the most part were however always straight through by reason of my suitcase sized cardboard sign which had Chicago on one side and Springfield on the other. June would usually take me on Sunday evening to a likely crossroad on the SW end of the Chicago metro area, her mom occasionally coming along. There she would wait out of sight, as she later told me, till I had gotten a ride. I can imagine her anxiety.

By Halloween, the routine of spending every weekend in Glen Ellen was made permanent by Uncle Paul landing me a Saturday job as a substitute mail carrier in neighboring Wheaton. It was difficult work at first, but the postmaster was willing to give me slack for Uncle Paul's sake. He also knew that my route surrounding Wheaton College was the most difficult route he had. This because it had many homes with boarding college students. These required excessive attention for forwarding mail when they moved or quit. However, I soon got the hang of casing (sorting) mail and sometimes wasn't actually the last carrier to check back in at the post office at the end of the day. I did valiant battle with many big and little dogs on my route, but was never bitten -- a big leather mail bag quickly dropped from the shoulder can be a good shield, or for effective intimidation.

The pay was great, but June also regularly deposited some of her earnings into my checking account so that I could regularly pay all my bills through the last year at seminary. Besides, I could concentrate on my study, not needing to find and work odd jobs. That ability to pay my bills was fortunate, in view of low pastoral salaries after graduation.

121

I finished school with only a small debt to sister Jan from the year before vicarage which we promptly paid off. June had gotten a job in downtown Chicago at a company which published the thick wholesale catalogues used by most hardware store merchants around the country. Her competence was quickly recognized and well rewarded. She made friends that year among coworkers and bosses which lasted till she died 30 years later.

Chapter 11 -- Graduation & Marriage - 1957-8

My final year at seminary was a refreshing reunion with classmates and professors, pursuing my studies with confidence. I had not made a specific dorm or dorm-mate application, so I was by SOP placed in a room with underclassmen, in fact two first year seminarians. And this was in the newer dorm in a suite of two adjoining rooms for three -- bedroom and study. We had a daily dorm room devotional period together, often joined by other more liturgically inclined seminarians. These were not just informal prayer, but the traditional prayer offices with assigned daily scripture. But other than that fellowship, I kept mostly to myself by reason of needing to study through the weekdays, since I was away from seminary to Glenn Ellyn for the weekends where study wasn't particularly feasible. There was consequently also no time for beer and bull sessions. Anyway, my own classmates like myself were also quite future oriented, not too much taking time to relax with each other, with few exceptions. Those already married, lived off campus, and many others were also spending weekends out of town for multiple reasons. I was content with the fellowship I could have with classmates before, during and after class sessions; That as well as during the recess period after midmorning chapel in the coffee commons in the basement of my dorm.

That break was also mail-call time, for which we unmarried graduating seminarians waited more than most. I myself eked out some minutes every day to write letters so as to receive some (email would have been nice). Both June and I would have been in tears for want of a daily note of reassurance. I wish now I'd have saved hers; She saved all mine, which I destroyed after she died. It would have been too painful to review them.

Our classes that last year were on a graduate level. Our parish experiences made us ripe with insights we were eager to share and evaluate. Our professors respected us for what we now better knew, yet also needing to guide and restrain us sophomore pastors-to-be. However, they were likewise keen to hear how the church out there was functioning. Consequently classes in pastoral theology and practice were high excitement. It might have been useless for the seminary to schedule more preaching theory and labs -- that would not have been palatable at our stage (better let pastors struggle for a few years and then.) But we still needed to take a third year of dogmatics. This focused on the third article of the creed with its teachings of the Holy Spirit and the church. And as ever, we had more classes with in-depth reading and interpreting key books of the bible in Greek. We also studied more church history which was taught by president Boepler, who was however often away on fundraising and synod matters.

Then on the morning of October 3, 1957, about 5am, there was a knock on the door of our dorm room. It was a summons to come to answer the dorm phone down on the first floor entry. It had arrested me from a wordless dream of Pa reaching out to me -- very mysterious and confused, without message or resolution. I don't remember any longer who the caller was, perhaps my sister Jan, or more likely Walter. The word was that Pa had died in New Ulm MN after a short hospitalization with his heart condition. I can't say that I was shocked or surprised since I well knew of his long cardiac struggles, and also that he was just then again in the hospital. But more particularly, I was quickly comforted by my certainty of his faith, which had never wavered; And there was relief for his freedom and peace. Together, we both had been relentlessly taught by the farm that life is lived with its inevitable end in mind, all in the embrace of a loving Father. He was proud of all six of us siblings; Yet I dare to think that I was unique in his hope; And his apparently coming in my dream at the moment of his ascending into our Father's care to bid me farewell, was very comforting, and has been a lifelong consolation.

I excused myself to the dean of the seminary to attend Pa's funeral, and then drove up to Chicago, and with

June drove on up to MN. (Till that time, I must have been driving my car back and forth to seminary each weekend.) Pastor Roth is remembered to have preached more lively sermons; At least the one he preached at Pa's funeral has been precious and remembered by me ever since. He told of having visited Pa on one of his last days. Sensing Pa's imminent death, he had a devotion with him in which he compared Pa to ancient Simeon who upon meeting the infant Jesus in the temple at his presentation, exclaimed a readiness to die since he had now seen his savior as it had been promised. -- Luke 2:22ff.

Simeon's song, called the *Nunc Dimittis*, is a key part of daily Vespers, and now frequently reminds me therefore of Pa, with thanksgiving for his faith and his tenacious abiding hope in me. He surely was not the only farmer who ever gave his firstborn son to the Lord, somewhat according to Mosaic command to ancient Israel; Pa never told me that he was on that account wishing me to become a pastor; Yet, I'm daring to believe that such was the special expression of his faith and devotion -- he frequently gave me reason to sense that he understood such biblical concepts. Perhaps, such an idea didn't from my birth dare to arise in him; But when he then had two more sons, he apparently dared that offering in his prayers. I glean this from such as his first remembered encouragement to study theology. I was in eighth grade when he counseled me that the farm was no place for me with my hayfever. Without meds, I was in fact a basket case at that stage of life. (With my appendectomy hospitalization that year, I did finally get medical help with hayfever.) Of this he had first hand experience. Yet, that was but his convenient argument, not having the piety of free spiritual conversation. Again, you have to be a Prussian yourself to see through into the soul of a Prussian, for reason of the inability of emotional words.

June and I were only about a hundred miles on our way back to Chicago after Pa's funeral when my little Hudson threw another main bearing near Austin MN. I had

125

not been driving more than the limit. (You who know that I drive with authority, will have trouble believing that, but...) We found there a garage where we were told that, yes, it's a main bearing, but we have no parts. These would have to be shipped overnight from Minneapolis. So they proceeded to tear the engine down. They had no waiting room, so the two of us sat in the car as they worked on it. Such a prison was never a real problem for us -- we had each other. We knew no one in town, but fortunately they had both a restaurant and motel in walking distance to which we went in late afternoon. By noon the following day, we were gingerly on our measured way to Glenn Ellyn. It had felt good to have June with me for this time of mourning for Pa. She so automatically helped turn me to the future for which Pa was now even more faithfully praying. But I keenly felt I had missed too many classes, so after taking June home, I quickly returned to the seminary where I must have almost immediately put my car up for sale -- I don't remember the details. So from then on I was a hitchhiker till after our wedding. That's when June's mom gave us the gift of a 1956 Ford Fairlane 500 with a big Thunderbird V8 engine. With it we were set for Canada.

I had rejoined the seminary choir that Fall, but now by October we were well enough rehearsed to begin the seminary PR of singing many Sunday mornings at area churches. These were all the more important since the choir was gearing up for a European tour the following Summer. I hadn't envisioned the conflict with weekends in Glenn Ellyn. In requesting an excuse from our director, he made it clear that such excuses couldn't be routine. Though he considered me his leading first tenor, I was very sadly obliged to resign with his blessing, having fully explained my situation. I was sad to disappoint him.

(Meeting Dr. Fred Precht thirty plus years later, after he had actually called me, having been pleased to review the publication of my first book, he had apparently forgotten that I hadn't gone on that European choir tour, so firmly and graciously had I been in his mind in memory of those three years of service. He had also been my much appreciated professor of advanced German, liturgy and worship. I was touched that he had remember me so well. I was especially also happy for his bringing his wife to that meeting with Me and Addie. In my seminary years he was married to a woman who worked in the IL state capitol where she had an affair, which led to a mandated divorce. She had always been invisible to us seminarians, obviously not in tune with our professors work. The faculty had also seemingly looked down on him, considering their preaching more important than the liturgies he used when doing his turn to conduct our daily chapel worship. He had by then left the seminary and finished the significant work of being chief editor of the then new LCMS hymnal. Now he clearly had a wife who loved and was loved. I was happy for him and was honored that he appreciated my work in his field of study. On parting, he touchingly blessed me in German.)

When that Winter of the last year of seminary had nearly passed, the seminary president, Dr. Boepler, began personal interviews with all member of my class in preparation for a call assignment, come May. That call assignment would be done in concert with all the presidents/bishops of the LCMS. Because he had once served in Canada where more pastors were needed beyond the number of Canadians in my class, he specifically asked some of us about our willingness to accept a Canadian call. Out of my believing that any call should never be foreclosed, I remember saying that I was open to anything the church considered best. Apparently he made the decision, because later on Call-Day after our calls had been distributed on that fateful day in St. Louis in early May, my MN bishop asked about my reaction to my call to Luseland Sask.., adding that he understood that I had asked to go to Canada. He would have had first claim on me for a MN call. I let it pass without comment. I was not at that time particularly pleased to be posted to Saskatchewan. Yet, it soon settled in as an adventurous possibility, both to me

127

and June; I had no thought to refuse the call -- if that had even been a possibility without serious consequences.

It has always been a sadness of that call time that one much loved class member was not awarded a call, apparently for lack of scholarship. The whole class loved him and believed that he would have become an effective pastor of souls. At the same time, one of our class, who had been a roommate in my first year, and who was clearly an alcoholic, received a call. His life soon ended in death and tragedy. Another, an erudite high-class black man, who didn't even have an accent, was assigned to an inner city black mission in southern IL. He had grown up in a cultured area of New York city. He was reduced to a class-misfit and was a casualty to the church. Such are the dangers of failed wisdom by leaders, specifically the failure to secure the willingness of a candidate for ministry to a specific place.

The month of June 1958 was nonstop. First, the seminary graduation attended by my mother, sister Jan and June (proudly introduced to classmates). Neither of these had been to Springfield before; So with enough slack time we went to visit the nearby Abraham Lincoln home and heritage park at New Salem. The graduation service was quite ordinary compared to present day seminary graduation ceremonies at our seminary now sited in Fort Wayne IN. (I witnessed that again in the year of 2018 on my 60th anniversary of graduation in their grand chapel, as I had on my 55th anniversary.) In 1958 in Springfield IL we had only a gymnasium large enough for such a service, and with a stage in place of a sanctuary. But we were nonetheless excited, and my dear ones attending were surely proud for me, no less than Pa who was not visibly present yet surely in spirit. He in particular, certainly had an UN-Prussian like beaming countenance. As for me, I felt like the farm-boy who had finally made good, somewhat vindicating myself. I had even accumulated a transcript more than sufficient for automatic admission to graduate school. No class ranks were published but I was proudly near the top of my class of 53.

My wedding with June was scheduled for June 22nd to coincide with the English District convention in River Forest IL. This would bring June's former pastor, Carl Harman, back from AZ so as to then also officiate at our wedding. We decided not to be married at Grace, both so as to avoid extended negotiations with Pastor Hartman, and because Grace had sold its church building and lot so as to eventually build a new sanctuary on the lot across the street where the parsonage would be raised. They had a relatively new parish hall where they then worshiped in the gymnasium. In that building June and I had met two years earlier. However, we didn't want to be married on the free-throw line. So we arranged with the nearby church in Wheaton where we were both well known. But our formal wedding reception was in the Grace parish hall/gymnasium with an extended party immediately thereafter at June's home.

It was a long way to our wedding from MN, but I was most honored that so many were to come down from there to see and pray with us. First there were Ma and sister Jan -- just recently having come to my seminary graduation. They brought along my grandmother Krueger, then 92 years old, and obviously greatly excited for my future by witness of her willingness to go through such a trip to Chicago. In addition they also brought along my Uncle Martin, Ma's brother-in-law. (I can't fully explain his coming, but apparently it was for his close friendship with Pa. He and, now departed, Aunt Ida, Ma's sister, were never absent from our family gatherings, or we from theirs. He must have felt like Pa's stand-in at my wedding, not having a child of his own, and apparently often having together celebrated my going to seminary. He and Aunt Ida -- Ma's closest sibling -- had always been special to me, and I obviously to them.)

Others of my family who came to our wedding were sister Bernice with my niece, two year old Ann; Walter, my

129

best man with his fiancee, Darlyne; Norman Sifferath, my high School best friend as groomsman; and brother Leslie who served as an usher. June had a small family, and they all came: three uncles, Arnold, Adolph, and Paul who gave June away to me at the altar; Also "Uncle" Bud & "Aunt" Mable Pittan; "Uncle" John & "Aunt" Edith Kromroy (actually cousins of June's mom and dad). Also the Burchard family of cousins, Ed and Ruth, and John and Ginny. These all came to June's home following the reception for opening gifts and more celebration.

That party was still going strong when June and I left about 8pm to stay in a motel somewhere in the NW suburban Chicago area on our way to a honeymoon in New Auburn WI, near Hayward. (We raised a few eyebrows among the elderly by changing clothes together in June's bedroom before leaving. My shirt was ruined from a leaking ballpoint pen, and June had to switch out of a huge hoop skirted wedding dress.) The fishing was lousy at that lake, but neither of us had come to fish. I'm not really sure we really tried, although one day we did row across the lake. The reason we went there was to be somewhat nearby to my home in Gibbon MN for the following Saturday for my brother Walter's wedding to Darlyne, at which I was to be his best man. Thereafter, June and I had a few days in the Twin Cities at Jan's vacated apartment before returning to Glen Ellen to start packing to move to Saskatchewan in mid July.

We contracted with Mayflower Moving to take our small partial load, resulting in considerable delay for their need to pair ours with other shipments in the general direction of Saskatchewan. In furniture we had only June's bedroom set and a bookcase. It was fully two weeks after we arrived at our new home before they were able to deliver our stuff.

Saying goodbye to June's mom seemed amazingly easy for June. I feel safe to say that this was for the great love and excitement she had for her own chosen life beyond home. I had had an amicable relationship with

130

June's mom, and appreciated how eagerly she worked to make June's new adventure one of her own excitement. We took the first leg of our moving trip to Canada, going as far as Gibbon. We stayed but a day to say goodbye to my Ma, Walter, his new bride, and Leslie. The next leg took us as far as Minot ND. That entrance onto the true prairie was essentially with the conscious sentiment and spirit of leaving home for good. Furthermore it was consciously connected to the prairies of Saskatchewan.

With some trepidation the next day, we approached our new world of Canada. It was high adventure to cross the US/Canadian border at Portal ND, where our car was searched almost as thoroughly as when going in or out of a hostel country. They confiscated several potted cacti and some fruit left from lunch. (Strangely, our moving van boxes, which followed us two weeks later, had apparently not been violated.) Since we were applying for residency, there was much confusion at the border over possibly paying import duty on the car -- the total difference between our cost and the value of such a vehicle in Canada. The question arose because we had declared it as a wedding gift from June's mom, which it was. They reluctantly passed on it subject to review. (Six months later we were forced to pay nearly $400 unless we returned the car to the US.) We were then forwarded to immigration officials in Saskatoon who ordered a full physical exam for both June and me. We both easily passed the exam; The only problem was that they noticed that I had a deviated septum. We were free to proceed.

Heading west from there we left paved roads behind. Earlier, on our way up to Saskatoon we had already traveled on a graveled highway for a hundred miles. That left all our belongings in the trunk covered with a good layer of dust. These last 160 miles likewise went over endless flat and dusty prairie. This was slowly discouraging us on that hot day (no AC). And for not having seen a hill now since MN. It didn't help our spirits then to see the town welcome sign when bypassing Bigger SK, which

131

proclaimed: "New York is big, but this is Bigger". There was brief excitement a little further on when driving through a major coulee -- ancient post-galcier riverbed with a small stream at the bottom of a mile wide river valley with trees. We both expressed the hope that perhaps Luseland might be in a similar coulee, as opposed to endless vistas, but it was not to be. It was hot and the farmsteads universally seemed to be nothing more than a collection of unpainted shacks, many of the buildings barely standing up, including some of the homes. For my woman who had always lived comfortably in the second biggest city, this could be thought almost more than doable, since we were not merely passing through but coming to stay; Yet she never looked-back. She was firmly locked to my side.

We arrived at Holy Trinity Lutheran Church, Luseland Saskatchewan on Thursday July 24, 1958. Both church and parsonage were deserted at our approximate 3pm arrival on a sunny afternoon, we both needing to find a place to pee. The doors were of course unlocked so we walked into what seemed to be the parsonage next door to the church. We quickly found the bathroom, but minus a stool. That was our first inkling that our plumbing would be primitive. So we quickly toured the church so as to find a toilet. But it had no plumbing at all. I finally found a toilet seat on a 5 gallon pail behind the furnace where June rushed to perch. (Only later did we find a similar utility in the parsonage "basement." That basement was a smaller-than-the-house dugout under the house, with dirt walls and a crude stairway.)

Almost immediately we were greeted by Alice Scholer, a member neighbor lady, who with her husband Max and three children became our closest friends. She had already called the official greeters who quickly drove in from the country a mile south of town. These were two more of the most genuine people in the world, Helen and Frieda Osterhold. They were sisters in-law and living as neighbors. Seeing us to have little more than our suitcases,

132

they insisted that we as quickly as possible come out to Helen's farm for supper. They were untouched by any estimation of greatness, and unaffected by the world such as we knew. They were content with but the rudiments of convenience and furnishings. Nonetheless, we were embraced by two families who were so hopeful of us that we could hardly help being what they expected. (We later learned that a few other families had a modern toilet and even TV, but with a snowy video for only a few hours each evening.) This welcome by the Osterholds was perhaps the most ideal entry into a problematic and strange new life situation. They had anticipated things very well, having had earlier experiences with young new pastors from the States: the kitchen shelves and frig had been stocked, and a borrowed bed had been delivered, anticipating the delay of our stuff. I now can only imagine that on going to bed later that night, we must have lain there embracing a long while, with endless thoughts spoken and unspoken swirling in the dark. But the most urgent question had already been tentatively answered: these would apparently be gracious people so easy to serve, and so it turned out to be.

Furthermore, the July prairie, which had troubled us on our way to the far west was later, on closer observation not entirely lacking in beauty, as we both eventually began to notice. The wildflowers were few, but they were therefore the more beautiful and spectacular. Just for that, within a month, I bought an expensive Olympus 35mm camera specifically to take pictures of these cheery roadside greetings. That then became our portal to a prairie we were almost reluctant eventually to leave behind.

It's now been more than 60 years since my August 3, 1958 ordination, having often pondered the strangeness of the process in my case. Yet it was the earthly way that God had to use to effect my "anointing." In such reflections I'm focused on the conflicted polity in the Lutheran church as it was when I began my ministry. It was then even more strange than now in the 21st century. In the LCMS in particular, this ordering of ministry was much confused. I had a call to a particular congregation, via their blind petition, and then authorized by the entire council of presidents (bishops) of the synod. That would seem to project where the authority for ordination was vested. These "bishops" were the visible embodiment and authority in the church, and the Gospel they espoused. They were its officers, and so had established a seminary, and regulated what was to be taught and believed in the church; And they had with the seminary judged and approved me to be an authentic representative of the church. However, in opposition to such a version of authority, the synod at the same time purported that the real authority in the church was God himself (Well, yes, of course!). He was however believed to act rather specifically through individual congregations of believers. Therefore, it was contradictory thought that the power to ordain someone to become a pastor was reserved to the congregations.

As of late July 1958, I was thus not yet a pastor since I hadn't been ordained. The synod had said that I was OK, but a congregation in far off Saskatchewan, who thus knew only remotely of my OKness, was to make a pastor out of me. Out of touch with me, or even my qualifications, they were to ordain me. This meant that they were to consecrate me for life to serve the whole church. They would stand me in the line with the ancient Apostles, and thus Christ himself. Still, they knew that this shouldn't be done by the congregation on its own, but by the authorized act of the area jurisdiction of the church. So by the authorization of the Manitoba-Saskatchewan District president (bishop), his local circuit counselor, needed to ordain me in the presence of, and with the blind approval of Holy Trinity, Luseland SK. That officer was the Rev. Alfred Lucht from Wilkie Sask., some 75 miles to the NE; He could come to Luseland on the evening of Sunday August 3rd. To assist with the laying-on-of-hands -- for the giving of the Spirit -- the Rev. Fred Kohler of Loydminister would also come; Neither of these had ever met me and knew nothing firsthand about my fitness for ministry. The only one there that day who knew me at all was June.

I do believe that the Spirit has done stranger things than my ordination, which I've never questioned as being authentic for all its confused order. I was at that ordination nonetheless given the Spirit by witness of what he still continually does through me. His power has often been dramatically visible to me in myself.

So I was then a pastor by that ordination, and by simultaneous installation was then specifically authorized and ordered to serve Holy Trinity, Luseland, with Word and Sacrament, as well as a small nameless Lutheran church 75 miles to the SW in Sibbald AB. (None from there had attended my ordination and installation.) It made sense to me that my installation was at Luseland so that Holy Trinity and I could pledge each other to faithfulness. But my ordination to serve the whole church ought to have had a more direct relationship with the whole church than by persons who knew nothing of me.

It still saddens me as well that services of ordination of that era were so bare-bones. Where was the lively spirit of celebration so appropriate on such an occasion? I was there only to publicly proclaim my ordination vows, but otherwise I was to sit silently in a special chair at the head of the main aisle. Pastor Lucht was the single efficient, Pastor Kohler only speaking a blessing at the laying-on-of-hands. There was no Communion, at which I should have been allowed to be the celebrant, spiritually wedding me to my people. After all this service was also my installation as their pastor. Such would have been a more grand and significant public and formal introduction of myself as their new pastor.

But there was, at the same time, a different unprogramed and also uncelebrated introduction that nonetheless also occurred that day: June's marvelous mezzo soprano voice -- trained in the music school of Valparaiso University -- was bright, leading the singing of the hymns; The congregation had unintentionally but providentially acquired an unofficial but true cantor, and with much appreciation. From the first bar of the first hymn, they knew they had met a musician with the voice of an artist. Witness that immediately after the service, the family anticipating a wedding on the following Saturday, rushed to secure her services as their soloist. The whole congregation was surprised and delighted. Perhaps, even if I didn't turn out to be able to preach with good effect, they might have been satisfied?

Following that service of ordination, Rev. Lucht greatly surprised me with the appointment to serve as the vacancy pastor of his own parish, since he had accepted another call, and would shortly leave his three-point congregations of Wilkie, Rockhaven and Leipzig. Suddenly, all in one day, I was the pastor of five congregations numbering more than 600 adult members. The plan was that I'd lead worship at Luseland every Sunday morning, and on alternate Sundays travel 75 miles either NE or SW for an afternoon worship either at my Sibbald AB church, or on the other Sunday for an afternoon worship at Rockhaven SK, plus an evening worship at Wilkie. (Leipzig was to come there to join in for the duration of the vacancy.) In each case it was to be a trip over graveled secondary highways, sometimes with loose cows appearing over the hill. In either direction I was leaving the essential flatness of the prairie. The travel to Sibbald could in good weather be shortened by 20 miles, using a 30 mile stretch of dirt roads; But over such a distance on dirt roads, the possibility of a storm made this problematic, given the state of weather forecasting, and particularly in Winter. I was glad for Mom Radtke's wedding gift of a dependable car.

By that Sunday of ordination/installation we had already become reasonably well aquatinted with our surrounding physical context. We lived in two-story parsonage (they called it a manse) with eight small rooms, constructed soon after 1910. It had two unheated bedrooms on the second floor. It had sawdust "insulation" in the walls, and wood floors over an unheated dugout basement. We needed to carry our drinking water by the pail from a member neighbor's well across the street from the church about a block away -- Summer and Winter. Our bathtub, kitchen and bathroom sinks drained into a barrel in the basement. When monitored to be full, it needed to be pumped with a garden hose out onto our garden, or anywhere behind the parsonage and single-car garage.

The garden had been planted with an assortment of root vegetables including lots of turnips. It was a goodwill gesture, but also a warning that gardening would be useful to supplement the bare bones annual salary of $3000 out of a total church budget of $7000. Had I not been married, the salary would have been $25 less per month; So essentially, that was June's salary. Individual members were however expected on a voluntary basis to come to church on Sundays with meat and produce as they had extra. When they arrived, they freely walked into our unlocked kitchen to deposit butchered chickens, eggs, or assorted other farm gifts into our frig. This was a gracious order to accord dignity to those who had little ability to bring a monitory offering. Obviously, these people were poor, mostly by reason of the state of the national government grain program. They were growing acceptable crops of wheat, even though they were then in a cycle of drought. Little of this primary crop could be moved off the farm and sold, since the grain storage companies were full for the difficulty of gaining world export markets. (Oil was just then being discovered all around, but there was yet no production for several years to come.)

Our single toilet was a five gallon pail with a seat in the dugout basement, vented into the chimney. This we were to carry out weekly to the alley behind the parsonage where it would be emptied into an open-top wagon by the town dreyman driving a team of horses. The same dreyman, with his horses and different wagon, picked up garbage on a weekly basis through the alley. And he also delivered packages or freight with a hayrack as it arrived by the once daily train. Furthermore, he could be hired to bring purchased water from the town well when rainfall, via gutters into our underground cistern, was insufficient for the pump to bring more water to our bath or kitchen faucets.

The church had likewise been built about 1910 but enlarged to seat 190 when a country Lutheran church of another synod had closed some 15 years previous. This addition was a transept to one side and had homemade plywood pews. It all had a full basement parish hall for meetings and SS classes. Except in fair weather in midsummer, the church was generally full, often with overflow, for Sunday worship.

The Sibbald AB congregation had no building, but rather used a small United Church of Canada building with "Methodist" theater architecture. It seated near 50 with a large wood-fired potbelly stove in the very center, slightly aside of the main aisle. Our attendance there was 20-30+/-. Sibbald was a minor crossroad on the highway from Sakatoon to Calgary of about 6 homes, none of whom were members.

The town of Luseland, founded in 1909, had a population of about 700. It's main access from the highway passed our church on the way to main street which had been built parallel along the railroad. The principal businesses were a gas station with repair shop, bank, 5(?) room hotel, postoffice, modern grocery, dry goods store, Chinese restaurant, butcher shop with rentable lockers for frozen food, coop gas & fuel oil plus hardware & lumber, senior fellowship cafe, municipal hall & office, plus a few small

138

businesses like attorney and insurance, and a car dealer and repair. On an upper side street to the north were a K-12 school, a medium sized brick RC church and a small frame United Church of Canada -- merger of various Protestant denominations. A new provincial medical clinic had just been built on main street, staffed only by a nurse. (Our provincial hospital was in neighboring Kerrobert 22 miles distant, where a new 25 bed hospital was under construction, with one doctor.) On a parallel street to the main street to the south there were five tall grain companies and elevators along the RR -- the prairie version of skyscrapers, visible from nearly 10 miles.

During the week following our arrival, June and I drove back to Saskatoon, a major city of around 100,000 with no lack of downtown stores for shopping. We needed furniture -- the moving van was only bringing June's bedroom set. There was need for a lot of typical home and office furnishings. Some dishes and cooking pots and pans from wedding gifts were also on the way, but the kitchen needed many other utensils. We had immediately bought a kitchen table and chairs in Luseland at the coop. Besides that, all we had was a borrowed bed. (Counting the nine months, it was in that bed Janet was conceived in love the week after we arrived.) We urgently needed a couch (where had we been sitting down?), living room tables, and a desk and filing cabinet for my study, plus seating for visitors. We found high quality items in Saskatoon that were equal to the best available anywhere even today. Pa and June's parents had taught the both of us to buy stuff that would last, so we indulged with the moderate savings June had accumulated (no credit was available). How to get all these things home was not a problem in those days. The RRs carried on a lively, if not next-day, delivery of freight, with the Luseland dreyman automatically making delivery and helping to unload on our end. By two days, we had all that stuff. The moving van then interrupted the VBS the following week, after my ordination, bringing my small library. By the following Saturday's wedding, we were

139

fully equipped, ready to be the host of the parish, as it turned out.

The week following my ordination had already been scheduled for VBS with a two week program compressed into one week by having both morning and afternoon sessions. This allowed for more far-out-of-town children to participate, some then boarding in town, and reducing the transportation project for parents from a parish spread in a 15 mile radius. (A few faithful members attended Sunday worship from 25 miles away, weather permitting -- over graveled or dirt roads.) Materials and lessons had been ordered and teachers were ready. June filled in as well to teach, and I had this as a good introduction to my confirmation class upcoming, by teaching the upper grades. The very active Ladies Aid Society provided a potluck style lunch each day, enlarging the program into a major parish fellowship. The closing program of Friday was almost like Christmass Eve. The participation and cooperation revealed the parish to be a lively and happy society.

Then on that following Saturday afternoon, I had my first wedding. It was for one of the men and his bride of a three-brother joint family farm 25 miles away on the border of AB. There was a fourth out-of-town brother attending who was a Lutheran pastor attending with his wife. That gives a dependable suggestion of the piety of the whole family. Their farm covered multiple square miles way out there to the west. Without their asking (June being a bit miffed by the surprise) the wedding family early that day virtually moved into the parsonage as their right -- out of necessity. They needed the manse for the dressing of attendants and small child care. The men got dressed in the basement parish hall. I myself, in getting dressed walked into our bedroom to discover a mother nursing her baby on our bed; Averting my eyes I simply got what I needed and all was quite OK, so cordial was the whole wedding and the spirit of these people. With the following wedding reception in the church basement parishhall, the parsonage was then the

140

nursery as needed. June did quickly adapt to the informality and sense of unembarrassed even intimate family relationships. She so naturally became the perfect pastor's wife, and I sensed that she was quite proud of herself for transcending the more uppity Chicago society. Her executive church secretary experience had been her school to be a pastor's wife. We were custodians of their parsonage/manse, and their guests and servants. So it was to be. Idilic? Enviable? It was comfortable!

I then led my first liturgy and preached my inaugural sermon at Luseland on the following day, Sunday, August 10. Two weeks later I traveled to the Sibbald congregation for the first time. I took June along, whose singing was there also dully noticed and appreciated. That especially because they had no pianist at the time. So we sang with June leading as cantor. (Unfortunately she went there with me only a few times before morning-sickness had her prefer to stay at home.) Wayne Osterhold, an active young adult (son of Carl & Helen), volunteered to go along to show us the way. He led us down south through Kerrobert to Kindersley, and then on the secondary (graveled) east-west Canadian Highway leading to Calgary. This took us straight west into AB. The service was held in the small United Church of Canada building in mid afternoon, a time that seemed to suit these people quite well. It was a solid but simple structure. (An indelible memory of it is of the sacristy with an outside door with gaps that allowed the dust storms to create a dirt floor. I somehow learned to vest without my vestments touching the dirt on the floor.) Not I believe on that Sunday, but quite often one or another of the families would invite me for supper before returning home. One family lived a dozen miles north beyond which was the short-cut dirt road back home, occasionally tempting me to use it.

That congregation consisted primarily of about six faithful families, some poor, and others wealthy enough to spend the Winters in Mexico. One family with a teen aged son, whom I almost immediately began to instruct in the

141

catechism for confirmation, lived in a home made under a large straw-stack. June and I and baby Janet were invited to stay there overnight when the son was in the following year confirmed at church. The home was basically a pole barn with straw bale sides, considerably covered over and around with straw blown onto it, obviously by a thrashing machine years before, and paneled on the inside -- I remember not by what. It must have had a floor. It was a proper home, cozy and surely warm in Winter, even though it stood on a slight hill without trees. Their farming involved beef cattle which roamed across the entire fenced and gated yard along the road.

Pastor Lucht must not have immediately moved from Wilkie after my ordination, since my first services in that vacant parish was first held on September 7, a month later. Our neighbor, Max Schoelor rode along to show the way. He often did this thereafter out of friendship and for my company on this trip that often lasted till about 11pm. He didn't do any driving. He just road along for my sake, particularly in Winter when snow was drifting, but not likely being plowed. (The two of us once shoveled our way up a north slope of the highway for 1/4 mile on our way back home, having no choice in an empty countryside in near zero weather about 10pm. That occurred after my powerful car finally bogged down in 12" of snow covering the highway for a half mile. Max did this even though partially crippled with MS. By then I had probably heeded our older ladies who were aghast that I didn't own a hat, nor carried a sleepingbag in the trunk for worst-case.)

Rockhaven held their services in the afternoon, but try as I may, I can't envision the building any longer; Probably it was a country school in their little village of neat yards and lots of trees. This, unlike Luseland which had only a few short boxelder and cottonwood. It was a community on the northern edge of the prairie, already somewhat into the "bush" -- aspen and birch forest country. Invariably one or another of the four or five faithful main families would invite me or us to come for supper in their really fine

142

homes. Two of these families were related. They were still Americans from the States, guarding their US citizenship; And they were moderately wealthy, with furnishings that reminded and pleased June in remembrance of Chicago. They greatly appreciated my ministry, and we had lively dinner conversations. They were homesick for the US, still after 25? years.

The Wilkie congregation, served that evening, had their own good sized church of a simple prairie architecture. They had an attendance of up to 200; But we never got to know the people well over the term of the pastoral vacancy which lasted till the following Spring. This was due in part to our having had supper at Rockhaven, and their previous custom of morning services. That evening time didn't fit them naturally to have much fellowship and refreshments with coffee after the 8pm benediction on Sundays. Besides, it was a full two-hour return trip for us, already tired after having led three services that day. June did go with me at first, and then also after her morning sickness abated, but not in the depth of Winter. When I had gone alone, those late nighttime Winter homebound trips were not fun, owing to the beautiful northern lights which however scrambled the Canadian BS radio waves needed to keep me awake with their classical music.

Getting back to the time following my ordination, it was a convenient time of year to become aquatinted with the member families of Holy Trinity. Perhaps there was still some farm work going on in August in the from of "summer fallowing." Only about half of their sizable acreage was planted each year, principally in hard Spring red-wheat. This was annually rotated, with the balance of empty fields being lightly cultivated, not only to kill moisture-robbing weeds, but especially to break down the capillary action of evaporating soil moisture. Yet this cultivation also generated dust storms. They didn't have enough rainfall to produce a significant crop each year on the same acreage; But with fallowing, they stored up the soil moisture into the next year for a respectable crop.

Otherwise our farmers were just at that time of our arrival in their community in a waiting time for the September harvest, when farms would become pell-mell busy to beat the onset of Winter.

There were some invitations to dine and visit, but June and I, or just I, often simply dropped in to visit other families, allowing poorer families to make-due hosting us with coffee and cake. However, mostly it wasn't coffee, but rather tea, which was more affordable. My problem was that I didn't particularly like tea. My salvation came with that it was automatically offered, not necessarily with sugar, but with cream. To make the tea go down, I tried that, and I liked it. That's how I now still drink it occasionally by choice. Almost invariably these farm homes were spartan with just enough comfort and beauty to get by; For real beauty they had the waving wheat fields, and the sky, and the endless vistas which stretched imaginations -- upwardly tending. Just a few also had a home in town which was more comfortably furnished and mainly used during Winter to avoid being snowbound out beyond nowhere, since many had no cattle to care for. A few others simply lived in town and drove out to their nearby acreage to farm. Still, the great majority were watching their nickels. The Sunday collection plate had more coins than bills, even many pennies. All this due mostly to the limited foreign wheat exports.

Then it was time for Sunday School and confirmation classes to resume after the Summer break, as well as an adult instruction class -- which had not been held for over a year. I was busy enough and didn't wish to follow the expected preceding pastor's practice of hiring himself out to one particular farmer to help with the wheat harvest -- he was silently "upset". This farm-boy had, other than gardening, left such work behind for good. I had after all, hundreds of people for whom to pray every day, and to study, so that God could become more holy among them. That was full-time work.

It had been the attractiveness of theology that had first brought me to the seminary. When I then took a multiphasic aptitude test early in my first year at seminary, I was unsettled by a measured low inclination toward pastoral ministry -- was I making a mistake? My vision of a pastor had been the kind of pastor I'd always had, that is, from my point of view. Namely a much reserved prophet, preacher, teacher and leader of worship. I'd never experience a pastor standing with persons clamoring for justice, or in prison, or ladling soup in a bread line, etc. But neither did my professors project such a pastor. In fact they were pointed about the distinction indicated in Acts 6 between apostles and deacons. However starting in my second year at seminary, we were sent out monthly in a team with upperclassmen to conduct one-on-one nursing home visitations with devotions and prayer in the Springfield community. Nonetheless, we hardly had much of a chance to get to know these elderly patients to construct a holistic relationship and to acquire the "fun" of being their pastor. Internship would then more properly initiated "pastoral" ministry, yet because of the sad restrictions of my supervisor in my case, I had barely experienced this joy.

Luseland, likewise didn't on the surface beg for me to be an "activist" pastor -- they'd never known one either. However, the voices of invitation, though faint, were heard and nudged me forward into a pastoral ministry from the start. It was obvious that I needed to get to know the many members; Else, how could I pray for and lead them by preaching and teaching? A few elderly widows had from the beginning been visible, which suggested an opening, and from there it grew. I heard no complaints about the previous pastor until later -- these people were too kind for that. But the need for launching an outreach to a good number of lonely and neglected people in the community quickly became apparent.

First there were elderly couples not being gathered into the church. Some of these spoke only German at home. They had been left behind and alone by others who had themselves made the transition to English society -- the majority of the community were German (those of English etc. extraction tended toward the United Church of Canada). These elderly were happy to have my interest and an opening into spiritual friendships; It especially helped that I could converse in German. Others quickly heard about that and passed it on. With one of these I served them in German at home during my whole pastorate out of their need; While with another, (appreciate how hard it might be to preach in German, not having polished theological language except in English) they bluntly said for me to preach and commune them in English as the better way for them to be served. They said they would rather do the struggling than for me. So I dummed it down for them. I got to know and love these neglected people, acquiring quite a list of shut-ins to visit and commune. (I was happier doing this than hauling grain to a bin from a combine for a farmer, supposedly because people were too busy anyway with the harvest for me to have much to do..)

Besides, there were the widows I'd already met at church whose additional attraction for me was their apparent deposit of history. (Almost as soon as I had arrived, I was informed that the church was to celebrate its 50th anniversary the following Summer. That to me meant that I'd need to prepare their history which hadn't been attempted. I did because no one else could, as was apparent form the fact that on one had. Anyway, their history excited me.) These widows were lonesome and needed personal encouragement toward their eventual home, even by the simple act of a visit with their pastor for tea, which quickly became an interview to learn their history. At church they were so easily greeted and passed by for more vital and active friends. To one of these I had early on expressed the hope that I'd be welcomed among them. This, after she had regaled me with much community and congregational history, stressing the extrema rigor of the 30s when many people drifted through, asking for charity. About that hope for a welcome, she bluntly said to me, "Well, we'll see." I didn't appreciate her stoic pessimism about me; However nonetheless her memorable scars needed spiritual salve.

Another bright spot was the meeting of the church's youth, which fortunately had not been neglected, even during the year of vacancy before I came. This was thanks to senior youth such as Wayne Osterhold and Adelia Heintz. These Walther League meetings were not pure fun&games, but rather mostly lite study and worship and spiritual fellowship. We did on occasion simply have a picnic. These teens were serious, probably influenced by the hard times which we were in, due to the poverty from the failed government grain exporting.

June was marvelous as my helpmate, etc. She freely wheeled her typewriter with confidence. She quickly projected that I knew what I was doing -- sometimes I did. I remember only one hiccup: I apparently was stymied by something or other, and she replied, "Pastor Harman...." (did such and so). She seemed to know immediately that she had put her foot in mouth, and quietly backed off. Otherwise her humility was sublime. Not only did she apparently understand and respect the need for me to decide and perhaps fail, so as to learn. But she recognized that this prairie-farm community was radically different from her suburban Glenn Ellyn. And she fully appreciated that she hadn't gone to seminary. It was only in fun that she once smiled about a reply to her weekly letters to our moms, that they were so well written that she might write some of my sermons. No, she took my dictation of letters, set up a whole new system of membership records so woefully lacking, typed my hand written sermons, etc. The parish had a secretary on the cheap, and as a "Mrs. Pastor" to boot; They and I had what was loved and required. Did I thank her sufficiently? Probably not.

Quite early after ordination, I was informed that the upcoming October area pastoral conference of our NW quarter of Sask.. was to be hosted by Luseland -- this, envisioning only the southern half of the province, the whole northern half being a wilderness. Obviously, Luseland had not taken its turn for a while since the parish had been vacant. There were 8-9 congregations and pastors involved; My congregation would need to be rooming them for two nights, with the Ladies Aid furnishing meals and securing those beds. It was at the same time to be a welcome to me; But it was also to satisfy their curiosity about what kind of stuff I was made. This was obvious by the other part of their announcement: Even through the host pastor was in charge of worship, I was also to present the main study paper. They even assigned my topic: *The doctrine of Angels according to the Lutheran Church.* Were they testing me? Cleverly so! I was already quite busy; Now this added work. I set to the task and decided to be exhaustive. Fortunate that I had brought along something of a library. I had barely finished when the pastors arrived at midday, all needing to travel +/- 200 miles. I had a hand written manuscript (time hadn't allowed June to type it for me). I read it, telegraphing my serious effort -- rather than leading an informal discussion from notes. It was funny to me that I was towards the end virtually being asked to cut it short by the observation that some of them were nodding off. Thoroughgoing theology was really not their specialty. I do believe I satisfied them all. They were a good group, however more keen about pastoral practice than theology.

My and also June's liturgical sensibilities were stretched by Holy Trinity Luseland. This was plain from the start, even before we met any parishioners or learned their very simple ways of worship. They had been using almost no traditional liturgy. The altar was simple and homemade, which was understandable; But the paraments for it was perhaps even an original one from 50 years ago -- faded and worn, and only that one set of green. (We later learned that there was a black one which had been taken home by a member, since there was little need for it, nor a place to store it.) In their poverty, and the apparent disinterest of previous pastors, they were unfortunately impoverishing their worship, limiting it to the spiritual without the aid of even a

148

semblance of physical beauty. They had no altar guild. So June jumped in to start. Neither of us could bear to anticipate Advent, come December, with green paraments, yet we patiently did. But come Lent, we could bear it no longer. Still there was no budget to allow for a new set of altar cloths. We decided to make due with a piece of a white cloth from the dry good store in town, which June dyed into the purple color. It was a statement, and an opening. The Ladies Aid eventually took hold to purchase all the missing seasonal colors, one step at a time over the course of the next few years. It was of course the perfect problem to have in that liturgically starved parish. It was my opportunity to teach them what the church had learned would enable more thoughtful worship, involving all the human senses for aid.

Church attendance at Luseland in the Summer prior to the harvest was very good, the church was generally full with near 200. The people needed to come in their need for each other, many of them far from town, living not even in sight of each other owing to the large acreage, so empty was their landscape across fields of waving wheat. However, early-on, on a particularly glorious Summer Sunday, there did occur a conspiracy well remembered. That Sunday there were only a hand full of members attending, to my confusion. The explanation came that "everybody" had decided to go to "the lake", and they were now going as well. "Why don't you come too?" I wondered if they would perhaps be embarrassed for their morning absence to see me there? It might be good to offer unspoken forgiveness, given their normal faithfulness, and for my self inclusion into their society. So we went per directions given, and had a good time, They were happy to have us. It was a lovely grove on the south shore of a small genuine lake, not a prairie "pot hole." It had a nice shaded picnic area with lots of play space for the many children. The beach was not much for swimming. June would later recount in her journal how graciously the women treated her -- almost like their queen -- and how she noticed their consistent and avid interest in my participation in the men's softball game. We were apparently fitting in.

It wasn't long before June's morning sickness began to somewhat curtail her activity. She was quickly on the couch most of the day, and became nauseated all the more from the smell of the simple foods I prepared for myself. She was not able to eat anything herself till late in the day, perhaps some soup I prepared for her. It was a rude awakening to have to be a nurse. We of course suspected what it was about. Yet it was frustrating to be limited by the sickness in living the joy of expecting. I took her to Kerrobert where they had the one doctor, a GP trained in Ireland, Dr. O'Halloran. Nice doctor, June liked him. He hated Sask.. and wondered why we had come. He too knew what June's sickness was about, but immediately recognized a problem.

Without telling us, and to be sure, he sent us to a specialist in Saskatoon where it was confirmed that June had an enlarged "cyst" in one ovary. It had to be removed, but her pregnancy was greatly endangered by surgery, unless perhaps if it was delayed till after the fifth month. The doctor knew not what kind of cyst June had, but waiting a few months seemed a reasonable risk for both of them. The specialist confirmed his diagnosis -- both the pregnancy and the cyst, as he called it. But O'Halloran was so confident that a confirmation was all he wanted. He retained care of June even though needing to serve in an outdated hospital in Kerrobert. June's surgery was scheduled for late November, and all went as best he expected -- not malignant. It was "like a simple appendectomy", he explained, only with the week long hospital stay to monitor and protect the pregnancy.

By then, June had outrun her morning sickness, and other things were fortunately settled to make room for the busy schedule of serving five congregations for the Christmass season. With so many children in these parishes it was a natural expectation and objective to focus on them on Chriatmass Eve, as well as in the vacant parish on the Eve afternoon. (We, in Luseland had had 60 children in VBS the previous August, a normal expectation.) The pace of ministry was exhausting, and especially as understood by the evidence of having just now reviewed those months via June's recorded letters.

June almost without fail wrote a 2-3 full page weekly letter in carbon copy for both of our mothers during our entire time of our ministry in Canada, and also about monthly letters to other family and her friends. Her mother saved her's and returned these to June years later. I've now reread these to check on details -- Priceless communion with a dearly loved companion. I was shocked for the forgotten relentless schedule that June recounted of us, and with which she kept pace.

In these she related a major blizzard, which I also still vividly remember, which occurred on that first New Year's Day. It amazed us and was fortunately safely endured. We had had rain mixed with snow and steady near freezing temps. I had celebrated New Year's Eve Communion at Luseland in the evening. During the night the temps dropped 50 degrees and a strong west wind developed; But the sky was clear in the morning. Undependable forecasts from places too distant from us spoke of a possible blizzard. That contradicted with what we saw and how it seemed. We were invited to Ed & Frieda Osterhold (brother and sister) for a 3pm New Year dinner, also to be attended by the Scholers, our neighbors, and Carl and Helen Osterhold, their neighbors. (These had given us such a wonderful welcome when arriving in Luseland in July.)

But first, I was scheduled for Communion in Sibbald at 11am. Should I go? There was no observable excuse, so I left at 9am. Osterholds would come for June if I was late. The wind was bad but the sky was clear the whole trip going and returning; Otherwise the weather and roads were fine. I was even back early, picked up June and went to Frieda and Ed's comfortable well furnished home. The Scholers tried to come the short distance of a mile from town by dinner time. But by then the wind was fiercely blowing snow with impossible visibility -- it had by then frozen and dried out the wet snow. So Scholers turned around and went back home, Max not easily deterred. As we ate dinner the storm intensified. Thereafter, the dark already descended, it was foolish to try to go home in town. The men explained that it was a ground blizzard, terribly strong wind simply picking up the snow with zero visibility; Yet they could pick out the stars directly overhead. The wind was 50-60 mph and the temp was already 20 below. So we accepted the invitation to stay the night. By 11am the next morning the wind finally slowed, along with the drifting snow. But our car wouldn't start, the engine oil virtually frozen stiff. After an hour or two with the block heater plugged in, the car was able to start. We drove home over roads blown clear of snow (they are mostly graded high for that benefit). With the strong wind and 24 hours of -20, the house temp was down to 50; But with the slackened wind, the house slowly recovered. There was drifted snow on our windowsills, even the following morning.

Let's try to go somewhat deeper into the spiritual nature of the life we experienced in my first pastorate in western SK. My intention with sharing our unique struggles from that time is that you might reflect on your own struggles to which you were or are divinely subjected for the sake of maturing faith. Everyone's struggle has the common denominator of being an ordeal for maturing faith, for which one has however been fitted or prepared in advance. Thus we should recognize God's hand and therefore be encouraged to see it through.

My experience of the squalid house of my birth is at most subliminal, since our family was blessed with the boldness of parents who somehow managed to construct a warm and modern house when I wasn't yet four years old. But that childhood nonetheless involved living through the lingering effects of the Great Depression, coupled with the restrictions of life during WWII. Such preparation doesn't directly give a vision with boldness; Faith wouldn't naturally thus be generated. In my case, I accepted my first call with it's privations at best as a testing, even as a ordeal of sorts. It was a place for ministry where I was needed, having been basically fitted and prepared. How June was fitted or prepared for SK, I can't adequately explain, other than that she had learned to subject herself to unchosen responsibility and was dedicated by love to be a selfless companion. She had lost her father near the end of university, and thereafter had to stay near home to care for one after the other of her grandmothers while her mother became a commuting breadwinner.

I have written about our shock when arriving at Luseland. We both would have preferred a city ministry with a modern parsonage. Yet in mysterious ways we were prepared to accept the conditions of a more primitive style of living so as to be able to sympathetically relate to our people. A very few of them did have modern plumbing, which speaks of our spirit when accepting the lack of it. The parsonage was "insulated" with sawdust and yet had either dust or snow drifting onto the windowsills, depending on the season because of old windows with ill fitting storm windows. But so did a majority of our people. We visited them over roads barely, or not even graveled. But so did they when they came faithfully to church. We drove to the hospital 22 miles across such roads, or alternately 160 miles to one in the city to visit them in need. We did it to encourage them, even if the highway was drifted nearly shut in Winter. Such living was all they had to offer. We ate the perennially offered gift of dressed chickens, or basket of eggs, because they knew by the necessarily adopted church budget that we were also poor. I drove to Sunday preaching stations, and for a year, to two congregations more that 60 miles over unpaved roads to pastor-vacant congregations.

They often took turns to ride with me when the weather was bad, knowing that it was inexcusable not to try. Once, e.g., Max Scholer, a struggling victim of MS, and I, returning home long after dark from a service in the

153

afternoon and another in the evening 80 and 60 miles away, encountered a half mile stretch of roadway drifted shut a foot deep with snow; with no detour possible, we shoveled a way through without despair or complaining.

Our preparation for endurance in many such circumstances was made significantly more easy by our mostly gentle people made so via years of their own struggle. That had produced the contentment that comes from faith matured by rigorous testing, by which they had been prepared. These people had become pastors to each other and then also to us, making for a peaceful community of saints. We parted with mutual tears. I am often touched with sadness for leaving, but for the perceived need for graduate study. We too easily regret the hand dealt us by God, for which, by reflection, we should be able to understand that we have by him been sufficiently prepared for the sake of endurance. Thus we sense service and pride in what God has accomplished in spite of all the imperfections we should be careful not to completely lament.

Lent was early in 1959, and with the pastoral vacancy duties, that season and Holy Week was like conducting a three ring circus, but somehow we managed. It was soon thereafter a relief to learn that the Rev. Dan Lentz had accepted the call from the Wilkie etc. parish. I was authorized to install him the evening of April 19. He was a 15 year pastor-veteran with five children, a friendly easygoing man who became a good friend, especially in relation to hunting and fishing. He didn't abuse his parish over that pastime, but he lived for that to the full, and was relentless in dragging me into that. Not that I resisted all too much in my need to have non-parish friendships.

To get aquatinted with all of us, he then quickly stirred up a crazy short getaway for five of the pastors in the NW Sask.. area including wives, and my less than a month old baby Janet -- next chapter.

154

Chapter 14 -- Luseland - 1959-60

Less than a year after ordination, I was so harried one week by many unavoidable pastoral duties, including a funeral, that I simply had to abbreviate the entire sermon preparation process for lack of time. (In seminary homiletics classes -- sermon preparation and preaching -- we were taught to move from careful text study, to exhaustive outline, to exact writing, and finally to practice delivery, so as to allow as much eye contact as possible. Such required several hours of rehearsal.) I decided to eliminate the time consuming writing of a manuscript, and instead prepared an adjusted exhaustive outline, simply stating the sequence of ideas -- a fat outline. That is what I then rehearsed as time allowed, thinking it through conversationally, rather than following a formal text exactly. It worked for me, and I was forever free with far better results. My list of ideas had careful exact phrases embedded which I often underlined. I could easily follow these, preaching conversationally, and engaging the congregation eye to eye. I had two pages instead of 5-6 or more of a full manuscript. And I was from then on no longer a reading machine. When June, who did all my typing was not available, I could even manage to shuffle the few hand written pages of notes. (I didn't teach myself to type till she died 30 years later.)

Having at the time a wife with-child for a secretary, some of that work was bound to be left undone or postponed. This was now all the more to happen as June's May due date drew near. Help had arrived in the person of my Ma who had flown in to Saskatoon from MN. She didn't type, but did however help with translating the German script church records and its brief recorded history that was needed for the 50th anniversary booklet for the congregation that I was busy preparing. More particularly, it was a blessing to have Ma come early to give moral support to a first-time mother nearing term. That also lessened the anxiety of a first-time father. Ma's confidence was reassuring for June and me.

June was also relieved by the fact that the new 25 bed hospital in Kerrobert had been finished and dedicated more than a month beforehand; And she had gotten a tour. She had dearly wanted me to attend her delivery, and been promised this by Dr. O'Halloran if the new hospital was done in time. I was however warned that if I fainted, they would simply ignore me. I replied that as a farm boy I'd seen enough blood, guts and tears, even death, that I was quite sure of myself. Although when at the last minute I saw the doctor needing to cut June with a scissors, I winced (and still do) with a shiver of empathetic pain.

It was not a problem to go about pastoral duties around Luseland in those last waiting-days, or even the Sunday afternoon worship on May 10th in Sibbald AB, 90 miles distant. June was overdue, but members and neighbors were eager, ready and excited to help. June urgently wanted me to take her and be with her all the way through. With no sign of her giving birth, I nervously went that afternoon to Sibbald, and returned. Duty had won out, June also having agreed. However, early Monday morning June's water broke. So we rushed to the hospital 22 miles away over a not-so-perfectly-smooth graveled highway. We made it, but it turned out to be a long wait. June was becoming dangerously worn-out by the time she finally gave birth at 10:58 am, Tuesday the 12th. Both of us had gotten little sleep the previous 30+ hours so I went home to share the good news with Ma, and by telegram with June's mother. Then sleep came easily before an evening visit for my first good look at a spruced-up and well dressed baby daughter - - given all the gifts of baby clothes already on hand. By then June's pains were already forgotten, glowing with pride and joy.

The normal maternity hospital stay was a full week, so Janet Ruth was finally baptized on Trinity Sunday, May 24th. Ma and Max stood as proxy godparents for my brother Walter and Dottie, June's college friend. By then the prolific wild peas along the highway were in full

bloom. That's what graced the altar that day -- Bright
yellow clusters of flowers on 12" stalks.

Pastor Dan Lentz, whose vacant parish I'd been serving till
April, was an avowed hunter and fisherman. Already by
June, only a month into his new pastorate, he had seized on
an offer to use a fishing cabin way up north offered by a
member of the church at Loydminister. He enthusiastically
organized a brief fishing trip to Loon Lake, about 230 miles
due north of us. Invited were the five NW Sask. area
pastors and their wives. It supposedly was a large modern
cabin -- it turned out to be large but not modern. It had bare
stud walls, electricity but only a wood cook stove, and no
toilets. Blind to this, we bit on the invitation regardless of
our month-old baby, and went up on a Sunday afternoon.
We had a great but crazy time. The men slept on the floor
in the main room, the women in the two bedrooms. Janet
was less than a month old. We had filled her bassinet half
full of diapers and plopped her on top. Ma was still with us,
and she also fortunately went. Cooking with wood came
naturally to her, so she took over all the cooking. She had
raised most of my family in similar conditions. So Janet got
an unconscious brief taste of my own infancy with Ma's
practiced help. The fishing was zero that first morning at
4am, but later that day we found the right spot via Dan's
expert survey. We stayed just that one day, all returning
home on Tuesday. Some hadn't bothered to fish, but had
enjoyed the fellowship and midnights that were no more
than deep twilight.

Unfortunately, that fishing trip resulted in the sad loss of
my wedding ring. All things there were very primitive,
including the set up for cleaning fish -- there was only a
table, but no running water. When I had finished cleaning
fish, I went down to the lake shore to wash my hands. To
do that thoroughly, I took my wedding ring off because it
was rather wide. I laid it on the gunwale of a boat tied up to
the dock. By the time I had washed thoroughly, I forgot to
take up my ring. I didn't miss it till we were back home
over 200 miles later. I had no contact person to look or ask

about it, and making a return trip seemed a hopeless chance. (June's mom sympathized and gave me her late husband's ring, not his wedding band, but a half carat diamond ring he had worn. She suggested I have a ring remade with the diamond to be a substitute wedding ring. I took it to a jeweler in Saskatoon who helped me to design a clergy ring with a cross and the diamond set in a black onyx stone. It had to be sent to Germany to be made. June was pleased, and I still wear it proudly as a sign of being married to her, as well as to the church. It now comfortably snuggles with the wedding ring Addie gave me.)

The reordered parsonage living with baby Janet went so well that Ma returned home to MN after just a few weeks. Thus we were on to the next challenge: celebrating the 50th anniversary of the congregation. I had all along been gathering an oral history by interviewing members, and Ma had greatly relieved my difficulty in reading the oldest records, being in German script. (Luseland was founded in 1909 by various individuals from miscellaneous places by the efforts of the Luse Land Company to develop land granted to the railroad. The sale helped finance the railroad construction. Holy Trinity Lutheran was organized in 1910, most of the members having settled west of town and arriving from Wisconsin, and especially Nebraska. Most of those settlers were Germans; Those from NE, were originally from Russia, to which they had immigrated under the German princess who became Catherine the Great. There they were in time being persecuted; And hearing of free land in NE, a large group had gone there with their pastor, only to find all the land already taken. So they acted on the Luse Land invitation and came up by train with their possessions: Their Pastor Buchner came with the intention to farm, having earlier been a missionary in India. He was persuaded to organize and serve Holy Trinity.)

I wrote the congregational history of those first 50 years, and edited contributions by the parish societies. A young woman far out of town relieved June from typing the

158

manuscript for a 36 page booklet. (Her farm had a pasture where we picked a "bushel" of mushrooms that we canned.) The Kerrobert Sun newspaper neatly printed our history in the nip of time. My predecessor, Pastor Moehring, had before he left, volunteered to come and preach; So that had long been agreed. He preached the sermon at the 10:30 morning service. A senior pastor of our district came to represent the synod and preach a 2pm afternoon service on the August 9th celebration. This was followed by a banquet at the town hall. June's mom and uncle Paul with his boys, as well as my Ma, had driven up in time for that anniversary. Thereafter, we and they took a week of vacation at Banff and Lake Louise AB.

Incidentally, Goggle Maps will get you lots of modern photos (360 degree) of Luseland, not much changed in general appearance from our days. However, the homes it shows are more modern, not so plain and poor, now that oil is being pumped all around. Our old 1910 church and parsonage has also been replaced.

The poverty, resulting from Canada's difficulty in exporting wheat, continued in 1959. Farmers were only reaching an annual 6 bushel quotas for the sale of their wheat. (When national grain storage space became available to allow all area farmers to sell as much as one bushel per each of their cultivated acres, a bushel quota was announced. Only at such intervals were they able to generate income, storing the balance of their grain on the farm awaiting the next quota announcement.)

Nevertheless, perhaps with some provincial help, Luseland was able to launch a town sewage construction project for 1959. (A city water system was proposed and done in the following year.) Many homeowners agonized about the cost of resulting assessments, even though a lateral to each houses was included. Only as the fever gradually caught on, did they sign-up with a plumber. Our church council had quickly agreed to connect the parsonage, but they passed on the church. (Men alone had a vote in the congregation, and no women were therefore represented on

159

the council which had decided. It was interesting politics to watch. The Ladies Aid was strong on account of this lack of franchise -- thus they were an unofficially house of Ladies. What made it tense was that a significant number of families had joined our church in town from the Lutheran church of another synod ten miles out in the country that had been closed a number of years earlier, where women did have a vote.) The women went home and lobbied, even demanded that the church would also be seward. Eventually the men agreed, with the Ladies Aid helping to finance.

The project down the streets went quickly with a giant trencher, but getting the plumbing done in the houses, which often didn't have a bathroom, dragged on into early Winter and beyond. With the parsonage there was a lot of hand labor to be done by volunteers, including myself. The dugout basement walls, plastered over on the inside, required a 5-6 foot tunnel to reach the outside of the house.

The trench in the unpaved streets had been quickly filled in during the super dry Summer -- which produced its full share of dust storms. Then the rains began, making that harvest slow and dragging it into the Winter. In town the rains caused street cave-ins where the sewer trenches had been loosely filled. June had difficulty even getting out of the garage with the car to do the grocery shopping in town via a circuitous route. Once we were finally connected in mid November, our cistern more often needed refilling from the town well because we had flushing toilets.

We had seen it already the previous Fall, but it was still an amazing spectacle to experience the Fall goose migration and hunt on the northern prairies. The wild geese were never seen there in Summer, not even many ducks. However, once the arctic began to freeze, the trillions of geese descended their ancient flyway that took the main flocks precisely across the Luseland area. Prior to 1900, when there were no wheat fields in which to feed, they undoubtedly had also stopped over in the larger lakes and potholes, till the advancing season urged them on. So this

160

country was long familiar to them by overlapping generations (wild geese live up into their 20s). If these were Snow geese, a 50 acre lake might be almost completely white in daytime appearance. The larger Canadian geese, of even greater number, kept themselves separate. Standing grain was not inviting to them, but harvested fields with straw, not completely threshed and stray kernels on the ground, were appreciated for their concentrated fuel. In the Luseland vicinity lakes (both 20 miles either east or west) the geese virtually covered the lakes all through the day of resting, as well as at night, safe from predators (hunters respected these sanctuaries). At dawn, and again in late afternoon, these geese rose in staged flocks of several hundred each, to find the threshed wheat fields. The great size of the fields and the level terrain afforded reasonable safety. They might circle the area from up high to gauge their chances, and then flip flop to slow down and descend almost vertically to feed, with older ganders, neck outstretched, keeping watch.

There were a few local hunters, but most were from the States, usually annual addicts, and wealthy -- a nonresident license in those days was $100. Some came in campers, a few staying in the very limited hotel rooms, many having long established connections with a farmer, affording hunting space, a place to sleep, or visit, or to park for the night or season, or to have a hunting party. During the day they were seen in town if they had already dug their hunting pits in the "prefect" place.

The method was to dig a comfortable pit in a harvested wheat field in which they were camouflaged, and wait for the successions of flocks seeking morning or evening meals. This meant getting to the pit in the dark, or shortly after noon, involving lots of waiting. (Lazy guys like me scouted for bordering brush cover, but then with prospects only of more distant targets. My first such hunt was with my neighbor, a high school English teacher from England. I, with only my Pa's 410 gauge shotgun, winged a Snow goose which I chased across the open field. Thus I warned

161

off several flocks to the great disgust of more experienced hunters waiting in nearby pits.)

I had limited opportunity to hunt (to the relief of the true goose hunters), as June's weekly journal recounts. Mondays were slower days of catching up on more personal and household tasks. Once in a while I had gone to play golf by myself on the town course with its sand greens. But the whole week was quite busy with the resurgent parish. Unlike my predecessor, I felt a duty and saw the opportunity to make hospital calls. It took a number of missed calls at first for them to learn of my willingness, because the previous pastor had not bothered. June's journal reminds me how often I was late home for supper, and then also to have quite regular evening meetings which I hadn't well remembered. I do remember though the quality time June and I had together doing supper dishes. It was a happy nonstop sharing of our day with the good classical music of Canadian Broadcasting System softly playing. That didn't change much when the more sanitary air-drying of dishes took over. To the end, we rested together after supper.

In late September, as farmers were struggling to harvest their drought thinned wheat crop, Dan prevailed on me (not with much protest) to go on a moose hunt in north central Sask.., near the end of roads and next to the fenced Canadian Air force bombing range. His uncle from MN came up for this and supposedly went along as our cook. We tented next to the road by a forest ranger fire tower. By then the leaves were off the trees and the nights were below freezing. We had sleeping bags but no stove in the tent; We cooked outside, breaking ice out of our washbasin to wash-up in the morning. (I had recently bought a brand new, with sporterized stock, 303 British Lee Endfield WWII military rifle, bolt action with 10 shell clip -- no bayonet. These had been for sale at the Luseland Co-op for $15.00.)

All three of us went in separated directions and hunted that way all week, never seeing a moose. Before I went my way the first day, I had climbed to the top of the fire tower to get the lay of the land. It was completely forested all

162

around, the road running north-south. To the west, almost a mile away ran a small river in parallel, and beyond it was the fenced bombing range. Both Dan and his uncle had gone that way to the west. To the east, about a mile distant, I noticed a thin line of coniferous trees, while aspen otherwise dominated. I set off towards that objective, never seeing it again till I got there. It felt like I had been walking over ground never before traversed by man, until I spotted a dead beer can.

It was disappointing that none of us were seeing any moose, though tracks were there. Dan smartly reminded us that tracks were worthless unless a moose was standing in them. So enchanted was this hunter that he was the fulness of optimism for us greenhorn hunters. We kept it up all week, and all day. Friday was to be our trip back home, some 300 miles. Dan suggested that we could still hunt till noon. He took his car and uncle about two miles north, and they hunted there. I and they were to meet by noon at the car and return to break-camp. I went west toward the river, slowly and generally following it upstream to the north. We met at the car and dejectedly drove slowly to our camp. I was sitting in the front passenger seat. Halfway to camp, coming over a small rise, there stood a bull moose broadside on my shoulder of the road, a football field length away. I had apparently disturbed it on the west side of the highway. Dan stopped and we all got out with our rifles. The moose seemed not to see or notice us. I had the advantage of speed, and dropped him with one shot where I estimated his heart to be. He was totally dead, but a shot in the brain made sure. By his horns he was about a seven years old male. Perfectly prime, if not with a majestic rack in his relative youth.

Now what? We had no trailer for this 1000+ pound animal, but Dan had it all planned. His car was an almost new four-door Pontiac sedan -- new wide-track chassis. We took out the rear bench seat, planning for all three of us to ride home on the front bench seat. With the moose skinned, quartered and loaded in the back seat area and trunk on plastic sheeting, we laid the seat on top of the moose. Dan's uncle asked to have the rack, and Dan had a jacket made out to the leather. I still have a leather key chain of it for my desk drawer key. Dan's butcher cut and divided it, giving the greater share to Dan with his family of five children. We found the meat more coarse that beef, the steaks a bit more tough, but the roasts out of the pressure cooker as tasty a beef. June felt good of herself for trying and liking the taste. For the next year, it was our red meat.

(All three of us did a repeat hunt the next September without success. Dan even went back for another try a week later. Two years after that, when we were already in the Chicago area, Dan almost lost his life on a successful moose hunt. He had gone alone, and even further north than before. In a canoe, and crossing a lake with a dressed moose on board, he capsized. Of course he was wearing hunting boots and warm jacket. Not a big man, he miraculously saved himself and his moose. Actually God did it to eventually provide another pastor for the Peace River country in far northern AB to which he soon moved.)

With Pastor Lentz arriving to fill the Wilkie parish vacancy the previous Spring, I was free to entertain having a preaching station in Kerrobert; This was to answer the petition of a group of families who lived there, and also farmers north of there who had a better road to Kerrobert than to Luseland. The Anglican church in town was willing to allow use of their building in the afternoon every other Sunday on the same schedule I had established with Sibbald. Under most weather conditions, I at any rate needed to go to Sibbald by way of Kerrobert. So beginning on September 27, 1959, services were held there in the early Sunday afternoon. The group attending was usually 15-20 or +. My Walther Leaguers carried out a town survey one Sunday afternoon which helped to announce our services.

The Sunday School attendance at Holy Trinity Luseland was very much weather related -- they were mostly from out of town. The usual number of children ranged in the

164

30s. Other than the main roads reaching out in the four directions, all the intersecting roads had not been graveled, so that significant rain mostly prevented travel. Once Fall advanced, and the roads were frozen, and as the harvest rush was ended, there were many more children in SS. This made the Christmass Eve service preparation and that holiday time far more active, barring an early storm. For Christmass Eve 1959 we had 75 children in the program we presented. How did we fit in the 300 total attendance?

During my final year at the seminary, on weekends in Glenn Ellyn, I had bought and assembled a high fidelity amplifier kit to better listen to my classical music records with my basic turntable. This was available from Allied Radio in Chicago. That gave us the idea for a Christmass gift to each other for 1959. We could already get a clear Canadian Broadcasting System station on our simple radio, but we wanted better fidelity music and variety. So we bought a high fidelity AM FM radio receiver kit and had it sent to June's mom in Glenn Ellyn rather than pay Canadian duty. She then sent staged portions of that kit for me to assemble and solder. I could do that change-of-pace and leisure work during free evenings in the living room, not needing to desert June. But how did I keep Janet from messing up the many tiny parts? Yes, those were heavenly evenings, making us overlook living on the northern edge of civilization. Still, we had the company of many others who knew how to love us. Their gifts of produce never ended. For that Christmass we even got a 20 pound turkey ready for the oven.

Chapter 15 -- Luseland - 1960

June's weekly journal to our mothers compares well with my date book for 1960, confirming that we lived then within the swirl of a fully resurgent parish. My self-doubt from the first year at seminary about having the aptitude of effectively serving in pastoral ministry were surely not even being remembered. Looking at the church attendance records of the Luseland congregation -- approaching 300 adult members -- we had a consistent Sunday morning worship attendance of near and even above 200, with the Kerrobert preaching station recording +/- 30 in addition. Owing probably to either Winter of Summer storms there were only but a half dozen low-attendances all year of 100 or the like. Obviously my leadership, preaching and teaching were noted and appreciated. This, despite my own lackluster evaluation of those early sermons prior to discarding then a few years ago. That evaluation fits with my inability to feel the same excitement when I on rare occasions preached an old sermon.

June's letters better record another record: the several nights per week -- allowed when there were no evening meetings -- that we used to meet and sometimes dine with various families -- not at all with a chosen few friends. I do remember that we made a serious effort to have spiritual fellowship with all who were able to host us as their happy opportunity to honor us as if it was the Lord. I recall that with such visits, my early idealistic thought had been of having a time of prayer to demonstrate and encourage daily family worship. But the Spirit morphed that intent into simply taking more general opportunities to informally celebrate their happiness' and blessings as being God's presence.

I had the sense that the Synod at times used the Canadian districts for trial runs of new initiatives -- we frontier areas were probably thought to be less bold to resist, nor enamored with our own supposedly wiser locally adapted programs. Such undoubtedly was their rationale behind our

February three day event in Saskatoon that year, whose program name is now forgotten. But not the interesting idea of having a lay institute during a slower time of year, built around four key parish ministry principles. Four of us pastors were assigned to lead seminars in prayer, stewardship, evangelism, plus another forgotten topic. I was responsible for the seminars on prayer, feeling at first somewhat overwhelmed with the program packet the Synod had provided. We from Luseland brought only 4 or 5 lay people, who with those from other outlying congregations, were hosted overnight by the members of the two congregations in Saskatoon. The Ladies Aids of those churches provided meals at church other than breakfast. Whatever else were its successes, it turned out to be a personal gift and revelation. Not only was my assigned program found to be within my competency, but I was virtually shocked at what I judged to be a sad proficiency with prayer by our laity -- consistent with many later impressions. I sensed a personal mission of the Spirit. I by no means felt myself an expert in prayer, but I was at least one who practiced it daily, and never gave up looking for better resources, humbling myself with such help. The experience of that institute served to set me on the trajectory of prayer as the means toward personal and congregational growth; That's been the central thread of my entire ministry, including my graduate study and extensive writing both before and after retirement.

June's mom retired from her work with IRS in the Chicago office at the end of 1959, and after an initial failed effort to sell her home in Glenn Ellyn, she flew up to visit us near the end of January, spending a month with us and her first grandchild. So there are no letters from June for that whole month to detail that happiness of hers and ours. Experiencing the exuberance of Janet must have been a high point in her life. She brought with her some more, or perhaps all the rest of the parts for the AM-FM hi-fi receiver that I was building -- a reciprocal Christmass gift between myself and June. A month later, we took her to Saskatoon for a return flight on leap year day. Then from home, she flew to Phoenix for the remainder of the Winter to stay with her brother Arnold, where brother Paul was already spending the Winter. He had also retired as chief postal inspector of the Chicago office. Arnold had earlier retired as a mailman in Phoenix AZ. And that was also the time when I panted tomato seeds in pots on the south bedroom windowsill in a determined effort of producing ripe tomatoes that next Summer to answer one of June's major craving.

Holy Week with Easter was a more manageable ministry that year, now that I wasn't also responsible for the Wilkie parish. However, Dan Lentz, their new pastor, was determined for me to help him with his passion of hunting and fishing. As soon as Easter was past, he began to plan a black bear hunt in the far north of Sask.. This was a new venture to him and surely for me. I got him to delay this enough to make the trip coincide with the opening of fishing season. We drove north that Monday, May 9th, as far as the roads went, and then continued on a trail that no one had used thus far that year. The trail was at first doable with my 56 Ford Fairlane, but eventually, still short of the supposed promising area, we reached swampy sections that had been cordorized (trunks of saplings laid side by side over soft ground, usually over a flowage). I awoke to the fact that we were many many miles beyond any source of help in case of a difficulty. Had Dan been driving, he might not have given up. (Fortunately, judging by subsequent information learned in northern MN where black bear hunting is well practiced, we would have had near impossible prospects. Stalking bear -- who are so keenly aware despite poor eyes -- is totally unlikely to meet with success; They must be baited to your site. That they would just then not yet all have been out of their Winter den also had no significance to Dan.)

We agreed to retrace our steps to a lake we had recently passed which had a river outlet with a dam equipped with a fish ladder on the far side. That lake with others were still ice-covered, although black and rotten; So river fishing was the only choice. We tented nearby and fished below the dam in a river 50 feet wide and about two feet deep with rapid flowage. The spawning run was on. It was almost too much fun to be fun. We used spoons with daredevil hooks, but no other bait. With about every other cast into the river we hooked a northern, walleye or sucker. The suckers were the most fun, being strong and reaching the test limit of our line; Determined to breach the dam to escape, they were gymnastic. We cared not to keep these and so released them. We also were in danger of too quickly reaching our limit of Northerns, so we released many of those not up to our gauge. We ate fish for every meal those four days, including breakfast. The limit was quite large so we both brought home enough fish to share, and also to last all Summer.

Already by April 10th, June had been sure she was pregnant again. Without seeing the doctor she already announced it to our mothers. She had wisely pondered her age and the limited number of safe years to have children. But her pregnancy with Janet had been so unpleasant, with over-the-top morning sickness that lasted all day until the last trimester, and particularly with a horrid taste in her mouth, that she had wanted more space. Therefore she was at first very upset that we had possibly miscounted days. However, the sickness was greatly moderated, and not growing over the following weeks as before. The bad taste was there but she was managing with lifesaver candy, and she was able to cook and eat.

Quickly she took heart and began to anticipate, even already weighing names. Should it be another girl, Louisa May it would be, but Karl Arthur was still our leftover firm choice for a boy. What a different term it was for her. She even felt able and energized methodically to do a thorough Spring house cleaning, even though I'd discouraged it by reminding her of the defeating dust storms surely coming shortly. At her venture, we moved my study into the main front living room, being used for classes and meetings. She started her cleaning with that small SW room. She

169

considered it perfect as a second nursery. It had a connecting door to both our bedroom and the front living room /study. She made nursery curtains with the new sewing machine I'd recently given her, which she was proud to master. (That was possibly because her mother wasn't a seamstress, freeing her from measuring up. She had always been timid with cooking, at which her mother excelled.) She was coyly determined that it would be a boy, knowing it would please me, but also really wanting it. Her brief disappointment about being pregnant again so soon had been understandable, and so uncharacteristically personal. God quickly gave her a vision that brought peace and energy.

July 3rd, will be a never-forgotten Sunday. Our teens (Walther Leaguers) had scheduled an afternoon picnic at Dillberry Lake 80 miles NW near AB. We had all the usual teen activities for the 18 attending. In addition we had lite worship and a brief meeting. It had been raining here and there, but the teens had gone boating, swimming and had their barbecue. It was a major success. June and Janet had gone as well. On returning, three teens girls were with us in our car. Nearing our destination they directed us to a shortcut to their farms. We tried one road that turned out to have a car stuck in the middle because that area had had significant rain. We managed to turn around and found another road supposedly even more direct. It was a new road, well graded up, but as yet had no gravel, and the soil was heavy with clay. We got to within three miles of Esther's farm when we get firmly stuck. The girls tried to push but it was hopeless.

Without a word they slogged away to Esther's place. I tried some more to get unstuck but got a flat tire. It was now 11:30 pm. I'm sure I had much fun changing the flat in that mud. There was not a farm light to be seen. We were alone in nowhere. About two hours later, Esther's dad, Mr. Turnan arrived with his large tractor, which the road couldn't deny. He totally pulled us all the way to his home, we a passive load behind. As a result the wheels of my car didn't spin-off any of the mud, so that the fenders filled completely. We got to their farm at about 2:30am, and were now on a graveled road leading to Luseland 8 miles away. But when the car was unhitched, my big V8 engine was unable even to move the car. The Turnans gave us their master bedroom to wait for morning. Sunup was at about 3:45am. Janet had already had lots of sleep, and was now lying between us on the bed. She was ready to play with us so near and handy. She climbed all over June, back and forth to look out the window The meadowlarks began to sing through the open window, and Janet could see and jabbered about the rabbits scampering just outside. June recorded how Janet would pull on my ears and nose and then laugh. When true morning arrived, Earl Turnan's two hired men removed the four wheels of my car to clean out the fenders. After breakfast we could then drive home. They had had 8 inches of rain, about their usual seasonal total.

Such an experience was not at all unusual during my travels to my preaching stations in Canada. There were many times during Winter when travel to Sibbald was unpredictable, but I went nevertheless. Since this involved secondary roads, and even some rarely maintained, I was a number of times pulled out of a snowbank too deep to manage. My car was phenomenal, but at times I overestimated its power.

Once this happened also in Spring with a flooded road. The Schaefer family at Sibbald, with two able-bodied sons, were faithful at worship. I was often invited in agreeable weather to come for supper after the service at their farm about 10 miles north, near the end of an occasionally maintained road (twice a year grading?). The after-supper trip home from their farm was a choice. Either it would involve a 10 mile stretch of dirt road north along the AB-SK border for a short 45 miles home. Returning back south to Sibbald to take the highway to Kindersley would have been 100 miles. I had driven about halfway on the dirt road north when I descended a hill and in the headlights saw standing water in a deeply rutted road. It had been detoured leaving deep ruts on each side through a shallow grass ditch. But neither side seemed safe. Turn around? I decided to trust my 56 Ford Fairlane with its V8 Thunderbird engine. I only made it about halfway through and had to exit the car through deep mud and water.

Since I hadn't remembered recently passing any homestead, I decided to walk ahead through the field to the NE which had a good sized hill about half mile distant. I was hoping to see a farmstead since these were often on hilltops. Gratefully I saw a yardlight in the dark night far more than a mile away. Return to the dirt road and find the driveway? I decided that I was already as dirty as possible, so I struck out straight NE across the field. I often lost sight of the light in the rolling country. Fortunately the farmer was at home. He like others who extracted me from snow or mud was ready and willing, also refused to be paid. (I carried no money in my pocket anyway because there was no place to spend any in that country.) I rode the drawbar on the back of the tractor and held on to the back of the seat as we drove about two miles via his driveway to the mudhole. This is one of the "angels" I will be glad to meet in heaven and thank once again.

Ma Lehrke and my sister Jan flew up from MN to join us for our annual vacation of two weeks in 1960. They came early so as to hear me preach on August 7th. We left town the next day. Our first objective was Edmonton AB and the national park at Jasper. It was an all day trip across the AB prairies, almost running out of patience to see the mountains. We rented a cabin on the outskirts of Edmonton and made day trips from there into the mountains. We found the scenery not as spectacular as with our vacation the year before at Banff, but we especially enjoyed a trip to the Colombian Ice Fields glacier where we went with a special vehicle up onto the glacier to walk around on dirty ice. Edmonton was a short stay because I felt obligated to attend a PTR central committee meeting (to the be later explained) at Lloydminister back on the border of AB and SK on that Thursday evening.

After that meeting we drove back into Saskatchewan, up into its primary vacation area in the north central part of the province. Prince Albert National Park is heavily populated in the Summer. It's an area of great beauty, with lakes, park land, thousands of vacation cabins, golf courses and scenic byways. Of special interest is the spectacular Lake Waskesiu in the center of the park. There we rented a lakeside cabin for our duration. We did some fishing, but not catching anything of note, except that when Janet briefly held a pole, she caught a fish. Mostly we toured the well tended park land and loafed on the beach. Ma bought a toy pail and shovel for Janet which was a big hit. I believe Jan and I wanted to, but couldn't manage to play golf on the truly beautiful world-class fairways. On our final weekend, we gave Ma and Jan a tour of Saskatoon before their plane departed for home. It's the gem of the northern prairie.

In October another new Synod program was being tried out in the "backyard" of our NW Sask. pastoral conference. There, any failure could be obscurely buried, while any success could be portrayed with a WOW exclamation: "It worked in that outback; surely it's a new form with promise." Its alphabet, PTR, represented: Preaching Teaching Reaching. It was a pilot program of Synod, really a new form of the old fashioned Protestant America Revival. However, there was an avoidance of having the likes of an "altar call" -- emotionally pressing people to come forward the "give their life to the Lord." All Summer we had been having planning meetings with Evangelism department central staff from St. Louis, attending and promoting. The idea was for each congregation in our conference to have a highly motivational preacher lead a "revival" service on the evenings of one week, Oct. 16-20, Sunday through Thursday. The Synod assigned the "missionary" preachers. Each congregation was to assemble as many evangelism teams of two persons from their members as possible, to make calls on the unchurched local residents, particularly on persons on their church's prospective member list. These calls were to be made in the early evenings after an early lite supper at church before the

173

services at 8pm. Statistics were to be logged of how many calls were made each day, how many of these came to the service, how many of the congregation members were present to welcome them, etc. And these statistics were on the following morning taken to a central meeting to be shared with the other congregations. That summary was taken back for the missionary or pastor to pep the growing success elsewhere at the following evening service, relative to their local statistics.

The resistance at Luseland for this PTR planning and organization was disheartening. They felt that this was the work of the pastor. At last, seeing I couldn't give up in the face of the other area congregations, a few key members agreed to serve on the calling teams, but the word was out that this program and not needed or wanted, and would not be supported. June almost single-handedly took over serving the light supper at church each evening, usually with only one assistant, at times even supplying all the food. The early kickoff service, to pray for success, before the "missionary" arrived, was attended by only 33; Not even half of the church council came. Our missionary was Pastor Meissner from Glencoe MN, who arrived on the Saturday before, preaching both Sunday morning and again that night, and then on each evening through Thursday.

June's postmortem of the PTR, written in the week following, interestingly doesn't attempt to explain the why of what happened; She writes that members were pleased. First they were surprised and then delighted with our success. Some even confessed being sorry for doubting me beforehand, and not supporting it. Was Meissner that inspirational? June never hinted of that. I'd judge him from memory to have been quite adequate as a preacher, but there must have been the mysterious wind of the Spirit. The nightly services slowly grew from a low of just over 100 to the final service of 175. The statistics, like Lloydminister gaining 35 for their SS, made an impression. Our callers gathered 6 persons for my membership class after making calls on every conceivable prospective family that I could list, plus a few suggestions made by our members. What June considered the most significant was that the seven teams of couples, who made the nightly calls before the services, were so enthused by their success that they then -- and on their own -- organized a couples club to continue both their fellowship, and making future calls of invitation. She also reported the eager passive and active welcoming of visitors by the members. They began to look for results with anticipation. (PTR was a pilot; were there repetitions? I never heard of any. Not saying, there were none. Great idea!)

Other results to celebrate in 1960 include my tomato project. Started very early in a major effort to please June with her favorite fruit, it was apparently slow for lack of its preferred warmer climate. It was an "in the face of Canada" effort. By the time of our vacation, my much babied 4 plants still hadn't produced ripe-on-the-vine fruit as I'd hoped. Our neighbor ate the first one while we were absent, and then (per June's report) we did pick 13-15 ripe tomatoes before a frost warning had us pick the remaining green fruit that might yet ripen. June had been excited by the early appearance to think of canning some. She loved me for the effort.

Another and unusual harvest that year was both pleasure and strange fun. Perhaps someone had alerted me, but I was delighted to find a large patch of horseradish growing wild alongside of the RR tracks near the Luseland depot. Digging it with the mystified depot agent's permission was quite a job, since it was so well established. That was also a problem since the roots were so old that most were hollow -- pealing wasn't enough. June was also a horseradish addict, so we both worked these roots one evening after supper; And then brought out our hand-crank meat grinder attached to a chair. The fumes were so eye-watering in the kitchen that we moved into the backyard in the bright moonlight. Not that we really cared, but "What will the neighbors think and report to the whole town about these Yankees?" We were pleased with the 2+ quarts, but then neither of us remembered how much sweetener and cream needed to be added, so we punted. It was hilarious fun.

When the November Deer Season arrived, Dan had made such a hunter out of me that I looked for and found a local hunting partner in the person of the Fruson man at whose wedding I officiated on arrival in Luseland. By June's account, the two of us went on multiple hunts, both around his farm way out west near AB, and then further north in the area that merged from farmland to bush. There it was that we finally had success. We were each hunting separately, but within rifle report of each other. I spooked a deer in a meadow land surrounded by bush. At a distance of about 100 yards, and with the young mule deer buck running rapidly directly to the left, it was going to be a lucky shot, particularly when adding in the bounding motion. I couldn't expect to have him stop by command, so I just aimed and fired without thinking. Fortunately, I'd had plenty of practice with hunting pheasants back home; So I'd learned how to lead the shot attempt relative to the speed, and pheasants always had speed enough to force that issue. The difference was the bounding motion for added difficulty. But my Lee-Endfield 303 dropped him with one bullet. He wasn't totally dead, but he wasn't about to go anywhere. Although deer will do the near impossible exertion when almost dead. I fully expected that, so I ran and did the coup-de-grace.

I did expect my partner to arrive, momentarily. Was it out of my pride, to show off what I'd done? Probably! I surely didn't need his help with field-dressing. I was wearing my hunting knife, bought as a 15 year-old with money from muskrat pelts. And I'd done it before, particularly with many farm animals. I'd have been in command anyway. Companionship was really more what I wanted. He later told me that he'd heard and interpreted the rifle reports: only one shot, and then after a pause, one less sharp from aiming downward, indicating the grace. He did good, not wasting the opportunity to be on alert that this disturbance might send other deer his way. By the time he did appear,

I'd finished the field-dressing, saving the heart and liver. But still, he earned his half by helping drag this 100+ pound mule-deer back to the car. I took it in to the butcher shop in Luseland to cure a few days before returning to skin and pick off the pesky hair. It was undoubtedly the best venison I will likely ever taste.

June had been negotiating with her mom to come for a more extended stay beforehand of Karl's birth. She told her that I too had wanted her to come early. But it apparently was her relator related efforts that delayed her, arriving eventually on Nov. 22nd, for the anticipated birth on Dec. 8th. Unfortunately, June then and therefore paused her letters, so that we have no other reports than my memory of Karl's birth. So let me report what I remember: It was a much less harrowing ordeal than the first with Janet.

June was delighted that it was again possible for me to be in the delivery room with her. She labored no more than eight hours, perhaps a bit less; And I was again at her side through it all for her comfort. And this time I had a better command of myself because there was less anxiety with extended labor. Thus at 4:45am on Dec. 14th, I was holding June's hand as Karl was born. He was 22.5" tall, forecasting his plus 6 foot stature. Fathers don't look too closely at their newborn, trusting the apparently healthy gift by the new voice, much more feeling grateful that the beloved mother's live was not sacrificed.

I'd left mother and son for them to rest and settle in; Returning that afternoon, I was at first alarmed. June was nursing a red flushed baby in her sunny room whose nose I thought was unlike any Lehrke I'd ever seen. I honestly wondered if the nurse had shuffled the nursery. In my anxiety, it actually took me some time to recognize that the nose I saw was unmistakably identical to June's, which I'd come to adore as the distinctive mark of royalty. He most certainly was June's, and thus mine. Besides, also by virtue of then noting his receding Lehrke chin.

177

So it was that on Sunday, Christmass Day, Karl Arthur Lehrke was baptized at Holy Trinity Lutheran Church, Luseland, SK. June's mother, Irma, and neighbor Max Scholer were proxies for sister Jan and June's Uncle Paul as godparents.

June and Karl were not yet even home when a momentous letter arrived addressed to me. I was being called by the English District of the MO Synod to serve as missionary-at-large (mission developer) in the south end of Elmhurst IL.

Chapter 16 -- Move to Elmhurst - 1961

Considering how well my pastorate at Luseland SK was succeeding, why did I even need to think twice about the tempting call to Elmhurst IL? The people of Holy Trinity were clearly more than satisfied with my ministry; They were thanking God as evident by continuing the shower of free will gifts of produce that always overflowed our refrigerator. But more important, they were faithfully attending worship in way above national average numbers. It would have been unreasonable to complain about their response. Yes, they were still naturally cautious about my leadership, well aware that I was young and still learning. Yet, significantly, their years of hardships didn't make them overly defensive and protective. They were not subjecting me to extended wait&see trial. Especially with their response to our PTR, they were showing excitement. It's not an overstatement that we had quickly come to love and trust each other.

And June was virtually adored as the first-lady of the parish, well on the way to being regarded as their spiritual "mother"; Her piety and poise was admired. The women in the Ladies Aid Society (a significant authority in the congregation) looked to her to lead. And although the male leaders were the older men, and much respected, they too were willing at every proposal of mine to give it a fair hearing, not standing strong to protect their status. I had, for notable example, their early and full support in scrapping their still original constitution and adopting a faithful adaptation of the Synod's model constitution. And the bell-weather was the acceptance by the congregation of the Synod's recommended liturgy. This had been previously ignored, but quickly accepted as their hymnal provided, without grumbling. Neither did they complain about my choice of hymns.

So what inspired me to accept this call? Mainly two things. (Some back home in the States, especially our families who were reading June's letters about life in Canada, which was

179

so different from their own, assumed that both June and I were anxious to "get back to civilization." It's true we felt almost like aliens, unable to avoid continually remarking about cultural strangeness; But although thinking many things strange to us, we were essentially comfortable, I perhaps more so than June.) The primary influence for me was an awareness that my seminary curriculum had been abridged. Springfield, at that time was constructed as the "practical" seminary. It was well enough suited to preparing men for becoming and being an ordinary pastor, but not so well for providing the foundation for becoming a serious student of theology. I wanted to be a better teacher, having a sense of already wanting and being able to teach pastors. Without some of such pastors and professors, the church could not grow into Christ. I sensed there was more truth than a restatement or spelling-out John 3:16. I had met professors whose deeper grasp of Scriptures and doctrine I admired. I urgently wished this for myself, and felt capable of it, thereby to be able to speak with more wisdom than pious exhortation. In short, I wanted to go on to graduate school. I craved becoming a theologian, plumbing the mysteries of God, not for private excitement, but the better to teach. I had found the exultation of opening minds to a fuller understanding of God's love in and through Christ.

Secondly, (a stronger emotional motivation for June), that call was into the English District, a non-geographical district of the LCMS, unique and well known for being progressive -- particularly, serious about theology. I had experienced the English District in my internship; And June had learned it from years of working behind the scene of the district conventions. Her Pastor Harman was a vice-president (assistant bishop) in the English District. Being his church secretary, she had been pressed into service to mange housing and travel of delegates to the conventions, which were then always held in nearby Concordia College in River Forest IL. In fact she had been the administrative coordinator for the convention arrangements for a number of years; She came to be aquatinted with the pastors as they registered and sought orientation. Consequently, she met

180

and by her charm gotten to know the many highly qualified pastors who honestly were a cut above. She had again been asked to oversee arrangements for the convention near the end of my internship, and I'd helped her with that. So I also got to know many more pastors from around the country besides those from the Chicago area. There were numerous ranking theologians among them, not common elsewhere: Martin Marty and Jaroslav Pelikan, to name just two of world class. I envied such company and anticipated growing into that. In addition, the Chicago area notably had seminaries with graduate programs.

Furthermore, this call to Elmhurst was from the Mission Board of that district. It was surely not merely on the strength of a personal connection with Pastor Harman, via June his late secretary -- which it undoubtedly also was. Pastor Harman had obviously heard of our success at Luseland; And most certainly, he and the Mission Board had confirmed that by tracking synodical parochial reports -- without which they would not have called.

Yes, in retrospect, it was too soon to leave Luseland, perhaps even to take up this choice challenge. But they all must have considered that too, yet nevertheless had called. It didn't then cross my mind consciously, but could I have expected to be eventually called into this fraternity at a later time? One doesn't reply to such with, "call me two years from now." Also, was it reasonable to expect the bishop to recommend me to one of his churches for a call after a number of additional years? Such a call would be to one of the almost universally larger thriving congregations under his care. My call seemed like a perfect way forward into this special synod; and I was specifically wanted. Was not the Spirit trusted to be operating, however seemingly mysterious? So I wrote in reply that I prayerfully accept.

I trust that I had enough sense not to spoil the Christmass holy days for the congregation in Luseland by immediately announcing my call to Elmhurst, nor my acceptance. Hopefully I waited till January, in preparation for the annual congregational meeting scheduled for the 11th. In the aftermath of that meeting, with the newly elected and continuing council members, a brief flare of disappointment erupted. I was criticized by a council member for taking unexcused days off for hunting. It was undoubtedly a reaction of anger for sadness about my leaving. One new council member however immediately and forcefully brushed this aside, and my final salary was not shorted.

Having quietly and successfully made moving van arrangements, I announced that January 22nd would be my farewell Sunday at Luseland, with the van arriving the next day. It was all sadly much too rapid. Greeting the departing worshipers at the door that final Sunday was an ordeal that still touches me to remember. The attendance had been 250, again an overflow. The tears were many, and not mine the less. I was additionally impressed that the Walther Leaguers invited me that evening to an impromptu meeting to pray the order of Compline as their spiritual farewell. There was so much disappointment all around.

Moving day that Monday was stormy, with light snow and stiff NW wind. The van driver was alone, with only me and Hans Scholer helping. By 4pm the van was on its way, leaving us feeling virtually stranded. On that very cold afternoon a ground blizzard was slowly building. What's to do? Our beds had left. The closest motel was 60 miles away at Bigger. We had not much choice but to eat supper and go. Consider then the empty parsonage, with the me, June, mother Irma, Janet, baby Karl, and with all the stuff we needed to make the three day trip piled up and waiting to be loaded into the car. There were no friends, even neighbors, to say a final goodbye. They couldn't trust their emotions, and we were likewise spared. But the loneliness was palpable. They were bitterly disappointed for our leaving, and we were sad for so soon disheartening them. Once the car was loaded, there was barely room in the back seat for Irma who held Karl in her lap.

The first 22 miles went fine with the NW wind on our back on a graveled highway built up high enough to keep the

182

blowing snow going across. Just beyond Kerrobert, however, it sloped down to the SE; And 10-12" of snow had accumulated for a distance of several blocks. Needing to cross open fields to get to a farm with a tractor to pull me out of a large drift on mostly unplowed weekend roads had happened all too often to frighten me now.

It was after supper and normal traffic had stopped. Others were comfortably at home. The procedure was to trust what seemed doable, and only then resort to shoveling. Besides, the shovel was buried in the trunk. Consider not my own concentration, but that of June for her newborn and a citified mother-in-law. They had never shared in such an experience on a deserted highway in 0 degree weather at night.

I took a run at the snow but got stuck midway. But worse yet, in the back and forth effort to wiggle my way through, I got a flat tire. (Why would one set out on a 1500 mile trip with an obviously old tire? But that's what poor people did, and still have to do.) It was below 0 and a minor blizzard outside. There wasn't going to be any help passing by. I simply had to do what I knew how. None of this was new to me. Irma had never seen the like, and she was afraid, doubly so for the month old baby in her arms.

There was no choice but to unload a full trunk into a blizzard to get at the spare tire, jack and snow shovel. To change the tire I would be facing the wind since it was the driverside rear tire. Then after shoveling enough to make a path through the drift, I was virtually frozen. Angels surely attended; My desperate efforts were blocked from consciousness by adrenaline; We did get through the drift.

Now I was greatly concerned with the deserted highway and no spare tire. Kerrobert, behind us and now separated by the rapidly filling snow drift, had no motel, nor tire supply I knew of open at 8pm. I trusted, as always, that when innocently beset by circumstances, one is subject to God's extra care if faith is engaged. Bigger SK, another 40 miles distant, was known to have a motel and a tire shop, so we prayed and drove on. It was many miles before I stopped shivering with the heater on full. The next morning I bought a used tire and uneventfully made our way back to the States.

I don't specifically remember much of the details of the trip to the Chicago area, other than that the weather was bitterly cold. This was fortunate for the venison we were carrying in an uninsulated box on the top of the car; For that we had to pay 1.5 cents per pound at the US border. I do remember that the car door locks were frozen shut. We must have stopped in Gibbon MN to briefly say hello to Ma and show off Karl. I remember that the English shepherd at the farm recognized me despite the years I'd been away.

When arriving in the Chicago area, it was then good for us that Irma hadn't been able to sell her home in Glenn Ellyn because the moving van was delayed, and we as yet had no house in Elmhurst, 10 miles further east towards Chicago. So that's where we stayed till a member of the district mission board, who happened to live in Elmhurst, was able to rent a house for us at 180 South Street. We moved in on February 6th, the day after I preached at Redeemer, our "mother" church so as to introduce myself. It was an older home butting up to a busy freight RR. When Spring came, we frequently had sewage backup into our basement after a heavy rain via the floor drain. It was a depressing place to me, and some distance from the mission field further to the south. By March 8th, we therefore already signed a contract for the construction of a new home of our own not far from the lot on Butterfield Road which the mission board had already purchased for the future church.

On that first Saturday in the area of my call, I was able to meet with my "boss", the district Mission Counselor, Rev. Harold Hecht, to get my "marching orders." (I don't remember where we met; Per the later common pattern, it would have been at an eating place convenient for him as he "flew through". More than once we met at a toll-way rest-stop. He was always in a hurry, coming from some seemingly more important meeting, and quickly on again

184

on his important way. I never got the impression that he respected me by reason of such hurried passing through. I don't believe he ever darkened the door of our home to sit on my couch to meet me as a friend or equal brother in the faith. He was later to be my bishop, so you are warned what was to come, as I wasn't. Good that I myself hadn't then been able already to add things up. I would possibly have been discomforted and discouraged, serving to defeat myself. The Spirit thereby kept me focused on pastoral ministry which was my call, and toward which I had been gifted and directed in Luseland.)

Hecht obviously felt himself to be quite important because he had a stable of some 15 missionaries across the country to oversee. He believed in his concept of mission development, focused on his process, which he expected would be respected and followed. It was a raw beginning, just from his treating me as a total beginner, lecturing me against having a lazy schedule because I wouldn't be punching a clock. ("What doesn't begin well, is likely not to end well." And so it eventually went, as I would experience. We were opposites in that my concept of pastoral ministry as a spiritual agency rubbed against his managerial efficiency with a focus on statistical and hard results.) I was too new to feel used, as it's now obvious to me, by his extra initial assignment to pinch-hit on Sunday for three weeks in a vacant mission field of his at Joliet IL, an inner-city Hispanic mission. At the same time I was to be preparing for an early start of the mission, yet without leads towards possible arrangements, nor more than a general outline of my field. My commissioning (installation) was held at Redeemer, our mother church in Elmhurst on March 12th. More particularly, the first service in south Elmhurst was to be held on the following Sunday. All that was up to me to arrange. And those arrangements were for the boss to review.

I remained blissfully naive about my boss, but I had all my life been able to focus on a doubling-down in a challenging situation, and so I did. The result was that everything went

185

amazingly well by divine blessings. Directly across the highway from the mission site was a junior high school with an auditorium seating about 300 with balcony; This I was easily able to rent for Sunday mornings. They allowed a storage room for lectern and altar, etc. (Where did I find these?) PR was arranged, a descriptive brochure for our mission printed, calling cards made, and so much more, all aimed at a first service in not much more than a month after arrival from Canada. How did I do it? Yet it was no more that the expected. If my boss was excited that in such short time we recorded 130+ attending the initial service, I don't remember it. And they kept coming at that rate and increasing. I was then consequently busier than ever calling on the visitors, and so easily getting commitments. For whatever reason, people believed in the prospects for the mission and climbed abroad. Already by April 7th we started weekly constitution committee meetings. On May 1st we had a "voters" meeting, and on June 25th we had Charter Sunday with 120 attending, almost all of them joining in membership. They had chosen to call ourselves Messiah Lutheran Church. Is it believable that by then we were paying all our own bills, including my salary, from our offerings, and from then on? It was all enough to make one dizzy with excitement.

June took over organizing the Sunday School which began with our initial service and an attendance of 34, increasing to a regular upper 50s by May, and upper 80s by years end. Teachers were easily recruited. It was enough to make the pastor of our mother church nervous because so many of his members were coming to pledge themselves to our mission; Yet the mission had been by Redeemer's initiative. That hit home when June sat down there at Redeemer with an agreeable SS secretary the more easily to sketch in SS children's statistics from their records for those committing to us. The pastor interrupted the meeting and scolded the secretary for sharing privileged information. June had to excuse herself and leave. He too was a lord.

The pace of the new Elmhurst mission increased significantly after Summer. This was facilitated by already having a nearby home of our own where meetings could be held. On the western edge of the family housing construction project, we had a split level home built for us. The living room and rear kitchen were at entry level front and back, three bedrooms were a half level higher to the left, and under those was a family room which doubled as my study and as a meeting room. There was also a basement under the living room. Conveniently, there was a rear entry to the study/meeting/family room to avoid disturbing our family privacy. We had moved in to this home in July.

We were able to buy a used piano from the Lutheran Children's Home in Addison, which could be used for choir rehearsal already organized on Sept. 13th; An Altar Guild had an organizational meeting Sept. 14th; An organ search committee was formed on Sept. 15th; A women's missionary and aid society began on Sept. 20th; A weekly adult membership class was begun in October. Besides, there was now comfortable space for the church council, deacons, evangelism committee, etc. to meet. For the Walther Leaguer teens we found a free space in a nearby new community center.

Another membership Sunday was held on October 8th and again on December 10th, indicating continuing growth in membership. A Sunday Adult Bible Class, which I taught, began meeting alongside of SS on Oct. 22nd. We had even managed to hold a two week VBS in August in the community center. In time for Christmass, we had an organ for Sunday services. A sure sign of stability was the formation of a building committee on Nov. 16th. Our average Sunday worship attendance was 136 for that first partial year of 1961.

Behind all this busyness, in which June fully participated, she was pregnant again, with a due date just past the New Year. Fortunately, her ordinary symptoms were even more bearable than it had been with Karl. But it became apparent

187

that this would have to be our last child. Not only was she reaching an age at which deformities become increasingly more likely, but varicose veins in her legs were reducing her mobility. She was able to avoid being confined to bed, but she did have a very alarming incident that I happened to witness. A vein burst open in her leg even though lying in bed, spurted an arch of blood two feet high across the sheets. Fortunately, after giving birth, she was able to recover her mobility.

Chapter 17 -- Messiah - Elmhurst 1962-3

With a home of our own in south Elmhurst, I and my family were blessed with some respite from the hectic pace of the new mission, even though many parish meetings occurred in our family-room. It was not only the obvious love of June, but of my children who greeted me with happy expectation at supper time. Besides, June's mom was nearby, and Uncle Paul was again spending the holidays and much of the Winter at her home in Glenn Ellyn. Christmass was therefore rich also with family time. Already during the Summer, with Uncle Paul's place in Michigan City IN, we had a place occasionally to more completely get away. It was only a two hour drive.

It would be nice if we had copies of the letters June did still continue to write to my mother after we returned from Canada. Thereby, though not providing an every week chronology of our family, we might then have more details of the birth of Philip Andrew on January 8th, 1962. What I remember is that June gave birth in a matter of a few hours upon my taking her to the Elmhurst Hospital. Both June and I were much disappointed that the hospital wouldn't allow me into the delivery room. We knew this in advance, and they were unrelenting. All I remember about his birth is my anxious waiting for several hours till I was rather impersonally informed that I had a son, but still not allowed to see him or June. Resulting from the hospital policy of being excluded, his birth isn't remembered with precious details. Strangely, not even a simple notation was entered in my date book. Apparently I was compartmentalizing work from family. But I can safely say that Philip's birth was celebrated. I remember, on returning home form the hospital after Philip's birth, proudly drawing up a big 3x4 foot sign and posting it on the inside of our living room picture-window: "It's a boy". June's happiness was in part focused on the milestone of realizing that our family was now complete. She was a proud mother of three, and they were all healthy. Our first two were demonstrating that they were smart enough, and this third couldn't be anything less.

Until a few years before, she hadn't even dared to think she would even be married, let alone have her own brood. That she had so quickly and eagerly agreed to marriage, pairs with the rapture I experience in her embrace, and with her unstinting love for our three.

Again, my date book fails me, but I'm reasonably sure that Philip was baptized on the following Sunday, Jan. 14th. I do remember it was a stormy day; That, by remembering that June's Uncle Bud and Aunt Mable were not able to attend from Chicago's near north-side as they wanted. It did save me from a awkward moment. Having recently returned from Israel, they had purposely brought home a bottle of water from the Jordan River just for Philip's baptism. I was quite satisfied that I could successfully baptize him with Elmhurst city water. Brother Leslie, who was at the time in the army in France, and Walter's Darlyne were named godparents.

So, how can we describe the community and people who were establishing Messiah Lutheran Church in south Elmhurst? This answer will help to understand the attraction and the long term result of the mission. I'll sketch my considered conclusions of now over 50 years of evaluation, and with heartache.

I can't say when the city of Elmhurst was established, but it's enough to explain that it was at first most simply a stop on the long western spoke of commuter traffic leading in and out from Chicago. This spoke was shaped by two RRs running mostly in tight parallel. My guess is that the Northwestern, a true RR, was not at first a commuter line as it was to become already before my time, with modern/comfortable AC'ed coaches. Alongside, was the "third-rail" Araora & Elgin (glorified streetcar/subway, which used the elevated downtown Chicago streetcar "Loop"). Both RRs used the same depot stops. I suspect that this route of suburbs was begun already in the 19th century, consisting mainly from east to west of River Forest, Maywood, Elmhurst, Villa Park, Lombard, Glenn Ellyn, Wheaton, etc. These were communities of

190

commuters, wealthy enough to escape Chicago itself, and congregating in compatible classes. Elmhurst, especially south of the tracks, was settled largely by professional and higher level executives -- upper middle class. (A slightly variation of these were also scattered, like in Wheaton for such persons as June's dad.) It was in this area that Redeemer, our mission's mother church, was located, indicating it's class of members. With the automobile, there was added the straddling parallels of two highways: to the north (North Ave.) and to the south (Roosevelt Rd.) serving all these same communities. "South" Elmhurst had been a rural area of 8-9 square miles between its original settlement and Roosevelt Rd., also bisected by Butterfield Rd. This area was being developed after WWII, and the main area of our mission.

Consequently, south Elmhurst attracted a broad mix of people mobilized by the automobile and freeways as opposed to the RRs. These new suburbanites couldn't and didn't want to reside in Elmhurst proper with its older more grand and expensive homes, but built more affordable housing. They preferred middle class three bedroom, suburban-like, homes. They were ordinary middle class, also many junior executives shortly out of college, as well as some "managers" rising up from laborers, reaping the postwar prosperity. Many of these had joined Redeemer church, merely by choice of denomination and lack of nearby options. But there they were unlikely to gain traction as active members over against its more elite members. Our mission was their chance to participate in church membership among people more of their own class. At the same time, we didn't appeal to the active and primary members of Redeemer. Strangely, Redeemer apparently didn't anticipate the almost wholesale transfer of their newer members living in south Elmhurst; These fled to be in more compatible fellowship, and to more directly participate. The surging activity of Messiah shouldn't have been altogether surprising. Our new members wanted the chance to express their faith as a vital part of their own compatible new community life.

191

My date book from 1962 reports daily activity in the parish documenting a schedule unsustainable except for one as young as I. It was a fulness of worship, education, fellowship and outreach. There was regular adult and teen fellowship, with the teens meeting most Sunday evenings in the community center. The adults had such a varied program that my memory no longer captures any form of it. Teen confirmation classes also didn't result in lasting impressions, suggesting that they were orderly and effective. There was just so much activity that its now hard to remember beyond the bare statistics. We had a full range of parish committees meeting mostly in our family room. The pace didn't let it even cross my mind to look into my own graduate theological education possibilities.

Among this activity, the building and organ committees became the stuff of the legend. The building committee was the more active, meeting every other week after the mission was barely six months old. Almost from the beginning there was a quiet conflict with the organ committee; That committee had been activated even earlier so as to find an alternative to the piano in the rented school. It was essentially resented by the building committee as encroaching on the vision of their supposedly all inclusive mandate. Yet, the organ committee was merely a serious expression for more aesthetic worship, its members having the necessary ability of art or ear. They were companionable spirits with the intention of simple service based of distinct ability.

Not so the building committee. The core was serving double time. These were the more determined members who were already serving on the church council and convinced of their general leadership ability. None actually had any unique talents qualifying them for the building committee. It was merely that of being forceful committed members. Unfortunately, one was an unreformed bully, and a second was his yes-man friend. The whole congregation, in fact, must in general be classed as people of the bureaucratic society, actually no more than clerical and mid-level managers. With that, came the temptation to exercise power. None were executives by vocation.

The rapid growth of the congregation gave them urgency. By March 8th of our second year, they had become satisfied to engage the architectural firm of Erickson. That led rather quickly to a design concept which they and I found acceptable, but was dismissively rejected by Hecht, as if by a higher understanding of a proper church. (I still believe after all my years as a pastor, that Erickson's original concept was superior for that mission. It was a somewhat traditional rectangular form as a first unit, all on one level. But to Hecht's dismay, it situated the mechanical on opposite sides of the entry from the sacristy/office/study. And the architect had dared to simulate a steeple with a chimney and a cross attached. In particular, Hecht couldn't envision the wisdom and benefit of the pastor's sacristy and study on opposite ends from the altar, instead of right there where people entered.)

Therewith the building Committee experienced the firm hand of my boss, and naturally, with whom I was seen to be allied. I was likewise viewed as the mission board agent. It served to gradually alienate me within the committee with their spirit of independence. Yet I dared not distance myself nor resign from the committee, being the only one who had a working knowledge of how a church plant needed to be arranged so as to function per the pattern of our worship. Particularly, Hecht refused to distance himself from the building process. Aside from my own regular contacts with him, he is recorded in my date book to have formally met with the committee on 5/22, 8/3 & 10/27. He held the purse strings for the construction of a church, and demonstrated authoritarian inflexibility. Such was not good when paired with that committee's sense of liberation and self-reliance.

Undistracted, our mission moved forward, mostly unaware of the conflicting notes associated with building a building. Few heard this noise, other than my deacons who admirably served as my spiritual councilors and counselors; They, in place of a boss who was not exercising his job of being my pastor, nor that of diplomatically relating to the building committee. He left me standing as the bad guy when relaying his veto. The mission was the project of the district mission board, and they had through him every reason to administer, yet with clarity and charity.

Significantly, Hecht otherwise stood aside from the mission, apparently quietly satisfied with the statistics; Namely that toward the latter part of the year of 1962, little more than a year after organization, Messiah had a regular worship attendance of 150+/-. On Christmass Eve the attendance was 297, with 98 on Christmass Day. And the SS attendance by years-end was consistently over 120; We had not even adjourned the SS during Summer, but nevertheless had attendances of 60s and 70s. The mission was thriving. Hecht let all that stand well enough alone and without comment or praise; For him it simply was what was expected.

He left me naked within the workings of a building committee wherein some were keen to establish their own kingdom with power for glory. This was not altogether surprising with our kind of suburban people. They were smarting under his firm control, in which I was implicated, not being free to take either side. I was the visible entity in the middle and safely opposed by the strong members of the building committee over issues that were mostly petty. Their expressions of opposition felt good to them but accomplished nothing. I simply had to smart under their quiet resentment.

By February 6, 1963, as my date book reminds me, the fat was obviously already in the fire. On that day, for whatever reason -- probably attending a pastoral conference -- I had a brief conversation with Pastor A.R. Kretzman the legendary pastor of St. Luke on the near north side of Chicago. I remember in conclusion asking this veteran and highly respected man how he managed such difficult and antagonistic members as the pair I had on my building committee and council. He replied, "I bury them." I didn't at the time consider that particularly transparent. Even so, I

194

didn't have the alternative of patience he was apparently encouraging. Going home and doing my best as a pastor was what I was already doing.

The building committee meetings proceeded apace. Working drawings were finished according to a radically different design (modernistic, with soaring roof lines) which Hecht had approved. The church office and sacristy was to be at the far end of the church from the entry, next to the altar. That would not be a ready welcome to anyone seeking urgent spiritual care. I preceded to do an in depth review of the plans and found numerous electrical services wanting. Such minor adjustments were grudgingly approved, none of the committee being capable of making much sense out of blueprints. Hecht apparently had a final meeting with us on March 14th in advance of a city council meeting on the 18th, at which our building plans were apparently approved. Bids were advertised and due on April 19th. Apparently some redesign was then called for to make the building affordable per mission board budget limits. This resulted in another advertisement for bids on June 20th. That resulted in groundbreaking on July 21st.

The ordinary life of the mission didn't falter due to the disturbances of the pair on the building committee. Several cycles of adult instruction were held, as were also membership Sundays; So the congregation was growing and none were leaving. The average worship attendance for the entire year of 1963 was 154, and the SS enrollment at years end stood at 158. A children's choir was functioning, and there had also been a men's retreat, with the women's missionary and aid society steady under June's special care. She was also the administrative secretary of the SS. The early rapid growth had somewhat slowed pending the completion of a church building.

Nonetheless, by Summer there was a growing stir in the church council caused by the two members who served on both the council and the building committee. These two were disaffected with my leadership at every possible turn, particularly smarting under the simple fact that I felt it

195

necessary to attend the meetings of the building committee. It was surely a reaction to the firm control of Hecht, to whom they related me by the known frequent conversations and meetings I was required to have with him, and for his firm directives through me. I was an exofficio member, and quite reasonably present so as to be a resource for a facility that was to be my place of work. The committee had limited insight into that work space. Probably by private discussions between these two antagonists, and who knows who else, they had conveniently fastened on the fact that I was not their pastor by call, rather an imposition of the district mission board. They argued that they were now well established and should have a choice of pastors. I wasn't acceptable to them, given their strong will to rule.

Eventually this all led to a special voters meeting of the congregation in the rented community center on September 11th, to which Hecht was summoned, and who in turn summoned the district bishop, Frey, with the implication that I was possibly failing as a pastor. Yet Hecht surely knew that this wasn't my problem. He chose not to tangle directly with the agitators. The attendance at the meeting was large, surely a sign of support for me and concern for the welfare of a church they already treasured. However, I was essentially put on trial and unnerved. I was seated in front of the voters (women were entitled), and with a table before us was seated Bishop Frey, Hecht and the circuit counselor, Kissling -- a pastor and area dean from nearby Maywood.

There were petty accusations. The only one I still remember is that I chose hymns for worship that were not appreciated, having nothing to do with the building committee's work. None of the three officials at the table displayed the majesty of their office. They simply listened to petty agitation, apparently not recognizing that they were on trial with me for having judged me worthy and placed me in charge. Nor were they ready to disarm the rebellion of the few, pointing to the statistics of success. It might be fair to suggest that the three district officials were nervous

196

about the continued flourishing of the mission which was part of their legacy. There was no attempt at resolution by them; Already they hinted that I would be replaced when the strategy of the two leading accusers brought up their wish to call their own pastor. Had a vote been taken, I'm very certain it would have been an overwhelming vote of confidence for me. A further meeting was held a week later between my deacons and Kissling. He had belatedly been informed of the "problems" and felt need to exercise his authority with his own meeting toward resolution. My deacons all stood firmly by me, meaning that I was being supported, not by my prayers alone. Nothing was accomplished in resolution.

It's apparent that the mission as a whole was still supporting me as their pastor by the simple fact that attendance at worship had not, and did not slacken. Through the last quarter of the year 1963 there were consistently 140+, even over 150 in church each Sunday. Had they lost heart, that would have shown itself on Sunday morning. For the third Christmass Eve of the south Elmhurst mission, there were over 300 worshipers, and on Christmass Day, 102. Nevertheless it's easy to understand that the spirit in my own heart was flagging for the likelihood that this would be my last Christmass with them. Two people had used the technicality that as a legal congregation they had the right to call their own pastor. Those two won because the synod preferred to simply reassign me elsewhere. I was a lame-duck, though I suspect that the congregation didn't yet know what was to happen. The mission board itself needed to meet and decide. Still many of the congregation surely sensed the uncertainty. Many cried silently with me and June.

I don't have any notes of when I was informed of the decision of the district mission board relative to my ministry. That was done without giving me their own hearing. Apparently, Hecht had decided and directed without further considerations. I was probably informed after the late December mission board meeting. Then on

January 20th, 1964, Hecht had the two of us fly up to Minneapolis - St. Paul to see their mission in Oakdale MN, and to meet with their church council. It was newly vacant. The mission board had decided to allow Messiah to call their own pastor, and to transfer me to MN. This, as if I was agreeable, or as if it didn't matter. They simply amended my call to serve as their missionary at large from Elmhurst to Oakdale MN. If that was a vote of confidence, it didn't quite feel like that.

The meeting with the church council at Holy Spirit, Oakdale, was cordial and agreeable. There was a mission board owned parsonage involved. All this I carried back to consider with June. There really wasn't much of a choice, other than to be unemployed with the general uncertainties of being called elsewhere.

We decided to approve the move to Oakdale. We immediately put our home up for sale, and made arrangements for a farewell service at Messiah on Feb. 9th, with the moving van to come for us the next day. Essentially Messiah's new church construction was by then already finished; Dedication was already in the planning stages. As a parting gift to me, the church council, pressed by the frustration of the general membership over my leaving, decided to worship in that unconsecrated new building on my final Sunday. It was a bittersweet celebration. The new church had a freestanding altar which I used facing the congregation, generating a parting criticism for doing so by one of the disaffected council and building committee members. These antagonists were not of a mind to leave or rest. It would be my peace to do so. As of now 50+ years later, the church stands in south Elmhurst as it was then, also its membership totals. They have failed to thrive.

Our move from Elmhurst IL to Oakdale MN in February 1964 may be characterized as a transition from living and serving in an affluent middle class suburb to that of an isolated blue-collar housing development at the eastern edge of the St. Paul MN metro area. The city of Oakdale was at the time an unincorporated township just into Washington County. It was largely rural, except for Stillwater on the eastern edge along the St. Croix River. Oakdale was a mostly rural township, a long narrow strip only two miles wide (eventually bisected along its length by the construction of I-694). It had no sewage system, though it did have water. This severely restricted its development for another ten, almost twenty years.

The mission of Holy Spirit was an effort based on overly optimistic community development. It was at first to serve two small housing projects: Oakdale Heights, a near 200 home cluster, and Tanners Lake, less than a mile south, an almost 300 home cluster. These were entry level homes of small three bedroom ranch homes. Most were identical other than paint on cheap composite shingle siding, and with alternately flipped floor plans. Tanners Lake did have some homes slightly varied, a few of them were split-level homes with tuck-under garages. All others in both projects would eventually need to build unattached garages in the back yards when owners could afford them. All had only graveled driveways. At least the streets were blacktoped. The bedrooms were so small that only one of those would accommodate a regular bed. All had septic tank sanitation with hope for an eventual metro sewage line extension.

However, Oakdale was located at the far uphill end of a long delayed metro sewage system, also affected by recession. Since the septic tank systems were quickly failing, no further housing development was by our arrival being allowed. Additionally, the mission was sadly ill advised. More chilling yet was the start in Oakdale of another Lutheran mission by the aligned non-MO Lutheran synods. They too had peered into and unrealistic future.

Gethsemane Lutheran, back across into Ramsey county to the west, was the inspiration -- our mission's "mother". They had simultaneously even persuaded the mission board to start a twin mission a few miles further south and west, called Afton Heights. It worshiped in a abandoned radio station which had been purchased by the mission board. Holy Spirit on the other hand had inherited the outgrown thirty-year-old church building of Gethsemane. They had built a new sizable parochial school nearby, where they were for some years to come satisfied to worship in its gymnasium. Their old church building seating about 200 was sold to the mission board and moved two miles onto a hilltop on a new full basement next to the Oakdale Heights housing project. The twin missions had begun under one mission developer, David Romberg, in 1961. After two years he had sensed the stagnation and taken a call to a church in MI. Was I now the miracle worker missionary who would recover the mission board's, or rather Gethsemane's dream? Perhaps Oakdale was no more than a place for the mission board to dump a spare missionary on a hopeless mission. The mission board hadn't expressed themselves to me. (All of this reflects on the questionable mission strategy of Hecht.)

Holy Spirit Lutheran was a congregation of mostly laboring class families. They were young and starting families, wanting to flee apartments, and honestly enjoyed their enlarged space and freedom in a semi rural area. Most families were supported by a single wage earner -- making it easier for me to canvass or call. Although there were numerous working mom secretaries. The school district was progressive, well staffed and funded. Most families were of rural MN background, even arriving from ND. Almost all adults had no more than a high school education. They brought their simple piety with them from the farm, may not have prayed every day, but they were faithful in Sunday worship, and in bringing their children.

200

There was one notably exception to this at Holy Spirit (and eventually a few more), a vice president chief auditor of 3M who had moved into a nearby 3M sponsored executive park of homes (with country club) from a northern suburb where his pastor had challenged him to help the new Holy Spirit mission. This humble saint was and did regularly serve on the church council, often as treasurer; He never failed to attend worship and tithe toward major support. Through the years he was also Holy Spirit's choir director. And by reviving his high school clarinet playing, he provided many exquisite duets of classical offertories with the encouragement of an eventual organist whose specialty was the clarinet. On the council and in voters meetings, he allowed all others the first voice. Only as necessary did he offer a caution or solution. (This was so radical from the pair of lordly leaders in Elmhurst.) He never failed me in the following 25 years. All members highly respected his quiet piety and wisdom. He reminded me consistently of my Pa, although in a far more cultured and educated version. Though only barely older than most heads of our other families, he was the effective grandfather figure.

Gethsemane, our mother church, was a parish just two miles to the west. It had been reluctant to part with any members who were related to its K-8 parochial school. Only two families, whose children were already older, had transferred to Holy Spirit to help initiate a mission of their own inspiration. That mother church may have wished us well, but we were expected to make it on our own. (Had it been a convenient way to dispose of their outgrown building? which itself would become our albatross!?.) Their pastor counted nothing more important than the parochial school. He definitely was not a theologian, focused instead squarely on parochial issues -- with inter-Lutheran cooperation as an ecumenical extra. He had little love for the liturgy, i.e., the traditional and proven ways of prayer. He was a pastoral opposite from myself. His liturgy was basically correct, but mechanical.

The other four pastors of the non-geographical English District of the LCMS in the St. Paul area were happy to welcome me with genuine spiritual fellowship. Somehow our circuit counselor (dean), Paul Schuessler, must have been immediately informed of how the Elmhurst mission had conveniently divorced me to call a pastor of choice. Therefore, to protect me, and on his own initiative, via the full approval of Holy Spirit's church council, he decided to install me at Holy Spirit on the evening of my first Sunday in Oakdale, Feb. 16th, not as the missionary-at-large of the mission board, but as the actual pastor of Holy Spirit. He used a liturgy which effected their choice by voice.

This pastorate in Oakdale was consequently an extremely challenging ministry. Though the cloud under which I had left Elmhurst was unavoidably felt by myself, I was steadfastly encouraged by June, and felt confident that I could start afresh on the strength of the two previous pastorates. Both pastorates had been free of any shame or personal fault, and successful by any unbiased measure. I still wanted, based on felt need, to pursue further theological study, but I owed the mission its priority. My pastoral skills were not wanting, either in my own eye, or even in that of Hecht, who was still my boss because of Mission Board subsidies. He didn't again offer basic missionary strategy and practice, but I was still so humbled that I might have patiently allowed it.

The parsonage was far too small to allow for any but brief and simple study. With many evening meetings and calls, it wasn't realistic to be in the office/study at Holy Spirit, by 8am. But by 9am with a mere two-block walk directly back and across a secondary main street, I was there in prayer. Prayer was always the first business, and I now had a suitable space, since a connecting door brought me into the sanctuary with its altar and a place to sit and pray. However, I was struggling at this for lack of introduction at seminary to better resources. At seminary, the simplest encouragement to pray for parishioners was barely mentioned, and of course hardly enough. And no personal biblical reading program or study discipline was taught beyond the admittedly already arduous weekly sermon preparation which stretched through every weekday. What resources there were to my knowledge, didn't personally satisfy, being primarily sermonic, seemingly pious and simplistic gospel meditations. It would still take many years before I could "sit" in comfortable peace with our Father, as Jesus had done in the night. I had no mentor for this, as was to be later encouraged. And I had no father-confessor. That would have been thought to be a weakness, and far too Catholic.

I then spent the morning at my nice oak desk (bought in Canada) doing sermon study, parish planning, miscellaneous church business, dictating letters and more, until no earlier than 12:30pm. This, was followed by mail time at home. For connection to the hired church secretary, there was an old wax cylinder Dictaphone. She used the other desk in my small office and came in after lunch several days per week for as long as necessary, typing letters, Sunday worship folders, etc. She also ran the Ditto machine and eventually a mimeograph down in the furnace room to produce the Sunday worship folder and newsletter. Kate Splittstoesser was a willing and skilled holdover who had transferred from Gethsemane at the mission's beginning.

Rarely did I not in the afternoons make house and hospital calls, along with doing church business, which might take me anywhere in the Twin City metro area. My date book is cluttered with the record. Fortunately, most hospital calls were at St. John's, on my east side of downtown St. Paul. This made it easier since there were as yet no freeways. Getting stuck in heavy traffic, particularly on the way home, was far more frustrating than modern freeways rush hours. But there were the exceptional afternoons at the monthly newsletter time. Further editing of dictation was needed, as well as supervision of copy and mailing arrangements. I always disliked that newsletter work.

The afternoon and evening calls had, as a first priority, the spiritual needs of Holy Spirit members. But an early overlapping responsibility with my arrival in Oakdale was the mission board's decision to close the twin mission of Afton Heights. Given their membership list, I was personally to visit each of these with a challenge to transfer to Holy Spirit, while also expressing freedom to transfer to another church more in their immediate area. This Afton Heights mission was located five miles to the SW of Oakdale. (I was also made responsible for keeping watch on that physical property until it might be sold. Many times I needed to secure the building after teen break-ins. One time I found a burning candle in the attic. This was mostly thankless work.) Only a very few of that membership were willing to drive out to join us. We seemed to them to be effectively beyond the current metro limits. However, there were two families who happily met the challenge. One of them was an upper level engineer who worked at the 3M corporate headquarters two miles from Holy Spirit. He became a faithful and strong supporter. (The main 3M factory itself was on the near east side of St. Paul some ten miles to the west.) So the hope of the mission board in combining the twin missions was somewhat in vain. It did not give Holy Spirit the anticipate significant new vitality.

It's hard to envision the possibilities that our children would have had, had we been able to stay in Elmhurst. But the Oakdale school district had a superior rating. And Oakdale did provide many childhood friends. Already before being of school age, they had a good number of fine playmates. Karl and Philip were especially blessed with well behaved boys their own age, including several directly across the street. Janet was not quite so fortunate in finding early close girl friends. Until of school age, she mostly made do with her brothers. She did have some good friends at Gethsemane where she started school, and then also at Eagle Point elementary. (That transfer was negotiated because Gethsemane was pulling Janet into their orbit, and with a piety of a different strain that was uncomfortable to me and June.) Janet's lasting friends weren't found till

Junior High. Altogether, Oakdale was a better than most neighborhoods in which to raise children. However, we took extra care to keep them focused on doing well in school for the advantage of being prepared for higher education, and a better life than was the expectations of their friends. June, especially, gave them the benefit of her encouragement by being a mom at home when they came home, interacting with their school experiences and homework. I had a more limited influence and credit for their superior scholastic development.

To compensate for the more extended family fellowship we would have had in Elmhurst with June's family, in MN we were blessed with opportunities to visit the Lehrke home with Ma and brother Walter's family. (In addition, my sister Jan lived in south Minneapolis.) That brought together cousins of the same age as our children. Even before the metro freeways were built, we often made the two hour trip to the farm on Sunday after church, returning in late evening. Freeways eventually saved us a half hour each way. Eventually, I built a small hard-shell camping trailer in which all five of us could sleep comfortably in spite of rain, making it possible to lengthen the farm visits to include my Monday day-off during the Summer. For a number of years it also allowed affordable Summer vacations, whether in northern MN or to visit June's family in Michigan City IN. Mostly, it was also more insect safe than tenting.

MN and the nearness of the Lehrke farm brought us the opportunity of more affordable meat. By then my brother Walter had replaced his dairy heard with Holsteins and began selling grade A milk instead of only cream. The male calves were then also kept and raised as steers and sold as beef. Actually, he also purchased from neighbor dairy farmers the male calves they would otherwise have cheaply sold as veal. The female calves were kept to replace aging cows. When these Holstein bull calves were raised as steers, the result was superior to beef breeds, having much less tallow.

An early Winter week-long farm project through my childhood had always been butchering time. Several hogs and a steer were butchered as a family project, and sausages made. Eventually, rural towns had butcher shops which then conveniently did the hardest part of that work. They did the butchering of live hogs and steers, cut and wrapped meat according to preference; But they didn't have the family sausage recipes. We now simply took back in-bulk what inferior cuts they had ground. With this we made our own sausage in a two day visit to the farm, I usually going alone. It was much appreciated that I was willing to come to help with this, now that we lived in relatively nearby Oakdale. So our family not only had a bargain by splitting a beef with my brother's family and Ma, but of cooperatively making our favorite sausage for year-round enjoyment. Thus we had a higher quality of meat, and far more affordable than from our grocer.

Ma had these sausage recipes in her head. I then had her season the sausage out of a measured container to record what she actually used. This made it possible to make up a recipe book of family sausages. In addition, I found a wholesale firm in Chanhassen MN which supplied butcher shops around the area for their work and with sausage making ingredients and supplies. Thus we had everything we needed to make use of the old sturdy family sausage stuffer. It was leisurely work and good family time. We usually made four dozen half-yards of summer sausage, the same number in rings of bratwurst, plus baraunschweiger, baloney, and even some others with recipes from a book from the wholesale supplier. Ma knew how to run a smokehouse, and Walter was learning. We still had the big chest freezer we had purchased in Elmhurst to save the venison brought along from Canada. With it we could store an almost annual supply of better meat than we could afford to buy. A month later we would return to the farm on a Sunday after church to get our sausages from the smokehouse. We could afford to live like royalty. So living in MN brought some special benefits.

Another back-to-nature benefit we gained with Oakdale was the chance to make use of my knowledge of having a vegetable garden. We had been doing that in Canada, but with much disappointment due to drought and short seasons. But I didn't want to till up the backyard at the parsonage for a garden since it was owned by our mission board. So I tried to do this back across the fence, under the powerline between us and the main street separating us from the church. It was property forfeited to the city and allowable for use. Unfortunately, it had been stripped of all topsoil; Even with several loads of discarded soil from a nearby mushroom farm, it yielded only disappointment. (That is, other than the infection of that area with spores yielding fruit for years thereafter.) It grew radish almost too bitter to eat. Consequently, the next year I had a gentleman farmer bring his tractor to an area behind the church to plow up virgin sod. That for many years was as successful a garden as I could wish. I even rototilled another adjacent area for potatoes; But that was more like adding work to fun. Years later we bought that area as a lot on which we eventually built our passive solar home in 1979.

What was it like to visit the home of my childhood after years away? When I had left home for university and then seminary, returning home was naturally great excitement far in advance, and it never disappointed. Our faithful English shepherd, Shep, by name, would greet me with obviously remembered love and unlimited affection. Ma and Pa, being Prussians by sentiment, glowed quietly and then left me to unwind among all that had been missed. The home garden got a quick glance, but then I was off to the barn, first standing on the top of the cistern south of the milkhouse that served like a viewing deck of the 30 acre pasture with its herd of Guernsey cows and older calves. Later I would tour the fields, but could already 20/20 see the crops beyond the pasture, knowing by the color and the calendar how well they were doing. Pa ran an immaculate farm yard; My tour was always rewarding, lifting ingrained spirits of youth. For however many days I could afford, I thoroughly enjoyed myself.

Then in the 1960s and 70s, my visits to the farm afforded the same scenes, but with nostalgia for the missing teams of Percheron and Belgian horses in the pasture. These had, since I was barely in school, been my charge and love. I could still visualize them grazing there, but now they were no more. There were now tractors in the machine shed. Reality thereby impressed itself; I was only a visitor. I had left for a life of my own. I had been married, started my own family, and brought them with me to experience what I had known and loved. I felt drawn to return. Visiting would get me excited in advance as before. Invariably, however, I was soon abused of former excitement. The scenes to be viewed were recognizable. Pa had ascended and Ma, and a brother and his family lived in the house; But the lovely house of childhood was no longer my home. Much was all the same but there was the reality that I had changed. Leaving it at the end of the brief holiday was almost a relief. I had left the farm by happy choice to seek ordination and ministry. I had always taken that seriously. Returning to the farm, provided a meditation check for the mind of the new life God has given and blessed.

My being installed as the pastor of Holy Spirit [HS] in Oakdale MN, instead of merely continuing my call there from the English District Mission Board as their mission developer, didn't change my basic responsibilities in that new ministry. Nor did it change the oversight by Harold Hecht, agent of the mission board. It merely provided a better and more direct relationship with Holy Spirit congregation, still being a mission developer. Or to put it another way, I was not simply the pastor of the Holy Spirit congregation. Rather, being a community missionary was to be the primary shape of my pastorate by the congregation's own directive. Thus they were committing themselves to outreach under my leadership. I was not simply their missionary, but their leader in mission.

My ministry therefore not only called for looking into every avenue of personally meeting local residents, but also that of mobilizing the membership to invite friends and neighbors to worship at HS. Building particularly on the positive and practical experience I had from Luseland, Canada, with the synod's *Preaching, Teaching, Reaching* mission program, we organized volunteers into a group we called *The Seventy*. (Named after the 70 disciples Jesus had sent ahead of himself.) I gave these willing members training in making house calls in our community on prospective members which I had already found. To start with, I had a list of prospects left behind from the first mission developer, Romberg. In addition, with VBS each Summer, when the church overflowed with neighborhood children, we had a valuable program to identify prospective members.

But I had especially been fortunate to be able to arrange with the Oakdale city water department to receive a monthly list of new residents from their records. On these I would quickly call, giving them timely information about HS. Furthermore, I was always quickly calling on any families who had visited our church on Sunday morning.

Thus our prospective member file was growing. And these lay evangelists didn't need to be anxious about ringing doorbells. They didn't need to do "cold calling", since those they were being sent to visit were those who had already expressed some interest in HS.

We made methodical headway sorting through my 4x6 card file of prospective members. These had my useful notations that could be used as conversation starters. That program of lay visitors was active and successful in view of my datebook from those first years at Oakdale. It logs regular training meeting of the 70, particularly each Fall. And that our missionary work was succeeding shows up in the fact of my needing to teach both a Spring and Fall adult instruction classes each year. Those attending were then accepted into membership on semiannually Membership Sundays along with families transferring their membership from other congregations.

Consequently the HS mission was growing, albeit slowly. When I arrived in Oakdale in early 1964, its baptized membership was 152, confirmed communicants were 80, and Sunday school enrollment was 75. By our fifth anniversary in 1966, two years later after I arrived, baptized membership was 284, confirmed communicants were 129, and Sunday school enrollment was 144. On our tenth anniversary in 1971, baptized membership was 265, confirmed communicants were 145, and Sunday school enrollment was 100. On our fifteenth anniversary in 1976, baptized membership was 270, confirmed communicants were 143, and Sunday school enrollment was 75. (The baptized membership and Sunday school enrollment over these years reflects the aging of the parish children and the stagnation of community growth.)

Significantly reflected in these statistics is the loss of five of our families to the other Lutheran Oakdale mission representing 10 communicants and about 20 baptized members. In the early 1970s, as the area children were growing up and becoming active in sports, particularly hockey, we were much affected by absentees in Sunday

210

school and church attendance, including their parents. At first this was simply being caused by Sunday morning practice sessions, eventually even by weekend games out of town. It seemed only reasonable pastoral nurture to write a newsletter article urging children and parents to tell their coaches that they preferred to go to church on Sunday morning in place of practicing sports, asking for this consideration in scheduling team practice. One outraged parent took violent exception to my advice and actively convinced four other families that the other Lutheran mission in Oakdale was more sport friendly. His wife slammed their door in my face when I called to talk. I stood outside crying in the cold for some minutes before getting a grip on my spirit. You must imagine my fervent prayer the next morning as I began the next day. The culture in Oakdale could at times reflect a simple and lovely spirituality, and then again, none at all.

Nonetheless, moving the HS mission to viability, especially financially, was a steep hill to climb. We were growing, but given the class of housing in our neighborhood, the families we gained came from the laboring class of people. Besides, these were struggling to establish a first home and beginning a family. Our prospects were very limited, considering that aside from our two housing projects of only around 500 homes, the surrounding areas, particularly to the east, was rural farm country. Residential urban community development had completely stalled for the reason of lacking a metro sewage system. Had it not been for the long term commitment of the mission board to support us financially for operating expenses, my family would have starved. I would have had to give up fulltime missionary and ministry and find another near fulltime job.

Nevertheless, it was understood that the mission board would not forgive the initial cost of land, building, parsonage, as well as capital improvements to our operation (we had to insulate the church and install steel siding to overcome hopeless paint deterioration on old wood siding). Their grace was only for day to day expenses of ministry,

211

including my modest salary. Member dared not dream into the distant future of self support, such as we had managed in the Elmhurst mission after only six months. It was in a way forgivable that Hecht wore a grim expression and attitude when he occasionally visited HS. Still, given the continuing commitment of the mission board whom he represented, a more upbeat approach would have been appropriate and more encouraging. I'm sure he knew how hard I was working and with what handicaps, but a frank discussion never ensued. It would have been interesting to overhear his report of the HS mission at the mission board's monthly meetings.

The way forward was bleak, but I faithfully kept at the work in a full-time mode. Since I was not finding some of my target families at home in the day, I regularly made evening calls. This to me was difficult in the cold of Winter, given my constitution -- After eating supper and quickly going out in the cold, I'd feel frightfully cold, probably due to my digestive functions calling for circulatory priority. But I also went regardless of the natural responsibility to wife and children which were often being set aside. They paid a price with the demands on my time, whether it was with evening meetings of committees, member visitations or contacting prospective families. At least we always had supper as a family, followed by bible reading and prayers. Even in Summer there was little play time with my children. Also later, attending their athletic games was a limited possibility. However, I made a practice of keeping Sunday afternoons free for my family, except that many Sunday evenings were taken by the Teen Spirits and Mature Spirits.. June always had a full family dinner ready for us when we came home from church. That would end her kitchen duty for the day. We all made do quite well finding our own supper. One of my standbys was a fried egg sandwich; My kids, especially Janet, would successfully beg for the same. However, that early Oakdale Sunday PM agenda was soon to be crimped by my graduate study.

My day was always full, and by this, discouragement was kept at bay along with the observation that my ministry was appreciated by the members. I felt particularly encouraged by a number of new members who had not been well served in other congregations, virtual outcasts. None of our members were criticizing or blaming me for anything, not even my choice of hymns. June was also more than doing her part as the hovering cheerleader, always the first to extend a welcome to visitors and members alike. This was her natural gift to me and our Lord; She was a most ideal pastor's mate. Significantly, the church council, and my board of deacons who met with me to discuss spiritual concerns and initiatives, were all part of a harmonious whole in the background. We were conscious of not being the typical suburban parish, and knew we probably never would be. We were a different sort of mission, concentrating on the need of those on the margins. We found those who had fallen through the cracks. In fact we had pride in practicing a more basic spirituality, less centered in mere sociability. We were in this way happy to attract marginalized people from elsewhere on the east side of St. Paul.

By October of 1965 the church was full enough to begin two Sunday morning services, alternating at first between Communion and Matins, with Communion at both on fifth Sundays. My rationale was to transition to Communion every Sunday, and thereby we did already offer Communion every Sunday, instead of only every other Sunday at a time when once a month was the standard elsewhere.

Quite soon in those first years at Oakdale, cumulating in a September 1969 rededication, I was anxious to renovate our chancel/sanctuary, i.e., the area around the altar. What we had inherited with our building was Gethsemane's old Lutheran, even Spartan or rural low church arrangement. The church was itself rather small, narrow with no side aisles. And the tiny chancel was unfit for any more activity than one or two pastors moving from their chair to either

213

altar or pulpit. There was a short communion rail, for no more than eight persons, which restricted the altar area on the east wall to barely six feet of depth. Two persons distributing communion were almost in each others way in that tight space. There was no room for acolytes, lectors or deacons assisting with worship. They hadn't been imagined as needing to be in place, helping in multiple ways, and in sight, magnifying the drama of the Word.. That necessary motion of worship was impossible, making prayer static and potentially boring.

Some of this work I eventually had to do myself, few of our people at first had the inclination or art to construct furniture grade furnishings to allow the liturgy to become more dramatic. Actually, this woodworking allowed me to learn woodworking based on the skills Pa had taught me. In anticipation I had bought a radial-arm-saw. Significantly, members not only didn't object, they enjoyed the result of making their prayer and worship more alive. They loved seeing their acolyte children helping with worship when we then finally had space for them meaningfully to participate. We enlarged the chancel by moving the communion rail into the front part of the nave. Thus, there was need for carpentry (structural work on the floors, carpeting etc.) which some of our men enjoyed as group fellowship. A much appreciated result was that there was a longer communion rail, speeding Communion and especially eliminating steps to receive communion. All this made it possible to have liturgical processions, so precious for promoting reverence, especially on festivals. There was then room in the chancel for all of the assistants, not just the pastor.

This entire project began with my building a credence table/cabinet at home on my day off. We desperately needed one since we didn't even have a place to store our communion vessels because we had no sacristy. And it eliminated cluttering the altar so as to project its sacredness. I'm still proud of that very first woodworking project. (I took that credence table into possession when HS closed, and still have it.) At the same time we made a closet on one end of my study as a place to hang vestments for myself and worship assistants. Next came separating the altar from the reed table, with a new back to the altar and a front for the reed table. This allowed for moving the altar into the center of the enlarged chancel, effectively symbolizing the presence of God amid his people. The reed table remained against the east wall to be used for candelabra and flowers. (Unfortunately, that innovation, inspired by the liturgical reforms resulting form Vatican II, is currently being undone in RC churches.) A front pew was removed with the enlargement of the chancel and it was used to become a humble place for pastors and assistants to sit behind the altar up against the reed table. The altar was then further uncluttered by making wooden candle stands, placed alongside and also serving as processional candles. All together this renovation allowed for HS to have a worthy spectacle that lifted up the gospel even when it wasn't Christmass or Easter. Worshipers were no longer falling asleep.

Through the week of July 5th, 1965, I attended a workshop at Concordia University in St. Paul that re-ignited my motivation to begin graduate theological study. It was led by the Rev. Dr. Walter Wangerin Sr. to introduce his three-year three volume catechisms for junior high age children, newly released by CPH. I don't remember the rationale for his assignment, but he asked each of those attending to write an essay giving expression to the spiritual motivation we had received from our more significant parent. I could easily have chosen to write about Ma, but I decided that it was more directly Pa who had through all my youth so subtly and tenaciously induced me, in spite of my reluctance, to study for the holy ministry. I've often wished that I'd have kept a copy of that essay for myself.

That was actually my very first effort to deeply consider Pa's piety and influence; And I believe I still remember the main conclusions. His quiet response, with a subtle smile, to my announcement in the Summer of 1953 that I had been accepted for enrollment at Concordia Seminary in Springfield IL, and his immediate determination personally to take me there was vividly impressed on me. But I had not before then taken time to try to put the pieces together. Perhaps it's too much to say that Pa had in mind for me to become a theologian in reflection of his own spiritual hunger. Possibly, he thought no further than my becoming a pastor. Yet when I wrote that essay I was moved to assess what motivated his piety; It was I trust allied with a thirst to know more about God. I wish I could have become aquatinted with his mother to confirm my suspicion that it was she whose spirituality he reflected. On the visible surface he was obviously dominated by my grandfather. A quiet piety, so visible in all those children of Gramma which I came to know, was surely hidden under her humility. And Pa obviously, by my experience, was a result of this which I suppose. Grampa's dominance over him, respectful negotiated nonetheless, had him gain strength from the more humble spirituality of Gramma. I frequently sensed something more in Pa than simple piety and humility.

Not often, but often enough, he showed amazingly faith, even jealousy(?), for my intellect and potential. That "envy" of me included even what he thought I knew about a variety of subjects. I sensed that he bemoaned the curtailment of his education and the sciences. He apparently didn't quit school after ninth grade by choice; Otherwise he'd have quit after eight, as most others did. He always proved himself to be inquisitive about many things about which he would ask or test me; He valued coming to know things. He asked me about things like the age of the earth over against the bible's symbolic account; And especially noteworthy, how was it that humans supposedly could actually give glory to God, as the Gloria in Excelsis proclaimed to be done. This had just then newly confronted him with the liturgy in English. In the German service, it had been sung as a hymn. He was capable of pondering theological questions. This I also did when monotonously cultivating corn; He surely had by his inquisitiveness spent

216

years in the field pondering the universe and the heavens. Subconsciously at least, he hoped that I would be better prepared to ponder, he having had the gift of study denied.

Grampa Lehrke most definitely physically leaned on Pa, his most able-bodied son. He was asked to quit school and take over some of the farming on his more than two farms, particularly as Gramma's health was slipping away. He was being diverted by his care for her. Pa obeyed his highly motivated father, setting aside his wanting to know things. Nonetheless, he always was an avid listener in family conversation. He never pretended to be an authority in his humility. Rather, quietly evaluating other's truth-speech, ready to learn. There were of course lessons in farming he had learned well, and thus he was quick to scoff to us about bad farming when so observed. Where experience had showed him what was true, he spoke up boldly; And he was particular about what he taught us. He didn't sleep through sermons, as I well know, sitting in my teen years on the other side of the balcony from where he sat with the older men. He had faith, only never the chance to study truth for more confident assurance; And yet also for the pure joy of knowing. He envied me the study I was already doing. He would do it through me? and I would do it for him?

That workshop essay at Concordia, the very school in which I had by him been encouraged to study pre-thology in their high school, didn't immediately send me to begin graduate study. The mission work in Oakdale was still a high responsibility which needed to be considered in a responsible balance. Until the following July I weighed the possibilities, and then apparently without discussing it with Hecht, I met with dean Hanson at Luther Seminary in St. Paul (following chapter).

First, I resolved to attempt a concerted outreach to make HS known in neighboring Woodbury, directly south of Oakdale, separated only by Hudson Road, later to become I-94. They were already incorporated with progressive, even vigorous determination. Since they were further down stream on the metro sewage system, they were already connected. Middle class homes were being built. That area had only an old rural-focused LCMS church several miles to the east which clearly would have limited appeal to these new residents. Perhaps we with our old church building were also out of the game, but I needed to try. I had no inside track to these new residents, so it was cold-calling as each house was built and occupied. And being of a different intellectual class from that in Oakdale, the receptions were not always cordial. The upwardly mobile are often naively dismissive. In addition, they were mostly not just first coming to the Twin Cities. Rather, usually from elsewhere in the metro area where they often had a church connection they wished to keep. So I often had nothing they wanted. Yet, I knew that even with freeways, this would be a temptation for them to laps. It was worth trying.

Finding these new residents at home was often difficult. But having strained my Oakdale prospect list to the point of making a pest of myself, I enjoyed meeting these new Woodbury residents. Additionally, I and they had a ready recognition of equality in social class. It was a pleasure to be again meeting people who had a better education and could carry on a vigorous conversation with substance. Over the time of the next few years I succeeded in gaining five families into membership at HS. Alas, in September of 1967 the geographic LCMS district of Southern MN noted the growth of Woodbury and decided to initiate a mission. They called one of my own seminary classmates to serve there. Their commitment included a very nice first unit church on a prominent location, attractive enough for us to immediately lose the families we had gained. It was very much a class decision. There was thereafter no point in continuing mission work in that area.

Chapter 20 -- Graduate Theology Study

On July 13, 1966 I met with Dr. Olaf Hansen, the academic dean of Luther Seminary, St. Paul, to discuss the possibility of doing graduate theological study. I had by then concluded that my parish, HS Oakdale, along with my related mission development responsibilities, had sufficiently stabilized. In particular, development in Oakdale had stalled, awaiting incorporation as a city, construction of a metro sewage extension into our area, and the end of an economic recession. I believed that I had enough time and energy to begin pursuing that persistent dream. Besides, I had had eight years of pastoral experience with which to form appropriate theological interests and questions. There seemed no reason nor benefit in further delay. So the process of determining my legibility was begun with Dean Hansen by making the necessary application for transcript of credits earned at Concordia Seminary, Springfield, and the University of MN. I had been sincerely welcomed by him as well as by the president of the seminary, Dr. Allan Rogness; And this, without prejudice for being a member in the ministerium of the LCMS.

A month later, on Aug. 18th, we met again to consider the possibilities. I was somewhat shaken by Dean Hansen's evaluation of my transcripts. What I had in mind was to begin a graduate master of theology program. However, as he reviewed my scholastic credits he pointed out that though I did indeed have the required theological credits to begin their master of theology program, I nevertheless did not have sufficient college credits as a foundation for my seminary credits. The seminary was bound by the standards of the national accrediting agency, by which they granted degrees. That standard required four years in a college liberal arts program (presumably resulting in a bachelor of arts degree), and then also four years in an undergraduate theological program leading to a master of divinity degree. Only with the equivalent could I be enrolled in Luther's graduate master of theology program. By leaving the

University of MN early, (without graduating and without a bachelor of arts degree), I was now short of credits for graduate school eligibility.

He suggested two options: First, I could enroll in any college liberal arts program, such as the University of MN. Then after earning sufficient college credits for a bachelor's degree I could reapply to Luther's graduate program. Or, alternately, I could enroll in Luther's undergraduate master of divinity program to earn the same number of credits; Total credits was the game. (Under that second strategy I was already eligible to enroll in some courses being taught for graduate school credit. Nonetheless, in my case, those credits would accrue rather as undergraduate credit. Luther's curriculum was however sufficiently large that I would not exhaust what courses I could later take for graduate credit.)

Besides, Dean Hansen, suggested that according to the standards of their own seminary undergraduate curriculum, I lacked some areas of study (like in church history, philosophy and pastoral theology). This, while exceeding their requirements in other areas (like Springfield's rigorous doctrinal theology, etc.).

I immediately chose the second option because general college liberal arts study was something I was already doing on my own, and would continue. What I wanted in particular was to study theology. It struck me that with the second option I could receive a better and much broader theological education. It would result in the equivalent of earning a second master of divinity degree beside the effective one I already had from Springfield. It would however stand in place of my lack of a bachelor of arts degree. I felt no need to posses an actual bachelors degree. So in September I enrolled at Luther Seminary. For three years I then took classes with each year's undergraduate class, eventually graduating with the class of 1969. Thus I effectively accumulated the equivalent of two MDiv degrees as a foundation for a MTh.

That first year, my courses were: Introduction to Old Testament; Psalms; Worship in the Reformation Era; Pastoral Counseling; and, Church & Community. Mostly my professors were cordial and respectful of my unique status, not actually being an undergraduate. The enforced humility was useful to me. One professor, however, because I dressed with a clerical collar as the pastor I already was, snidely made fun of me about my wearing a collar to students gathered around him after class as I was leaving. I dressed in clerics for possibly needing to stop by a hospital on my way home. He couldn't see my collar as quiet humility and simple identity; And, after having gotten to know him as a professor, I might snidely suggest that there was no humility in the parading of his scholarship.

The course on Psalms was a major frustration because the professor used the historical-critical method of biblical interpretation, then becoming increasingly popular. (This by now has been discredited by orthodox Christian theologians as a primary method of exegetical study.). By this method, a psalm's message for us today is supposedly to be restricted to that from its own era (the original message, not our reading of subsequent fulfillment of prophesy). One day he asked the class about the meaning of a particular passage. In the silence, with no answer forthcoming, I spoke up defiantly that the passage was a prediction of Christ. The result was a deafening silence (the class gasping at my rebellion). Ignoring me, Dr. Milton volunteered his own answer. The exams were a farce to poor orthodox me. I accepted his B for the course.

But in retrospect, I should perhaps have been even more bold in my convictions, the result of which might have netted me a failing C. It had been a course so potentially rich in the development of what nevertheless later became a central element in my theology of prayer and Christology. By that orthodox theology it is taught that Jesus became sure of himself by recognizing that Psalms had predictedly spoken of himself. The whole underlying motive in my graduate study had been to come to sit more comfortably

221

with God in prayer and life. I firmly believe Psalms to be God's most particular lesson plan for developing the art of prayer, as I eventually was gifted to recognize -- walking in Jesus' footsteps.

The course in the history of Christian thought was likewise a mistake. Its assumptive thesis was that all Christian thought has developed along and out of a continuum, and is still growing. Namely, that modern Christian thought is beholden even to preceding Greek philosophy, as well as the insights by countless philosophers in recent centuries. My objection was that Jesus' theology was not a world view, but constructed by him on that of the OT prophets; Nor dare we build on more. The so called progress of theological Christian thought was to me little more than an arrogant human exercise over against the consistent changeless "philosophy" of the bible itself, in which I was thoroughly confirmed. I was so disturbed and apathetic toward the thesis of the course that I was unable to concentrate and master the charade; And so I earned the failing grade of C.

In my second year at seminary my courses were: Ancient Israel--Church & State; Seminar in German Reformation; Christian Faith -- Task of Theology; Social Ethics; and, Perspectives on Ministry. None of those courses made any direct contribution to my prayer life and its ultimate goal of being more at peace with God; Yet the study was intellectually invigorating. The pace was rigorous when placed alongside of my pastoral duties. Often my main block of time for reading and study was Sunday afternoon and evening. Sometimes there was not enough time for satisfying excellence. With term papers required in most courses (heavily weighted toward my grade) I resorted to dictation into a tape recorder after carefully assembling my notes and research. Then it was June's chance to help, naturally often retyping a paper after corrections and refinements. Still, the final submission was at times a personal embarrassment per shortage of time.

With the third year, my courses were: Readings -- History of Christianity in America; Seminar in American Lutheranism; Topics in Liturgical Theology; Church & Sacrament; Ecclesiastical Council -- Vatican II; and, Marriage Counseling. With those courses I had accumulated the required number of credits to become eligible to enroll in Luther Seminary's master of theology (MTh) program the following Fall. In recognition of that, the seminary gave me the degree of Master of Divinity on June 1, 1969 at Central Lutheran Church in Minneapolis.

All the while, parish ministry at HS continued with little time to relax. But during the Summer we did find family time, often longer weekends at the Lehrke farm, or at Wise Lake north of Brainerd MN. To make such outings, as well as vacations more affordable, I purchased a trailer chassis in 1968 from Bethany, a camping trailer company in Burnsville. On this I built my own hard shell camping trailer. Walter, who had become proficient in welding, made an angle iron frame which I then finished with metal siding, insulation and inside paneling. It was only slightly over 6' wide, 8' long and 5' high; But it sported bunk beds fore and aft, and another over the far wheel well. It slept all five of us in sleeping bags. When the rain pattered on the roof at night, we praised God for liberating us from a tent.

The previous Summer of 1967 had us raising two dozen ducks in the parsonage backyard. Purchased just after hatching, they created domestic responsibility for the whole family, and a continuous excitement for dozens of neighborhood children, also much fun and frustration. It was instructive to me that the two different breeds we had, did not live in harmony, and that they made a great deal of mess in their fenced-off part of the backyard. With October, there was the responsibility of turning them into food. On three evenings, with hovering neighborhood children not to be denied, they were decapitated, plucked and butchered. The boys insisted on front row positions, and the girls nonetheless not looking away from a distance. You can imagine the reaction of parents with this lesson of nature and food, particularly when a child brought home the claimed head of a duck.

There were in those years -- not entirely restricted to the Summer -- work nights at church for our handy men. These, I mostly needed to direct and supervise. We had inherited an old cold church building which two furnaces struggled to heat. The basement walls were concrete blocks and the whole space was one room. It made sense to divide it, making it possible to heat one half for a meeting for a confirmation class in mid week. We couldn't afford to heat round the clock. We started by firing the walls, insulating with Styrofoam and attaching wood paneling for a warmer look. A dividing partition was made in four foot removable sections. The end sections were permanent, one with a door. The partitions were normally in place, unless there was occasional need for a single larger space.

We had also insulated the upstairs church and roof by a contractor, but the single pane windows couldn't be weatherized. They were hinged at mid-height, the lower half pivoting inside, and the top to the outside. Storm windows were therefore not even feasible. There were eight of such double windows plus two singles. After much shopping I found a double replacement casement window -- hinged to the outside, and it had insulated double panes. Yet this double unit was 1" too wide for the rough opening. So we disassembled the entire new unit so as to reduce the thickness of the outermost jam on my radial arm saw at the parsonage. Reassembled, glued and foamed into place, bought us an end to drafts that drained heat the furnace couldn't overcome. Furthermore, when those windows were installed, they provided a possibility for memorial gifts of stained glass. All were eventually subscribed by member families for departed loved ones.

July 1967 brought a memorable opportunity. I was chosen as a pastoral delegate to the NY City triennial convention of the LCMS, one of the representatives of the English District. For eight days we assembled and deliberated at the Hotel Hilton in Manhattan, with a Communion celebration

224

at St. John the Divine. It was the occasion of having earrings made for June as a ninth anniversary gift -- nine rubies in each. They were an ongoing testimony of my first love. Janet now already has these.

Finally, in Feb., 1968 the township of Oakdale was incorporated as a city. That made way for the possibility of city sewers etc., which in turn won approval by a further election on Sept. 15, 1969. Yet it would be a good number of years before any significant residential development would result. This was due to the retarded reputation Oakdale had acquired. Community leaders were few and this intellectual vacuum would need to run its slow course to resolution. Nevertheless, I succeeded in having leaders of HS meet with a land surveyor in Jan., 1969, toward the possibility of subdividing our surplus church property. The plan was to offer lots for sale to reduce our indebtedness to the English District. We platted our 27 acres -- some of it was a small lake. The idea was too optimistic and too early, and nothing came from it; But the hope and the idea never died. Eventually, a few years later, when Oakdale had sufficiently developed, I was vindicated in that inspiration with a sale that completely repaid our capital debt to the Mission Board.

Perhaps it's fair to suggest that I was with the foregoing impetuous, particularly in those early years in Oakdale. I sensed that I had the gifts to make things happen, over against the frustration that progress on all fronts was painfully slow. (This had played into my seeing the way open to do graduate study while doing full-time parish ministry.) It seems to me now that I was always running on ahead, sometimes proposing things before their time, like with the surplus church property development. I had smoldering energy that broke out in assorted volunteering.

Already at the very beginning of serving in Oakdale, the pastor of our mother church, who was deeply involved in local ecumenical work, particularly cooperating with the various other Lutheran synods, and who was chairman of the St. Paul Lutheran Council, invited me to serve on that board to represent the LCMS. Other synod pastors had been reluctant to participate. I didn't hesitate, in fact I enjoyed working with veteran and leading Lutheran pastors of the other synods. I dared to think I could bring something to the table. I soon took over editing the Lutheran Church ad in the St. Paul newspaper which ran a weekend church page. Then in 1966 I responded to the council's growing concern over escalating divorce rates. Pastors were judged to be failing in preparing couples for marriage. When it was suggested to have metro area premarital classes, I boldly agreed to lead such and effort. I arranged for use of a classroom at St. John's Hospital, assembled materials and presenters for sessions over six weeks of weekly evenings. I myself was at first one presenter. I generated publicity to be included in area church newsletters and Sunday bulletin announcements. It resulted in annual Spring and Fall sessions, usually with at least 15 couples attending. It was judged successful and continued for many years, eventually attracting professional presenters.

I was likewise fair-game to help the chaplain at St. Paul Ramsey Hospital whom I had gotten to know as a good friend when making hospital visits. He was Lutheran but served as the Protestant chaplain of this major county hospital. Beside the Sunday worship in the hospital chapel, for which he was responsible, he wanted to introduce a midweek Protestant worship. He would spend the morning personally inviting patients, and then come with them to an 11am worship which I would conduct. It was easy for me to simply come and use the hospital vestments and vessels in their chapel. I presented a brief sermon, a condensation from memory of my previous Sunday sermon, and celebrated Communion. It was at the same time a much appreciated ministry to the chaplain himself. It gave me valuable experience and provided a good spiritual friend. He paid me by thereafter taking me to lunch in the cafeteria. I continued this weekly worship for several years till graduate study in a tight spot forced an end. But not long thereafter, I was tempted to resume such a weekly hospital ministry, this time for the Episcopal chaplain at St.

Luke Hospital (later named United). The process was the same, as was my satisfaction. It too continued for at least a half dozen years.

On the strength of that experience, I was recruited in the early 1980s by the chaplain at St. John's Hospital to serve there as a night-chaplain. There were six of us pastors and deacons who were by him trained in monthly morning meetings. We were introduced into all the operations and procedures of the hospital, (other than maternity) observing surgery, and prepared to step into any kind of emergency. After that, we were each scheduled to serve at the hospital one night per week from 7pm till midnight. Our first task was always to call on every patient scheduled for surgery on the following day -- there being few outpatient procedures in those days. Thereafter we made complete rounds in ER, ICU, etc., excusing ourselves only if the patient's own pastor was already present -- It was disturbing how rarely this occurred. I was thereby involved in many deathwatches, also ministering to family members present. Fortunately, I had had some positive experiences and practice for not having hesitated to serve my own members through the years in similar crisis. Hospitals have become quite familiar to me -- home territory.

Once again it was my position on the St. Paul Lutheran Council that got me involved in a new venture in the early 1970s: the MN Lutheran Episcopal Dialogue. I came into it already accommodated by the Episcopal hospital exposure. It was at first led by a well meaning priest from suburban Minneapolis, who couldn't stop talking. We were about a dozen, and had representatives from across the state. Somehow, after a year of frustration in which there was virtually no dialogue, I and a young Episcopal priest managed a coup detat. The group appointed the two of us as cochairman with full program responsibilities. We met monthly and eventually sponsored occasional joint Lutheran Episcopal worship in the metro area to bring the lay people into an ecumenical occasion. This, for the wish of greater denominational respect and cooperation in the

227

work of mercy and Word. On one occasion, we filled the Episcopal Cathedral of St. Mark in Minneapolis to hear a sermon by Martin Marty. I served as a cochairman until I left MN in 1990.

The contrast is stark, hard to believe, between what I'm now recalling from memory or date-books of life in Oakdale in the 1960s, 70s and 80s, and that of Oakdale in the present 2019. I was overwhelmed by its state of development when just now making a brief tour through what should have been familiar streets and intersections, but now was almost unrecognizable. Its current equality of pace in the Twin City metro area makes my tale of its humble origins and early struggles hard to believe.

Our pain was also then difficult for others to appreciate. Witness a particularly infamous meeting from about 1970 that was not noted on my calendar by reason of my bitter frustration. Three of our district pastors, led by my neighboring pastor -- who had been the original inspiration to begin our mission in Oakdale -- came for an uninvited conference to discuss his embarrassment that Holy Spirit wasn't thriving in step with his expectations. We sat in my study in that nostalgic old building on a hill. It might have evoked nostalgic sentiments in people passing by. However, it was not in tune with the spirit of people moving to the city. This, even if they would have recognized ours as a suburb aimed at financially challenged families. That pastor himself had judged the building no longer serviceable for his congregation. Yet he didn't understand the most fundamental need for a mission church to thrive. The discussion was instead about my possible inadequacies. The most galling is the only one so painfully remembered: That my tenor voice had a pitch too high to be comfortable to the ear of a "seeker". I had to take comfort that at least one of the three pastors stood by me over those insults.

It seemed to me that our efforts were virtually heroic. June was only the most visible in welcoming members and especially visitors. We had functioning and effective evangelists reaching out into our community. We had good SS teachers with well led classes, a great organist, choir and director. I was attracting people from some distance for the strength of my sermons. We were a Spirit led congregation of friends without cliques. Besides, a good number of our able men were never failing in my leading them with making improvements to our building. With no office space other than my small study (which also had to serve as a sacristy) we turned a tiny closet into a stairway to a cramped attic space above my study for secretarial and office space. We insulated and paneled basement walls for more comfort in the cold, and for the eye. We installed efficient new windows in the nave, but could do nothing about having only a center aisle with the resulting off-putting poor traffic. We had remodeled the sanctuary for more graceful worship -- but there was nothing to do about our physical handicap of directing worshiper up a long stairway either outside or inside. With a parking lot behind the church, invisible from the street, we had the liability with visitors who would be uneasy about possibly driving in and being almost unaccompanied by others. We all did want to grow and prayed about it.

The nature of Oakdale, reflected in the family spirit of HS, was quite unlike our surrounding suburban communities. Woodury to the south, was a brand new well-orchestrated venture; While, Oakdale along with HS and its hand-me-down building had for a decade been an venture "on the cheap". Ours were blue-collar people; Our neighbors were our betters. Woodbury's new well funded mission quickly built a fine church suited for their higher society. They thrived even with a bumpkin for a pastor. Maplewood to the west and across the county line, was a mature 50+ year old community with all the necessary community and commercial facilities, which we in Oakdale were expected to support in our poverty. We had virtually no commerce of our own, and till late, but a bare township administration. To the east it was farms and large estates. Oakdale was still limping with failing septic utilities and streets without curbs at the end of the 60s when the I-694 "bypass" was constructed -- a fitting label of the metro attitude toward Oakdale.

I felt "under-used" at Holy Spirit, abandoned and mostly forgotten by the church. Many a morning I walked home for lunch fantasizing on approaching the mailbox that there just might be a letter of call awaiting me to a challenging ministry. I was not about to beg for it, believing that the Spirit must be free of my vision of the future. But I also knew that the bishop had no inclination to think of advancing me. My failure to keep the peace when in Elmhurst -- not withstanding its spectacular success when in my care -- was apparently a blot in the eye of the bishop, not to be erased. What kept me going was a healthy family life and the appreciation of my congregation. Filling in to use up my energy was graduate study at Luther Seminary were I immediately began a master of theology program as quickly as I had finished a second master of divinity in June of 1969. My mind and spirit was thereby stimulated with subconscious prayers for future service in the church.

Mark 10 provided a good lesson to me in how to approach the difficult stretches of pastoral ministry. He pictures Jesus along the final miles of his last road to Jerusalem: "Jesus was walking ahead of them." I often noted that with amazement. Mark compares this with the notation that the disciples, who knew what lay ahead, were lagging behind. We might say that Jesus was *gritting his teeth*, determined to be responsible with his eternally significant work of loving his Father in spite of any dread.

Many visits of a pastor with individual parishioners are joyfully anticipated, while a few are not. I freely admit that I at times dreaded the house calls I needed to make after supper. It was occasionally a relief to have a meeting on the schedule, deferring the more unpleasant assignment. Yet, I went, consoling myself as I got ready that I wasn't already at the appointed door -- it still would be x minutes. Just keep putting one foot ahead of the other in the meantime.

It had been the same a a child when the assigned work for the day was hoeing the field garden with its peas, potatoes, sweet corn, etc. Before the actual work, there was still a pleasant stroll down the field road with gopher holes to

231

monitor, meadowlarks to enjoy, and a brother's company to appreciate. As long as we moved towards the work, we could already feel responsible, and then the work was only an ounce at a time.

I was once dramatically unwelcome when making a house call on a parishioner -- angry rejection with the door slammed in my face. Hence the possibility was at times in mind, producing dread; Likewise when canvassing new residential housing. Usually, however, any dreaded visits ended with satisfaction, confidence increasing and determination building; Although it never equaled the amazing ease by which Jesus endured each step toward Holy Week, fully anticipating the brutal confrontation.

Our family's one or two day visits to the Lehrke farm at Gibbon, to stay in touch with Ma, were now fairly regular, enabled by the camper I had built. Our children made the most of the free-for-all play time on the farm with cousins their own age, and I much enjoyed being an un-hired-man with assorted farm work. Additional extended family support came that year with sister Jan moving to nearby Lakeland on the St. Croix, having wedded Andy Anderson. That in turn brought the gift of Rex, a Belgian-German shepherd who became a full member of the family for the evening. He thoroughly made use of the church acreage as his kingdom. Later that same year brother Leslie, who had moved to Bloomington MN, was married to Darlene, making for three Lehrke siblings in the metro area, and its family celebrations.

Our family vacation in 1968 was quite unusual, but then also memorable for all five of us. I was nearing completion of a second masters degree at Luther Seminary in St. Paul and had the inspiration of doing a Summer School at the St. Louis seminary with the thought that on that tenth anniversary of ordination, there might be some classmates from my 1958 Springfield class present and enrolled in Summer School at Concordia St. Louis. And it turned out that I was right. There were 5 or 6 of us, though not any in the two classes I took.

It was scheduled to start in mid-June; we left our camper behind. I took my family to Michigan City IN to stay with June's mom and uncle Paul; I then drove on to St. Louis for the June 18 to July 11th session, staying in a dormitory with an assigned roommate from IA. The classes were full semester 3 credit hour courses concentrated into four weeks, with daily sessions. I took two courses. One, which had immediately tempted me, was taught by the famous professor of liturgy, Dr. Arthur Karl Piepkorn. Its exact title isn't now on record but it was a study of the Lutheran Confessions (16th century Lutheran doctrinal declarations) and their commentary and teachings about the historic Christian liturgy. An extended study I was required to do in lieu of a term paper (later submitted with resulting praise) was a survey with analysis of communion practices by Lutheran pastors in the Twin City area. I was gratefully successful in gleaning over 100 replies. The second course, whose professor's name is now forgotten, was a theological and sociological study of the Western Christian liturgy. Each day there were four hours of class time requiring many hours of reading in the afternoon and evening. It was exhausting, leaving little time for exercise or leisure.

To soften the rigor, I invited June to come down by train to St. Louis for a weekend at the halfway mark. She arrived Friday afternoon to spend time with me in Forest Park, with dinner in a five star restaurant -- with violin serenading -- on US 40 nearby, but now gone. I had been led to the place one evening by study mates to experience their famous half-yard glasses of beer. With my roommate gone home for the weekend, June stayed in my room, using but one bed. It had been a lonely separation. We needed to be that tight.

June returned to Michigan City that Sunday afternoon, leaving some hours yet for my study. Then coinciding with the end of the Summer session, she and our children enjoyed a train ride back up to St. Paul. They had all been spoiled rotten by Uncle Paul with fresh sweet rolls every

233

morning. But that train ride home is surely locked into indelible memory for its first-rate exciting adventure.

In 1971 several things combined to start me in beekeeping. There were two beekeepers whom I had met in canvassing our own residential project. They were having envied success. It stirred my memory of Pa's brief experiment with bees in the mid 40s -- thinking to supplement the rationing of sugar during W.W.II. In visits to the farm I became aware of Pa's beekeeping equipment still being stored in the attic. It was not quite enough for a proper beginning, but my new beekeeping friends supplied the connections to acquire that and more. One of them even placed an order for two two-pound packages of bees for me, along with more for himself; He delivered them, even helped me install the screened packages. His full confidence and fearless practice was not to be outdone. And Karl was immediately involved, whether willing or not, I'm not remembering. We had a seemingly remote area back behind the church that seemed ideal; There we set up the two hives which so immediately prospered that I ordered another package of bees from Sears, even though it was really too late in the year. (This third hive never adequately strengthened before Winter, and dwindled to a handful by the next Spring.) Sadly some neighborhood children once tipped over our hives, yet I harvested 360 pounds of honey that first year.

Our family took a spectacular unforgettable vacation in late June and the first half of July in 1971. We first spent a week near Lake Michigan in Indiana, at June's Uncle Paul where her mom lived with him. This included a tenth anniversary celebration of Messiah Lutheran back in Elmhurst IL, where I had been the mission developer pastor for its first three years. We then drove and camped our way to Aspen CO, where June's cousin Ginny lived with her first husband Richard. On the first weekend, they and our family drove to Crystal City CO (now apparently called Crystal Mill) where they had the use of the dilapidated abandoned saloon in what became a ghost town after the

234

demonetization of silver in the 1890s. In its time it had a population of near 1000. But that year it had 15 summer residents in a half dozen restored Summer homes along a wide main street dirt road. Adjacent was a deep 20 foot wide turbulent mountain river flowing in parallel on the south edge of the town with the relic of a mill. It was Spring snow melt season. It's valley was accessible from a public highway only by way of an ever-upward six mile crude and treacherous mountain trail.

Our cousins were driving a 4-wheel drive truck, while we were traveling with a new ford Failane sedan (Toreno) and our camping trailer. We left the trailer in the parking lot down by the highway; But we decided to try to take the new car up to Crystal City since we were planning to stay for two weeks while our cousins returned to Aspen during each week for work. The trail had no impossible sharp curves, but it was heavily rutted from storm and snow drainage, and from Jeep traffic on that south slope ascending to the east. Several times I had to stop to survey the possibilities to avoiding bottoming-out. There was no turning around. The steep ascent made it hard to see the right edge of the trail which had no forgiveness on many section of cliff. Once I did have the right front wheel over the edge and needed to backup unto the track. June was terrified and the kids were mesmerized with the view and the unimagined adventure, apparently considering me able.

There was no electricity, telephone nor plumbing in Crystal City. The boarded-up weathered wood saloon had a two-story keepers living quarters attached to its back side, separated by less than 50 feet from the raging river. An outhouse stood ready in that back yard. It had an eastern entry shanty for storing firewood which led into a generous kitchen with an old traditional wood-fired kitchen stove for preparing meals. Behind and to the left was the main bedroom, which we never explored and where our cousins slept. Beyond the stove to the right was a large booth-like dinning area that served also for lounging and game space. Back at the single entry, a stairway led to a sizable bedroom above with three beds and worn-out mattresses. On these we used our sleeping bags. There was a south window overlooking the river, without panes, standing wide open. The roof shed starlight; Fortunately it didn't rain by my memory. We went to bed with outdoor sounds singing us to sleep, as well as the scurrying of rodents across the floor inside.

No house cleaning had been done there in many years. One might not call it dirty or disordered, rather littered and crunchy under feet. Particularly, there were peanut shells and other litter covering the floor. Once we were on our own after the first weekend, June swept the floors only to be silently rebuffed by Richard on the following weekend as he dropped peanut shells on the floor with visible deliberation. I also received a rebuff, though quite verbally pointed, for being a tenderfoot, for using dry firewood for June's cooking instead of only as a fire starter. Otherwise it was a happy family togetherness with games and even religious discussions invited by Richard, affirming (or justifying?) his liberal principles.

There were endless exploring opportunities begging us in every direction, for all except June who mostly kept herself busy inside reading and knitting. The kids loved the old hitching post alongside for their gymnastic play -- a 20 foot long 3 inch diameter pipe 3 feet parallel to the ground. (On returning home I therefore built what it inspired: a 12 foot tall set of two A-frame 4x4" and a 10 feet long pipe with climbing rope etc.) I chopped wood and went hiking and photographing with the boys. We were pleasantly out of touch with the turning of the world, including astronauts about to walk on the moon for the first time.

When the first weekend brought our cousins back for the 4th of July weekend, we all together made an expedition with their truck further up the valley to the east, as far as the trail went, and from there we hiked several miles further up to the north through landscapes of early Spring wild flowers. We found a deep snowbank from which we took icy snow back to Crystal City to make home churned

236

ice cream. On the second weekend, with the outdoor wood pile all split and stacked in the lean-to, Richard took me and the boys to a steep mountain hillside where the trees had been broken down by a Winter avalanche. With his chainsaw we made up a load of firewood. I was impressed with what a man with an artificial leg could do.

We camped our way home to MN through Wyoming and SD. The MO synod had experience a revolution that Summer with the election of a renegade president -- bishop -- J.A.O. Preus.

At my sister Jan's petition in 1972, I made the first two (of eventually ten) grandfather or tall clocks. She had seen what I could do with my radial arm saw when I had, in a cramped corner of our basement, made a stereo cabinet and speakers out of oak plywood and a credence table for Holy Spirit. (June never complained about the sawdust in the opposite corner from her laundry.) Not yet having found my way to a hardwood lumber company, as I did for subsequent clock construction, nor at any rate being able to afford hardwood, I found a beautiful 4x8 sheet of high quality walnut at a wholesale lumber yard. I had studied a way to make two clocks from one sheet, as well as a way of construction so that few would recognize the ply. It would be one for Jan and one for us, justifying the $60 price.

What a heart arresting experience that was when manipulating such a large expensive sheet for the first critical cut. June had learned to help hold and lead such a sheet through the saw in a space barely large enough for the path. It was easier to set the saw and cut the same piece twice, stashing the second. (That successful plan years later had me again cut out two clocks at the same time, one in maple for Philip and one in cherry for Addie.) I assembled Jan's clock first, and with great difficulty made the hood properly to conform to the case -- the hood needing to be removable for installing or repairing the clock movement. Jan bought her clock movement locally which I successfully installed; But I was not fully satisfied with its quality.

When I had built our clock case a year later, it stood empty in our living room for quite a few years because of not affording the works. Then for our 25th wedding anniversary in 1983, Philip and Karl gave us a gift towards the cost of a German movement which still runs well.

We had tried to make a vegetable garden under the power lines behind the parsonage the year after arriving in Oakdale; But since there was no topsoil, all of that was stunted. Then when I had placed beehives behind the church in 1971, I estimated that area (which we eventually bought, and on which we also built our own home) finding very fertile soil but with deep sod. So the following year I had one of our members, who had a small garden and vegetable stand nearby, plow it for me. There was enough space between the trees for a 50x25' garden. The ground was virgin and benefited from being on a downward slope, with ageless accumulation of nutrients. It never required fertilization and began to produce more than our need. That year I had increased my beehives to six and moved them behind that garden area, somewhat more insulated from teenage vandals. In 1973 when the six hives had matured and increased to seven, I harvested 2029 pounds of honey.

Following the small grain harvest in the Summer of 1972, our family was again visiting at the Lehrke farm north of Gibbon for several days. Walter happened to be baling straw on a neighbor's field for extra animal bedding. Wanting to help and needing exercise, I was hauling the bales home and throwing them off the hayrack into storage. The straw was very dry and the bales seemed so light in weight compared to the hay bales I remembered. I was delighted to be able to pick up a bale and throw it. After unloading several loads of bales in such a weekend-warrior mode, the twisting body motion of throwing a bale suddenly resulted in a sharp pain in my lower back. I had trouble straightening up, but I continued as possible.

Over the next days, weeks and months, I managed to accept the pain which never let up, though it was often not consciously noticeable. I had learned to bend slightly to ease the pain. But by the following Spring, it gradually became unbearable. Finally in July, my doctor had me admitted to the hospital and put me in traction -- a harness around my hips connected to weights over the end of the bed. Thus confined to bed most of the day and all night for ten days without results, I agreed to have a specialist do herneated disk surgery. Not surprising, I was immediately without pain. But fortunately in this process I met a man across the hall who was going through that surgery a second time due to not diligently following the post surgery instructions and therapy. It sufficiently frightened me to obey the specialist with his post-operative care instructions. After those three weeks of hospitalization, I spent three more weeks mostly resting in a recliner. In addition, I learned to lift correctly and sleep flat on my stomach for most of the night to keep my spine straight. (It's good that I was never addicted to golf or bowling. Such activity of twisting, or with too much weight being carried by one arm will always be problematic for me.) Though I've ever since needed chairs with good back support, I've been able to boast of complete recovery.

With Oakdale becoming a city in the 1970s, no longer a rural township with a few small residential clusters, it was taking on some of the disorder of a modern city. Particularly, we were having more teenage misdemeanors. So the police department was reorganized and a chief of police was hired from LAPD (Los Angeles). He brought with him the veritable opposite of the small town police enforcement many of the Oakdale residents remembered, and which we had till then experienced. He hard-nosed it with the teens, going firmly by the letter of the law, and without particular respect to human dignity. The solution of the city council after many complaints was to organize a Human Rights Commission with the mandate to write a city policy to which the police department in particular would be bound. In 1973, the mayor appointed me as chairman of this new commission to serve with two others, and eventually two more. Our process involved meetings with the police chief to learn department policy, but with the obvious awareness by all that the police department was in the process of being policed. There was resentful compliance by the chief, while we felt insulated with a sense of right. Fortunately there was never a question of getting the police chief to humanize his department. We did more than a year of research with regular meetings for debate, review and recommendations for city council legislation. The effect and appreciation of the mayor and council was felt almost from the moment of our existence. I served for two years and then resigned as the commission broadened into other city human rights issues.

The family Christmass gift in 1975 to us from June's mom was airline tickets to Phoenix AZ. We all flew down the day after Christmass to stay at Uncle Arnold's home, which had been inherited by his siblings, Uncle Paul and June's mom. We were joined there part time by cousins Dick, Paul's son, and Ginny, a cousin of June. We took day trips to places such as Tombstone etc. I had no accumulated vacation time; So on the following weekend, Janet and I flew back to MN, arriving in the midst as a super cold spell.

Mike met us at the airport; He was by then was Janet's intended.

By 1976 our boys were able to enjoy more adult recreation, so I was inspired to purchase a small fiberglass sail boat -- a 14' Kolibra, made in Germany. It had a centerboard with main and jib sails. We took it along for our Summer vacation to Park Rapids MN, carting it on top of our camper -- a heavy lift for several hands -- leading thereafter to buying a trailer. The lake wasn't well suited for sailing, being too small, and the weather was too calm. We did launch it and did sail to the far end of the lake. But returning took forever, tacking back and forth against the breeze. It was a primer nonetheless. Philip wasn't much inspired, probably turned off for being way too slow. Karl was willing to try again on White Bear Lake (north of St. Paul), to which we several time returned on my day off. There we occasionally had more wind than we could completely harness. Karl tended the jib while I had the main and the rudder. He thrilled with the maximum speed we could generate, which was however dangerous with our small boat for its likelihood of taking in water in the stern and swamping, or even capsizing. I once tried my boat on the St. Croix with sister Jan tending the jib, but the speed boats there made for difficult sailing. They didn't respect a sailors right-of-way, and created a dangerous wake. Several years later, when vacationing on Gull Lake with June, I tried sailing alone, having limited fun. I wasn't experienced enough to tend a jib from my seat in the stern. I capsized but had no way to bail out the boat; Fortunately I was not too far out from shore. I had a good appetite for sailing, however, for a bigger boat which I couldn't afford.

By 1973, Dr. Jack Preus had been president of the LCMS synod for four years. The tension in the synod was increasing, particularly in relation to the faculty at the seminary in St. Louis. He demanded of the faculty a simple and literal interpretation of Scripture. Undoubtedly some professors were suggesting that not everything in the Bible was factual history -- like the creation of the world in six 24 hour days. (More than likely, it was rather a parable of Moses similar to the teaching parables of Jesus.) Such debates must be done with charity. At issue for many people in the synod, myself included, was the high-handed way almost all faculty members were suddenly being accused of denying the Gospel itself; And they were without honorable opportunities to defend themselves and even being dismissed by the synod president. His was a crude power play unbecoming the church. Consequently, the synod was split between loveless accusations and opposition groups.

Eventually in 1976 my English District, in convention at River Forest near Chicago, after careful debate, inspired a majority of delegates to walk to a nearby church to reconstitute its predecessor English Synod. I went along and then home to consider this with Holy Spirit. It resulted in a September congregational decision to leave the MO synod English District to join the English Synod. Subsequently, the five other English District congregations in the Twin City metro area, (except a mission in Forest Lake too financially indebted to leave) likewise voted to leave for the English Synod. We were joined by several other LCMS congregation in the metro area from the geographic MN district. Sadly, we at Holy Spirit lost several member families who rejoined LCMS congregations.

What were we thinking then when inviting Hecht to preach on the Sunday of the annual congregational meeting in January of 1977? With the re-constitution of the English Synod -- which Holy Spirit had joined the previous September -- he was no longer the mission director of the English District of the MO synod. He had rather become the bishop of the English Synod. After over a decade of being my critical boss, why were we courting him for anything now that he was our bishop? Surely I didn't really imagine that he might consider advancing me after our history. As the trickle of pastors wishing to leave the conflict ridden LCMS looked to the English Synod for refuge, he did find quite a number of places for them. Perhaps I still hoped.

I know I did think it possible that he might appoint me to a position on the commission for the new hymnal, then having already begun. This eventually resulted in the *Lutheran Book of Worship.* I did feel qualified, and he did know of my studied liturgical practice. I remember asking him because I knew that he, now being the English Synod bishop, was in position to nominate. Again, it was a foolish hope, particularly since I had long suspected that it was precisely my interest and practice of traditional worship which he thought was contributing to my "failure" as a mission development. However, what is memorable of that visit by Hecht is that there was the usual potluck dinner following worship. This was always preceded by great fellowship as the final preparations were made in the kitchen. He rather waited in my study upstairs till it was time to sit down to eat. Per always, he asked me how my garden had done, as if that's what mattered most to me, never how I was doing.

The decision of Holy Spirit to leave the LCMS had been problematic in view of our debt to the district mission board. Consequently, the process of cashing in our surplus church property, already underway with a land survey company, was accelerated. The 27 residential lot plat was submitted and approved by the city; And the mission board agreed to hire an excavating contractor to prepare a rough grade for streets and lots. We had furthermore negotiated for sewer and water construction with the city, to be paid by assessments to the lots. The plan was to advertise and sell individual lots. I had first dibs, choosing the lot we were already using for my bees and garden. However, the contractor turned out to be hopelessly too small to do the site work. He himself proceeding with one bulldozer for most of the Summer. Fortunately, our advertisement attracted a home builder who wanted to purchase all the lots available. A contract was singed, and he took over the site work. The end result was the repayment in full in 1977

243

of our $150,000 debt to the mission board. I had done all of the management to bring it to completion. Since we had for some time been meeting our operational expenses, there was considerable relief in the congregation about our future.

There had been optimism in the church council from the start with the vision to develop our surplus property to pay down our capital debt to the mission board, or was it desperation for the lack of any other vision? Our leading charter member at Holy Spirit -- always the last to speak up, yet consistently helping to define our direction -- was again at the time on the church council. He was not being pessimistic, but rather cautious as always, when he had then challenged our faith with a promise: "If this works out successfully, I'll take you all out to dinner to celebrate." And he didn't forget. Shortly after the mission board had been satisfied, he took all council members and spouses out to nearby Tartan Park, a members-only facility for 3M employees from its main headquarters. There we had an evening of fine dining.

Our family had no well-laid plans for our 1977 vacation -- which was not unusual, preferring always to allow blessed surprises to develop out of general plans. By using our camping trailer, we were well supplied from home and well prepared to meet whatever we encountered. Leaving Janet in the care of the two Carols (so as to work at her Summer job as a waitress at a restaurant called Farells. It was there that she then met Mike Grant, her eventual husband.)

We loaded bicycles for Karl and Philip onto the top rack of the car. As so often, we drove the North Shore, this time all the way up into Canada. Our general plan was to circle back westward from Thunder Bay to MN through International Falls. Once in Canada, we looked and asked for possibilities and found Antikokan OT, a fishing resort on a rugged chain of lakes in Precambrian shield country. We pitched our kitchen tent beside the camper and were comfortable and pleasantly surrounded. But it didn't start well, only because I blamed June for not packing my elaborately planned family devotional material. Eventually, I forgave her and we blessed each other. But the fishing was very poor, and the old outboard motor which I'd inherited from Pa was a big pain -- always slow to start. Yet the boys enjoyed swimming, and June and I went boating to enjoy the views of the rocky shoreline -- the fishing prospects were that bad. But per usual, fishermen love to talk, at least in general of new found success. So I heard of a nearby lake where the bass were biting. Karl, Philip and I eagerly went to try, and had great luck, catching our daily limit. We went again after a few days when our twice-a-day feasting on bass had nearly used up our supply. Again we caught our full daily limit. But for some reason, after another evening meal of fish, we didn't feel like fish for breakfast before leaving for home that day.

Heading west along frost-heaved roads, without roadside service or even habitation for may miles, two disasters struck in succession. First, the load of the camper when tossed and jerked by major frost bumps broke a rear spring on our four year old car. There was nothing to be done but to drive slowly on. Then, finding no service station, we ran out of gas. I hitchhiked ahead some 25 miles and hitchhiked back with a gallon, only to be fearful of running out of gas a second time. We did make it to the US border. But then we frightfully remembered that for lack of having had fish for breakfast as planned, we might have more that our possession limit of fish. Perhaps we wouldn't be checked, but we were apparently recognized as fishermen -- perhaps by the old outboard motor in the trunk; So we were asked to pull aside. I forget how many too many fish we had, but it resulted in a painful $79 fine. Returning home with three strikes in a row, regardless of how much other recreation we had enjoyed, took some time to process.

Fall of 1977 was the dawn of the time much discussed as our children were growing up: college. June had, matter-of-factly, encouraged them regularly with memory and comments about her having graduated from Valpariaso

University in IN. Even before they started elementary school, it was mentioned because she was aware that none of their friends had parents with college degrees. There was pride and determination in mind, not wanting our children to fix on the vocations they became aware of from around our small neighborhood. After all, almost as soon as children begin school, they have graduation in mind. She wanted them to realize that we were justifiably expecting something more of them than the visions of those with whom they were growing up.

She realized that this conditioning was important because it was impossible for them to understand her advanced sort of motherhood for them as a worthy benefit of having gone to college. She was hard put to explain, in their childhood, that she intentionally didn't have a regular job like many of the mothers of their friends because, in large part, they were her job out of college. The reward of having them grow up well was greater to her than their growing up with better things by her having a job. It didn't matter to her that they might not be wise enough to thank her till adulthood. She felt a sacred duty of love to stay home for them, ready to be a tutor or counselor. And she did faithfully keep up and facilitate their study. Besides, she already had a full-time job of being a Mrs pastor. In addition, she had become church secretary when Kathleen retired. She (nor I) ever felt sorry about all this. Particularly, not now as I write, as the reward becomes ever brighter.

It would be hard to explain the resulting trepidation for both June and me on accompanying Janet to Moorhood State College in 1977. It was the more so for reason of those many years of our vision. We trusted that we had always tried, and we had some confidence despite getting nervous as Janet simply coasted through her final year in high school. We both went along to Moorhood to haul her things and to see her settled; Her casual goodbye was a shock. That she was "gone" was dramatic. Were we at fault for not clinging? Was she so dismissively confident because she was, or because her friend Mike had also

246

enrolled? Hopefully she not only appeared strong, but in fact was by our nurture. Mother-daughter relationships are typically often tense, as it was in her case. We drove back home troubled by a flood of emotions -- June's much deeper and more anxious than mine. What's to do? Having tried, all we could do was wait in faith. We should not have questioned ourselves and failed via faith to imagined her eventual *summa cum laude* graduation after less than the normal four years later.

Chapter 23 -- Hallmark Hills House - 1979

By the mid 70s I had finished the course work for a master of theology degree (MTh) at Luther Seminary and was to be working on a thesis in church history under Dr. Fevold. I was very comfortable under his direction. For this thesis I had for some time been planning to analyze the sacramental theology of MO Synod's founder, C.F.W. Walther. I had the impression that his theology, and particularly his piety, was rather word centered; Namely that the sacraments were merely pro forma, i.e., not a lively act of his faith. I had not read or found such criticism by others, but believed it should be considered. So I had begun sorting through his many published sermons; He had not written books or papers about the sacraments of the church, which itself aroused my concern. Was he not enlivened and dramatically assured by remembering his baptism and by faithful communion? That he so seldom celebrated Communion or received, made me uncomfortable.

I already had a tall stack of his sermons printed out, chosen because the text would have required disclosing his position on the spiritual significance and practice of the sacraments. These were original German sermons. As I began reading, it wasn't the reading of German, nor the older style of writing, nor the method of his theology that bogged me down. I simply couldn't any longer prolong any excitement about proving my thesis. Partly it was because I sensed that the church had on this issue moved beyond Walther. It was too much a matter of old dry bones.

Therefore my thesis assignment was being neglected; It nagged me for a time, but then its topic was decidedly abandoned. There was then the haunting frustration of being unable to get enthused about some other worthy issue of church history to debate. I had a full load of parish ministry to excuse the procrastination. Besides, we had purchased the parsonage from the mission board and built an addition for another bedroom and a family room. Therewith I had the work of finishing the inside of that addition in any spare time. Furthermore, we then had a dining room for which we had no table. The work of constructing a table filled my days off for a while, Karl helping with a pleasing trestle design. Thereafter its new chairs needed to be finished; And there was always the garden and the bees.

It wasn't till the new hymnal, *Lutheran Book of Worship*, was published in 1978, which included many new first prayers for the Sunday liturgy, that I was indirectly led to a subject for a thesis. Still, that was not conclusively recognized for some time. My thesis eventually was a critical review of the work of the LBW subcommittee on prayer. That topic eventually came to mind while assuming the consuming years-long project of creating a new translation of the Latin traditional prayers, as I believed the hymnal commission should have done. In this I was much encouraged by hundreds of pastors who came to know what I was doing and helped by trial use of my prayers. They too were disappointed with the new prayers in the new hymnal. (That work during the 1980s will be covered in a subsequent chapter.)

What intervened was the building of a new house in Hallmark Hills -- the name given to the subdivision of the surplus property of Holy Spirit. That work was the significant cause of my much delayed master's thesis.

The inspiration to build a new home for our family followed on the 1973 Arab Oil Embargo. This had raised concepts of more efficient home construction, and alternative sources of energy. We didn't as yet own the plot behind the church were we had a garden and my beehives, but that gracious space worked its magic in concert with tending the garden and the bees. It had charm in its relative isolation, vistas, wildlife and ancient oak trees. My thoughts while tending that garden and my bees were often intruded by, "Where would one build a house down here? It's such a peaceful place." And becoming convinced that energy conservation loomed as a crisis, I studied the many ideas being suggested. I found myself discussing them with others similarly inclined. I also remember play-designing homes, even underground and earth sheltered. I did lots of reading then flooding the magazine racks of new housing concepts inspired by the energy shortage. Eventually, I drew up crude floor plans that actually resembled the home we eventually built, particularly its split level and earth sheltered concept. My key thought was always solar, via a south facing greenhouse as a passive collector.

Realizing I needed help, I interviewed architects in the metro area who advertised their interest in solar. Finally in 1977, I chose Truman Howell who was just then starting his own firm after working for one that had experience with solar. We shared ideas for over a year, along with conversations with the home builder who had built our addition to the parsonage. Repeatedly, we encountered the difficulty of choosing designs that were buildable, i.e., using a residential contractor who was interested in new concepts. There were of course commercial contractors who had residential experience, but these were unaffordable. Through all this study, June was passive, yet supportive. I took that as permission to follow the dream.

It took a year to find a commercial contractor who could build what Howell eventually designed for us. It involved a concrete lower half of a partly earth-sheltered house. There were to be three horizontal split levels of poured concrete walls, and floors of precast concrete. This was part of the passive solar design. We wanted lots of concrete as a heat sink for the solar heat to be generated by a south-facing "greenhouse" to prevent rapid overheating. This contractor was experienced and agreeable, though he was busy.

We scheduled construction for the Summer of 1979. Consequently we listed the parsonage with a realtor. It quickly sold, with a closing in mid September. I hired an excavator to dig out the lower earth sheltered levels. Then with Karl and Philip, we spent much of the month of June digging the footings by hand, and waiting for this contractor to arrive. Many promised arrivals of his crew were disappointed, while I kept prodding him. It was well into July before he sent a crew of three.

Fortunately they were highly qualified and very interested in our unique concept. And they were faithful from then till the last, nearly three months later. They quickly built forms for footings in the excavation long ready. Cement delivery was schedule, only to be interrupted by a major thunderstorm just as the truck arrived. That storm flooded the forms. (Other than that, it had been a mostly very dry Summer with little honey and few vegetables resulting.) Our cement truck had already backed down the slope and was now stuck. It was decided to pour the cement into the forms, simply displacing the water. There would have been no way for the cement truck to leave when full, even with a tow. When the truck was empty, it still needed to be pulled out by a winch from the street. It was dirty work, far from standard procedure, but this highly qualified crew were always in control.

There were further delays (with some new anxiety) for the return of the crew after we removed the forms and installed a perimeter footing drainage system. They eventually brought bulky metal forms into which to pour the first of the three levels of walls. Thereafter, all went ahead as rapidly as possible. There were only the necessary delays after each of the three levels, waiting for the poured walls to cure sufficiently before removing the forms. And then another delay each time for the arrival and installation of the three sets of precast concrete floors lifted into place by a crane. During that entire time, Karl and I were regularly the fourth and fifth members of the crew. Karl was my paid laborer all Summer; He was awaiting enrollment at the UofMN, having graduated 3rd in his class of 420 at Tartan HS. Philip worked a full shift at McDonald's and helped as able.

Soon it was time to move out of the parsonage, but no place into which to move. We therefore rented a semitrailer for storage which was parked out on the street beside my pile of shop material -- some of which was consequently stolen.

Our furniture was placed in storage with a moving company. And for living and sleeping, we rented a 24' RV trailer which we had them park alongside of our construction in the neighboring church park. June was most faithful throughout that ordeal which lasted through November. She fed us well, but I lost 15 pounds that Summer.

Finally, in September our contractor -- who had built the rough construction of the parsonage addition a few years earlier -- was able to come with two additional carpenters; They constructed the rough double frame walls and roof of the final three levels of the house, as well as a three car garage across the full north front of the house. Karl and I were added to his crew as well. The contractor bought premium lumber and was highly practiced with our praise. I believe I and Philip eventually shingled the roof. A subcontractor of his came to do some of the interior sheetrock after I insulated the double thick walls. He also had an associate who applied stucco to the inside concrete walls on two of the lower levels -- three bedrooms and a family room. Through all of this carpentry work, June was ever ready to clean up. She was a proud observer of a unique project. Meanwhile, the excavator associate of our carpentry contractor performed landscaping with his little cat and hauled in fill with his little truck after the exterior of the lower concrete walls were sealed with a bentonite material as water proofing.

All Summer long, we were visited with a steady stream of parishioners wanting to observe and bless the construction of our unique new home. They stopped by, particularly after worship on Sunday, all of them supportive. There was also nonstop neighborhood and city interest in our building project. The fire department came to understand this new type of construction. Endless strangers stopped, looked and asked. The interest by the congregation never let up even after we had finally moved in.

Moving in was high excitement since by that time the cold late Fall weather made sleeping in the unheated trailer not much fun. Nevertheless, although we still had no heat in the house, we were comfortable with the partial solar features. The heating contractor caused a frustrating delay because of at first being unsure of load requirements. Being an ordinary residential heating and cooling contractor, he was baffled by needing to use the hollow cores of the precast floors as heat and return air ducts. The solar furnace -- the "greenhouse" on the south face of the house -- was postponed to the following year while thirteen 3x8 thermapane window panels were being made to order. These also required special aluminum channels.

In the interim I erected a common plastic sheet greenhouse that worked amazingly well all that first Winter. By Christmass we were highly pleased for enduring the many Summer ordeals and delays, delighted for our perseverance. What a home it turned out to be for June's last ten years!. She had all along been passive, but became quite proud of it, and happy in our comfort. She took special delight in its brightness, allowing for her care of an accumulation of over seventy house plants; These were our humidifier.

In the following Spring of 1980, Philip graduated from Tartan High School near the top of his class of near 500 and then enrolled in Fall at the UofMN in aeronautical engineering. Meanwhile, Janet had graduated early from Moorhead State, yet *summa cum laude,* and accepted a job with our Washington County in child protection. Karl came home for the Summer from the U and built a large storage shed for me in the backyard to use for beekeeping and gardening. He also helped me build a three-season side porch by the back door leading into the kitchen. That provided somewhat of a handicap entrance to the most critical level of the house -- kitchen and dinning room --.of our six split levels. Another major project that Summer was construction of the permanent two story 22' wide "greenhouse", its second story with a slight shed slant. This construction, with cedar frame, called for very precise workmanship so as to accurately accept the 300 square feet of solar glass. It was a major functional success, exceeding all expectations. A year later our all-Winter heating cost was only $65. Not surprisingly, the power company came to our door to make sure we had not tampered or bypassed their meter. When they stepped into our warm living room on a bright but cold Winter day, they exclaimed, "Oh! We understand! Sorry to bother!"

I had not made much progress during the Winter with the finish trim of the house. That was always being placed at the end of the line of things to be done -- the last of it waited till just before we moved out ten years later. I well remember a common pattern with my Monday-day-off. As with every other day, I felt the gift of the house and its blessing. On Mondays, when able to do some work to finish remaining details, I'd first stepped back to reveled or luxuriated, not having had time to decide which project to start or advance. I was instead made conscious of the already. The wonderful view of the backyard with the two acre pond in a large open field beyond, also attracted my attention. It was always a leisurely beginning, taking me well into the morning. Wanting to live in the house, tools and material had not been left waiting for me. June was content, and we were happy to be together in that place.

It speaks to the greater contentment we both felt in our new home that we began celebrating life in extra ways. One was becoming season ticket holders of the MN Orchestra for concerts at Orchestra Hall in Minneapolis, and then eventually in St. Paul after Ordway was constructed. June had in childhood come to love opera, and then in college taken operatic voice lessons. But she had come to enjoy symphonic music as well. I therefore didn't need to be sad for the lack of opportunity in MN of taking her to the opera, as would have been possible in the Chicago area. It would have been an uphill struggle for me, while the symphony wasn't that for her. She and I both enjoyed dressing in our best and attending concerts. It was a rising above ourselves, a meager expression of an appetite for the celebrations in heaven.

The Summer of 1981 is memorable for making and installing the stairs for our split-level home. Our carpentry contractor had made stair-horses out of common lumber, and I had added plain 2x12 stair treads, which I had not bothered to finish. That Summer I used up my entire two week vacation time to make an open hardwood stairway system, with the impression of furniture. For the four half flights of seven step stairs, I bought 2 inch thick yellow poplar, a sturdy hardwood. My shop was now in the third stall of the garage, allowing expanded work space with autos on the driveway. No longer was I making sawdust next to June's laundry. It was a major learning experience to correctly operate a large new belt sander. That Craftsman sander I bought was not naturally well balanced, requiring a new skill, which took time to avoid gouging. It was also my first time to cut stair-horses. Fortunately I had the ones that were in place as a guide, but they were in place, requiring lots of measuring. And this was cabinetry work, not carpentry, to cut stair-horses from hardwood planks. I enjoyed the work by the north facing open garage door where the hot weather was not a problem. Then after installation, with windows open, I strategically applied stain and urethane, staging it with our need to use the stairs. Considering the hard work and the time, I was highly pleased.

Later that Summer with the stairs in place, we had a grand chance to show off our entire handiwork. Having published a Lehrke Family Tree, I invited a host of relatives for the first ever all-Lehrke family reunion. We began with worship at Holy Spirit next-door in a later Sunday morning service with near 100 attending -- my congregation having worshiped at an early Communion. This was followed by a potluck dinner at church, and then we walked down to our home. There we had a family tree program in our large living room with its open balcony level. I shared background history of our ancestors dating back to 1724; Also the Civil War history of my great-grandfather Gottlieb Lehrke. It was a happy meeting on a beautiful Summer day.

Many had never met each other before. A few even stayed into the evening for a beer following light refreshments.

In late Summer Karl began going from the U with a bus load of other students to work in the corn pack at Green Giant's Glencoe MN plant -- 60 miles distant. Because that involved time consuming travel, I took him to the town priest to ask for a recommendation of a room to rent. He quickly connected Karl with a room in Glencoe, having Mom Radtke's old car to come and go. Philip then also went to join that work force.

With the resumption of U study, Karl transferred to its school of architecture from liberal arts, being one of 60 out of 300 applicants accepted. He as well as Philip continued living in the U's men's dorms. In the following years they would rent an apartment together with a friend.

On September 13th Holy Spirit celebrated a well planned and festive 20th anniversary. Seventeen and a half of these years, June and I had led them. Spirits were high as attendance and membership number were growing. It felt good to be self supporting and debt free.

The day after Thanksgiving, Ma Lehrke died of a massive stroke at 86. She had had a productive life, even surviving a heart attack for 25 years. Her last years were spent in a Gaylord MN nursing home where June and I often went to visit on my day off, making it a holiday that June and I much enjoyed. This, not only for being with Ma, who thought much of June and visa versa, but also for June's leisurely time with me. Ma had eventually become content and active there in those last years. She was survived by two older sisters, Aunt Molly and Lena, and two younger brothers out of a family of eight children. We were proud of each other.

Chapter 24 -- *Prayers for the Eucharistic Gathering*, a book

The year 1981 was auspicious for me as a scholar with a lifelong subconscious call to write. Even so, it would be a preliminary stage. (The trajectory has however slowly but faithfully led to my final book, now awaiting publication: *The Incarnation -- A Life of Faith and Prayer*.) Already in childhood, I had had a poorly formed consciousness of a desire to write a theology of prayer, trusting that timely transforming inspirations would appropriately follow. The vision was vague, at first a figment, the strand of which I'm only now able to describe. It was there in an abiding interest in prayer, and on intermittent pause for coalescing what I was called to say; The mission itself was not quickly clarified. (Authors are well aware of first needing to have a clarification of a worthy subject. Yet there is for them a prior interest and dedication with determination to contribute to a special cause.)

What was finally set into motion for me that year actually had its beginning when I was a preteen in the early 1940s, and by then attending English language worship at St. Peters Lutheran Church near Gibbon MN. My spirit was strangely excited by the centuries old first prayer of the liturgy being recited by the pastor each Sunday and festival. Earlier, when they had been prayed in German, though they were the same set of prayers, they had escaped my special notice. These English translations of the original Latin were prayers prepared by martyr Thomas Cranmer, Archbishop of Canterbury in sixteenth century England. They were prayers which had in turn been composed in the fifth through seventh centuries, and been set in their Sunday and festival order by the twelfth century. It had fallen to Cranmer to translate them into English, as various others did into German in Germany, etc. When Lutherans began worshiping in English in America, they were glad to simply choose the excellent work Cranmer had already done. He had convincingly matched their original truth with incredible poetic beauty, seemingly virtually impossible to surpass for all this time, although by the 20th century somewhat archaic.

These old first prayer of the Sunday liturgy had originally intended simply to open the spiritual ears of worshipers for the reading of the Scriptures by way of teaching the various fundamental truths regarding prayer -- worship. Nevertheless, it wasn't till I attended undergraduate seminary lectures in liturgy by Professor Fred Precht at Springfield that I became aware of how precious those prayer already were to me. This, by the fact that I realized that I already knew them virtually by heart. Not having till then studied them, and only having heard them once each year on their assigned Sunday, they had nevertheless become my unacknowledged yet functional compendium of a theology of prayer, particularly a classic expression of incomparable reverence. For me, they had the force of scripture itself. Consequently, they were my as yet unrecognized call to learn and write on the art of prayer, eventually to be focused on the prayer above all prayers, the Lord's Prayer.

What had finally happened to set me into motion was that the major Lutheran churches (synods) in America (the LCMS left late in the process) had in *Worship*. It 1978 published a new hymnal, *Lutheran Book of* unfortunately reached and expressed the mistaken conviction that the first prayer of the liturgy each Sunday should relate to the assigned scripture lessons as a way of introducing them. They proposed the abandonment of the traditional introit which had subtly previously done so. (That idea still stands as an unrealistic effort since there are three largely independent scripture lessons per Sunday, and even three annual sets of lessons in a three year cycle. No one prayer for a specific Sunday of the year can possibly accomplish this unification.)

About half of the centuries old prayers had consequently been abandoned by the LBW, and the rest reassigned from their historic order, supposedly to fit a particular Sunday's lessons. Lost in committee was the traditional

258

understanding that these prayers were essentially an independent component of the liturgy designed to teach the art of prayer. It was true that Cranmer's translations were four centuries old, and like the King James translation of the Bible, they needed to be updated. Hopefully this could be done without shedding their incredible beauty. But that early hope was quickly abandoned by the committee, deemed altogether intimidating. It was safer and easier they thought to write new -- predictably inferior -- prayers; This project was justified by their unfortunate theory of a better liturgical use of that time of prayer, i.e., stating a theme for each Sunday. They failed to recognize the original and long successful role of simply teaching the art and practice of prayer.

After the new hymnal was published, I was quick to grumble to other pastors about this loss of the stately old prayers. I considered this tragic. Other than that, we and the whole church was quite pleased in general with the new hymnal. Our shipment at HS was one of the first, and our church council had decided in advance to use it immediately on arrival. It would replace all the assorted materials in our pew racks which we had been using to supplement the aged *Lutheran Hymnal* of 1941 with its limited liturgical offerings.

Many across the church sympathetically heard my complaints about the loss of the traditional first prayers; One pastor actually encouraged me to be the Cranmer for the modern age. I had no illusions about that, but then in 1981, I decided to try since, no one else was making the attempt. That is, other than some Roman Catholics in Canada who got in touch with me when they heard what I had started. With the course work for my graduate degree long done, I felt I had the time to work on such a new translation. It wasn't yet the work of writing a thesis in the area of church history, as my seminary graduate advisor was expecting of me. But it eventually led precisely to that.

I started with the original Latin version, then already more than a thousand years old. Each week for the next whole year I copied out the Latin first prayer for the following Sunday. And then I secluded myself in the Luther Seminary library book stacks where the Latin dictionaries and lexicons were kept. Usually for an entire morning or afternoon, I poured over the original intention of each of the less than a hundred words. Once I had decided the proper meaning of each word in its context, I went home to compare my rough, virtually literal, translation with every other available translation, particularly with what Cranmer had decided. And once I was confident about what the prayer was attempting to teach about prayer, I opened myself, not to some expected sudden rush of the Spirit, but to a protracted session of contemplation, striving for the most felicitous way to duplicate in modern English, what the Spirit had already so long been teaching about prayer in Latin.

This work had to be done early enough each week to allow the "finished" translation to be printed in the worship folder of my parish for the following Sunday. Traditionally, the first prayer is to be recited by the celebrating pastor. But I however decided to ask the congregation to pray the prayer with me in unison. My reason was to test its fluidity. If I heard a difficulty in the congregation with smoothly reciting a phrase, I then knew it would need more work. Usually there was a sense of joyful accomplishment every Sunday. It took only a minute of worship, but it excited me for struggling with next Sunday's first prayer. My people were therewith learning the fundamentals of prayer.

This work of translation was no secret within my circle of pastors, even across the synod. Before these prayers had their first anniversary, my work was announced in several national Lutheran newsletters, and with an invitation to participate. I invited other pastors to subscribe for a trial use on their own. June gathered and duplicated my prayer translations in monthly sets, and we mailed these out free of cost. The mailing list quickly passed 100, indicating that I was far from the only pastor disappointed with the prayers in the LBW. It was a good feeling to imagine the number of worshipers in the US, Canada and Australia who were being blessed with these modernized yet reverent ancient prayers.

It wasn't long before there were calls for me to write other liturgical prayers for each Sunday. Historically the liturgy included two more short prayers for each Sunday which had for Lutheran usage been terminated by Luther in his liturgical revisions during the Reformation. One was a prayer at the offering of the congregation's gifts, the other, a prayer at the conclusion of Communion. Luther had judged the existing prayers to be hopelessly infected with doctrinal errors. He simply decided to eliminate those two prayers from the liturgy, probably for lack of time to create better ones -- a major effort. But then he partly demurred, offering several post communion prayers of his own for repetitions use. In particular, he spoke against the practice of an offertory prayer out of fear that the people might believe they were contributing to their salvation, paying for salvation coming in the form of bread and wine. However, that resulting Lutheran discussion had never been resolved. But ever since there had been strong sentiments to pray at the presentation of the offerings, and in thanksgiving after Communion. This reflected the ancient piety which had originated this addition to the liturgy That issue was again considered in preparing the LBW, but again without agreement. The preparation of those additional prayers had been left undone; probably the LBW subcommittee on prayer was intimidated by such a major effort. Composing the many new first prayers had already been overwhelming.

By two years later, my apparent success in meeting the approval of many pastors via their trial use of new translations of the historic first prayers encouraged me. Therefore, I dared to begin in 1983 to see if I could do better at composing entirely new prayers than the LBW subcommittee on prayer had achieved with the First Prayer. It seemed indeed possible, since it would not be by a hopeless committee process. The urgency was recognized by the fact of the unresolved 400 year-old debate about the offertory prayer. Yet there was no one daring to make an attempt. There clearly was a felt need of praying a prayer at those critical intersections of the liturgy. In particular, it struck me that these weren't only fitting junctures in the liturgy for the congregation to be in concerted prayer, but the best opportunity to teach prayer.

With a different prayer every Sunday at the time of offering the gifts, the entire range of stewardship could be addressed; And this better by far than by an annual stewardship campaign, as had become common in most churches. Likewise, as Lutheran churches were at the time increasing the frequency of celebrating Communion, attendance was improving. So there was urgent need for remedial education regarding the blessedness of that sacrament -- many were still asking why they were being encouraged to commune every Sunday as only the Roman Catholics did.. So after a year of writing one offertory prayer every week, I was eager to continue in 1984 to compose a post-communion prayer every week; I was responding to many pastors who confessed to being tired of using to same one every Sunday that Luther had prepared. The feedback was positive, and the batches of liturgical / Eucharistic prayers were faithfully mailed out to subscribers every month thanks to June's unrelenting dedication.

Meanwhile, the work on the new house continued during the Summer, like with installing cedar shingle siding, with which Philip helped when not working at McDonalds as a shift supervisor. But there was also the effort of tending 15 double colonies of honeybees -- each hive had two queens for the Spring brood rearing season up till into the start of the honey flow in June. That was a way to multiply the harvest. It was also a simple way to have a young queen going into the Winter. During the year of 1982 I used the wheelbarrow to bring in from the backyard a total of 4000 lbs of honey. In fact for all of the 1980s and also late 70s, this happened almost without fail. I took off about one 65 pound super from each hive every Thursday afternoon, starting in mid July till well into September. After supper, often till midnight, I worked alone in the basement uncapping and extracting honey with a 12 frame motorized radial extractor, usually resulting in 30 gallons in the settling tank. Then on Friday after supper, I would skim the wax particles and bee parts (to again settle in a jar -- to be later skimmed and returned for the bees to recycle). Then cases of mostly 2 and 3 pound jars were filled via the bottom spigot till the tank was empty. Sometimes I got help with printing and attaching labels to each jar. After this the cases were carried to the garage and loaded for an early Saturday morning trip to the St. Paul Farmers Market. After a few years we went rather to the Minneapolis Farmers Market where June and one of my children helped sell honey from about 6am till about noon. By this I eventually gained bulk customers of individuals and whole-food store concessions, some of which continued to buy through the Winter.

Both Karl and Philip had sufficiently tired of dorm life at the U of MN by the Fall of 1982 to agree to rent an apartment together nearby to be shared with a childhood friend and neighbor who was also in IT. It was a happy arrangement with the three taking turns at cooking, leaving each with more time for study. They ate well, sharing with us in one of Walter's butchered steers. It was their time of experience towards becoming excellent cooks, and their study habits made for good company and lasting friendship.

It was sometime in those early 80s that Janet and Mike Grant announced a long anticipated engagement. Janet had graduated with a degree in social studies, and was working for MN Washington County in child protection. She had been living in an apartment and owned a new red Mazda 323 with sun roof. Mike had transferred from Moorhead State to the U of MN to finish his study in business, and had taken a position with NCR in Dayton OH. Meanwhile Janet moved back home, and they started planning their April 16, 1983 wedding. Janet took responsibility for virtually all of the wedding arrangements. They were

263

married at Mike's Methodist church in Maplewood with a reception in a stately home among the mansions in the Summit Hill district beyond the St. Paul cathedral. It was a fine wedding attended by many relatives, but also by their many friends who conveniently lived nearby. Janet interrupted the rite with tears and sniffles of emotion; I had to hand her my handkerchief (a real one) which I still have, never again in use.

They had been nervous about it, but I supplied sufficient wine from my own cellar for the whole evening. It didn't run out and the guests were quite pleased. (I need to look up what recipe I had used.) The next day, a Sunday, the families gathered in our living room to open gifts and continue the celebration. The weather that weekend had not been pleasant, beginning on Thursday with 13 inches of snow. Now 35 years later they are still well married. Monday morning, they left through the deep snow for a honeymoon in DC at cherry blossom time, and then returned to live in Dayton OH. By August, Janet found a position as a social worker in a 460 bed hospital that launched a spectacular career in health care.

That same year June and I celebrated a quiet 25th anniversary in June. Walter and Darlyne, married a week after us, had a major family celebration at the farm; so we decided to avoid everyone's double duty. Instead we took a whole day for a leisurely trip down the Mississippi on the MN side to Winona, and then back up along the WI side, enjoying the river and parks with romantic interludes. After a fine dinner in Prescott, we went home to bed.

Those years are remembered as "fat" times. Our children were prospering beyond our most daring visions, and Holy Spirit congregation was slowly growing and flourishing. That put out of mind, at any rate, the unrealistic thought of securing a new ministry elsewhere. (The bishop, at any rate, not rating me above average, was content to have me fill a post that he would have had a hard time filling.) We were delightfully comfortable in our mostly finished new solar home, and June and I were deeply bonded in love. Besides, the economy was booming.

So we were able to take in stride the distress in November 1983 when June's mother, Irma Radtke, soon to be 88 year old, fell and broke a hip in Michigan City IN, where she lived with brother Paul. After a brief hospitalization, she was at home, but not fairing well under Uncle Paul's reluctant care. He demanded that June would come down to live with them and care for her mother (and himself?). I was not about to let that happen, and June wasn't ready for such an ordeal. It would have involved caring for her mother in Winter, in what was at best an totally outmoded Summer home.

We decided to give them no option. We would come and bring Irma home to live with us; How that could work itself out, we left to faith. It would be a 500 mile trip which would need to happen in one day. My car, a small 1981 Pontiac 2000 hatchback, had a reclining front passenger seat which would make for a reasonably comfortable bed. We managed to do it, and without Irma grumbling. Surely she was relieved to have care from loved ones, with compassion and a warm new modern home. Actually Paul didn't protest, probably because he would then be free to fly to Phoenix for the Winter, as was their custom, living in what had been their brother's home. He seemed quite done with making a home for his sister.

Irma had of course been reduced to a wheelchair, but how would we manage her in our multilevel home? To begin with, our family room became her bedroom, it being on the same level as our main bathroom, as well as our bedroom from where June was ready to help. I then found it physically possible to pull her backwards in her wheelchair up a half flight of stairs to the kitchen for meals -- dangerous without a doubt. But I was in robust health and felt comfortable doing it. Fortunately the stair treads were extra wide. June, as ever, trusted me and didn't even need to help. Following up the stairs after us would anyway have

265

endangered her in case of a mishap, which fortunately soon wasn't even entertained.

I marveled how even Irma was quite willing to be so carted. Soon it was so routine that we moved her to a regular bedroom another half level down. A nursing home was never entertained as an option till several years later when Irma's Alzheimer symptoms became more pronounced. (By then, June and I were in over our heads.) She did however have short stays in a nursing home when June and I were out of town. The only difficulty remembered was Irma's reluctance to trust me with her finances, June not herself confident to advise her. But it took only one firm lecture on my part for her lack of trust to set it straight. I had in our earlier years always gotten along well with her, and been able to ignore her dogged Depression era financial paranoia and hyper conservatism. Eventually, she believed me that I was honest and wealthy enough not to covet what she owned.

Philip made us proud in June of 1984 by graduating from the U of MN with Highest Distinction (*suma cum laude*) in aeronautical engineering. But Karl wasn't present to help us celebrate. For the Spring quarter he had gone to study architecture in Europe with a professor and others of his class. Philip was a "first-round-draft-pick" exercised by Mcdonald-Douglas of St. Louis to work in their military aircraft division. (Now, after these 35 years, he has risen to the top at Boeing as a configurator -- design.)

After June once more retyped and mimeographed my 100 page second study edition of Eucharistic prayers and sent them out to over 200 interested pastors for continued field trial, we placed her mother temporarily into a nursing home and drove up to Luseland, Saskatchewan, Canada that Summer of 1984 to help my first call parish, Holy Trinity, celebrate their 75th anniversary. It was paired with the 75th anniversary celebration of Luseland itself. The sole difficult council member from my pastorate was found to be the leading local editor for gathering Luseland's history within two oversized volumes of Saskatchewan's history -- done

266

with provincial sponsorship. As part of the town celebration we met him and bought the history books ($70 ?). He was very cordial and friendly, forgiving the past and by his cordiality seeking reconciliation, with which I gladly reciprocated.

The celebrations at church were both nice and enjoyable. By then I was no longer MO synod and wondered about my allowable part -- probably they were not aware. ("Don't ask, don't tell!") I had no speaking role anyway, neither in the morning nor afternoon worship. But I was vested and marched in a grand procession with all the other pastors attending -- very difficult to arrange in their still original 1910 building, with its equally large transept. Moehering, who had immediately preceded me, had again inserted himself as the preacher for the morning service, as he had 25 years earlier (he was not the preacher he thought he was). A district representative of the president (bishop) preached in the afternoon. Then following, there was a reception on the lawn between the old church and the new parsonage for the visiting pastors. (We sadly didn't get a tour of the new parsonage, which would have been interesting to compare with the pioneer version in which we had lived.) It was a cordial gathering through the round of introductions and biographical updates of each. All of them had served after myself, and whom I had never met, other than Moehering. Interestingly, I thereat reflected as most others also did who were apologetic for having left Luseland, a place of good ministry and memories.

The visiting former pastors had, for lack of a town motel, been quartered with member families. June and I were hosted by a Scheid family 20 miles west of Luseland in their lower level "apartment." That, without being otherwise accorded fellowship with this host. June was hurt and disappointed since she had bonded with Mrs when the two of them each had at the same time given birth to their firstborn (Janet). This lack of hospitality was somehow noted by another neighboring Scheid family which I had counseled, married and forgotten. They then invited us to

267

visit on the Monday following the festivities, which we much enjoyed and appreciated. It was nice to see and know I had tied a good knot 20 years earlier. Later that day, an older couple, who lived in town, invited us to stay with them for several more days of great hospitality. (I had served both of them in the persons of one of their parents -- both widowed and then married to each other in old age; Each subsequently dying after my much appreciated hospice ministry.)

June and I thereafter drove north as far as any roads could take us, staying for a week at Lac La Ronge, SK. It was the entry port by aircraft to many more miles of the province further north. June and I one day drove even further north on an unpaved trail as far as we dared. It was a unique experience to worship the following Sunday with a congregation of native Canadians. We could follow the rite without understanding the language.

I had had an interest in fishing, but we instead bought fish to take home from their commercial fish freezing factory because, as Americans, we would have been required to hire a guide, aside from the $100 cost of a fishing license. Sadly the frozen fish tasted so old when we ate them at home that we were minded to feed them to the dog. Actually, I believe Rex, our Belgian-German shepherd had by then already died from a stroke at age 14.

It was June's work of typing successive field editions of my Eucharistic prayers which in 1985 precipitated my first computer ($2500 -- NCR) and printer ($1500 -- Epson). I installed it at home, not comfortable or trusting it in the church offices where room was also limited. I made a computer center in half of our balcony where it was out of the way of living. Already I was mostly doing my studies at home with the church offices hard to heat in Winter. Thus June also didn't need to do all of the church secretary work in the cold attic office with but a space heater.

With each new edition of the prayers, she had needed to retype nearly 100 pages of text including the Latin original.

This would incorporate suggestions and corrections from field use, as well as my refinements inspired through contemplative editing. She wasn't comfortable to learn the MS DOS operating system, which I did slowly manage; But she enjoyed the smooth typing of the text on the electronic keyboard. Her fingers (carpal tunnel?) had been cramping on the harder key strokes of a typewriter. Her two smaller fingers on each hand no longer worked. She was by then reduced to typing with index fingers alone.

However, after saving a new edition into the computer, we allowed a young man, supposedly computer able, to use our computer during which he erased all her work by mistakenly reformatting the hard drive instead of a floppy he had brought to use. So still once more June retyped all my prayers. (I at times through the succeeding years think of this when I appreciate the convenience of cutting and pasting what is still essentially her work -- she is still helping me.)

Karl graduated that year "With Distinction" from the U of MN school of architecture. Godmother sister Jan and husband Arthur Luckwell attended with us, and had the pleasure thereafter of a tour of the school, and Karl's still functioning cubicle followed by a dinner of celebration. Again this graduation was unattended by siblings, as with the two previous graduations, Philip hard at work in St. Louis, and Janet in Dayton OH.

June and I decided that it was time that Summer to celebrate on a larger scale. The new house was essentially done, Holy Spirit congregation was at peace and slowly prospering. I had finished graduate theological education (all but for the required thesis -- although I thought my work on the prayers of the liturgy might somehow suffice -- not yet knowing what to do about it.) And we had seen our three children successfully through college with spectacular scholarship. It seemed right finally to do our dream vacation -- Europe. Life might otherwise have become boring that Summer in MN.

With the cancellation of Janet's high school European choir tour following her junior year (for which June and I had agreed to help as chaperones) I had again promised June a trip to Europe. I myself had lost out on a European seminary choir tour in the Summer of 1958 following my seminary graduation because it would have resulted in a delay of our wedding and my ordination in my first call parish. Being a four year member of the 35 voice seminary choir, and the leading first tenor, I would have qualified to sing in the 16 member touring choir that went to Europe. I had even then told June that some day we would, if possible go together. The exchange rate was unusually favorable in 1985, telling us, "It's now or never."

Furthermore, Karl was graduating from U of MN and was planning another trip to Europe. He was interested in joining us for the main part, a trip to Poland. He planned to join us a week into our trip in Luxembourg. Specifically, I had wanted to find the birthplace of my great-grandfather Gottlieb Lehrke and his Henrietta in what had at their time been known as West Prussia.

I had purchased a small Renault from a dealer in Amsterdam, to which we flew nonstop. Imagine arriving in the early morning hours with only the address of the car dealer in hand. We negotiated the transit system in that foreign city with our multiple suitcases. A further difficulty was that we were able only to speak the related language of German. We found the destination to be in the city's not so elegant quarter.

Fortunately, all went as trusted that first morning in Amsterdam, but we were dead from an overnight flight. We could think only of getting out of that city. Intentionally, we had no detailed plans. We found our way with maps up the coastal highway and along on top of the many-mile (kilometer) dyke to Harlingen, a harbor city. There we spotted a small family owned hotel a half-block from the sea, where we crashed, slept, showered and had a late breakfast of celebration late in the afternoon. Thus the pattern was set: drive wherever we felt momentarily inclined, with only a general tourist guide in copilot-navigator June's hands. We always serendipitously found a gasthouse to drink, dine and sleep when we had had enough of each day. When we saw tour busses, we did and "end-run".

The following day we crossed into Germany and came upon the old city of Bremen where we spent some time in the city center among big old buildings. I was rainy, but fun to be almost overrun on that Saturday morning on the steps of the cathedral by a boisterous informal wedding anniversary parade. From there we stayed three days in Hamburg. We had a small flat where we could do light cooking. That precipitated an interesting German grocery shopping experience. We did a lot of walking around the central city area that weekend. People were in a holiday mood in nice weather. And there were those who seemed to be there precisely to meet any foreign tourists, of which there were few -- northern Germany was an out-of-the-way destination. We stood out for gazing at the buildings and thereby attracted self-proclaimed guides. For example, I chatted an hour with a 60? year old man who had been a Nazi youth and then a clerk, but by then retired. We worshipped that Sunday at St. Jacobi with a liturgy that used the same text and melody I had at home in my youth. It had a Schnitger organ!!! The people everywhere seemed happy and friendly. My conversational German had been quickly refreshed and surprised them when introducing ourselves as Americans. It's still a city in which I'd enjoy a longer second visit.

From there we took a long side trip to the north toward Denmark, even briefly entering. Just across the border, we were halted by a large herd of about 50 Holstein dairy cows being moved right down the center of the main highway into Denmark and then off into another yard on the opposite side. They were being herded on bicycles. It took

271

fully ten minutes of interrupting the two-way traffic. We drove this isthmus up into Denmark since that Schleswig-Holstein area was supposedly the ancestral area of Ma's family.

It was then time to head south by stages to meet up with Karl. In route we spent one glorious evening, night and morning in the still totally medieval-like city of Glosar. The beer was good, and the gasthaus was quaint, clean, and comfortable, through built in the 15th century like much of the surroundings. It had a grand castle overlooking the city and prominently visible from our window a half mile away. A few days later, June and I met Karl's plane in Luxembourg and we immediately turned our sights toward Berlin, in route to Poland. It was to be an anxious time till we returned to West Germany nearly two weeks later.

The highway through East Germany to West Berlin, an Allied powers corridor, was considered to be a safe trip. We managed it with only a parking fine, paid on the spot at a rest stop oasis. Of note was the occasional sight of East German or Russian autos disabled for repairs on the shoulder of the freeway, even straddling the ditch to allow for owner under-the-auto repairs. We felt quite alone and on our own, driving a small Renault with French plates, quickly attracting police attention. Not being part of a charter touring group, we were not shielded, but rather quickly in the police spotlight. We had to find all our accommodations on the fly, and shift for ourselves. We felt watched as they deviously intended. My bold daring was our freedom -- faith through righteousness.

Arriving in West Berlin, we went immediately to the tourist accommodations office and settled on an apartment without bath, only a public toilet far down the hall. I think we had a hot plate and were allowed to do a minimal amount of cooking. Karl quickly went his own way, and June and I went ours. We walked the West Berlin central city area created after the city was divided. We went to the Zoo, and of course made a trip to the Wall. There I walked a short way along the Wall to the right, toward the south from the

Brandenburg Gate. Using my car keys, I scratched a cross in the fairly soft concrete of the wall as my prayer for the future of the city and the country. Already, I was in deep sympathy for the plight of East Germany, a concern which was growing by the hour.

On Sunday, June and I decided to enter East Berlin with our car via the famous Check Point Charlie -- the only entry point allowed. We were required to purchase a certain amount of East German currency which had to be spent or left behind on our exit. We went directly to the original central city with the old government buildings and churches. It had become a national showplace, some of the public buildings still being in stages of repair from the war. Actually our hope was to get a travel permit to go down to Leipzig and worship in the St. Thomas Kirche where J.S. Bach had served as organist for many years.. But though that was supposedly possible, we were curtly, quickly and belligerently refused without explanation. Instead we then decided to worship in the Lutheran cathedral, since the adjacent St. Marian Kirche didn't have a congregation nor services scheduled -- It apparently was merely a show place to off-put the anti church state policy. The cathedral was still under repair, looking yet very bombed and burnt out -- still partly open to the sky. But they had a congregation that worshiped in a side chapel seating about 100. It was full and we felt very much alone among people equally as somber and cheerless as all the other East Berliners we had or were to meet.

After the service we introduced ourselves to the Lutheran pastor, but were greeted with a passive and suspicious blank face. I could only conclude that my German (my mother-tongue without accent from birth) was too good to pass for an authentic American -- trust was dangerous for them. We then walked and drove wherever we wanted, including the shabby, decaying and dirty residential area to the NE. Then also back to the west to see the eastern side of the blocked off Brandenburg Gate. It was "open" but guarded by impregnable Soviet military, with tanks and wire barricades.

To spend the required money we ate at a restaurant which obviously served only the few fortunately better-off, meaning that it was rather exclusive. Frequently I used my German to engage people in conversation. I was never rebuffed, but also never found anyone who dared to stray from the official East German propaganda. All were as dispirited as those in a prison. The contrast to West Berliners was like night and day, with those in the west feeling, acting and thinking freely even though they lived in a besieged city.

Later that week we were ready to leave for Poland. That freeway was not part of the Allied corridor and therefore had a very large checkpoint at the West Berlin city limits. It was shear terror with swaggering police intentionally intimidating. We were not searched, but interrogated at length, and in German. (I never understood how cleverly they had always tricked me to indicate that I could understand and speak German, thereby to possibly put me at some disadvantage.) There were no problems with our plans and documents, but their power needed exercising with demonstration for the effect of insuring our obedience. I sensed the similarity to the Nazi regime.

Finally, after many minutes, we were cleared to go. The autobahn to the NE was like a modern expressway (it was after all the main route of political connection -- Russia.). After skirting the north edge of the city and then turning toward Poland, we were already pulled over by the conspicuous East German police patrol and asked for our documents. Everything was in order (perfunctory authority) but since Karl wasn't wearing his seatbelt, we had to pay a fine on the spot, something like $15, which probably never found its way into any official treasury. They had probably fixed on our French plates. It was a simple, "Better behave!" parting lesson.

We eventually crossed into Poland, and drove East along the Baltic Sea coast toward Gadansk. Here there was a notable presence of the Russian Navy and other maritime shipping activity with heightened security. At the same time, I was noticing the fertility of the country, which was however, with the eye of a farmer's son, visibly retarded from its potential by the practice of collective farming.

That night was spent in the seaport of Salpulsk where we were able to find a 12x12 room with three beds, plus a toilet and shower combo -- a toilet with a shower head above, and a concrete floor with drain. There was only cold water.

Gadansk, renamed from the centuries old German Danzig, appeared to us as a decaying city. The buildings and infrastructure were much neglected. It had fallen on hard times. We could still see evidence of the prosperity from earlier centuries of lively maritime commerce under German domination through the 17, 18, 19th century. But these Poles now were people who had been reduced to working with their hands against a tide. They had already become poor before Germans again took over in 1939. Then, following WWII, they had no means to modernize their occupied country. Russia was not a generous patron. We saw public works welfare servants: women sweeping streets with ancient brooms made by tying coarse bristles around the end of a stick. Everything was dirty and drab from lack of money for paint. At the hotel, which gave the impression of serving foreigners by being almost nice, there were many young boys with pails of water to wash auto windows. They didn't even wait to be hired, hoping for a tip through embarrassment.

The hotel clerk was a woman in her 20s, very pleasant and able to speak English, seemingly anxious to be helpful. But it eventually became apparent that this was a shakedown in the process. "Yes, we may have some rooms later." So we waited by going sightseeing in the surrounding city. For instance, we visited a very large Gothic church, more than likely originally Lutheran but now clearly Roman Catholic.

275

It was stark in its bareness, giving the impression of a black and white colorless world.

When we eventually returned to the hotel to check on availability of rooms, there were still no comfortable words, so we went out to eat at a restaurant, one most certainly not being used by the locals. Then back to the hotel to check about rooms. Finally, well along into evening, the clerk informed us that she had found a room elsewhere but with only two beds, to be occupied by only two people, fully knowing that we needed three. I still pretended not to know that she was waiting to be paid. Instead I elected to take the room with two beds, intending to let June and Karl use them. She then soon offered that she might find another bed elsewhere. She was now taking control of the situation, trusting that she had us. She made some phone calls and then told me that I could have her boyfriend's apartment; she would have him sleep at her apartment. It was now getting late and sleeping in the car was illegal as well as impractical, so I gave in to her "kindness".

After checking June and Karl in at the boarding house nearby, with June braving a stiff lip but near tears of fear, I followed this clerk and her boyfriend in their car with my car several miles to the NW. With some desperation, it seemed like a safe exchange for $20 American. But I remember being nervous till I was done with it -- black market transactions could have gotten us into deep trouble so far from home. The apartment was in a concrete high-rise typical in that time of Soviet influence, style and cheapness (they'd rather pay for their military in that cold war era). I was pleased with the possible use of the Stereo hi-fi, but decided to leave it alone. There was a bathtub, but I had to bathe with cold water.

Morning blessedly came uneventfully through the east windows. As soon as possible, I made my way from memory back to the rooming house across from the hotel. I found my much relieved June and a stoic but wary son, both of whom had not slept more soundly than I.

We did enjoy the Polish countryside and usually had a roadside lunch of good dark bread etc., as we were able to find it in local bakeries. From Gadansk we set out to find Neu Paleschken, the small town to the SW where Gottlieb and Henrietta had lived and been church members, and were married in 1854 just before immigrating to MN. The Poles now call it Noe Polaski, and the maps I had been collecting led us there without confusion. It was midday as we excitedly approached the town from the NW. We passed an old farmer seated on a mower drawn by a team of black horses on his way home from a hayfield out along the main highway. I couldn't resist stopping to ask if we had found the right town, knowing that the older people had all learned German in school during the German occupation. He assured me that it was indeed Neu Paleschken, and gave us directions to the church.

The church surprised me in that it merely looked like a large old half-timbered building. In actuality it fit with the poverty of near 300 years ago; They wouldn't have built a grand church. But we were disappointed since the building was locked. We had only a few minutes to consider what to do next before we were approached from virtually next door by a woman in her 50s. I greeted her in German and she responded in kind. I explained who we were and what we had come to find; She promptly told us that she was the janitor and would be happy to unlock the door for us.

I then began to question myself whether this building was in fact where Henrietta and Gottlieb had worshiped because Helen, the janitor, told us that this was the Roman Catholic church; We had inquired about the Lutheran church. However, I knew from the parish records I had found several years earlier in the Mormon genealogical library that Neu Palesechken had had only a Lutheran or Evangelical church in earlier centuries. It then quickly made sense that when most Germans or Lutherans left by the end of the 19th century, as I knew had happened, that the mainly Roman Catholic Poles would not have hesitated to reconsecrate a usable building; They were unlikely to afford anything more. Still my question reverberated, fearful that we had merely found the town, but not the real place. Nevertheless, the instant we were inside and I saw the font and the altar, I knew that this was most certainly what we had come so far to see. The church furniture and furnishings spoke from much longer ago than from when the Roman Catholics would have claimed it. It seated about 400 and had a balcony wrapping both sides halfway to the front.

I was at the point of tears standing and touching the generous baptismal font which I was certain had been used not only for my great grandparents but also for at least four more generations of ancestors before them. This church and its appointments were easily as old as the mid 1700s when my ancestors would have built a church soon after founding a Lutheran congregation in 1728. We took pictures and all too briefly looked about.

My next question of Helen was about the location of the cemetery. She at first said that there was only a Roman Catholic cemetery, confirming indirectly that the church had not always been Roman Catholic. I pressed her a bit and finally she disregard her embarrassment and admitted that there was an old abandoned Lutheran cemetery, but in serious decay outside of town. I reassured her that I perfectly understood its neglect, and that we would like to see it nonetheless. She was then brave to get into our car to take us there. It was a short distance and seemed at first like an overgrown wooded pasture land separated from the road by a brush lined fence on the south side. We crawled over the crude fence and saw that it was indeed a cemetery.

I felt some shame myself as I looked around at this sad cemetery with ancestor spirits in communion with me. There were bits and pieces of tomb stones lying about among the cow-pies, a few even almost upright. I tried reading what had been inscribed, but the poor people had been able to afford only soft limestone, and even concrete headstones. None were even remotely readable any longer. At least we were standing where a resurrection of loved ones by blood would take place, and anticipation of fellowship. I thrill to meet them and learn of their weal and woe, and to thank them for their faith passed down to me and mine.

We drove back into town to take Helen home, where she then insisted we come in to have a bite to eat. She wanted us to meet her elderly mother whose last name was Schneider, just possibly, a very distant relative through a now indecipherable network of marriages. She too spoke German, and so possibly was according to her name. She was quietly delighted to meet us.

Their home was small and very poor, made of industrial brick; It was uninsulated. June was much concerned that we shouldn't be eating their scanty provisions; I assured her that we had no choice lest we shame and embarrass them. The food was simple: bread and homemade preserves like pickled beets, sausage, etc. It wasn't food for snooty Americans, but we did it justice to show them love and communion.

Helen was quickly excited to telephone her nearby sister, who she said had two teen boys. Both sisters apparently were widows -- by the war?? Their poverty was obvious and I heard a reverberating unspoken Kyrie in the air, amplified by reasons of their obvious faith. I was powerfully drawn into communion. We asked what we could do for them, what they needed. Without shame or opportunism, they replied with a plain childlike straight-face, such as comes out of desperation seizing a divinely sent opportunity. They listed the need for denim jeans for the sister's boys, asking nothing for themselves.

I believe we gave them $20 American, which we knew would be quite worthwhile on the black market. We exchanged addresses and promised to send much needed clothes for all of them. (All this memory even now brings me to tears. On returning home, and over the next few years, we several times sent large boxes to Helen, and she would write in reply. The last time she wrote was after June

279

had died. I had sent many of June's clothes which I thought would be serviceable to them.)

We were euphoric for these experiences on leaving town toward the east, not knowing that another excitement awaited us as we headed north at the first main crossroad. After a few miles, I was astounded to see a crude sign pointing back to the west to Christovo where Gottlieb and Henrietta, and also his brother Johann, had lived with their families before 1854.

So we took this unpaved wagon trail or field road, wondering what we might find. It was perhaps 4-5 miles to a dorf of possibly 5-6 homes up the south slope of the road, with several barns down the hill to the north and all bordering a small lake with geese and ducks spilling up the hill on the grass. Apparently, as my maps later confirmed, it was an extension of the meandering chain of five lakes that separated this village from Neu Paleschken by no more than a few miles to the southwest. No wonder that Gottlieb had chosen a MN homestead on the shores of Hydes Lake.

It was late afternoon and the only person around (other than two teens on bikes who wouldn't have understood either English nor German) was an older man tending his bee hives. I engaged him in German about bees and then quickly about who I was and why we had come. No, the name Lehrke wasn't familiar. He seemed friendly, but I understood him to be busy and anxious to get on with his open hive. Too soon we took leave after taking photos. I, wishing that there had been a motel anywhere nearby so we could have delayed leaving this special place. Surely our saints smiled to know that we cared enough about their humble life to visit from so far to see what remains of their place, we admitting that they had given us a running start.

The worst of the nights spent in Poland without doubt was a few days later in Redone. It had been a very hot day. We found only an old dirty hotel with a room available upstairs. It had a north window overlooking a squalid low lying city under a forest of TV antenna. We went out to eat, walking to the nearby restaurant. The food was good but the presence on the street of Russian soldiers serving as police was quite unnerving. We returned to our hot rooms and would have paid a lot to have a shower. But that wasn't available to us without renting certain unavailable rooms. Again we appeared unqualified. On the floor below, I had in the hallway seen an obvious public shower room which was locked. I considered waylaying an occupant on their exit, but couldn't pull it off. So we sweated through the night, with an open window.

Our destination the next day was Auschwitz, expected to be a most sobering experience. When arriving at the main SE gate with high electrified fencing still intact, though rusted, we saw the improbable sight of a woman on a horse drawn sickle mower cutting hay just outside the south fence. It was as if this place had lost any current significance to the locals, an ignored relic of an evil past, but ready to be swallowed by the relentless march of more basic and beneficial interests. The gate had a railroad dead-end running through it, which quickly brought the barbaric scene to mind of trainloads of Jewish prisoners to be securely and hopelessly interred. Most of the barracks, along with the administration building lay to the north, but our attention was on the road running a quarter mile straight west along the south fence to the crematorium furnaces. The whole place was rusting and starting to decay, giving one a ghost town edginess. The crematorium furnaces looked as if they had been dynamited and left in that fallen crumpled state. Alongside were prominent Russian memorials with multi-language markings. Obviously the western allies had no part in administering this site. The primary marker proclaimed, not the Jewish martyrdom which had happened there, but rather the even larger Russian casualties of the entire war at the hands of the Nazis. The day was sobering, appropriately dark and overcast. It was a good place to leave behind.

From there we drove a short way south to the Czechoslovakia border, hoping to be allowed a short trip through to Vienna, Austria. Unfortunately, our travel documents didn't authorize this crossing in advance; So we were summarily refused entry to Czechoslovakia. Instead we had no choice but to head west and reenter East Germany with the intention of circling back to reach Vienna. But first we needed a nights rest and a plan to get the gas necessary for the trip; We had no more gas coupons and no way to get more.

God smiled in our finding an amazingly modern motel in Kosernya. However in getting there according to the directions we were given at the border, I accelerated too quickly on leaving one of the smaller towns along the way, and was stopped by a "cowboy" local policeman. He gleefully announced that he had caught me with his radar. I don't remember the language we used, but the fine was collected on the spot. He was as excited as if this had been his first ever catch. He projected nothing of the usual police state intimidation. Surely, he was pleased to pocket the fine to feed his family; So it was fine with me.

The motel was a welcoming place so unlike most of our experiences in Poland. It made me bold to confess to the clerk that we has insufficient gas coupons to reach the East German border. "No problem!" At a prescribed time, "Be out in the back parking lot with your car and someone will meet you with a can of gas." The price was paid in advance, and memory is that it wasn't unreasonable. I didn't dare tell any of this to June or Karl till the next day because of justified suspicions and concerns for our safety for breaking the law. I didn't want them to inadvertently trip me up. But the Spirit gave me leave on the spot, and I sensed the benevolent spirit of the angelic motel keeper. I went as directed while June and Karl settled into our room. And it was as promised, allowing us to rest the night and reach the border on that tank of gas, augmented with the few remaining gas coupons. We slept well and comfortably after June and I took a luxurious warm shower together in a room size stall.

The next day we did uneventfully cross lower SW Poland and southern East Germany through what almost seemed like the American Midwest countryside. Again, it was the impression of being in a breadbasket going to waste for its collective farming system. Then came a terror to be remembered for life: the exit from East Germany back into West Germany. In 1985 this wasn't a friendly border crossing. The police state atmosphere of the East German border police was suffocating, with curt and cold commands. Normally a border crossing has more to do with the country you are entering, not the one you are leaving. But this was rather an exit from a prison. June was terrified and Karl was quite subdued as well. They literally turned our car inside out as we waited standing outside, out of the way. I was confident that their searching wouldn't uncover anything actionable, although our car was often parked out of our control. Mirrors were used to thoroughly check under the car and every content unloaded. Our luggage was opened and searched piece by piece right in front of us on the ground. Psychologically, it was a strip search. Finally, after at least an half hour we were free to go, with no hint of apology for our innocence. Our relief was equal to being cleared from a major felony accusation.

We then headed toward Austria; But we quickly decided we had had a full day. So we found a nice modern hotel and relaxed from the fear of being watched. I took a walk and conversed for a long while with a group of young adults on the street about politics and the US role in Europe. They lived in the shadow of totalitarianism; and appealed to me as an American that we would not leave them defenseless. Karl had his own room that night, and June and I let down all our pent up reserves and fears, celebrating our joy and blessed life together in a night that still lives.

Vienna was for Karl a rich experience, but to June and me, it was totally anticlimactic after Poland. We had difficulty finding affordable accommodations in an overpriced city being visited by too many budget conscious, or not, young people on Summer break from college. What we found wasn't much to our liking, a room with three beds and simple cooking accommodations. June and I were not much impressed by the Viennese show of recovered greatness amid its storied historic buildings and bravely renewed culture. After walking the city for a few days, June and I were ready to leave. We went on excursions into the countryside. One day we headed north toward the Czech border -- from where we had at first planned to enter Austria. We found a delightful and simple pleasure, compatible with our nature: a huge sweet cherry tree overarching the highway, loaded with ripe and falling cherries. We had found a free lunch and celebrated our humble appetites before returning to the culture of Vienna. It was so like the happiness of being with June at Uncle Paul's place in his garden of plenty.

The following day, June and I explored the country to the SW of Vienna. Some 25 miles away we found a tranquil valley which had become a resort for those in Vienna who needed the refreshment of pastoral peace, yet with rest in luxury. We couldn't resist immediately renting a large comfortable room in a gasthaus at half the price of our small room in downtown Vienna. We tried out the luxurious bed though it was only mid-afternoon. Later, I backtracked alone to Vienna to find Karl, who was not really ready to leave. That gasthaus had first class dinning for the three of us, again at half the price we paid for ordinary tourist fare in Vienna.

The next day we headed into the Austrian Alps with two days in Salzburg, and then to Innsbruck where we stayed in a hotel half way up the mountain overlooking the city and valley. Karl and I took the cable car to the top to Der Berghof -- Hitler's retreat. Its been restored after the Allies blew it up after the war. June was not comfortable to go along on the rickety ride. The next day we took Karl to the train station from where he parted for Rome. (After his Italy visit he eventually went to England where he took a job till November at Hull, working as an architect, restoring historic buildings.)

June and I then elected to skip Switzerland in order to spend more time in the Moselle Valley which we had briefly visited in route to meet Karl early in our tour. We found the wine to our taste and bought several bottles which we snuck home, not anticipating a problem in advance (luckily we were not required to open our suitcases for customs). That final weekend was in Cologne where we worshiped at the cathedral on Sunday morning. We had the distinct experience of being communed by the cardinal himself. He looked intently at me, as if trying to decide if this tourist was Catholic, but I put on a practiced Roman Catholic piety without flinching. It was but a half second before he gave me a host. June, of course, was a natural.

After the mass I introduced myself to the head usher and explained that I was an American priest composing Eucharistic prayers for American Lutherans; I said I wished to find a place to buy a German breviary to see what Germans had done for modern offertory and post-communion collects. He gave me instruction for returning on Monday to a nearby book seller (which I did). Then with special hospitality he offered to give us a personal tour of the cathedral, including (for VIPs only) the crypt several levels below the altar where many previous cardinals and bishops are resting for resurrection.

It was time after six weeks and 5000 K to sell our Renault back to the dealer in Amsterdam. We stayed well out of the city that last night. I decided to drop June off at the airport with our baggage, and for me to go alone to the auto dealer. I trusted a smooth transaction and finding my way back via public transportation. I had to be my own guide. It worked, this time with more confidence, in that my destination would not be strange to the person I might need to ask.

The return flight was in clear daylight, taking us over Greenland, a unique sight from our window seat. It had been a life enhancing and enchanted vacation. We felt blessed, but at the same time, glad to be home again.

In 1986 Karl returned from Europe, and soon into the new year he was hired by the Minneapolis MN architectural firm of Bentz-Thompson-Rietow. Rietow had been one of his adjunct professors at the U of MN. While serving there, Karl participated in the design of several buildings, notably the reconstruction of the old St. John's hospital buildings on the eastern bluffs overlooking downtown St. Paul to become a campus for Metropolitan University. It's signature structure designed by Karl has a F.L. Wright flavor.

Then on August 3rd my first grandchild was born, Alyssa Ann, daughter of Janet and Michael Grant, who were living in Dayton OH. So, not long thereafter June and I drove there to meet her. I had the privilege of baptizing her back at Holy Spirit when they paid a return visit for the Christmass holidays that year. On another later occasion we visited them in Kettering with June baby-sitting Allie while they were at work, and I attempted making a new concrete driveway for them. Their old driveway was badly cracked, separating and heaving. I had thought, "I've paved several driveways; I can do this easily in a week." What I didn't know was that instead of a normal 4" slab, it had been constructed without reinforcing and probably for that reason the slab was 6+ " thick. I worked like mad for many days with an electric jackhammer, but finally we had to hire a tractor to finish the breakup and removal. Then on the day we were finally ready to pour the new driveway, it was so beastly hot that the concrete set up way too rapidly for me and Mike to do the work properly. An ordeal never to be forgotten.

October 25th had us joining Philip and bride Karen at St. Louis for their wedding. June and I did the traditional hosting of the groom's reception the evening before. Not being nearby residents, we brought all the refreshments, including wine from my cellar in MN (possibly illegally brought across state lines). We celebrated in the hospitality room connected with the apartment where Philip and Karen would then live in St. Charles. There were a considerable number of MN relatives and friends of Philip from childhood in attendance, and then also for the wedding at Philip's Zion Lutheran in Florescent, with a following reception nearby.

Holy Spirit's 25th anniversary was celebrated that September in a well orchestrated event that was much indebted to June's loving attention. As preacher, we invited the organizing pastor, David Romberg, and as special guest at the dinner following we had Pastor Krause, from our neighboring parish, which had instigated, but not actually sponsored our mission. It was a true celebration for the congregation. The spirit was one of optimism and faith, now that we had, a few years before, become self supporting and independent of the mission board. We were gradually growing. We were even winning back key families that had left over the decision to leave the MO synod. Part of the overall celebration that Fall was a grand Pig Roast fund raiser. For it, I was the supervising chef in the overnight roasting of a whole hog in a rented outdoor charcoal covered grill; I was then also the carver at the feast. It was a very lively event, especially for children. They were fascinated, freely viewing the roasting hog and carving session, with generous offerings of a taste on demand from a chosen part of the carcass.

1986 is particularly special in that sometime that Summer we met Addie (Atalie Meier Stocker). It seems to me that it was earlier, but Addie believes she otherwise would have then remembered my European vacation with June and Karl the year before. One Summer Sunday morning she strolled into our parish hall via the parking lot door and, of course, immediately met June who was always ready to greet any visitors. She was alone, since she lived alone in a mobile home park some five miles to the east. She was unchurched but of Lutheran upbringing. June invited her to sit with her in church, and learning of her unscheduled agenda, invited her to Sunday dinner. June always had this

287

ready and waiting for us when coming home from church. So I got to meet Addie at Sunday dinner in our kitchen. By then she and June were already friends. It proved to be a lively dinner, thanks to Addie's ready and playful wit and humor, so lively in those years. She dared to tease and poke, which I could hardly let go unrequited. June joined in, but couldn't keep up, yet immensely enjoying the company and friendly sparring. Thereafter she was seldom absent at church to begin a routine of the two siting together on the south side in the fourth pew from the front.

That then became a pattern; Addie joined us for Sunday dinner virtually every Sunday thereafter till June died two years later. We became her family in place of her brother's, who had grown tired of helping a struggling sister. We took it on with ready love. She was after all repaying us with delightful company. (LPNs were not well paid as now under Medicare.)

When I came home from church, the two of them would be gabbing away nonstop while getting dinner ready. Addie has often reminded me of their typical kind of exchange: Addie asking if she should also set out knives, to which June would playfully reply, "Oh, Gene always needs a knife." Every Sunday consequently became an intimate family celebration of love. Then after dinner the two washed the dishes while I deprogrammed and napped up in the living room. The two would then commonly retire down to the family room for more friendship until Addie would need to excuse herself to return home for a short nap before going to work at her LPN nightshift at the pain clinic of Midway Hospital. June was as hungry for truly close friends, as was Addie. They were a gift to each other, virtually became like sisters.

Addie had never married, not even ever had a boyfriend. She had lost her mother when 12. And with her father's poverty, he often struggled at two laboring jobs, never much concerned for Addie -- self absorbed, even physically abusive. This twin loss resulted in only average grades at school, though she is obviously far above average.

Fortunately, she did have the determination to graduate as an LPN from Bethesda Hospital, and then worked for years in nursing homes in the St. Paul area. Along with her affliction of depression, she was financially insecure and consequently irresponsible. So she struggled to meet her obligations. Her only sibling brother, John, had already on that account disowned her. (I did get them reconciled, now that there were no financial entanglements. That is, until more recent disgust for Addie's resurgent mental illness, has again resulted in estrangement.) In her innocence and trust, she soon admitted her struggle to June. She had difficulty with paying her auto expenses and rent, etc. June appealed to me, and we gave her a "loan", more in the nature of a gift. Addie's need was June's happy love. I was at first but a related friend and agent for care.

I was considerably embarrass for Addie when I eventually made a visit to her in her mobile home in Lake Elmo. Her lonely and depressed spirit (early sign of un-addressed mental illness) had resulted in a chaotic and cluttered home. She had confessed to being on the verge of giving up on life when she had finally made the effort to find us at HS. We found it irresponsible to ignore her. Our love was so critical. We recognized ourselves as her way to salvation, but she still needed much love and help to stand. I could think of no other way than to ask June and Carol Lynch to give her a hand with a general house cleaning -- it might give her a real sign of hope. I'd have done it myself, but as her pastor, it would have been highly inappropriate. June was quite unhappy to become a "maid", but she loved Addie so sincerely that she went to help. June and I continued to agonize within the context of our own love over how to love Addie, who seemed heaven sent to benefit from our love. She did have so much enviable charm when she felt safe in our care, virtually more than enough of a reward for our effort and expense. She became our holy charity. It felt good to us to pluck at least one brand out of the fire. Without our anticipation, God had far more in mind.

1987 was the year I finally managed to finish our living room. (Not far off from a smart-aleck observation of a crusty carpenter soon after moving in: "It will take you ten years to finish.") It required oversized sheetrock for the unfinished walls in the living room in the upper lever, which had all those years sported plastic sheeting over insulation bats.

Fortunately, there had been a lucky break for us at Knox Lumber (not the usual Menards). They were for some reason discontinuing their stock of tongue&grouve 1x6 cedar. Yet I found they had a sufficient supply, which I just happened to stumbled across. I needed 1000 sf, for the living room ceiling, and they had more than enough. I quickly went home to get my boat trailer and June. We were allowed to sort out the imperfect lengths, and June stayed behind while I hauled one load home. She held off another interested customer in the interim, and we loaded what more we had sorted for ourselves.

It was late Fall. I belt-sanded and polyurethaned two coats on the whole lot of boards in the garage. It took longer to dry in the unheated garage, but we therefore didn't need to smell them. It was quite an assembly to rack that many long boards for drying -- most were 12 feet long. (It would have been near impossible to do after they were in place.) June eventually had to help get the boards into place with my needing to nail over my head; She held the far end of each board with another long board from below, while I climbed a tall step ladder to a ceiling that started at 9 feet and reached up to 15 feet before it continued over the balcony. I did intend to fill the nail holes but decided against it since they were barely visible from below. Did it ever made a big improvement with our stereo classical music!

June was still with us in 1988 when we heard from Augsburg Publishing House that they weren't interested in publishing my now well field-tried set of Eucharistic prayers. They of course were the publishers of the new Lutheran hymnal (LBW) and were not willing to consider an improvement over its set of prayers. Understandably!, also since the national synods had to give authorization for such liturgy. But concurrently an unofficial Lutheran publication house in St. Louis, then making waves with supplementary worship resources, Creative Communications, signed a contract with me and serially published my prayers. The next year, after my further refinements, they signed a second contract and continued royalty payments for a number of years. Thus many hundreds of churches were blessed with the prayers I had been gifted to compose; Many are possibly still using them to this day, as in fact I'm aware that some are.

That Spring, Karl took the MN state boards to become a licensed architect. In a week-long set of all day tests, he proved equal to the ordeal of understanding the state regulation of construction. It baffles me to imagine passing those extreme exams on his first try, only two years into his profession. June too was immensely proud of that accomplishment. She had been deeply concerned in prayer for him, calling him each evening to hear how he thought he had managed that day.

June and I had been married on Sunday June 22, 1958, the same date in June of 1988 on which we were to bury her in Union cemetery, Maplewood MN, exactly thirty years later. She died of myloblastic leukemia 24 hours after first diagnosis. Had I known that we would only have thirty years together, I'd have married her just the same, in spite of living in such a shadow. Having found and bonded with so grand and faithful a woman as she, I'm sure I'd have nonetheless accepted those thirty years as the gift it became. However, I obviously would have tried to make more of the time -- if such an oft considered regret actually makes any sense. With a quiver in my voice, I remember saying to several couples standing by her casket at her wake on the eve of her burial, "Love each other now; you never know..."

Those last two days before we lost June are seared into memory, as are the three days following. In retrospect, I honestly don't understand now how it was that I was not more outwardly overcome. Apparently, the Lord gave special strength for that ordeal. And yet, what would a more outward expression have served except to have obeyed the narcissistic celebration of personal feelings, as opposed to sensing divine intervention. I must have seemed like a person of cold steel at the grave: With but a sober face, I was surely observed to have with my fingers traced a cross over her casket after Pastor Brunning's committal and then simply turned to walk away. I was to be often enough confronted with the bitter reality of it all, frequently awakening in the night, suddenly painfully alone in bed. I'd ask myself if I had just dreamed it all, and then shed tears with fully dawned reality, feeling sorry for myself in prayer. Out in public, I would jealously notice couples going along together with life, and fight back my loss compared to their companionship.

It had made me sigh in sympathy on the Sunday previous to the Sunday of her death, watching from my upstairs study window at church as she walked up for worship. I had already finished reviewing my sermon and must have been looking out onto the parking lot to see who had already arrived. I saw her coming up the gradual slope from our home. At the far edge of the parking lot she stopped to rest. It was obvious that she was out of breath. Feeling no lack of vitality myself, I cried inwardly that my dear mate of 30 years was failing before I was ready to accept a slower pace myself. And there had been similar experiences and thoughts at various time stretching back about five years.

There was no warning beforehand, other than the ones no one understood at the time. She had always been under regular doctors care, and for some time she had a frustrating inability to tolerate more than a very light breakfast. Often she had a shortness of breath with angina pains if she walked too fast in order to keep up with the pace I set. (I'm ashamed to admit that I always set the pace till she would alert me.) Those symptoms were at that time not that unusual for a person 61 years old.

June had just had a doctors appointment the week before which resulted in normal test results, including blood analysis (as I was assured after the fact by special message from her doctor). But as that week wore on, she gradually lost energy. Finally she was unable to sleep in bed at night, choosing instead the partially upright position of her recliner in the den across from our bedroom.

We were to celebrate our 30th anniversary on the Sunday she died, and the responses to our invitations had given promise that many would be coming from far. It was to be the first time since our wedding in 1958 that we would attempt a large gathering to celebrate our happy union. They were all to join us at church and then in our spacious home.

On Saturday morning Janet arrived for the anniversary from Dayton with two-year-old Allie. They stopped in to visit. Allie was overly shy, not remembering June. In preparation, June had showered, but was so weak that I had to help her. It was shocking to see her exhausted and virtually helpless as I toweled her dry and then made her comfortable in her recliner.

Janet too was concerned about June's ability to manage our celebration the next day. To help decide what to do, I called Addie, an LPN, who came immediately and advised us that June wasn't up to our plans, but should be taken to ER. We quickly made a few telephone calls to activate a grapevine to the effect that our anniversary celebration was being canceled. And then I took her to St. Johns Hospital in Maplewood where she was admitted for tests and evaluation.

It was quite late in the evening when, first the hospital and then the doctor called me at home. The first was to invite me in for a consultation and the second, to tell me that June had leukemia and was being transferred to United Hospital in St. Paul where the family was to meet early Sunday morning with their team of doctors. It was certainly a restless night, but I was of no mind to cancel the Sunday worship at Holy Spirit.

The doctor's consultation very early that Sunday morning was unbelievably agonizing for its slim hope that the prescribed treatment would even gain any time. She had myloblastic leukemia, normally always fatal in six weeks. My three children were present, and thereafter both Karl and Philip agreed to come with me to church with the understanding that there was nothing better for us to do than to worship and pray as June was rushed into treatment. The congregation at Holy Spirit needed their pastor and be told and invited into our need. They too were our family.

Unanticipated, attending church that morning was June's long-fast friend, Nureen and her husband, from Chicago who had come for our anniversary celebration. Apparently she had been privately invited by June; She was unaware of anything amiss. At least she was thereafter able to go to the hospital for a brief visit with June.

At the hospital after church we found the Red Cross leukofloresis team desperately at work filtering out the excessive and defective white cells from June's blood which were clogging the circulatory system, making the red cells unable to carry enough oxygen. With no immediate change in June's condition, Philip and Karen then flew home to St. Louis that afternoon. Janet and Karl eventually left in the evening for the night.

Addie had excused herself form her nightshift at the pain clinic and came to join me in an anxious prayer vigil in the waiting room. She was there for me through the late afternoon and evening till after June died shortly before midnight. She was a comfort in brief recesses from June's bedside while they frantically attempted intervention with rapidly deteriorating results.

By 10pm, June progressively showed more difficulty in breathing. They advised putting her on a respirator as the situation became progressively more alarming. I called

Janet and Karl back to the hospital, along with several close friends, the two Carols.

Near midnight it was clear that the respirator was only keeping June clinically alive. Janet had been upset when returning to the hospital to see June on a respirator. We jointly elected to have it removed and then face the inevitable. We barely had time for a short prayer with June already in a coma before she left us to go on ahead to be with our Lord.

On Wednesday, we buried June at Union Cemetery, Maplewood MN, after a funeral at Holy Spirit attended by a full house of family and friends. Her pallbearers were all ordained pastors as an intentional tribute to the selfless life June had lived in the service of the church.

My children and I had a family restaurant gathering the following day. Reassured by my apparent coping strength, they returned to home and work, confident that I'd be OK. Addie stopped in on Friday to check on me, finding me busy writing a eulogy sermon for the following Sunday before taking a week off. She was thereafter a major source of consolation, coming with effectively sympathy. In her own lifelong loneliness, she had in June had a best friend who had provided several years of stabilizing support. Quite soon she and I, already knowing each other well, both of us needing friendship, and being compatible, why now go our separate ways?

After all these years since then, in spite of the struggles of Addie's accelerating mental illness, it still seems divinely appropriate that Addie and I soon decided to go on together. It felt good to both of us in the fear of God, as love quickly brought peace.

Mysteriously but consciously, I was consoled by a conviction that I had not reached my intended potential, particularly as a theologian. More ultimate accomplishments for this life, I dared to believe, still awaited me. I was being called to go on. And God did have work for me, as is still being realized, June still a partner in my prayers. Even as the parish of Holy Spirit in Oakdale was to melt down the following year through the incompetent vision and decision of the St. Paul Area Synod of the ELCA, I would find alternate excitement in researching and writing my long deferred MTh thesis. This served to widely open the door to defining a theology of prayer. Though with a limping heart, I was given the will to move into a whatever future.

Already in April, Holy Spirit's organ committee had led the congregation to select and contract for a new Rogers organ. Our original vacuum-tube electronic organ was a frustration by then to keep alive. The $30,000 cost had at first been unthinkable until a member gave a gift of half the cost with the challenge to the congregation to raise the remaining. I then pledged $1000 at the congregational meeting considering the new organ, and quickly enough sufficient other $1000 gifts were announced The new organ was installed on Sept. 9th and dedicated on Oct. 30th. It was a true sign of the vitality of the congregation.

That process suggested a memorial for June. The new organ was a new generation of electronics, and was capable of having organ pipes added to it for a truly astonishing pipe organ sound. $5000 had been received in memory of June, and I added another equal amount to purchase two ranks of organ pipes, the principle and a flute. Sadly, we were only to enjoy that enhanced organ for one year before Holy Spirit was dissolved and the organ was lost.

Chapter 27 -- Holy Spirit Closing

The city of Oakdale MN had originally been a semi-rural unincorporated township; It was only two miles wide from east to west, but six miles long. Since the 1950s, it had been the metro Twin Cities border territory on the east. It lay just beyond the Ramsey County border of Century Avenue in Washington County. With only scattered development on that border, the MN DOT then built I-694 in 1969 -- the metro interstate bypass. It ran exactly through Oakdale's length, forming a new barrier beyond which it would then effectively remain rural. Holy Spirit was just inside that new barrier, and struggling to survive in this even narrower strip of territory. By the mid 1980s that territory had gradually been developed. And then finally, the area beyond, east of I-694, was showing life. The barrier had been breached. Earlier, we from Holy Spirit could have thrown a stone across the barrier to the east, but there had been nothing to hit. Now we saw that we had perhaps at last been opened to the future in line with the original vision. And we felt more than ready and willing. We had managed to pay off our organizing debt, and were self supporting. Our parish rejoiced in the prospect of growing apace.

I was calling on every new resident as soon as they moved into this new territory, just as I had been doing in our immediate area. And our lay welcome teams followed up on any I considered prospective. We were gaining new members and excited over long delayed possibilities. What had however never crossed our mind was that our St. Paul Area Synod was looking over our shoulder, eager to score points in the ELCA by notching new mission starts. Credit them with noticing, but not with companionship. Supposedly, as they later maintained, they had driven through our empty parking lot during the week and assumed that no one was at home or alive. I may well have noted their passing from my upstairs study in a morning hour; I walked to church, so my car was not in the church lot. I can testify that they had not knocked, phoned or written, asking about the new church pasture.

Finally, we somehow indirectly heard that the synod was considering a new mission in Oakdale east of I-694. June and I were devastated when we heard this in 1987. I went to confront Bishop Erdahl; But the dice had been irretrievably rolled. We at Holy Spirit had been judged in absentia of being too ossified to appeal to the expected middle class newer residents of the city. And the interstate was quoted as a barrier to them from us. (The fact, however, it also was that the freeway made it possible for such new residents to remain at their old congregations in the metro area -- it was a new day of shaping a parish.) In nothing more than a lunch meeting with myself, the bishop and an ELCA district mission director -- me being the only one from Holy Spirit -- explained their strategy. I asked in frustration why we at Holy Spirit could not instead be redeveloped, even relocated, if such was considered to be the need. I would even resign and move on, so they could call a mission developer to take over HS, they could build a new building, etc. After all, this was our assigned and long-identified parish territory. I was willing. However, that did not fit their paradigm.

Little wonder that when June had then died, Bishop Erdahl was rebuffed when he called and wanted to speak at her funeral. He insisted on it as his right, so we reluctantly let him come. He popped in just in time, spoke with stilted compassion from the pulpit for three minutes after the procession and invocation in which he didn't participate, and then left. Good! Holy Spirit could cry and worship without one who had not considered our welfare. We had been left to our own council, and we clearly understood the synod's threat to our very existence. They had purloined our mission territory. In council and congregational meetings we discussed our possibilities, yet minus any synod offer to guide or help. At first, when June was still among us, the mood was to just doubled-down, continuing our invitations in our reasonable territory surrounding. But then with June no longer present to help lift the spirits, the congregation began sagging in their mourning.

As 1988 rolled on after June's death, Addie and I came to decide that we could both better go on together. Half of my family urged us to wait, but for what?, for them? We were sane mature adults feeling divinely led and blessed. We had a right and duty to proceed with our hearts and inspiration.

It was several weeks later when Addie made a frightful but also reassuring confession. She told me that she had flushed down the toilet an accumulated stash of lethal drugs. I then realized how far to the end of her rope she had come when she had made that life changing decision to attend Holy Spirit about two years earlier to meet June and me. She had from then on had some reason to hope, but now with a conviction that we had a dependable relationship of love, she was daring to live.

Therefore when New Year's Day in 1989 fell on a Sunday, we were married as part of the Sunday congregational worship, with Communion, overflowing the church. Pastor Brunning from Gethsemane celebrated and Rev. Mrs Breckenridge from the synod staff preached. I was dressed in my church vestments and Addie as a bride, a sign that she was being married into the congregation as the new Mrs pastor. (Very consciously we were married for better or for worse, and eventually when her mental health, suffering under poor medical support, gradually struck, it would, for a while, be for the worse. But neither of us would today rue that New Year's Day wedding. In many half-mysterious ways, we see the hand of God.)

The fate of Holy Spirit was then still nonetheless under debate by the congregation. At the same time, I was well aware of the growing unlikely-hood of Holy Spirit's survival, given the steadfast mind of the synod. Our congregation's spirit also seemed deflated, while I myself still felt a strong sense of ministry in the church, somewhere else if not there. Remarrying was like being outfitted for continued ministry either at HS or somewhere.

299

Soon, June's mother, Irma Radtke, for several years by then in a nursing home, suffering severely with Alzheimer, died on April 6th. I had had to succeed in being her legal guardian after June had died, and then also seeing to a probate of remaining assets. She died owning only her half of her brother Arnold's home in Phoenix AZ. Her brother Paul flew up to contest my appointment, but was quickly dismissed by the judge. I led her funeral myself at Holy Spirit. We buried her alongside of her husband in a Chicago cemetery without the attendance of this only surviving brother, Paul, nor his sons. Besides my family, the burial was attended only by her Burchard cousins, Ed and his son and wife.

Holy Spirit continued to discuss its prospects with no other wisdom as yet than to go on. Till we inevitably ran out of spirit? Finally, later that year I proposed that we present our whole selves to the synod to do with us as they chose. It was calling their bluff. I'd resign and move on, while the congregation donated themselves and all they had to the new mission, since the synod was determined to start a new mission. The congregation quickly bought into that. As a way to quit a hopeless situation? Perhaps! And the synod? They were nonplused! Eventually they had to take up sale and distribution of assets. This did include a modest severance package for me to tide me over into a new call. The church was sold and briefly owned by an evangelical church; But it was soon again sold, intentionally burned down and replaced with an apartment complex. To crown the tragedy, within another year the new synod Oakdale mission, not yet two years old, failed and was abandoned by the synod.

Holy Spirit set its last worship and dissolution for February 25, 1990. Only a half dozen families transferred to the mission. So the congregation essentially evaporated. I was then on-leave-from-call and placed on the bishop's list of pastors seeking a call into the synod. The latter was entirely ridiculous since there were less than 200 congregations in the synod , but the list already had 500 names; Apparently

300

there were many pastors from outside the synod who were jealous to live in the Twin Cities. The Minneapolis Synod had the same surplus of pastors inviting a call, with obvious duplications. For other reasons as well, I therefore requested the bishop to nominate me for a call in every other synod within 500 miles. I was fortunate to be owning the parsonage so as to have a place to live while I waited. I called it a sabbatical, such as I'd never had.

There was no hesitation in deciding what I'd do while waiting. My unfinished graduate thesis at the seminary had been left hanging for almost ten years, mainly for lack of a commanding thesis of interest. But I had in the meantime been working hard in what was comparable, namely studying and writing liturgical prayers. I went to see my faculty advisor with lots of questions about a way forward. No, my independent work can't after the fact be admitted as a thesis, nor as a starting point. It would need to be focused on research into a field of original study; And that new work needed to be under faculty supervision. And if this was the area I wanted to address, then I'd need a new faculty advisor since, Dr. Fevold of the church history department, who had been assigned, felt unqualified to serve me.

Another faculty advisor was then nominated who was however too preoccupied with his own postdoctoral study. So I was then accepted to work under Dr. Carl Volz, who taught in the department of pastoral practice, which included liturgy. We bonded quickly. When he heard of and saw the work I had already undertaken with liturgical prayer -- already essentially a postdoctoral project -- we agreed on a new thesis. My concern had already for ten years been dissatisfaction with the prayers in the new hymnal; We decided on my studying the work of the Subcommittee on Prayer for the LBW hymnal. And my preliminary research would need to be a study of the Christian liturgy since the early church -- namely when, how and why did these prayers come to be inserted and been required in the liturgy. I was quickly excited, and never looked back. There would be no reluctance along the way of completing my thesis which came to be titled: *The Prayer of the Day in the Lutheran Book of Worship in Relation to the Western Christian Liturgical Tradition.*

In addition, the academic dean considered it to have been too long since I'd finished the course work for my degree. He therefore recommended I take two additional courses in the graduate curriculum. Dr. Volz was to be teaching, *Pastoral Life and Practice* in the Summer quarter, and Dr. Nestigen taught a course in *Theology of the Cross* that Fall. These fit in perfectly with my interests and my thesis.

As an accepted masters degree candidate, I was assigned a carrel (simple steel desk in the library stacks) along the window side of the stack level that contained the books I'd need to study. Actually, I did little work there other than to park my notebook, and as a gathering place for books I was finding and consulting. Gradually, I checked out about 45 books which I read at home where I'd be more comfortable, and note taking was more easily done. I settled on a system similar to the time honored index card system -- hand written notes in a full-sized notebook as I read, later cut apart and sorted into order for the composition.

All through the years, I had anticipated and dreaded the prospects of such a project, and of writing such a lengthy work. But it went quite smoothly. The only frustration remembered was the preliminary requirement of producing a highly detailed outline for the thesis prior to composition for faculty approval. (How did I fully know what I'd write till after I'd written?) Creating incredibly detailed outlines had always been disturbing.

Addie was still working her night shift at the hospital pain clinic, so I had lots of quiet time to read. If I got sleepy, I took a short nap in comfort, and was able to plunge on, never loosing interest till bedtime around midnight. But it was not quite a relentless seven day week. When Addie had some days off, we headed up to the North Shore. She had seldom had such freedom and affordability. Tent camping

302

in state parks in good weather was quite enjoyable to both of us. Otherwise, we also stayed at the more affordable resorts with lake view cabins on the North Shore. We did lots of hiking, and in addition we explored every derivable side road in reasonable reach of the area, eventually with extra exploration when encountering a for sale sign. Not that we were very serious about it. It was something to do, but the exploration slowly created the consideration of possibilities. Because of the depressed North Shore economy, there were may such for-sale signs.

It was on a late Summer return trip home that we got to discussing what kind of North Shore property we might conceivably buy. I had explained that I didn't want to buy a fancy expensive property for its lake view, such as we had usually found. I said that we should look for a run-down shack with a good lake view. Addie interjected as she pointed to something on my side of the highway, "You mean, like that one." I spotted the for sale sign, slowed down, turned around, and stopped in front of a vacant and sad looking small house with many shingles missing, and an unkempt yard -- a ghost house. We got out of the car and briefly looked at a building that gave me shivers of revulsion. Well, it was for sale, so we felt it allowable for us to see what kind of lake shore it had. In that late Summer, everything was overgrown. There were some deer trails which of course didn't lead to where we wanted to go. Four blocks of thick forest separated us from Lake Superior. We fought our way through were no one had gone for some time. Without walking sticks, we finally managed to overlook a large bay with a long and wide beach -- extremely unusual on the North Shore. It was steep and treacherous to get down to the beach. I turned to Addie and said, "We can't afford this." The house was nothing, but the property was one in a thousand.

What would it hurt to call the phone number on the for sale sign? We were informed that the price had just been reduced. A divorcing couple wanted done with it after much delay and without response. (The Silver Bay taconite plant had gone bankrupt after court ordered anti-polution efforts for Lake Superior. Unemployment was off the scale in the area. Homes in town were selling at $10,000.) It was 9 acres with 500+ feet of Lake Superior frontage, then priced at $79,000, down from $135,000. We drove home, I went to the bank, mortgaged my debt free home valued at $200,000+, and paid cash. We had a first use of the "cabin" on September 21st. It was so filthy, we put down our big tarp, usually used under our tent, and slept in sleeping bags on an air mattress. Remembering the view and the beach, we gradually managed to clean and convert the cabin into a home away from home.

Meanwhile, I had a grandson on June 27, 1990, Ryan Michael, born to Janet and Michael Grant in Kettering OH.

I have noted earlier that I had never learned to type; June had been my faithful secretary for more than 30 years. She never once hesitated, nor ever showed the least sign to indicate that this work had ever been less than a privilege of love. I could never have managed the thesis without my computer. For this work of preparing an academic thesis, not one word dared to be misspelled nor mistaken; no corrections were allowed. If a mistake was made, that page needed to be retyped. All this beside it being required to be formatted according to precise rules. And there needed to be multiple original copies. The computer allowed me to correct and shape everything to satisfaction before printing; And the multiple original copies were no problem for my printer. June could have retired with grace.

In good time, by late March of 1991, my thesis was done and in the hands of my advisor, as well as two faculty readers who prepared themselves to conduct my oral exam. That session of face to face examination without any supporting notes in hand is naturally feared, and the stuff of legends. I had already had any number of private consultations with my faculty advisor, and was confident that my thesis had satisfied him; But what would I run into with two other faculty members whose face I had merely come to recognize, and with whom I'd merely passed the

304

time of day? It was to be a four hour grilling of any claim I had made, even including my competence with the whole field of my study. The three of them huddled for some time beforehand, while I waited outside imagining the worst. It however went without a fault. Dr. Volz was in fact so pleased with my thesis that he unbelievably declared it worthy of publication, assuring me that it would have been fully satisfactory as a doctoral dissertation. I wore my red tassel with excusable pride at the commencement on May 26th at Central Lutheran in Minneapolis.

By then I had already had an invitation to interview to become the pastor of Zion's Lutheran in Pershing (or East Germantown) IN. Addie and I drove down for a weekend, including a church council meeting, to conduct worship and preach on Sunday April 28th. The pillars of the congregation greeted us cordially. On the way home we stopped in Indianapolis to meet Bishop Kempski. I asked him point blank what I needed to know about the congregation, since they had given me no direct signs of warning, yet having been vacant for a year. He replied, "What you see is what you get." -- a most dishonest evasion. In all charity, he apparently dared to believe that I was up to the predictable ordeal he already knew it would become.

Zion's is the oldest congregation in the Indiana-Kentucky Synod, having been founded in 1822. It was worshiping in a red brick building, built in 1900 according to a Protestant or auditorium floor plan. The building was already 90 years old. It had a Moeller tracker pipe organ that had unfortunately been installed in the space of its sacristy. It took some time of actual residence to recognize that there was much pastoral work to be done in a congregation that had had over forty pastors. That itself should have signaled that the pastors had through the years been treated as hired-hands, rather than as agents of the Holy Spirit. What the Spirit had intended had been made impossible by small but firm self centered minds. I was eventually to learn that the pastors had been the one considered in need of being taught how things were to be done. These pastors quickly saw what seemed an impossible impasse, and soon enough moved elsewhere. In fact, as I was to understand, things were insisted to be as they had been. I was, in particular, no different to them than a fresh seminary graduate, one who may known something of Scripture, but little of how a local church actually does its daily work..

But I had a spine, a full education with significant experience, and a spirit with a determined dedication. So we walked in cold, trusting ourselves into the Father's mysterious hands. I should have been more concerned for Addie, who nonetheless made me proud by being a true Mrs pastor. Yet we were both to be often discouraged by the insincerity we met. Some on the council had already balked at the estimated moving cost, offering to come and get us with their open farm truck. But we said, No. That was but the first issue. And so we moved into an Indiana Summer overly hot and dry. The MN North Shore was far away, but we knew it would always be there for us when we needed a retreat for spiritual recharging. Even to dream of it often quieted the storm. It would be a long seven years.

Chapter 28 -- Zion's - Pershing IN - 1991

Zion's Lutheran Church in Pershing IN was my place of ministry beginning in July of 1991. It's located just off the old National Road, US 40, and in view of the parallel I-70. It's a saga that brings back the memory of many unsettled days and years, yet with satisfaction for doing the hard work of refreshing the Gospel in that place. I was recently again reaffirmed in the trust that this was accomplished because I was able to visit on a recent Sunday, and they are alive, though smaller. The reformation of leadership and spirit we launched had taken hold.

It's the oldest Lutheran church in IN, founded in 1822. I was the last full-time pastor out of over 40 who served there through many difficult times. Essentially the community is rural, but by my time it served a mix of others, along with a few farmers, and with significant numbers of senior citizens. The majority were Germans, but that language had long been abandoned. Quite universally they were very conservative in culture and philosophy, and unashamedly parochial. Unfortunately a number of older men and women vied to be the acknowledged pillars of the congregation. But one man, who had the right surname by tradition, unofficially claimed that honor, having never relinquished aggressive leadership on the church council. Alongside of that council there was then no structure or voice. The women's organization was considerably more evangelical but effectively neutralized. It was quite telling on arrival often to hear a leader proudly talking of Zion's having "trained" numerous seminary graduate first-call pastors, and this to my face, with its subtle message, even though I was a 30+ year veteran. It didn't register with them that those pastors had so quickly fled causing the rapid pastoral turnover..

Was there a mad wisdom in the bishop by nominating me as Zion's pastor? Once the parish came into focus after a few months, I resented his not having clued me in advance to what I was getting into. Surely he knew, but when I had asked before accepting the call, he had replied, "What you see, is what you get." Without full disclosure he was attempting to solve a troublesome responsibility. His "wisdom" came to light several years later after there had already been two conflict resolution interventions by the synod -- never directly involving the bishop. The second time, to a fully assembled congregation, his assistant announced the verdict: "We (synod and bishop) have often reassigned your pastors at your request. We will not do so again. Pastor Lehrke will remain as your pastor with our blessing."

Did the bishop realize from the start that his long-troubled parish needed an experienced pastor with a sufficiently thick skin, fortunately also with a studied orthodox theology, to successfully reorient ingrained congregational politics? What a gift of encouragement it would have been to me through the long struggle had I known that he stood behind me. Instead, his assistant had at times merely informed me of having fielded another complaint, all remaining anonymous and unspecified.

Visiting Zion's upon receiving the call, I conducted a Sunday service and attended a specially called church council meeting. Asking the council about the communion schedule, I informed them that as their pastor I'd want to celebrate communion every Sunday as I had been doing for twenty years. They objected and insisted on their schedule of once per month. Not yet being their pastor, I responded pastorally that I was willing for some time to teach them about its importance. (I should have said, I'd like to celebrate communion every day; so let's compromise and do it every Sunday.) It was undoubtedly such, albeit gentle, forwardness on my part over such a critical issue, which effectively threatened their leadership. And in my subsequent teaching there arose a smoldering friction with those who considered themselves the pillars of the congregation. It was indeed a most worthy issue for me, and ultimately, nonnegotiable per the Gospel. Through the resulting friction and discussion I soon learned that their previous pastors had either been intimidated in their youth, or chose to bend with the politics to get along. I rather treasured my studied integrity and call through the Spirit; The issue went to the heart of the church.

Three of the six council members thought and spoke as one, led by one. All three were elderly men. One of these, an elderly subordinate with his wife, sat on our front porch swing watching the moving van being unloaded at the parsonage. Naively, it was a gesture of welcome, but also a statement of authority and an invasion of privacy. Sadly, my salary was not negotiable -- there was at the time not even a recommended synod salary guideline. Salary was simply what they were willing to pay; it amounted to about the same as a seminary graduate would have received. Is was really a matter of avoiding more responsible stewardship. That was apparent at the start when the estimate for the moving van was shared. Through seven years, there would be only nominal salary increases, or occasionally none. One year an amendment for a raise was moved at the annual meeting but voted down, clearly intended as a rebuke. (A noteworthy saint came to the parsonage the following morning with two $100 bills as an apology.)

Thus you might correctly sense that there were as well numerous spiritual pacifists in the congregation with a long history of being intimidated. Many others no longer cared, or tried to stay in the shadow, surely dreading intimidating confrontations. That visit to Pershing to inquire into my call had included Addie and I being guests for dinner at the home of an evangelical family with a number of other like-minded guests, cordial and welcoming. They represented the disenfranchised membership for whose sake the Holy Spirit led me blindly to accept their call and attempt a reformation. Unfortunately, this didn't factor in the lesser strength and ability of Addie, whose spirit was nearly broken after seven years, even though we had by then managed a victory of sorts.

309

When Addie and I arrived for our interview, we had with that visit stayed overnight with the acclaimed principle leader and his wife. The heavy authoritarian spirit in that home inspired me to agree with Addie to purchase an air mattress on the way down from MN to assume the pastorate, so as to already stay at the parsonage while awaiting the moving van. We dreaded being again assigned to that home to spare motel costs.

Not counting on the heat of Summer without AC, it helped that the parsonage was well shaded, and there was a shaded porch on the east front with a bench swing. It was too late to plant a garden, but some members shared their surplus. Most people were genuinely welcoming and optimistic for the resumption of a resident ministry. I attended as of first importance, visiting and communing the half dozen shutins. These I found most grateful, except for one who was universally bitter about everything in her marginal disability. They had been without pastoral visitation for some time. Generally all the members were welcoming and Addie and I enjoyed many evening visits among them. The parsonage lawn was even graciously being mowed un-requested, giving me generous time for pastoral and hospital visitations.

Few were the remarks about my unexpected traditional liturgical practices and vestments, they not having been exposed to how the church did church elsewhere -- it had been as they wanted. Most likely the pastors had asked what the practice had been, and meekly followed suit. Significantly, the congregation was proud of and enjoyed the use of their large bell to signal the time of worship; A slow adult was thrilled to do that part. I'm not sure what they thought of then also tolling it at the praying of the Our Father according to tradition. Not quite so well appreciated by the "leaders" was my rearranging the chairs in the sanctuary, as if this was their sacred space rather than my work space. But we were managing and worshiping. After more than a year on sabbatical leave from parish ministry, during which time I finished graduate study and the writing of my thesis, it felt good to be in a pastoral harness once more. The rest of that year was basically peaceful service, and Addie made me proud for her partnership. She had a deep desire to be a true Mrs pastor, likewise to honor me. Her smart wit was lovable to all, particularly with the teens, with whom she worked with natural skill.

But it didn't take long to notice that there was an elephant in the room. The self declared leaders "strutted," and greeted the occasional visitors perfunctorily, projecting that Zion's was their church. There were also those who projected love, both to other members and visitors, but the contradictions were hard for visitors to ignore. I called on these visitors within the week, but Zion's was a hard sell because it didn't consistently and successfully sell itself.

Nevertheless, with the new year of 1992 the parish and parsonage rhythm was more than manageable. Confirmation classes which had been adjourned during the pastoral vacancy involved some catching up, but were progressing and orderly. My "office" at the church became a classroom since my study, also for church and secretarial work, was on the second floor of the parsonage overlooking the church yard. I had to be my own secretary, which was possible since I had the use of my computer, and had rapidly learned how to type after June had died. There were at any rate no prospects for secretarial help involving a computer in those days. I did easily recruit monthly help with the mechanical parts of preparing and mailing a newsletter, happily renamed the Bell. My computer was already nine years old, so I replaced it that year with a kit that I was able to assemble myself, having some courage and practice in building stereo amplifiers.

There was no hesitation that next year with planting a sizable vegetable garden behind the parsonage on a very fertile plot. It was in my genes to do so. Belatedly, that Summer I brought from MN my rototiller and wheelbarrow. It was a good day-off routine that gave me pleasure. That was supplemented with my bicycle, brought

311

along at the start for many a 25 mile ride on the universally blacktopped country roads.

Then a special good fortune struck in late Spring. I was teaching confirmation class at church one Saturday morning when Addie interrupted to inform me that there was a swarm of bees on the front porch of the parsonage. By the time the class was over, they had already settled in under the capstone of a brick pillar which had a cavity the approximate dimensions of a bee hive. There was only a small hole where a part of the mortar was missing. I had sold my apiary in MN, but somehow I was able to quickly purchase the main parts of a hive. Now how?? I found it possible to tip up the heavy capstone and found the bees hanging from it with a small newly built comb already constructed. My frames fit perfectly alongside and were suspend in the pillar for a few days. Then I again tipped up the capstone and removed my frames with the bees attached. Unsure of keeping the bees at the parsonage, the Sowers agreed to have me bring them to their small farm south of town. From there I brought them back to the parsonage the next year. And there they stayed without problems till we moved them with us back to MN in late 1997. Every year they produced a significant harvest with all proceeds going to the local food pantry.

That Summer of 1992, son Karl began a masters in architecture at the U of PA. He came to Pershing in a U-Haul truck, towing his Honda to leave with us pending whatever. We then followed him to Philadelphia and helped him unload and settle into an apartment. From there we went to visit daughter Janet and family who had recently moved to NJ. It included taking my two grandchildren to the beach on the Atlantic for a memorable wading party, and then later to witness Allie off on her first day of school.

The annual congregational meeting of Zion's at the beginning of 1993 included a motion from the floor by some members who were satisfied with my year and half of teaching the basic importance of communion. But to begin every-Sunday communion was however defeated on a voice vote. I made no immediate response, but in that week following, I decided to take my ordination vows in hand; I'd simply begin doing what the Gospel and the church taught and required. I celebrated communion that next Sunday and every Sunday thereafter, just as I was required by the church to preach a gospel sermon every Sunday. To have or not to have communion with Sunday worship was not a matter of democracy, the same as not asking the question of whether the Bible was to be read at Sunday worship. The response of the leading families was at first disbelief, but sullen silence. The leader soon dropped out of church and refused to meet or talk with me. His wife refused to intervene (long intimidated) and also gave me a cold shoulder. When the Spring lawn mowing season began, he elected no longer to mow the parsonage lawn nor any part of the 50 foot wide strip of lawn between the parsonage and church driveways, implying but not saying that it was all my responsibility -- not merely the half part next to the parsonage. It was a deliberate but ham-fisted protest in place of even facing me on any issue.

His chief buddy also then dropped away; When I visited his farm home, he angrily lectured me for 30 minutes with no chance to reply before he stormed out of his house, (like a sergeant dealing with a raw recruit). It left me standing with his quiet (and embarrassed?) wife who advised me to resign my pastorate. Another family, in which the husband was disabled, and whom I visited as a shutin, shortly thereafter had their non-attending son waylay me on leaving their home. He lecturing me in the hot sun, brooking no defense and likewise advising me to flee Zion's -- their church. So, who was I called by God to serve? Was it to grant the personal wishes of the few abusive leaders who had co-opted this church as their own? Did it not more fundamentally resolve on those who rightfully hungered for the sacrament which Christ had taught, even commanded the apostles to celebrate with his followers? He had not even instructed the apostles to worship every Sunday or to preach a sermon; Rather, simply to celebrate his memory with bread and wine -- consistently!

Besides, sensing and being committed to my ordination, with its nonnegotiable duty of preaching the Word and administering the sacraments, I was also not about to be bullied when an issue like mowing the lawn came to be bound up with God-given duty. So I refused to mow any more than half the lawn between the driveways. It looked a fright for some time until an effort was made to find possible parsonage lot markers. I wasn't informed of those results, but thereafter the church half of that strip was again being tended. As it was, the parsonage lot was quite deep with much lawn beyond the garden that was of no use to me. Somehow the thought came to me to fence it and buy 5 goslings to graze the extra pasture of very uneven ground which was quite difficult to mow by hand. What a treat those geese became to the parish children, including the public school children, whose playground abutted the back fence.

The Sowers knew that Addie was voting for a dog, so when some irresponsible person dumped off a tiny still un-weaned kitten along the road at their small farm south of town, they called and offered it. It had managed to find shelter in their goat barn. With difficulty, Kenny managed to capture it and handed it to Addie who never let it go. It was a yellow tabby, barely 4" long. I relented and we took it home. There it disappeared for two days when hunger apparently somewhat overcame its fears. We called her Wunderlein -- German for little miracle, given that it had survived heartless abandonment. She became a dear pet for many years. She loved to go for a walk in the cemetery with me and our soon to be acquired cairn terrier. She would race ahead and disappear among the tombstones, dashing out and on when we caught up to her. We buried her years later in MN where she loved to roam and catch field mice, as well as the many house mice which lived in our basement with its porous and cracked cinderblock walls.

The behind the scene lobbying of the few opposition leaders at Zion's about the shameful new practice of celebrating communion every Sunday, apparently with numerous complaining phone calls to the synod office, had the desired result. The synod sent out a conflict resolution team. It was entered in my log as occurring on June 25-26, 1993. I don't specifically remember any details about that ordeal. Perhaps that's understandable for being merged in mind with the second synod conflict visitation three years later in 1996, at which synod then refused to take action against me and effectively told the opposition to desist.

Taken as a whole, it bears witness to the unrelenting background of gossip and rebellion by a few, of which everyone was quite aware. The few leading opposition families either no longer attended or transferred to distant congregations, although continuing the effort of undermining my ministry. I privately and rightly faulted those fellow pastors involved for requesting a transfers for them instead of giving wise council. It was admittedly hard to be Christ like. Although, Jesus had refused without compromise when his call to teach was questioned. He had stood up for who he was when the Jerusalem leaders questioned his authority, even braving death for integrity sake. Addie and I will bravely stand before the throne, as we already did in Pershing.

My pastoral ministry at Zion's continued to be stressful both for me and Addie in 1994. In the aftermath of the synod conflict resolution intervention the previous year, with which there was no resolution, there was only a feeling of having eluded but not escaped impeachment. Opposition wasn't at all abated from behind the scene. I was determined, however, to equip the congregation for new life. Therefore, an antique constitution needed to be replaced and fully implemented to pave the way to shared leadership. This had already by then been done, and surprisingly simple by lack of the old leaders to anticipate or object. To run everything in the parish through a monthly church council meeting, consisting of only six old members, did not allow for brainstorming a new program, even if there were no alligators on the council pressing their authority. Time didn't allow for this.

Especially, we needed a select board of deacons who had a serious spiritual interest and point of view, and who could be trusted with confidentiality. I needed these -- either men or women -- with whom to discuss spiritual matters and new pastoral programs or practice, especially including personal member issues. Forwarding a question or plans to the church council through the chairman of the deacons with voice vote on the council, as also with other committees that were created, provided a better chance and broader representation and deliberation. It served to equalize things over against a headstrong council with a few still holding assured veto power. Had I from the start shared this rationale for a modern constitution, I wouldn't have had a chance.

In addition, I dared to seek out and engage reasonable persons about the wall Zion's was facing which threatened its future -- particularly community outreach as opposed to merely being a chapel for established families until they died. I had by then learned that Zion's had a long history of patriarchal family government which had virtually no mission consciousness. Nor had it understood the needs of all members to have a place to worship and serve. I specifically remember the likes of an extended informal conversation with two promising new leaders (they are yet today leading well). We had come home from a workshop at Muncie of our district of synod, considering congregational organization and leadership. We were sitting in my car at church yet for some time after coming home, because on the drive home I had dared to open our "can of worms". They were sobered by my evaluation, and it apparently also gave them heart over against years of intimidation by senior pillars.

This fortunately coincided with some genuine interest from several families slightly beyond the immediate Pershing area. And with these there were a few who had a Sunday morning work conflict. No one objected when I offered to begin a 5:30pm Saturday low mass. My sermon was already fully crafted by then, and we would need no organist, etc. We read the liturgy, I led the singing of only one key hymn, and from memory preached the main parts of my sermon, whose text I had left at home. We celebrated communion and we were done in about 30 minutes. It had the spirit of a serious rehearsal, and yet quite real. These families brought a half dozen teens into the catechism classes and served to launch another adult instruction class. We usually were a happy crew of a dozen, or plus, at this low mass. The difference in the spirit of fellowship was refreshing.

Eventually we did constitute an actual properties committee, but to start, the old leaders, for whom this was their primary interest, were the trustees and focused on property. However, they ignored the parsonage, only casually monitoring the appearance of the church itself. One man, who by then was struggling with cancer, had in the past taken the lead with the property, including the parsonage. But now there was no one. Only once, and quite early, did one council member even enter the parsonage for an inspection. He came at my request to approve a redo of the stairs to the basement so as to authorize payment for my invoice for supplies. It had been treacherously steep and with short treads. I feared for Addie carrying the wash up and down, since the washer and dryer needed to be down there. I saw the possibilities and requested council permission to reconstruct the stairs. For the shortness of the space, I made a landing half way down and a 45 degree turn, making for a safe descent with hands full. My work was offhandedly approved, but the project and inspection confirmed that no one was really interested. No one had offered to help.

There surely was no mercy on the council for lack of AC at the parsonage. There wasn't even a line in the budget for any maintenance and repair at the parsonage. So at my own cost and engineering I installed a window unit in the living room beside the fireplace. At least it took the edge off. That involved some serious electrical rewiring; But nonetheless, we often kept blowing fuses. The electrical in the parsonage was in primitive shape. Since finances were tight, and I did know how to do virtually any ordinary electrical work, I offered and was gladly given permission to do their work. They would have grumbled about an electrician's estimate. Fortunately, they agreed to pay for the supplies. This involved replacing the old fuse box, which had only six fuses for six circuits. I installed a control center with circuit breakers for dozens of circuits. It was fun for me -- I could have happily been an electrician. I staged the work so that we could have the power company come and first disconnect the power for one day, during which I installed and wired in the new control center. Thereafter, I proceeded to divide the existing circuits in a leisurely project on my days off. That then also solved a critical problem with my computer work. It's obviously very frustrating when composing a document if the power is suddenly lost from a blown fuse, needing a start from scratch -- in those early days there was no continuous saving of computer work in progress. None even had a computer so as to understand.

During our Summer vacation in 1994 at our MN North Shore cabin, I managed the first stage of a total reconstruction spaced over the following Summers. In advance, son Karl had drawn up blueprints which we submitted to the county planning and zoning via our attorney. Since the cabin would eventually need to be moved away from the highway (scheduled for reconstruction, unpredictable years hence) the county was reluctant to approve the application for a building permit. Fortunately the attorney who presented this in our absence managed to persuade them with great difficulty. We had only four rooms in a 24x27 house, with an attic. A tiny bath had been created out of the pantry. That plumbing was connected to a non functioning collapsed septic tank. I was able to contract for a new septic and mound field. But I wasn't content to continue with that bathroom. So in only three weeks, and by myself with Addie, I tore off the small back entry cubicle, and over a temporary set of supports, I built the rough construction of a 24x16 two story addition. It provided a proper entry and stairway system to an eventual second story, and included two bathrooms. Addie helped wherever possible and nailed all the exterior hard panels, often from a tall ladder. I even managed to put on shingles; And all the windows and door were installed before it was time to return to IN.

That reconstruction was a lease on our emotional life; We now had this livable place of our own elsewhere when we returned to Pershing. (Our home in Oakdale was being rented.) It projected a personal future amid the vagaries of a pastorate from which I still might be impeached, given the underground efforts of now sidelined pillars. But the following year of 1995 did bring promise with a 15% over all improvement in the parish life of Zion's. Yet the stress was getting to Addie who got some relief by working at her vocation as an LPN visiting homebound patients for the county, monitoring their vital signs. Fortunately one of the saints at Zion's also effectively became her mother. Without that family we might well have given up.

319

I had not been able to give much of anything to son Philip at his wedding several years before; So upon finding a wholesale lumber company north of Richmond, willing to allow my purchase of hard maple, I began a grandfather clock for him. Almost immediately, I then also started one for Janet and Mike. That was also of maple and by the same basic pattern -- Alexander Hamilton. However that one was finished with a medium stain rather than left natural as with Philip's. This was a good days-off pastime in the garage with my radial-arm saw. Naturally, I also had a garden to tend which yielded more than we could use. And that year I bought 8 goslings to mow the back yard that lay beyond the garden.

With my continuing interest in renewing the life of the parish, I then chose to specially announce my willingness to hear private confession, emphasizing its confidentiality. That was in view of (though not explained) the gossip and intimidation factors troubling Zion's. I was also seeing divorces without being asked to help. I didn't really expect much chance for a renewal of this ancient and also Lutheran practice of confession, but it was a dramatic way to announce and offer myself as Zion's pastor to anyone troubled in body or soul.

Little did I expect a tempest. One member who had never become involved as a leader, but who considered himself a staunch Lutheran, took strong exception. He apparently had been consistently lobbied by the out-of-power opposition. When I visited him, he vociferously attacked me with the argument that Luther by his 95 theses had overruled private confession. After gently explaining that those 95 theses had nothing to do with private confession, he angrily ordered me out of his home, and refused for a while to attend church and communion. Fortunately this never directly caught fire, but it was in the mix the following year when a second synod conflict resolution effort was begun. (He never apologized; But in my recent visit at Zion's, at the sharing of the peace before communion, he was willing to shake my hand. He even put his other hand on top of mine

320

as a special embrace. I accepted that as his unspoken request for forgiveness.) Forgiveness was so hard in that community.

I might well have expected a similar disturbance when my deacons approved a monthly healing service. At the time of the intercession, we invited anyone with health issues to come to the altar rail to be anointed with prayer. Not having a memorable history of public use, this might have caused a stir. Its happy acceptance surely was a thing of the Spirit for so immediately and broadly being appreciated -- just the sort of wholesome unifying spirit that was so desperately needed at Zion's.

Our 1995 three week Summer vacation on the North Shore was again used for the second stage of cabin reconstruction. Even though we entertained a parade of visiting family and friends interested to see our beautiful Lake Superior property, one can hardly believe that Addie and I tore down to the first floor level the entire front half of the old 1935 cabin and rebuilt it new in the rough with dormers above a tall cathedral ceiling. That brought in beautiful light into the living room. It was a very hot few weeks; Working nearly naked, fully exposed to the nearby highway, we sweated it out with not a day to spare. I still shudder to have in mind our joint work of shingling the roof. I had to carry 90lb bundles of asphalt shingles up a ladder. Addie handed the shingles to me on the steep roof from inside through the sides of the incomplete dormers. Addie had also helped with the deconstruction, disposing of the debris which I made by smashing things apart with a splitting maul. She made quite a pile in our front yard. That pile had to wait till the following Summer when I dragged it further away for a giant bonfire. (This attracted the police and fire department who had not been informed of our fire permit by the permit agent.)

After returning to Pershing, I harvested 12 gallons of honey, selling it through the Medicine Shopp for a $200 gift to the local food pantry. There was moderate peace at Zion's during this time, but the annual meeting gave

321

evidence of the continuing unrest from background agitators. A static salary had been included in a budget submitted by the council. When a motion to raise my salary was defeated, it prompted a saint to visit us the following morning at the parsonage with two crisp $100 bills. It was encouraging that I wasn't serving without many prayers, and there was much appreciation nonetheless.

In 1996 there was increased conversation about the coming 175th anniversary of the congregation. I chose not to become directly involved since it was in capable hands and most of the planing was about physical preparations, things that didn't much interest me. Instead, I contributed significantly by what I was uniquely capable of doing. I did know how to do research into the history of the congregation, beyond talking to older members, which I did as well.

There were only a few newspaper reports from earlier anniversaries and a partial log of pastors with no biographical notes. I was able to correct and add considerably by connecting with the synod historical society library and office at Trinity Seminary in Columbus OH. They had all the stuff related to Zion's early history since we had branched out from Ohio. It became a passion once I became aware about more of the internal struggles and controversies Zion's had experienced. I was finding a history of a pattern that compared with the current unrest. I spent many days and hours there freely gathering whatever pertained to Zion's. I eventually published a 98 page book in time for the 1997 celebration and dedicated it to Pastor Isensee. He was a tragic casualty of the controversy in his time in the mid 1800s connected to the "Second Great Awakening." That was a revival movement arising out of frontier Methodism. His health was thereby broken and he was buried in Zion's cemetery. I thereafter began to pay regular devotion at his tomb when strolling the cemetery to excise my dog and cat.

By 1996 the patriarchal families had for several years retreated to the shadows or altogether left, not meaning that they were pacified nor quiet. Twice, I was then again accosted at church and angrily lectured by individuals connected to the old principal families. It was as always about trivial issues, and to the point of emphasizing that the pastor was hired help, subject to the congregation. Many simply couldn't even begin to see the pastor as being sent by God to do this work of the Gospel, and to be respected for inspired spiritual leadership. The first one was painful since she had from the start stood up for every-Sunday communion. I simply let her vent and said nothing. She has never apologized; I wait in hope. But the second was by the one remaining old befuddled one of the original three. He raved with crude bluster about my lack of obedience. I couldn't resist telling him he could no longer come to communion for his anger and disrespect, knowing however that I couldn't make the excommunication stick in public. It would have raised the forces of hell, not worth the fight. I never even discussed it with the deacons, though I should have. I bound it over to the Spirit and judgment day. He even kept coming to communion, even every Sunday. I fed him, and he will be answering for himself.

Apparently a few continued to lobby the synod for my removal. Apparently, the bishop had had enough. Surely he by now knew the substance of the matter; He knew even before I became Zion's pastor. He must have wanted finalization with supporting documentation. So he sent a crew of three pastors who conducted two days of interviews at church. Members were free to come and complain about whatever. His assistant came for an evening congregational meeting at the end of the second day. In a filled parish hall, he announced a stunning vindication: "We have often reassigned your pastors at your request. We are not doing so again. Pastor Lehrke will stay with our blessing." I was of course relieved, but subconsciously also angry for needing to struggle alone for five years to reform a parish for the bishop.

Our three week vacation on the North Shore in June of that year called for the final and third stage of basic reconstruction of the cabin -- the back half. I had been forced at the end of the previous Summer to temporally sheet-over the disjointed height of the gable from the new front half of the house and the old lower one of the back half. Fortunately, the rolled roofing patch had held through the Winter. Now we then needed to completely destroy the whole back half of the cabin down to the floor. We even added five feet of depth of new construction, again over temporary supports. We didn't want to make proper footings and foundation since the house was slated to be moved further away from the highway once the MN DOT was ready for its reconstruction.

Addie and I struggled with a hand post-hole tool in hard clay and stony ground to make those temporary concrete support piles. Finally help arrived for what we knew was too-big-a-job for just the two of us. Addie's friend's unemployed husband came with his vacation trailer for the final two weeks, though he ate his meals with us. And brother Walter came with his construction know-how for almost a week. By that time we had the deconstruction nearly done. Once the 17x27 new construction area was cleared and ready, we built up two stories and topped this with trusses that we winched up by hand and sheeted the roof. I knew we didn't have time to shingle, so I hired a local handyman as a roofer. We managed yet to install all the windows, except those in the south facing two-story solar. I felt duty bound to return to IN on time to avoid complaints. Instead, I came back in midweek in October to cover the new solar with plastic sheeting. (The proper windows were installed the following Summer.) What a job that all was! Too big for one Summer's vacation time, but it was of one piece, and needed to fit into those three weeks.

That's when the writing of Zion's history began in earnest, but I had till Fall of the next year, 1997. I was able to find a photo for all of the 41 Pastors except for 13 . The bios were in some cases brief, but I was certain of the accuracy and completeness of the list and details. I had been

324

disappointed on arriving in Pershing that there were few members with which to sit down and hear the history of the congregation and community. The only one who gave some help was handicapped for having only relatively recently moved back into the community of his youth. But then, the early history was from so long ago. Unfortunately, Zion's history records were almost nothing. Without the synod archives, and the book I was glad to prepare from there, the 175th anniversary would have been a good party, but hardly a proper anniversary. I gave the congregation a history and an identity that it had not known. With it they acquired dignity via the opportunity for repentance, which it must have inspired. It dramatically served to set aside those who had coopted leadership, by which they could surmount their immediate soulless struggle.

That year leading up to our celebration was relatively peaceful at Zion's. But Addie was really struggling with depression; forgiveness for all the never ending pain was hard for her. She was almost irreparably broken. I subconsciously sensed a need for us to leave Pershing. Better anyway for another pastor to hopefully make a fresh start on the strength of the new more evangelical leaders now firmly and properly in place. But though I was at near retirement age, my probable pension plus savings made it impossible to retire. So on the whim of the Spirit I stopped in at the NE MN synod office when driving back up to the North Shore for our 1997 Summer vacation. "Was there a possibility of a pastoral call back to MN?" I was immediately informed of the situation at Finland MN, near in fact to our cabin. They were preparing to call a pastor. "Are you interested?" Well, why not? So the synod quickly arranged for me it interview there, yet within the time of our vacation. It seemed a welcome fit, though the probable salary was admittedly only somewhat better than basic.

Our vacation that year was more leisurely. Finally after three years we didn't need to be concerned with having a roof open over our heads. About the only thing I did was instal the 28 windows in the two story solar. Everywhere we looked in the house we saw the need for sheetrock on the exposed stud walls and ceiling. But there was no deadline, and patience was easy as we made plans. It felt like we were already victorious. So, refreshed and having the possibility of a new call to ministry, we trudged back to Pershing, silently announcing to them, "We know something you don't!" That Finland call became official on the very day of Zion's 175th anniversary celebration, Nov. 9th. Our IN bishop was attending, but we chose not to tell even him, nor the congregation. Let's first celebrate, each in their own way.

How could we not already even on that day feel even more inclined to accept the Finland MN call because of being accosted at the close of the festival by a previous protesting member as people were already leaving the celebration. She and her husband had transferred membership to a church in Richmond in the early stage of Zion's conflict. Her complaint was regarding her grandson, whom I had given private catechism instruction for his failure to join a catechism class at the normal maturity. His family were still members, but never attended church. He had some time before been killed in a farm accident. I hadn't even been notified of it. The family instead contacted a former pastor of Zion's living 50 miles away in Indianapolis. He did a private funeral for them. This grandmother was still angry with me for not serving the family in that grief. I should properly have lodged a complaint with the bishop for that other pastor's pastoral interference, but I didn't. As I already stated, forgiveness was so hard in that community. *O Father, forgive those who didn't intend what they have done.*

Chapter 30 – Zions - Finland MN - 1997

The move from Pershing IN to Finland MN was a do-it-yourself project. The poverty of the Finland church was quite plain and inspired empathy. Fortunately, there was then a U-Haul dealer at our interchange with I-70, three miles away. There we rented a truck that seemed large enough. Addie was dreaming of possibly driving it to MN, so I let her drive it back to the parsonage. That short drive shattered her dream – it was not like driving a car. She did manage, but turning corners with its very different steering was no fun for her. Rather, she gladly drove the Pontiac Grand Am with August, our cairn terrier; I drove the truck with Wunderlein, our cat in a kennel – for fear of her slipping out on me.

The truck, however, wasn't large enough, so after we filled it, we had to also rent a trailer to tow behind the truck. (How did we by ourselves manage to load the heavy bedroom and office furniture from upstairs? There were no offers to help.) Unfortunately, the truck was older and under-powered. Besides, on the way, it lost a breather contraption for the engine oil, so that it was spewing and loosing oil. I lost several hours sitting in a parking lot waiting for them send repair service, anxious for the lack of a cell to stay in touch with Addie. It wasn't really possible to stay in sight of each other. We managed as planned to go only as far as Janesville WI that first day. The second day we drove to Oakdale MN to drop off a few things at our house rented as a retreat. We stayed there overnight. The next leg was up to the North Shore where we stayed the night in our cabin and dropped off some more things, including my bee hive. The cabin wasn't yet suitable to live in fulltime.

So the next morning we called the contact person at Finland who had already arranged for good and happy help with unloading the truck at the parsonage next door to Zions church. It was a three bedroom home with two full baths on one level, and a two car garage tucked under on the downhill side. We considered it a comfortable arrangement awaiting the finishing of our cabin seven miles down the hill at the Lake.

We had arrived slightly before Thanksgiving Day. The leading Nicolai family very graciously invited us to spend the day with their extended family for a traditional dinner, having had a service at Zions on the eve before. It was an enjoyable time for us. We found these families pleasant, though a typically sober bunch of Finns. Such also were most others in the community. It was a reassuring celebration which provided hope in this situation of again having a patriarchal family with primary responsibility for most things at church, both in physical and organizational matters. But here there was humility.

Finland is a community of mostly Finns who, starting in the 1870s, had settled a broad valley inland from the coastal ridge of the Sawtooth mountains along the shore of Lake Superior, 60 miles up NE from the tip of the lake at Duluth. They were anti government, including especially the DNR. This was consistent with their reactionary polity from Finland. Actually both church and US government had basically ignored them till well into the 20th century. And there still was a noticeable hostility for the lack of support during the Great Depression. No church of any denomination had been interested in their existence till the 1950s when an early warning radar station was built on a mountain another five miles to the north. The influx of service men, many with their families, finally moved the American Lutheran Church synod to organize a congregation and build a church. But one couldn't say that the Finns then gladly flocked to the church. Yet there were enough of them who joined so that when these service families left when the air base was closed after the Cold War, their church property having been paid off by then, they were on a thin budget able to keep the church going. This even with a supposedly full-time pastor -- salary was however no where near the standard level.

328

Zions had no problem with my firm statement at my call interview that I would be celebrating communion every Sunday. In fact there was no reluctance although they were having only a once per month Communion. That is, except for an infrequently attending non member who was ignored. It didn't even come to my attention till some time later when a shutin I normally visited told me of this friend of hers and his objection. Likewise, I was quickly able to assemble a crew of three deacons, all women, and this readily approved by the council, whose chairman had a welcome seat on the church council. These three, plus Addie, took turns being my liturgical deacon at the altar each Sunday. These deacons took on all the worship and member related issues.

But therewith, I did have a short anxious time. The husband of the organist had been on the call committee, and so I had asked him to consider my call to be a deacon. He seemed stable and qualified, but he was reluctant, apparently wanting to weigh his standing in the congregation. When mentioning this tentative choice of mine to the already sitting deacons, they were all aggressively against him being seated, but unwilling to explain. I never did find out their reason, though it probably involved occasional drunkenness, of which they knew only secondhand – there was a temperance element in the community. Some months later with smooth progress, I explained to him that we were doing fine with the three deacons who were serving. He was notably dejected, probably feeling rejected. But I had no difficulty retaining his favor. He was however never elected to the council. He lived in a small community 15 miles north, an independent pulp wood farmer, as were many men in this forested part of MN.

We quickly settled into a happy congregation of serious worshiping Christians, not filling our pews for about 125, except for Holy days, but consistently had around 75 attending. We also introduced a much appreciated monthly rite of healing. We thereby didn't heal our much loved MS member from her physical infirmity, but she also never lost heart that we stood with her in the Spirit.

The confirmation or catechism classes were the only dreaded part of my ministry at Finland. Right from the start, I had a boy who was incorrigibly disruptive. After a month I had no choice but to expel him in mid-class till his parents would come with him to talk. These had never attended church and had no interest. They never did come, and he never returned to the relief of the whole class. He had been enrolled by the initiative of his grandmother member. She was then upset with me that this family was now supposedly lost. But the sad fact was that they and none of her other children's families cared at all about attending the church, and her own husband was an agnostic, whom I couldn't even engage in conversation.

I attributed such disinterest, which was quite common in the community, to the failure of the Lutheran synods to have had any earlier interest in starting a mission. These Finns had been living there out of reach of a church for 75 years; And if their hearts had been warm before immigrating to MN, they were in many cases now callously cold. Most in the community did attend funerals of relatives and friends when held in church, but they never showed up even for the Holy days; And when I visited them in their homes to invite them, I sensed I was bothering them. Even when I'd connect with such, as with one of their shutin elderly, the prospect of death didn't inspire them to any more than matter-of-fact hospitality.

One such case was slightly better. This particular family was still on the membership rolls (only index cards which I was carefully grooming). I found this family, in their 70s, some 20 miles north on the highway to Ely. They had not attended church in a long time. None of the deacons even remembered them. They were desperately caring for a bedfast grandson in his late teens who had CP with the mind of a one-year-old. They were needing to take turns staying awake through the night to care for him. I went home to explain this situation to Addie who thought she could help. She began serving there immediately, at first by grace. But we then got them connected to a company of nurses serving such persons not normally hospitalized, but needing nursing care in the home on a daily or continuous schedule. For multiple years Addie then had this as a regular night-nurse job, being paid by Interim Health Care which related to the county for reimbursement. And she was very good and happy at it, also relating well to the grandparents, to whom I also then gave regular pastoral care with communion as one of my monthly shutin visitations.

That relationship between Addie and that Aldinger family is how it was that she wrecked Karl's Honda the following year. We had at first left it behind in Pershing IN in a member garage. She was now driving it to work at night on this wilderness highway after my 86 Pontiac hatchback had been exchanged for it. (At 12 years old, my little Pontiac was so badly rusted that I could no longer find a place to use a jack to change a tire -- June had had an accident with it years before. So I dared to drive it back to Pershing IN to a junk yard, and retrieve Karl's Honda. Living in Manhattan, he no longer had need for it. So we bought it from him.)

On her way to Aldinger's in the dark, along a deserted highway and miles from any habitations, she hit the rear end of a moose with the right front of the Honda. Being tall, this 1000 lb. bull was lifted over the hood and crashed into the windshield on the passenger side and thrown off into the ditch; All this at about 50 mph (their color makes them invisible in the dark of night). She missed the devil-of-death by inches -- for not striking the animal fully broadside. She called me on her cell and I called the highway patrol, getting there before they did. The moose was still alive. The officer killed it and called someone on his list who got it to the butcher in Finland.

The Honda was still derivable but without a windshield; It had moose stuff throughout the car. I drove it to and left it at Aldinger's for a few days as Addie drove there in my car.

331

I then borrowed a snowmobile helmet a few days later and drove it home. After making arrangements, I drove it on to the collision repair company where it was mostly repaired with the insurance total loss money. (Eventually, Addie had an accident a few years later, totaling it a second time – falling asleep on her way home after a night of working at a nursing home in Two Harbors.)

Working through Zions membership list involved creating proper computerized membership records. (We had already in Pershing been able to purchased church computer software for this, and left our work well tended; But not being understood, it was abandoned and lost.) The church membership record system at Finland had been a 3x5 card file. I had a secretary to prepare the Sunday worship folder, but she wasn't able to learn the membership software. (A few years later, the next church secretary did manage the membership records and kept them in good order. This served well, but all that work was eventually lost when, after my retirement, Zions church burnt down from a lightning strike. The computer and all records were lost. By then I had purged my own computer of those records.)

As a child, I had witnessed the celebration of the 40th anniversary of the ordination of several pastors. That significant milestone, normally also coinciding with retirement, had always been in the back of my mind. However, my 40th in August of 1998 was only a year after beginning a new pastorate; It was unreasonable to consider that anniversary the time for my retirement. Yet it seemed necessary to celebrate it; The future might possibly deprive me of another opportunity. Zions was obliging, inviting the bishop's assistant to come and preach. And they prepared a festive dinner to follow worship. Somehow they quietly gathered a few of my friends, including a U of MN dorm roommate who was an MD in northern MN. And all three of my children made a non-obligatory trip to come and smile with me. Janet even commissioned an artist to draw a framed sketching of the buildings of the five congregations I had served: Holy Trinity, Luseland Sask..; Messiah,

Elmhurst IL; Holy Spirit, Oakdale MN; Zion's, Pershing IN; and Zions, Finland MN.

That Summer we had been able to live at our Lake Superior cabin, returning to the parsonage for the Winter. The cabin with an ancient oil furnace was not yet quite ready to be a home. But in my days off, I had been able to make it an enjoyable retreat for the Summer. Addie in particular was relieved not to have the church five feet from our back door.

1999 continued to be somewhat uneventful. Church work went ahead peacefully. I prayed, worked and studied at church every morning Tuesday through Saturday; Then making calls on shutins etc. in the p.m.. My secretary came for several hours each week, relieving me of much office work. The church had no lock or keys, so people came to or pray at nearly any time. Our leading member, who was a supervisor at the taconite plant, came after hours or Saturdays to do most of the mechanical maintenance. The complicated and fussy furnace was not understood by anyone else.

He also helped with my project to install plumbing in the sacristy, both water and sewer. I bought a double kitchen sink with cabinet -- one sink was plumed to the sewer, and the other to the ground for cleansing holy vessels. In a congregation that had had a very low-church practice, the generous sacristy had only been a clutter of storage. I installed cabinets for sacred vessels and supplies. We began a very traditional worship and practice, including crucifix led processions every Sunday, properly vested liturgical deacons and acolytes, etc., at every worship and with much pleasure. Particularly, there arose a deep appreciation of the sacrament of Holy Communion regardless of only having had it celebrated once per month. For its distribution, we made large standing circles up and around the altar, including wheelchairs below the steps. It had quickly become a deeply sacred time.

During the first Winter in Finland I lost my bees being kept at the cabin, because the race I had brought from IN wasn't hardy enough for northern MN. After research, I purchased the better breed of Carniolan. I placed them in an electric fence behind the parsonage since we knew of often having roaming bears through the village at night. To have them with me at the cabin for the Summer that next year, I had tried to move them one day to the lake, but then couldn't because the weather turned sour. I'd however turned off the electric fence and forgot to turn it back on. That next night a bear waiting his chance, struck. He or she totally destroyed the two hives, bees, frames and boxes. Thus I had a too-late restart with bees that year to have a harvest. Thereafter I kept them at the cabin by the lake without problems, but always was careful to have an electric fence.

The work of finishing our cabin went on successfully using my days off. I did most all the work myself, all except the sheetrock. I could have done it, but hated it intensely. Actually, I was not equipped to do cathedral ceilings, nor any other ceilings by myself. Fortunately, Finland had a good father and sons company for that. In my basement shop I made all the trim using 1x4 Douglas fir floor boards with the grooves removed. It was also used for a floor upstairs. In addition I was fortunate to find a supply of traditional maple flooring to match the partially existing first floor. The baths and entry floors were finished with ceramic. So by May of 1999 we were happy to move in once more until late October when we again returned to the parsonage in Finland because of the old furnace.

Meanwhile, we knew that ALPB was finally at work on publishing my first book of liturgical theology. They had promised to do it more than five years earlier, but for a backlog of other publishing they repeatedly asked for patience. They chose the title: *Prayers for the Eucharistic Gathering.* It included a complete set of the traditional prayers for the Sunday worship for the entire church year. These I'd done in the 80s. However the first half of the book presented the full text of my master of theology thesis

334

from 1990 at Luther Seminary. This had traced the history of the origin of the First Prayer of the Sunday liturgy starting in the third century. My graduate advisor, Dr. Carl Volz, had been so pleased with it that he had strongly urged me to get it published – an excellence seldom achieved with work done at the masters level.

Therefore that next January I finally saw the many years of my work and study in the form of a book. I had not really seriously imagined such an accomplishment. I had dreamt without steadfast hope. I was so proud of it that I sent a copy to my undergraduate seminary professor of liturgy, Dr. Fred Precht, who by then had left the seminary to work at CPH. There he was in charge of the new hymnal for LCMS. Shortly thereafter he telephoned me one morning at church in Finland. I had not seen or spoken to him in 42 years; But he remembered me well, partly from being in his seminary choir for three years. He was embarrassingly full of praise for my book, obviously proud that one of his students was succeeding in his own field of study.

That Summer of 2000 we made a permanent move to our cabin, thereafter having difficulty for some time in referring to it as a house, which by then it was. (Zions then rented out the parsonage.) We had gone deeply into credit card debt to make it a house and home. We really didn't have much of a choice, since retirement was scheduled for the following year; That was where we would have to live. The solar house I had built in Oakdale, which was being rented as a retreat home, was a possible home for us, but we were in love with the North Shore. The anticipated settlement with the MN DOT when reconstructing Hwy. 61 was trusted to eventually retire the credit card debt. We were assured that when they were ready to reconstruct the highway past our cabin, there would be a reasonable buyout to pay the costs we had assumed in making the cabin a home. This financial juggling made me nervous since my projected retirement income was a paltry sum. We were hoping to make it by in spartan style, plus Addie working yet a while as an LPN.

Our vacation that Summer didn't need to be used working on the house since it was already reasonably finished. So we elected to visit my first parish in Luseland SK. They were celebrating their 90th anniversary. Addie, who had not ever been to Canada, was interested in seeing where I started my ministry. It proved to be a major disappointment to me, except for our Canadian mountain excursion in the weeks that followed. The church in Luseland was currently vacant, but their previous pastor returned as promised to lead the celebration. They had built a new church which was a joy to experience. But the pastor ignored all of us previous pastors in attendance. There was even no festive procession. We pastors and wives just sat together in a front pew; And then we also stood or sat around in the parish hall at the festive dinner, with but a brief chance to introduce ourselves. It had not been like earlier anniversaries, nor as was appropriate.

I had brought vestments but the pastors were not vested. Previously we had processed and done parts of the worship, and had been hosted by willing families. We were rather given the name of their new motel in town, to make our own arrangements. I did enjoy the brief chance to greet a few I well remembered, particularly those who had been teens forty years earlier. One still single middle aged wealthy farmer stopped yet at our motel the next morning to say goodbye. He lived 25 miles west of town. His mother was the daughter of one of the pastors who served Luseland in the 1930s. That family was as faithful and pious as they come.

Thereafter we headed west across the harvest-ready prairies to the mountains, I intending to camp in our tent, but that never happened. Addie was apparently done with that style. We crossed into AB to see the Banff park area and on into BC. Eventually, we reentered the US through the Montana Sweetwater portal where we had a major hassle. Declaring that we had purchased nothing of consequence in Canada, they tore into our full trunk and found two Christmass tree ornaments which became a "criminal" issue. We were ejected from the car to wait inside the station. After a full hour of their not finding anything more, we were soundly lectured. I seethed all the way home and lodged an official complaint by telephone with an upper level supervisor. I had some satisfaction when hearing of his own dissatisfaction with that entry portal.

Chapter 31 – Retirement & House Moving - 2001

Addie was my liturgical deacon on June 24, 2001, my last Sunday before retirement. As always, she read the first lessons with polish and spirit and reverently administered the cup at Communion. She always served like an angel. In fact all three regular deacons had also been the most reverent and best I could expect. For the sake of our emotions, it was good that we were no longer living in the parsonage, and could simply drive away from Zions, Finland MN after that service. We could more easily let be what I would no longer direct. My watch there had ended, while the future of things, as it seemed to me on that day of retirement, and now still are, made me sad for the sake of the love I had for these Finns.

Living in the parsonage was a renter whose wife had joined him from PA. She had recently resigned her ministry in a parish of the Church of Christ denomination which had joined into fellowship with the ELCA. Consequently, Zions immediately "hired" that available "bird-in-the-hand" to be their new pastor without call. Not all things Lutheran could be predicted to soon be undone, at least not every-Sunday communion. That would hold throughout her two year pastorate. After that, a two-point Lutheran parish with another congregation further up the Shore was arranged. Nevertheless, the door had thereby been opened to a more liberal theology and practice which would eventually lead to a split of Zions' congregation, Thus it would no longer be a viable congregation (which is as things stand today). Not withstanding, they were able to rebuild their building with the insurance money after it was struck by lightening and burned down.

Addie and I struggled for several months to find a church to attend after I retired. We finally found two that were comfortable to both of us. Addie liked French River Lutheran and decided to join there. I preferred the better liturgical fare at Pilgrim Lutheran in Superior WI, where I joined. Therefore we began alternating between these two.

With both of them, I quickly became a pinch-hitting pastor on a fairly regular basis; I did this only because I had gotten to know and love many people in these congregations and could therefore better relate as a preacher. It was a colder feeling when preaching elsewhere, so I decided not to accept such invitations any longer. I was busy enough as was.

My goal for 2001 was to build a garage before Winter, which most especially was to finally include a shop for my woodworking. However, it was difficult to find a crew after getting a permit. Everyone was too busy to help that Summer. I was finally promised help from people I had gotten to know in the Finland congregation. But after my excavator dug footings, we couldn't get a concrete crew on site till September. We were desperately hanging on against the clock of Winter. We were building forms for the footings, when on Sept. 11th the crew's radio announced the attack on the Trade Towers in NY and the Pentagon.

That added a new anxiety for my having planned to drive out east the following week to MD for a retreat of a new order of Lutheran pastors, STS (Latin acronym for Society of the Holy Trinity). I was planning to join now that I was retired and need not justify or explain this to a church council. I went regardless of the national restlessness. My construction crew was judged to be able to get along without me.

That STS retreat was like homecoming to a home I had never even felt or known. Pastoral conference meetings are supposed to be like a home, a time of refreshment with others of like mind. But mostly such are just plain church work. This religious order was rather about worship and spiritual fellowship for mutual encouragement with our ordination vows. I felt especially embraced because many of the then 60 pastor members of this two year old society already knew me by name from already having and using my book of Eucharistic prayers. They admitted to using it in their congregation's worship, and with deep appreciation. I almost could have cried meeting in person my editor who proudly introduced me to many others. I met dozens of pastors from across this country and Canada who immediately became friends. Mostly we prayed the six offices of daily prayer and engaged each other about our dreams in Christ for his church. One almost didn't want the retreat to end.

Once the footings and concrete floors for the new garage were finished, involving a lower split level to the rear towards the Lake for the shop, it was my own carpentry project. I worked mostly alone with August our terrier supervising, and Addie occasionally helping to lift such things as trusses up onto the walls. That 24x36 structure kept me racing the clock. Finally by a week before Thanksgiving it was ready for the steel roof. That work was more than was possible by myself, and Addie was not able to work with 3x16 foot sheets of steel. I took up the offer of a saintly couple from Finland to help install that roofing. After making a pattern for Shirley to drill the holes for the screws on the garage floor several sheets at a time, Kenny worked from a ladder at the eves while I walked the roof securing the sheeting with screws. We were relieved to beat Winter and even get to St. Louis in time for a Thanksgiving celebration with Philip and Anna.

My attending the retreat and joining the Society of the Holy Trinity (STS) the previous September, with its many endorsements of my book of Eucharistic prayers, got me to consider how I might get these prayers into use in even more churches. So in 2002 I got a list of email addresses of all the members of STS. And besides I advertised what I was offering in international church newsletters. I would prepare an every-Sunday four-page church bulletin insert, called *Word for Today* including my Eucharistic prayers and the assigned scripture lessons. At first I added a meditation on the First Prayer, but was soon inspired to begin a seven year project of meditations on the art of prayer. With preparing one such meditation per week it would take seven years to total the 365 needed for an almanac. (These meditations were then extracted in 2010

340

and published by Amazon as a skeleton breviary in an almanac format, *Lord Teach us to Pray*. Just this year of 2019 a third edition was issued by Amazon, this time also in a 670 page paperback. A final two volume 4th edition followed in 2020.)

I felt confident, based on my years of ministry, that I was qualified for this, even to teach pastors about prayer. After all, I had done significant graduate seminary and personal study in this discipline during my entire ministry. But it had been a true piece of work which had taken many hours each week, often a whole morning for the first draft of a lesson on prayer. But I was retired, and so had the time. Even more so, I owed the church what had become my gift from the Spirit. Just to be more sure of myself, I was able to get oversight from a well trusted and gifted pastor friend to check these one page meditations for clarity and propriety. She got a month's bunch at a time, and then I sent these worship resources on via email to those who had subscribed. In no time I had a hundred subscribers from the US, Canada, even Australia. By the end of seven years of such email publication, without further publicity, my subscribers mounted to way over 250, growing by word of the users. It was a joy to consider the multiplication by 250 times of the Sunday attendance in those churches. By 2010, I converted all of that work, minus the meditations, onto a CD which I then sold for a song, and am still regularly giving away to interested young pastors as they begin ministry. All this for the joy of providing good prayers for countless Christian worshipers. (That CD is still available.)

We felt settled enough to take a Winter vacation in March of 2002 to the far southern tip of Texas. Unfortunately, our brand new Pontiac Grand Am, unlike our old one, no longer sported a drivers seat with adjustable back rest; Thus for not using a lumbar pillow on that long trip, my back came seriously out of joint. It thoroughly crimped my enjoyment, needing repeated chiropractic help. We returned to MN via St. Louis.

Thereafter, Addie applied for an LPN night shift position at the Silver Bay Veterans Home. However, the purely pill-pushing duty was not to her liking. She had served many years in nursing homes enjoying the interaction with the assorted handicapped patients. Consequently, she was let go for not expeditiously doing her rounds, spending too much time consoling patients. So she applied for a similar position at the nursing home connected with the hospital in Two Harbors, 28 miles back SW. Things went along better for her at that home, even though she was there also regularly falling behind with pushing pills for the same reason. As you may know, her light hearted and smart humor personality made her a perfect nurse from a patient perspective. (Even now as a patient herself, she has the skill of lighting up the nursing staff. It's her gift, but not one much in demand in today's medical facilities.) This gift was exactly what was then to get her fired at Two Harbors MN in 2003. (That is, after she totaled Karl's Honda, falling asleep one morning on the way home after a night at work.)

She had encountered a female janitor making a lot of noise at night with a metal pail. In fun Addie scolded her for waking up her patients. But it was taken as a verbal assault and a complaint against Addie was filed. She was suspended for two weeks while an investigation was made, after which she was dismissed. A truly sad ending of a gifted career in nursing. I didn't have the heart to allow her to look for another similar job, considering what nursing had become. So she was welcomed into retirement and then was able to qualify for SS disability benefits.

In May of 2002, we were able to sell the solar home I had built in Oakdale MN in 1979. It was a long ordeal. For the sake of very high property taxes, I had trusted this nonprofit religious retreat facility (RC affiliated) with the title to the property. They cared for the property well enough. But the resident manager got it in mind that I personally owed him some compensation for that -- a portion of the sale. And their board stood by him and started a series of negotiations. I finally contacted their

342

supervising sister who ran another of their facilities in AZ and explained the situation. Fortunately she immediately gave orders for them to desist. But still the managing board insisted on listing the property as if they actually owned it, instead of simply transferring the title back to me. Possibly they were afraid of county repercussion when learning of "fraudulent" ownership, with they then owing a hefty back-tax. Eventually, it was fairly listed and sold. I also received the full sale price. (Several years later I stopped to knock on the door of the new owners. They were overjoyed to meet me. They had unsuccessfully attempted to get in touch, for no other reason except to thank me for building a house they had come to love. They wanted me to know of their great pleasure of living in that house. On another later visit they assured me that though they were soon to retire and move, their son was claiming the house for his family for like appreciation.)

It was about this time that Addie and I began a most enjoyable regular Saturday night canasta card party with Gary and Mary Nelson, alternating between our place and theirs up near Finland. Gary was a shark, playing with me as a regular partner, never allowing the ladies to win, which they too seldom did. They had been members at Zions Finland. Without abandoning our previous pastor / member relationship, all four of us were very compatible. We thoroughly enjoyed each other as lively Christians. Too seldom are two visiting couples so well matched with another set, each with the other three. They had stopped attending Zions after I retired and eventually moved and joined a Covenant church in Duluth. Gary has since died after many years of battling leukemia during which I served him faithfully.

That November, after several colonoscopies in which my doctor thought he saw a suspicious spot, I was scheduled for surgery. But even with another colonoscopy an hour before the surgery to mark the spot, my very skilled surgeon couldn't find the offending spot. For almost an hour he sorted through my colon, fearing meanwhile for resulting trauma. He finally found and removed a six inch section. It didn't then even look suspicious to him. A day or so later the biopsy came back positive for colon cancer. He was immensely relieved that the ordeal he put me through was not in vain. Fortunately, I recovered without too much difficulty.

Every year we had been hoping for MN DOT to find the money to reconstruct MN highway 61 past our home. We knew about that plan already when we bought in 1990. We also knew it would entail moving our house away from the highway, all of it our own responsibility to arrange. They would pay us for its value and that of the additional land they would be taking. So we were long in suspense, occasionally checking and being told, "not yet." Finally, they got the appropriation for that work to be done in 2004.

Meanwhile, I was working at finishing our guest suite above the shop on the lake side of the garage we had built in 2001. That was where we would have to live during the moving of the house. It was itself a gift we had not planned. When excavating for that building, intended to be only a garage and shop, the slope towards the lake taken down to the bed rock was such that the shop floor needed to be almost six feet lower than the garage. With a common roof, that left an attic the height of a full story above the shop. Thus it was decided to finish this attic, not just for storage, but as a guest suite. It was snug, but we had a full bath, a bedroom large enough for bunk beds and a generous kitchen and living area. I did my best work on this project and was quite happy with the result. My insurance agent remarked that he paid $200 a night for such accommodations on the North Shore.

Also in 2003 we went ahead with drilling a new well since our old one was on what would be the new highway ROW. In preparation our driller and I separately witched for water, meeting only three feet apart via different tools. So he set up there and drilled to 250 feet without finding more than a trickle. His solution was fracking the hole. A bladder was lowered to the 200 foot depth, then capped and filled

344

with water under high pressure. It held securely for about 20 minutes and then gave way, the pressure falling dramatically. When uncapped, the water ran out over the top for a half hour before it quit. When a pump was installed 180 feet down, they couldn't pump it dry. It yielded eight gallons per minute without failing. Unfortunately, the water had a slight calcium chloride taste (not sodium chloride -- salt), impossible to use to make coffee, yet safe and good to drink and wash. Our old well had been similar. So we would need to continue to get water for coffee from Tetaguchee, the state park next door.

I also used that year to finish and insulate my shop and garage. I had a propane wall furnace installed for year round use of the shop. Without heat, the garage then never dropped below the mid 20s even in long sub zero weather. What a joy it was to finally have that shop after 40 years of woodworking -- a real shop with generous space. I already had most all the tools I wanted, just never knowing where they were all tucked and scrambled. Now I would finally be able to build Addie's grandfather clock out of the cherry I'd gotten and partially cut already down in IN. (That was my first new project in the shop during the year of 2004. It turned out to be my most admired clock of now ten. Even now in Addie's nursing home, where it now stands, she regularly compliments me, and gets many compliments. Always a tease, she has frequently asked me "Where did that nice grandfather clock come from?"

That Summer of 2003 it was also time to get the area ready to which the house would need to be moved prior to the highway reconstruction. This was an area the length of a football field down the hill towards the lake, forested with birch, fir and aspen. A few trees were as big as my 14" chainsaw could bite. I was proud of making most every tree fall in a chosen direction. As I felled each tree, I de-limbed it and piled up the brush out of the way to be later burned. I cut the tree trunks into firewood sections, but left these lie till all trees were down in an area larger than a basketball court. Then came the heavy work of splitting, right there

345

where they had grown. But I had no good place other than there to make a wood pile -- the wood shed was already full. Unfortunately this was down the hill from the house from which it would be a pain to bring up that Winter on a sled. I tarped a pile of more than two cords – a cord being 4x4x8 feet. (A year or two before, I had built a 12x12x10' tall woodshed, large enough for four cords, with a steel roof, all out of free slab wood from a sawmill near the airport.)

2004 was an anxious time of scheduling and executing the moving of the house. (Meanwhile, I was building Addie's clock in the shop.) I had found a skilled house mover from Duluth to take the place of a Silver Bay contractor whose bad reputation was legendary. This man could have come a year earlier when he had first come to survey our project, but now wouldn't have time till October – late, but it would have to do. The real frustration was scheduling the construction of footings and concrete walls onto which the house was to be moved. The preferred crew for this was being delayed by their current project which was encountering major problems. And I couldn't find another crew. Besides, they were highly skilled and trusted. It wasn't till well into August that the excavator dared come to dig for the footings. With this there appeared a problem of too quickly hitting bedrock. At that shallow level, the house would either stand too high, or the upper end of the basement would be less than a full story. The solution was to site the house further down the slope toward the lake by another ten feet. (With the house then built on this bedrock, while having a fierce storm on the lake with towering waves pounding down on the beach, we were able not only to hear but to feel the vibration when standing on the floor in the lower level; This, although the shore was 500 feet away and 400 feet lower.)

The concrete and building crew was then finally able to arrive in September. Prior to that, I repeatedly had to pump out the rainwater from the excavation during that very wet Fall. The crew used a concrete pump once the forms for the footings were finished. With that we had a near tragedy. We had excess concrete for the job. In anticipation, I had made forms ready for a cement pad out the back of my shop door. This would be "No problem!" With the pumper truck still standing above the site, the operator could by remote control lift the boom-hose above the small forest of forty foot tall fir trees between the site and the back of the shop more than 100 feet away. When that form was filed, the workman having just let go of the hose, the concrete boom touched the 15K power line above. There was a huge explosion as high voltage jumped through the truck, over the rim of the truck wheel, and to the ground; It blew out one truck tire. Otherwise the work went well. They crew then built forms for the basement walls out of Styrofoam units. A concrete pump truck was once again brought to fill the foam forms for the walls, and still again to pour the basement floor after the water and sewer lines were dug in. With no time to spare, we were ready for the house mover who arrived in mid October. Through all this, I worked as a full member of the crew, fortunately always present to give updated directions as needed.

The house mover had a crew of only three including the owner, and there was little for me to do. Once they were ready to lift the house on two huge 50 foot steel beams under the length of the house, Addie and I moved out into the guest suite because the furnace and ducts had all been removed. That is, all of us moved except Wunderlein our cat. She braved it in the cold house fully open underneath for several days during which the night temps went below freezing. Finally she came mewing at the door on the deck I had built on the back side of the guest suite, with its incredible view of Lake Superior. Addie was also content with the well equipped kitchen, with TV and phone in the bedroom – I had installed a Direct TV dish and we had dial-up internet. We were all quite cozy while the house moving went ahead by inches.

I kept busy in the guest suite with, among other things, publishing the first annual edition of a 100+ page skeleton breviary. (After four more years of the same, it inspired the more complete almanac breviary now being published by Amazon, *Lord Teach us to Pray*.) These breviaries were printed by an office supply company in Duluth and sold in bulk for under $2 to interested churches who were already subscribing to my *The Word for Today* worship resources project via email attachment. It was mainly a way to bundle the previous year's meditations on the art of prayer from that email project, on the way to finishing my contemplated almanac book.

The house mover had quite a project, and a show for those who drove by on the highway on a daily basis. He needed to take it 300 feet down a hill, lowering the house in stages about 15 feet, and in that process turn the house about 45 degrees to realign it to the four directions. But it also involved carefully fitting the house under the 15K power line that ran behind the house. The beams mentioned above, were transsected beneath with two heavy wooden beams resting on four trestles with numerous 6 inch wooden rollers separating these from the steel beams, and the house above. By building ever new sets of trestles in the direction of the move and attaching a heavy rope to his truck with a winch, the house was moved a few feet at a time. When the house had been moved into a proper alignment with the destination, a lazy susan plate was placed under the proper corner, and an arch of plank tracks built for the other corners. The house was turned 45 degrees with the winch of the truck. It was like clock work to this crew. Then came the encounter with the power line. It could have just barely fit underneath, but the mover was unwilling to take chances on having a possible disaster. So the power company was brought in to place a temporary power pole, displacing the swag of the wires drastically upwards. Once there was no more room for the truck with its winch between the moving house and its destination, he move the truck off to the side and used a very long rope across the site to a big tree beyond the site towards the lake, where a pulley was anchored and the rope brought back and attached to the house. For reason of some office work I needed to do in the house, I rode along in it that last day for the final dozen feet to its perch above the new foundation.

My other crew had by then already constructed the double wood stud walls on two of the sides to complete the foundation level on the lower walkout end of the house. They had measured well enough for a fit, only an inch and a half off, which was easily adjusted. That crew was moving fast to get things completely enclosed before a possible Winter storm. The house was quickly set down, the trestles inside on the basement floor and beams removed, and the perimeter buttoned up yet before Thanksgiving.

It was a Spartan Thanksgiving in our newly positioned house, but a true Thanksgiving nonetheless. Electricity and phone had been quickly reconnected. The furnace was not yet reinstalled but we were comfortable with our wonderful wood stove. We had been anxious about our enforced timetable so late in the season, but were blessed with a reasonable stage of completion to bow in thanksgiving.

My crew of five continued through December 2004 with the carpentry and sheet rock work in the new lower level of the house after it was set down. They installed windows, a patio door, interior walls, a temporary stairway up to the house (later replaced with finished wood) etc. I was meanwhile responsible for quickly insulating outer walls so they could do sheetrock. And before that, I needed to do the electrical wiring in those walls. Then there also was all the plumbing work. As owner, I needed no electrician's or plumber's license, though subject to inspection. Then after Christmass, the two with master's skills went back to work at the Silver Bay taconite plant where they often contracted to do carpentry work. The other three then continued through January doing more sheet rock and a suspended ceiling. The NSOP company reinstalled our almost new high efficiency propane furnace with all new heating ducts, also the water heater which had been stored in the garage. (We had installed a top-of-the-line freestanding fireplace stove in our living room several years before. It heated the whole house – our new high efficiency propane furnace had seldom run.) Fortunately, one of that crew had a truck with a snowplow, since January was a snowy month. He opened us many mornings to let us and the others in and out.

Finally, in February, after many months of daily having workmen pushing us to get up early each morning, we could relax. I could more leisurely attend to the endless odd jobs of finish work like wood trim, interior doors, installing a water softener, and then eventually a complete ceramic floor. Besides, when I wanted or needed to write, I could do it in peace.

All that was interrupted later that month with a NM vacation with brother Walter and his Darlyne. They had a two-week timeshare scheduled at Ruidoso for which they invited us to be their guests. All four of us were quite compatible, playing cards and making day trips. We took August our dog along but needed to board him there in a kennel for the duration – his first such experience; He was glad to see us thereafter and get a bath!

On the way down there, we were in a four-car accident in Ames IO at 50 mph. On a four-lane divided highway, I was following a car in the right lane which had signaled and begun an exit. But when I was almost alongside, that car with a young driver and his mother, decided not to exit and sideswiped us, blowing out my front tire. That car spun out of control into the ditch. But this threw me into the left lane, sideswiping a car alongside. I managed to get control of my car even though I was bouncing off of a car on either side. The car in the left lane spun out of control, was hit by a car following; it went off into the median. Fortunately, no one died, nor was seriously hurt. The highway patrol took us to a motel within sight of the accident, and had my car towed for repair. The next morning we had a new tire, and with a crude unbending of my front fender, we were on our way again.

Already in the 1990s, when living in IN, Addie was suffering from depression; For several years running, both of us went for monthly counseling in Indianapolis. Visibly she was seen to be in control, but the counseling sessions revealed that the distant affection received from my children was disturbing her. That in turn questioned my love for her because she observed my love for my children whom she claimed I was favoring over her. So she looked for and found fault with incidental things that demonstrated to her my insensitivity and insincerity. Those sessions were bitter trials to me which never reached resolutions. I tried harder and harder, but with her depression not being addressed medically, things were simmering inside of her. Then after 1997 when in MN she connected with a now questionable mental health clinic in Duluth which had a satellite office in Two Harbors where she did receive medication. Thinking to trust the psychiatrist and counselors, and hopeful to avoid becoming the ready focus of her problems, I elected not to go to her sessions. Only after several years did I find out that they were buying

351

Addie's excuse of my being the whole cause. Basically, Addie thought her way into sidestepping ownership of her mental illness, and the counselors abetted her with their preferred nondirection.

In 2005 Addie's depression gained renewed intensity with open hostility at the slightest supposed provocation. Often after placidly sitting together for an evening of reading, she would suddenly verbally begin accusing me of loving my children, implying that it was in place of loving her. It was her continued protest for their apparent insufficient affection from the start of our relationship. This, without even a phone call, or letter from them for weeks. I was walking on eggs, and praying a lot of psalms as my only way to consolation. It waxed and waned defying resolution. Ineffective medication lay at the root, though sadly not understood by anyone till much later. Such is the curse of largely experimental mental health medication.

Addie's depression apparently was further aggravated by her no longer being employed, while I had plenty to do. Mornings I was either writing or trying to finish my new study and library room in the lower level to finally get my books out of the boxes where they had been since Finland. It had been frustrating to look for a book in the many boxes. With plenty of room, yet not enough wall space, I made two-sided shelves projecting from the wall like the stacks in a library, made out of Douglas Fir. It created a classy physical setting, making me feel more intellectual than I was. I also had lots of yard work outside, weather permitting, landscaping and constructing flower gardens around the newly repositioned house. That, rather than lawns – with which I was done -- in favor of natural vegetation.

Late that year I contracted to have steel siding installed on the house. The parade of highway traffic, particularly the locals, must have been glad finally see our home with siding, and to view what gave the impression of a normal home.

352

One morning in 2005 we woke to a loud tractor sound up near the highway. In preparation for the highway reconstruction, DOT had contracted with a local pulpwood farmer to clear the forested portions of the new ROW. He had a large back-hoe like machine on tracks with a grasping arm in place of a bucket. It grasped a tree, even as large as near two feet in trunk diameter and fifty feet tall. It trimmed off the branches, cut it off and laid it down on a pile -- All this in one operation. It was a wonder to watch, having myself cut down and harvested many a tree. I introduced myself to him and found him to be a confessing Christian, quite willing to give me the gift of the trees in my area to use for firewood. With the highway contract, he just made piles of the trees to be later burned up. He agreed to make piles of my tree trunks off of the ROW for me to harvest with my chainsaw. This came to be a gift of around 15 cords of firewood. So I obviously had plenty of exercise for each afternoon after a morning of writing.

A bit later that Spring there were much angrier sounds to awaken us each morning. The highway reconstruction was finally under way. There was swarm a of bulldozers and earth movers removing the hill in front of Palisade Head to fill the valley in which the creek bordering us on the east was seasonally flowing. Eventually the creek was made to run in a huge concrete culvert deep under the highway. But on that day I still had stacks of firewood down in that valley on the ROW. I had harvested the mature birch trees knowing they would simply be destroyed. With just a wheelbarrow, I set desperately to work, dodging the deep ruts of the earth movers, to rescue my firewood. Fortunately the construction crews were patient with me.

One weekend that July, Addie and I had an invitation to attend my sister Caroline and Rev. Norbert Gieschen's 50th wedding anniversary, and Norbert's 50th anniversary of ordination, a bit south of La Cross WI. Norbert was standoffish Wisconsin Synod, so we went only to the afternoon reception -- We didn't feel welcome at their morning worship. I had never been invited to their home.

But after the anniversary reception, they invited everyone including us to come to their home some few miles down along the Mississippi. We felt welcome and accepted it as regret for a life of wasted family fellowship. That would be the last we met with either of them; They both died just a short time later in quick succession.

That year my one beehive made 13 gallons of honey – 156 lbs., three times the national average. Winter that year came on with full zest one day when I was getting more building supplies from Duluth with my trailer. I had stopped to drop off a chainsaw chain in Two Harbors for sharpening, and saw them getting snowblowers ready for sale. Inspiration came after driving away. I had already had difficulty in previous years getting the driveway plowed after we had the long driveway down to our garage built in 2001. Recently, we had been lucky to have had workmen during the previous Winter, plowing as a gift. I decided to buy a self propelled 26" snowblower. I picked it up on my way home since I was towing my trailer with enough room. Great decision! Even on a Sunday morning after 8-10 inches of snow over night, I could in a half hour clear the long driveway to get to church in time. It served me well till we moved to MO when I got my price within hours after parking it up by the highway with a for sale sign. Philip and new friend, Anna Maria, not yet wed, came to help celebrate a great Christmass that year.

In March of 2006 Addie and I took advantage of the gambling culture in northern MN to hitch an economical flight part way to CA. Allegiant flies gamblers from many cities including Duluth to Las Vegas nonstop every week for a week of gambling -- They even have gambling in the plane on the way. From there we rented a car and drove to and around CA for three weeks and then back to LV. We were merely interested in the country side: the coastal highway, the agriculture, Yosemite, Sequoias, vineyard country, Redwoods, etc. We made a special visit to an apiary in the northern part of the central valley from which I had for many years bought honeybee queens; I wanted to

see that operation. Our headquarters was a housekeeping
motel in Monterey where we played a lot of canasta in the
evenings. Once back in NV, we spent a day at Hover dam.
After nearly a month, we were weary and glad to be home
again.

That Summer I split a lot of firewood, but also tackled
some needed home improvements: namely, constructing a
front door deck with a view of the lake on one side and my
emerging perennial flower bed on the other. I also hired a
contractor for a sidewalk to run from the front of the garage
and alongside to the rear with access to the shop and my
apiary. It then continued on to the back lower level of the
house with its entry to my study etc. I really needed that
sidewalk for ease in carting heavy honey supers into the
house for extracting, and also for bring into the house
heavy items like water-softener salt, etc.

The biggest project that year was preparing a new
vegetable garden just off to the side of where the house had
been near the highway. The garden I'd previously had was
far down near the lake with marginal soil and serious
animal problems. The new one had far better soil, but it
was infested with rocks. After breaking the main chassis of
my rototiller with the rocks, I resorted to doing it by hand. I
carted many wheelbarrows full of rocks to the drainage
ditch along the highway. About a half dozen rocks were too
big to lift; These I simply rolled out after prying them up
incrementally and filling in under. One rock I never did
manage to remove. It was the size of two bushels. All I
could do with it was to wiggle it with a long heavy pipe. Its
top was almost level with the surface. I decided simply to
farm around it. Another project begun that year was an
orchard behind the new garden with the first tree being
moved from near the old garden where it had not after five
years done more than stay alive.

That July began the deeper frequent hospitalized stage of
Addie's mental health care. (It was then to continue
basically unabated for the next ten years. Dementia has
now erased this terrible conflict from her mind, in a sense,

355

to wondrously give her back to me. She has forgotten all the previous hostility and conflict. Not that she is by any means cured, but I again have her in a reciprocal relationship of love. For years her depression had effectively questioned God's love; It was resented that I had a confident faith. Today we have the miracle of her hunger for the weekly Communion I bring with me from church, and she eagerly looks to me to explain the Gospel for each Sunday.)

As a pastor I'd made many visits to hospital psych wards to serve church members. I could do that well, but this was now for my own wife. How does one then not feel greatly afflicted? Compounding this was the distinct impression that Addie was not being helped. The medications were even much admitted to be guess work. Yet the sadness was greater for her inexplicably still blaming me. The loneliness of those ten years was far more terrible than if I had become a widower. I didn't need or want anyone telling me what I knew perfectly well. My contest was with God, and so I engaged him as he invites, with a heavy diet of Psalms to attempt a dialogue, morning and evening, to dare to sit with our Father for presence and consolation. Fortunately, these psalms were already familiar and appreciated. They were gradually to become a spiritual lifeline. What is more, via Psalms, I have more perfectly come to claim our Father as my friend.

Eventually, in the following year, I did find a counselor for myself, a competent psychologist who was not ashamed of his Christianity. He was after some time judged to be helpful enough that I dared think he might also help Addie. That, far more so than her mental health clinic counseling. He was willing for me to bring her with me. He really tried to help for many months; But he sensed the impasse firmly founded in Addie on reigning sociology; Eventually, he sadly told us to consider placing Addie in a home, something I was not yet desperate enough to consider.

Always in the background, even from first finding our North Shore place, I had a dream of it becoming a retreat for pastors etc. When I retired from pastoral ministry I made a proposal to that effect to the bishop of the NE Synod of the ELCA. He gathered a group of five for us to explore the possibilities. Eventually, an architect from Duluth, being a member in what then became a board related to the synod, drew plans for up to four hermitages to be sited overlooking and close to the lake. In the next few years we were three times denied approval by the county zoning and planning commission. The US DOJ, aquatinted us with a federal law forbidding such exclusions for religious organizations, and was for a time willingly involved. They worked with us to prepared a case, but eventually elected not to proceed for lack of resources. They however advised us that we had a just claim. Briefly we considered a law suit against the county to force the issue, but the bishop adamantly told us, "No law suit!" I then even offered our property to the Roman Catholic diocese in Duluth which confessed insufficient resources to develop a retreat center.

In February of 2007 Addie and I, both long being in admiration of the Mississippi, decided to tour its valley below St. Louis, which neither of us had experienced. After a visit with Philip and Anna in St. Louis, we drove along the eastern side, finding much civil war related interest, particularly at Vicksburg, where we spent some time. From there we drove on south and eventually crossed the river on a long ferry. Then not minded to do more that pass through recent hurricane devastated New Orleans, we toured the Gulf coast of MS, with extra time in the storm ravaged city of Gulfport. There Karl had built a large Federal courthouse in sight of the gulf. It too had been damaged but was again in use. We talked our way into this very secure facility, and did an independent walking tour of allowable floors, unfortunately having to leave my camera with security.

We then drove the FL panhandle and on to the Atlantic coast, staying a week at Palm Beach in a housekeeping motel, and making day trips from there through the country side. This included a trip down the hectic interstate through

Miami, intending to go all the way to the Keys. We repented for reason of the traffic. Again we played lots of canasta in the evenings. We did manage to see the ocean between endless opulent homes and their private beaches. Actually, we did find a park with a public beach and got to dip in the Atlantic with more than toes.

That Summer I enjoyed my shop for the building of another "grandfather" clock. That one was for Karl who specifically wanted an English Tall Clock. I had only a catalog display for a guide. I was fortunate to come for the boards at the wholesale cabinet company in Little Canada, where they allow me to buy from their supply of hardwood. It was on the very day when they had received a shipment of cherry. It was still lying outside on their driveway. Through this I was allowed to sort out the boards I wanted. It was a scrambled pile four feet wide and a foot tall, with most boards 12 feet long. It was beautiful stuff, including one 18 inches wide, such as I needed for the front of the clock case. Good that it was a hot day because I had to load my purchase sticking out the passenger side window and back through the car and out through the trunk for the 200 mile trip back to Silver Bay. It was quite a project, including laminating a dial face onto a sheet of aluminum. After building the clock and mounting the special movement, I had a lengthy experiment to determine the proper length of the wood pendulum rod that was supplied for it. This was to tune it for keeping correct time -- I needed to incrementally shorten it.

The delivery of the clock to New York was a further challenge. That year my religious order of pastors (STS) was to meet at the Fort Wayne IN seminary in late August -- that was half way. The clock rode in the front passenger seat with the seat-back reclined, strapped in with the seatbelt. (That seminary is my undergraduate alma mater, though having been moved from a campus in Springfield IL. Their new campus was built on a spacious site in the 1950s and all of one piece by famed architect Eero Saarinen.)

After that retreat, I drove to the upper west side of Manhattan, braving the NY traffic with some trepidation. Typically, there are no curb parking spaces to be found anywhere near Karl's apartment. He was at work, but his doorman had been alerted, though offering no help. Asking about double parking, which I was already doing, I was told it was at my risk. Once the clock was inside the building, I was able to find a curb parking place a block away. It was so tight that I almost gave up. The doorman let me and the clock into Karl's first floor apartment where I reinstalled the movement with pendulum. Karl was well pleased, but I was embarrassed for the very pronounced mark left by the seat-belt – it had shaded the clock from the sun, which had elsewhere already significantly developed a patina during the week of the trip to NY. Soon enough, I'm sure it disappeared.

Addie and I drove to St. Louis for the October 13, 2007 wedding of Philip and Anna Maria in St. Charles. Addie was not emotionally and mentally fit for such an ordeal, but she went, perhaps to render token sympathy to Anna for becoming a Lehrke. With her, Addie had come to be comfortable and devoted. I was most pleased to acquire a daughter so far above the pick-of-the-lot.

My wedding gift to Philip and Anna was delayed till 2008 because it involved serious deliberation which was not quickly resolved. It was to be a dining room table built with the left over legs of my grandfather Lehrke's dinning room table. These I had seen from childhood stashed in Pa's garage. For some time I'd now had these legs, claiming them since Walter had no interest in them. Since Philip didn't have a dinning room table, these inspired me to construct a personalized gift these newly weds might prize. It had the additional aspect of being a virtual family heirloom. The legs were now near 150 years old -- (Greco-Roman design). Actually, it apparently had not originally been a high quality table, but I thought I might somewhat overcome their humble origin. I had taken one leg along to the wedding. I remember showing it to Karl, who was not impressed with my possibilities. Whether I showed it to Philip and Anna, I'm not sure. Probably I waited to tell them after, or if I'd come up with a dependable idea of how to proceed.

The legs were of oak, 2¼ inches square, thus not particularly substantial. And they were short because of probably originally being toped with a table expanding undercarriage. So my solution was to use them to create a four legged pedestal which would then be substantial. I also planned to add new feet to the legs. I could easily buy 1½ inch oak stock for those feet. But then after partially making a table top out of ¾ oak plywood, I discarded that and went again to the Little Canada cabinet shop where I was allowed to buy lumber. I purchased oak stock for the table top 12x1¼. To make the table more elegant, I bought a high quality undercarriage to expand the top for adding three table leaves. I spent days upgrading the old almost crude legs. In retrospect, I could have done even better with the pedestal; But I was reasonably pleased, and son and new daughter made a believable show of appreciation when they drove up to MN for Christmass with their pickup to haul it home.

My writing project that year was a two hour paper which I delivered to the members of my MN chapter of STS. It was a distillation of a significant inspiration that I had received in my endless study and contemplation of the piety of prayer. It was the fruit of the Spirit teaching me that the Lord's Prayer was meant by Jesus to be prayed in bond or fellowship with himself – we speaking and praying his words to invoke him, and he doing the real praying with us. He would add what we are not wise nor spiritual enough to ask by ourselves. I called this Christologic prayer. It literally blew away that retreat of two dozen pastors. Yet, I knew something more still needed to be said, yet without for several years conceiving of a way forward. I thought someone smarter than I would need to pick up this significant truth which no theologian apparently had yet developed. (Eventually I proceeded to do this myself.)

Actually, I had developed most of that theology over the term of the previous three years, and that paper was by then old stuff to me -- a summation. What rather occupied me theologically in 2008 was a different paper. It was the fruit of years of nagging consideration of the Brief Order of Confession as the opening part of the Sunday liturgy. Again as usual, my study was worship and prayer related. It was a problem to me that the Lutheran church had now centuries after the Reformation begun to start the Sunday liturgy with a confession of sin. And no other church, including the Roman Catholic, was doing this. I had not been exposed to that till my home church occasionally began to worship in English with the 1941 Lutheran Hymnal. It took many years for me to fully sense how inappropriate it was to begin worship with a confession of sin. That conclusion became somewhat more definite through my research into the genesis of the Christian liturgy with my master's thesis. Never before the Reformation, nor for centuries thereafter, had the church done this. It had rather invited Christians to private confession when they had sinned, yet were struggling with an accusing conscience, seeking an elusive assurance of forgiveness. They had been instructed to go to confession and receive absolution from their priest or pastor. Confessing sin in this new way on Sunday morning, and simply in general terms, I was convinced, avoided seriously considering and acting on the specifics of repenting and amending life. Doing it together with a congregation in a public worship was to me a cheap way to claim forgiveness. Sin is after all specific, and needs to be specifically repented, and then addressed with specific newness of life. One shouldn't suppose that with such a one minute general confession to be able to wipe sin away, and claim to be holy. It's virtually as if the following sermon then didn't appropriately confront worshipers with specific sins, since at the start of the service they had been completely forgiven and were wiped clean and free. I can't just now explain this more fully, but I did fully develop a convincing argument in a near three hour paper.

I sent that paper to the senior of my religious order of pastors, STS. He was my best authority, being an acknowledged authority on the Christian liturgy. He agreed that this issue needed consideration, and therefore invited me to present my paper before the entire society in September. Generally, the one or two who were thus invited to address the annual assembly were notable professors who had already written a book on their subject. I trembled to accept and stand before 200 assembled pastors who were not run-of-the-mill, but rather leaders. However, I managed by not straying from my text; And I was not refuted in the following discussion. It was an amazing victory over self. In the years since then I have occasionally been thanked for that paper, even recently receiving a request for a copy.

More than a dozen years before, I had made my own copy of a microfilm of the main church member records of the church in West Prussia in which both of my paternal grandparents and assorted other relative had been members before they immigrated to MN in the 1850s. This film had come from the Mormon Genealogical library in Salt Lake City which has a branch in suburban Minneapolis. It was entirely in German script, making it hard work to decipher.

It began with the organization of that congregation in 1724. They existed till a century after my ancestors had left West Prussia. I tried to take this film with me to read at the Duluth public library, but that was unworkable since it called for endless hours of study. So that year I searched Ebay for a microfilm reader, and successfully bid on one for $700. I installed this cumbersome machine in my study and set to work. It took most of my spare hours for much of the whole of the Winter of 2008-09. (Eventually, Ebay later sold this machine for me.)

With that microfilm, I uncovered a huge family tree of hundreds of Lehrkes reaching back to the late 1600s when three Lehrke families had come there from Westphalia. It was quite a puzzle to connect the individual baptismal records into families, and those families to each other by finding the baptismal records of the parents, etc. It was exciting for me successfully to trace my roots back through seven generations. Always in this search I had the memory of having visited this church in 1985 with June and Karl. That church must have consistently totaled 2000 or more members, since there commonly were 100 or more baptisms per year. I had touched the baptismal font where those baptisms had occurred. Sadly, the marriage and death records left much to be desired for their incompleteness. Possibly those other rites weren't always held in church. Wives were suddenly found to be different in the baptismal records, signaling the death of the first, but without definite resolution. Apparently, only the baptismal records were more complete since they needed to serve a civil end, birth being of greater importance to the state.

I had with retirement in 2001 taken over all the cooking and baking of bread and pies. Addie's illness brought a careless attitude -- she said she was done with all that. Only for a while longer did she wash pots and pans, or load the dishwasher; Then she was done with that as well. However in 2009 she began a brief recovery, knitting and reading veraciously. She spent most of the day upstairs in our family room watching TV and doing hand work I myself

363

never ran out of work. Addie only sporadically helped with the perennial flower garden -- Irises were her favorite. To get her out of the house, I left to her the getting of mail from our box by the highway, a scant block up the hill. She rarely used the deck even if I was enjoying it, because she had no patience with insects -- even fearful of my bees flying far overhead. That year I had five hives of honeybees – two were non-producing splits. My harvest was 234 lb., for an average of 78, compared to the national average of near 50 lb. Besides there was the need of splitting about four cords of firewood each year.

Ryan Mills and I had formed a mysterious and strong spiritual bond and friendship at near the time of his graduation from seminary. This, by the simple accident of his attendance at a MN chapter Easter retreat of STS in Minneapolis -- which society he also later joined. He had accepted a call to a church in Texas, as did his friend Kathleen who was in his seminary class. In October of 2009 they were to be married in Kathleen's home church in Portland ME. Addie and I were invited. I could not resist attending and even became one of three pastors officiating. We needed a vacation anyway, and Addie did it quite well. She was however overwhelmed with attending the grand wedding reception following. Both going and back we drove through Ontario, providing a view of lots of different styles human flourishing, and natural views at a colorful time of year.

The oldest of my five siblings, Bernice, age 84, died that year on July 9th. It was good that we had not long before all been together at the farm with a photo taken of us six siblings, to be long treasured. That funeral was sad for a special reason, also to be long remembered. Her pastor subscribed to the minority theological position that the dead will indeed be raised on the last day, until which time they are however simply dead. That's an early Old Testament belief uninformed by the breakthrough Jesus was able to teach us based on David's psalms. He also pointedly taught that when God spoke to Moses, identifying himself, he had said that he *is* the God of Abraham, Isaac and Jacob. Then Jesus added, "He is not a God of the dead but of the living. In him the dead are alive." Being the Son of God, he dared to realize that no way would his Father let him remain dead after dying for us. Bernice's daughter Jane was much comforted by my explanation to her of this at the following funeral lunch. I have ever since added Jane to my daily prayer list. I was not her godfather, but have taken it on via prayer.

On January 20, 2011, our faithful Cairn Terrier died at age 18. I had named him in German so as to remember his birthday: August der zwei und zwanzigsten – August the XXII (22nd)). I buried him behind the house beside Wunderlein. We wasted no time with extended grief for the joyful memory of those happy years of companionship. Addie soon launched a search for another Cairn. We drove clear across MN in May in our yet almost new 2011 Chevy Cruze to claim Rusty, born March 30th. He gradually became all black but for rusty whiskers; At first he was all rust colored. Another super faithful dog. (With great sadness, I note his recent tragic death in January 2020.)

That whole Summer and Fall went by quite normally, Addie being more stable. No hospitalizations for her, but I had surgery in December. I feared I was having a gall bladder attack, drove myself into Duluth to ER, not trusting our Silver Bay clinic. They diagnosed a bowel obstruction which needed immediate surgery; But this required a pre-surgery physical. Since I wasn't connected with a doctor in Duluth, I asked for Addie's doctor, who however wasn't available. In his place they sent his associate, who became my much appreciated primary care doctor till we moved to MO. All went well with the surgery. Janet flew up to Duluth to visit me daily till I was ready to go home. She even drove out to Silver Bay to bring Addie in for a visit. At discharge, Addie came for me with our old Pontiac. Our friend from Finland, Kenny Nelson, rode along to drive my car home.

I had a near empty woodshed by Spring of 2012. Asking around, I was connected to a pulpwood farmer who was willing to bring a truck load of birch logs at the price he got at the paper mill. He came with a load of 13 cords, enough for almost three Winters. The truck was so long that he had to wiggle his way down our curved driveway and almost didn't get back out. His truck had an attachment to grasp a half dozen 12 inch by eight feet logs. He dropped these on my septic mound – out of the way. I was determined to get them cut, split and under cover by Winter. First I, however, needed to upgrade and enlarge my woodshed -- wood posts connected with 2x4s and a corrugated steel roof with slab-wood sides, with pallets underneath. (My original woodshed had by then been converted into a storage shed for beekeeping.) Good that by then I had a chainsaw worthy of a woodsman. It was dangerous work, not just for working with a large chainsaw, but for the possible avalanche of big logs when disturbing the pile to select the next log to be cut. Once a log was sectioned, I'd split each piece with a wedge and sledgehammer maul. When the pile of split wood got in the way, it was wheelbarrowed into the new woodshed. This worked better and faster for me than a powered wood splitter. I could do only about three hours of such heavy work, working mostly in the afternoon after a morning of writing. They say splitting wood is about the heaviest sort of work one can do. It both generates an appetite and slims the waistline.

Over the previous Winter I had built another grandfather clock in advance of Granddaughter Allie's wedding coming up on June 16, 2012. I almost managed to totally surprise her with that gift. For some years I'd had a John Kirk Co. grandfather clock ad clipped out of an Indianapolis newspaper that I believed I could make some day. The ad was for a clock made by Stickley which they named Hallmark, from their Mission Oak collection of furniture. The advertised price in the ad was for $5348, and the ad was dated 1997. Mission furniture calls for oak, but I decided to do it in cherry for more elegance. I again bought the needed three 12'x12" boards for this clock in Little

Canada north of St. Paul. I had little trouble making working drawings simply by considering standard grandfather clock dimensions in comparison with the clock ad. It was clock #8 for me, and pure fun because it was to be a surprise. I had it made, and with a running movement in time for the wedding.

Then came the "fun" of taking it to the wedding in Dayton. I thought it would fit into my trunk and back seat area with the back seat folded forward. But though there was enough length, the case couldn't slip in under the top of the back seat. I had to go to the Chevy dealer to entirely remove the back seat. Then it fit, although Addie's front passenger seat had to be so far forward that her knees were almost wedged against the dash for the whole 775 mile trip down to OH. Karl and Philip, who had paid for the clock movement, and I managed to unload it, hiding it in the basement while Allie and Jason were gone. Then we brought it upstairs after the wedding with the couple away in their nuptial suite. Allie and Jason were quite pleased with our gift the next day, but apparently not totally surprised. Perhaps that was no more than, on Allie's part, there was hope for a clock from me.

With all of the above, could there have been any downtime for me in 2012? I do believe I did also sometimes work on those 13 cords of firewood in the morning; But mornings were usually spent in my recliner with my laptop writing this or that. My notes however tell me that in that year I published the first edition of *Lord Teach us to Pray*. That involved significant editorial work with my accumulated files on the art of prayer which had been composed over the ten years previous. That book was published by Amazon in a digital Kindle format. At the time it was simply a matter of giving finality to a significant piece of work, knowing that it was little more than putting it on the shelf. And true enough, it generated little interest. Still I was unable to let it rest. Every year, thereafter, I have each day methodically read through that almanac as part of my evening devotions, making minor adjustments and refinements. (In 2019 it was republished as a paperback with greater hope. So far, it's selling well. My royalty is only $0.10 per copy so as to stimulate circulation.)

Apparently in 2013 I did have down time, looking for something to do. After all, the woodshed was still 2/3 full with enough for two more Winters. So my woodworking shop called me to do another clock, just for myself. This, even though I still fully enjoyed my #2, plus Addie's grand clock facing it from across the living room.

For several years I had been admiring a simple new clock movement in the catalog of one of the main German clock smiths. It was a simple and inexpensive "skeleton" movement intended for a shelf under a glass dome. It had a key spring wind. Its attraction was the visibility of the many gears. Then they developed it further according to the familiar cuckoo wall clock concept, driven by a weight hanging down on a chain. The idea struck me to use that movement in my own idea of a simple tall hall clock case. I made it 12" wide, 10" deep and 7 feet tall. It has a full glass front, beside glass windows at the top of the sides to allow viewing the skeleton movement. In its simplicity it's a "not-much" but I consider the case to be elegant. I call it my #9 even if it's not a true grandfather clock. I love to hear it ticking from behind my recliner.

At our French River church we had a member who had transferred from Milwaukee, a medical practitioner, who for several years had with her church and synod gathered a team for a medical mission trip to El Salvador. She was going again in January of 2014 with others from Milwaukee, and invited any of French River members to join them. They still didn't have a chaplain volunteering, so I decided to go. I could be a chaplain to the staff of 20 doctors and RNs. But I didn't know Spanish to pray with the patients who would be coming to their clinic at the site of a refugee camp left from that country's civil war. That was where there is now a Lutheran congregation for the pitiful poor of that desolate area. They said my lack of

Spanish wouldn't be a problem; There would be Spanish language pastors from the area, as well as some from San Salvador, the capitol city where we would stay each night in a small hotel. The mission was being cosponsored by the El Salvador Lutheran Synod in cooperation with the Milwaukee Synod of the ELCA.

However, to hopefully make myself more useful, and to prepare myself, at least for elementary communication in that country, I bought and studied a beginning Spanish language lesson book, as well as a Spanish Bible, in the month beforehand. I also taught myself to pray the Lord's Prayer in Spanish with the help of a pastor of a Hispanic mission, a long dear friend in Joliet IL. I was quite excited and gladly bought my plane ticket, and paid a modest hotel fee. This was to be my own responsibility. It was worth this unique three week experience. The clinic was only a week long, but I was to go with the advance team to set up the medical part of the project, and then stay the following week to wrap up and store whatever over-the-counter etc. stuff was left at the synod's headquarters in San Salvador.

My flight down was through Atlanta, so I had the unique experience from my window seat of crossing the Gulf of Mexico, belonging to the Atlantic, and on arrival, landing after a brief loop over the Pacific. My first impression was a pleasant shock, coming from northern MN in January and seeing a profusion of flowers in San Salvador; But the third world impression was quickly there as well, reminding me that this was not heaven. Some other members of the advance team, two of whom I already knew quite well, were there ahead of me, waiting to welcome me. They waved to me reassuringly across the customs and immigration divide till I was processed. We all were then ferried, as happened most every day as needed, by a commercial van and driver, to a small family owned hotel near downtown San Salvador. They also served our minor meals in an open air courtyard with wild birds, trees, flowers and city sounds, serenading us from beyond the

369

secure walled enclosure. We were safe from the crime infested city with its scary barbwire dressing.

Our early team of course conversed in English, but the hotel staff knew only Spanish; I could manage their greeting and simple waiting questions. I leaned on others to understand more complex things – they spoke far too rapidly for my new ear. Our team retrieved leftover supplies from earlier missions from the synod headquarters, and then worked to make up packets of common over-the-counter medicines and health supplies some others had brought with them through customs. These would be gifted to the natives attending our clinic the following week. We had pleasant days of work followed by short excursions to the nearby city center shopping area, and for dinner at assorted restaurants trusted by team leaders from earlier visits. One day we strolled a verdant nature park in the cavity of a very ancient volcano within the city proper.

The following Sunday we were driven by our commercial van to worship with a Lutheran mission out in the province 30 miles outside of San Salvador near where the clinic would be held. They had a concrete block church building constructed over several years by volunteers from the Milwaukee synod churches. They have a pastor assigned by the bishop -- having an episcopal governance. It's located in a government resettlement community made for refugees from the civil war. There are several hundred small half-open-air hovels on narrow lots about 25 feet wide. Gradually they are only now after several decades installing sewers. There are major gang problems. We worshiped in Spanish, our leader sitting with me whispering interpretation. I also spoke to the congregation with her as my interpreter, and was even asked to concelebrate at the communion with the local pastor. That was regarded by them as a special blessing. It was a faithful mass according to our western catholic tradition.

Late that Sunday the medical people arrived in stages, some assorted 20 doctors and nurses, most all from Milwaukee. It was a privilege to lead them that evening with vespers on the open air rooftop court at sunset (this in early Feb.). Early Monday we were all carted off by commercial coach to the pitiful abandoned original refugee center where one of the bishop's pastors serves the surrounding community of poor peasant people in a building also built by Milwaukee Lutherans. The people of the area live on rural subsistence farming plots. (There is much unemployment after the mechanization of sugar cane company owned farms.) These families were driven to the clinic from far and wide in every imaginable full vehicle.

Their 50x40 foot church has open sides -- basically only a roof. It was divided for the various health teams, including our chapel area by the altar. There we pastors practiced healing by anointing and prayer. Sadly the doctors of various specialties had to set themselves up in the adjoined derelict abandoned row of refugee residential quarters. Each had only a single small room, and worked with little more than a stethoscope. The bishop had led an open air worship that first morning for a hundred early attendees. The whole complex was worse than primitive. The men's latrine was a large bare room with a long urinal trough along the wall, but no sink.

On Thursday the clinic was held in a remote area some 50 miles into the mountains at another synod church, half way back to the Atlantic coast, in a community where coffee bushes are cultivated. There was a developed community at the base of a volcanic mountain, which had just previously begun erupting with visible smoke arising from it when we were there -- possibly two miles away. For some mysterious reason the church had been built some two blocks up the fairly steep side of this volcanic mountain on a small plateau. There wasn't even a road up to it, only a walking path with many steps. So our coach was parked below for the day, and we all trudged up on foot. I believe they had an ATV which hauled up supplies, like for the pharmacist. Now the doctors were even more at pains to set up their place for diagnosing illness. Some set up inside

371

and some outside the small church; They were side by side with their assigned nurses, barely several feet apart, and with no screens on a wide verandah. Our pharmacist likewise, was on a verandah on the other side of the church. Our healing area for the pastors was under a tree in back of the church. Many of the patients who came to the clinic, working all their lives on the side of this volcano in sandals picking coffee beans, had visibly deformed toes from the radiation. It was a truly pitiful society of sober humanity, apparently resigned to their margin of society. They were all far more desperate in appearance than any pictured in appeals from LWR.

It took me a while to size up that entire project. There surely was an obvious need among these people suffering from various illnesses. And our little bit, apparently helped a little. Mostly they were out of reach of effective government medical care. However, the lost earnings of this group of medical people from the US over the term of a week alone would have gone a long way to take or bring health care with better technology to such disadvantaged humans. I flew home with mixed feelings and much empathy. From the comfort of my recliner and laptop I did, file a review, encouraged by conversations I'd had with one of the nurses who was part of the advance and wrap-up team, with whom I often reflected.

On returning to the North Shore for a frustratingly late Spring, that refused to want to come, I made good progress with the start of a new book on the Incarnation, inspired by my earlier paper on Christologic prayer, which had begged for further theological development. Now five years later, it's still not published as I continue clarifying. I'm however already assured by my peers who have reviewed it personally, or in part at pastoral conferences, that it'll be my best and lasting contribution. The Spirit has slowly dribbled insight as he is able, considering my not being capable of running on a full complement of theological cylinders. But what can one expect when a plowboy from the farm is plowing new theological ground for the church.

(That book, *The Incarnation -- A Life of Faith and Prayer*, has now in 2020 been published in a preliminary draft edition.)

I had often demonstrated to myself and others that I was able to write worthy theology in the format of papers, successful even with a graduate thesis in theology. In 2015 I dared to proceed with an attempt at writing a book of theology. As expected, I found it hard work, but was somewhat surprised with myself that I was methodically progressing, chapter after chapter. I was following my outline and advancing my thesis with conviction and excitement. It was an attempt more completely to develop the concept of Christologic prayer -- praying in fellowship with Jesus. To say it quite simply, if we are indeed called to pray Christologically, then there must be a foundation for that in the prayer life of Jesus during his life on earth. As a corollary of us now consciously praying with Jesus to our Father, we need to be able to recognize that we were consistently in mind in his life of prayer with his Father -- he already praying with all those who would come to have faith in him. For that, I proposed and pursued a study of the four gospels as deeply as I found possible to discover Jesus' spirit and piety of prayer.

I was addressing a problem in the church as I saw it through years of pastoral ministry, namely, that such an invigorating form of Jesus' prayer was being overlooked. We do know from the gospels that Jesus was a man of prayer. But there has been no study and direct discussion about what and how he prayed in those lonesome sounding prayer sessions before-first-light. The gospels provide no report of Jesus sharing with the disciples, after they found him in the morning, what had him praying half the night. And when we finally begin to read of his praying his Lord's Prayer with them (Luke 11), that discernible prayer burden of Jesus has been largely ignored by the church in favor of discussing what Jesus seems to be suggesting that we ought to be praying today by ourselves. To explain what we are to think to ask when we now use his prayer is not the same as understanding how Jesus prayed in his existential setting. Furthermore, he surely hasn't changed his intentions when

He now prays with us as we pray his words --
Christological prayer. That is., not about our earthly
concerns about ordinary welfare, rather about his concerns
for us, the eternal spiritual realities and promises.

Recognizing that the Lord's Prayer must be, and is in fact
our primary window into the piety (faith) of Jesus and his
understanding of his mission on earth to live by faith, I
determined to comb the four gospels to note in particular
the spirit and underlying rationale for Jesus' seven petitions.
To put it crudely but succinctly, How did Jesus pray his
Lord's Prayer? What were his fundamental concerns and
dreams? What and who inspired him to pray and how?
Certainly the Holy Spirit was working within him, but like
every human he needed a natural and concrete means -- he
didn't operate on direct inspiration. If it was only
Scriptures, then which? Jesus was a man with his divinity
disabled so that his prayers were not face-to-face
communion with his Father, receiving truth directly from
him. This was obviously for the reason of thereby living by
faith, and on our account. He learned to pray just like we,
so as to live for us.

All this is over against what Christian theology has
essentially been simplistically doing with Jesus, as I see it.
The church has simply almost collapsed the life of Jesus
into his sacrificial offering on a cross in payment for our
sin by way of suffering. That, instead of recognizing the
faith of Jesus in his Father's steadfast love by which he
lived from birth (living out the primary expectation God
had with his creatures since creation). Jesus expressed this
saving faith through works of love, showing to us the way
and shape of faith.

Hollywood has been abetted with its show-buisness story of
Jesus accomplishing our redemption via his physical pain
on a cross, implied as having enough value to save
humanity, since he was actually the Son of God. We ought,
it strikes me, rather to champion Jesus as our lifelong
offering of faith and prayer, with the climax of that faith

being his martyrdom of dying for the truth of who he was, our substitute, magnificently having faith in his Father's love for a resurrection. That's the thread of my new book, *The Incarnation -- A Life of Faith and Prayer.* By December of that year, I had finished the first draft -- only a first draft to address a significant truth.

Meanwhile, life for Addie and me had been stumbling along. In the relative isolation of Winter on the North Shore in 2014-2015, we in our Winter depressions began to talk of becoming snowbirds. (Snowbird was a term I well understood. All my life I was keenly observant of birds. And I was alert to how the birds announced the changing seasons and take advantage. It impressed me that they instinctively sensed weather for the sake of survival. In particular, I watched for the Slate Colored Junco, which is by many called the snowbird for good reason. One hardly ever notices their northward Spring migration. But when I began seeing them in very late Fall, I knew they were only briefly stopping to feed for strength for their journey, with snow driving them southward. They announced the imminent arrival of snow which handicaps these ground-feeding birds. The most hardy of these finally pass through after the first storm, desperately searching for a meal in the snow. For these I had been spreading millet on the sidewalk, since they generally refuse feeders. The majority had already moved south, and had found their plenty with the ripe weeds on the ground.) Addie and I talked that Winter of the appealing possibilities of various regions to which the snowbirds had presumably fled.

Finally in early May 2015, after the Winter had already passed, we got-a-move-on and headed to central MO. Jefferson City or Columbia seemed like a possibility to us. Realtors in both places had been alerted and did their best. Addie was not excited enough to be of much help. It was quite confusing also to me. And by the weekend we'd had enough, and headed to St. Louis to stay with Philip and Anna for the weekend. Janet and Mike joined us for supper in their favorite roadside dinner in Defiance. They naturally wanted to hear what we had found, or not. Soon we were persuaded to have their Realtor show us what was possible in the western St. Louis metro area. We looked at a few yet on Saturday, but headed home on Monday with the promise of receiving email listings.

That MO trip had not been useful or comfortable to Addie's spirit, rather a serious aggravation. The road home was a testy ordeal. By late May and again in early June, Addie was then twice hospitalized for out-of-control emotions. She was becoming violent again and they weren't helping her. They simply recommended a nursing home. We even looked at a few, but groaned over the pitiful prospects we found in northern MN. And what sense did it make to place her in a MN home in what now seemed to be on the edge of nowhere? How would that fit in with a place in MO? Would it work for Addie if we could by Fall move to a MO condo? We then quickly agreed to purchase a condo in July by long distance negotiations. I went down alone to look, not daring to stress Addie with the trip. We closed on it July 25 in absentia.

Now there was much to do to get ready for Winter in MO. Added to the press was the plan to install a steel roof on our North Shore MN house, already long delayed. This was now even more wise with our home possibly being unoccupied in Winter. That work was contracted, but still left me with many extras. I needed to safely winterize the house and guest suite. We decided on how we would divide our furniture and furnishings so that we could come back to MN for the Summer. As of then we had no plan to sell and leave the North Shore. I was relieved that Addie pitched in, capably dividing and packing dishes, pantry etc., including her clothes. Perhaps she had faith that a more southerly Winter in a new place offered a new lease on life. She was accenting.

Once we were into October 2015, it got more real and hectic since we planned to move via a U-Haul truck; But we were frustrated in finding help with loading. Eventually, and after being thereby delayed a week -- risking the weather -- we were able to hire two men from Duluth. This was after I had almost killed myself with loading things too heavy and bulky, Addie not usually good at doing things my way, nor the strength for it. The weather then already turned quite cold, and the helpers finally arrived one day at nightfall, making the heavy loading in the cold dark a most disagreeable ordeal. It was near midnight before we were done. Earlier that day Addie and I had driven our two cars to Silver Bay and left mine at the U-Haul dealer. The next morning, Addie was in deep despair with impenetrable emotions, reluctant even to get into the truck when it was time to go. We drove to town with the loaded truck to hitch up a trailing dolly, onto which my car was loaded and strapped. We had a late breakfast in Duluth to cheer Addie with her favorite breakfast dinning.

That was October 31, 2015. We drove as far as Waterloo IA that day, parking near enough to the motel to connect our frig with its perishable food -- though it was cold enough not to worry. The second day I had to constantly console Addie, assuring her that she would yet sleep in her own bed and new bedroom that night. She hadn't been there to see the condo, and couldn't be comfortable with my promise. We did get to the condo in good time, where Philip and Anna were waiting, along with two men Anna had arranged, who quickly unloaded the truck and set up our bedroom and furniture. (We found that the car had not been properly secured on the dolly. We had almost lost it.)

Addie was reassured by the welcome of family, who then went to get a take-out meal eaten around our own dining table that evening. She was beginning to function and it seemed that a fragile peace might slowly come. After the hectic previous weeks, we leisurely began unpacking boxes. I let Addie set the pace. That next Sunday we already found Living Lord Lutheran Church in nearby Lake St. Louis. This happy encounter allayed my concern of finding a Gospel preaching and Communion celebrating fellowship. (A potentially dry search for a church had me anxious. I now felt ashamed for my fears, which the Spirit had made unnecessary.)

I had brought my books, desk and computers; But for some time it was chaos for me not to have a dedicated and comfortable space to write. We had no place for me to set up a study. The advance plan had been eventually to finish the bare basement when possible, to include a study -- it has a walkout to the north. I wasted no time getting started with that work and made good progress. I set my computers up amid the construction. But first we went to buy new recliners for both of us, installing one in Addie's large bedroom and getting her TV connected with hope for its pastime.

That Winter of 2015-16 passed with only two light snowfalls. Our routine became comfortable, and Addie was connected with a far better quality of mental health care in our own neighborhood. She had a psychiatrist even I could trust -- after the fraud in MN who to my face had accused me of causing Addie's illness. Yet she had a crisis which had her hospitalized over Easter in St. Charles. However, they made a dramatic step forward (by accident?), taking her off of a long used medication that had probably been toxic to her -- lithium, still a standard.

By the middle of May we had had enough Spring in MO to hunger for a Summer in MN. It would not yet be real Spring in MN, but we had in previous years been schooled to be patient. MO was already getting too hot for us. It proved to be worth going and waiting. However, Addie bitterly regretted a whole Summer of no TV, we not being able to be connected for the slowness of the county's installation of underground internet -- Direct TV wasn't willing to sell us less than a whole year of TV, and their big new dish antenna didn't fit on our house, nor could be high enough to get a clear signal above the forest. Apparently I made do with dial-up internet.

After Memorial Day, our church attendance became a problem for the earliness of worship at French River. For a while we tried worshiping at Finland where the church had burned down from lightning, and they were holding church in the community center. But with a 2009 split of the congregation over the ELCA sexuality controversy, they were by then a small fraction of their former self; And Addie was not comfortable. Sunday had anyway been our day to celebrate in various ways in Duluth, including some shopping. So after fits and trials we settled into worshiping at the RC cathedral. Their main mass fit our schedule with coming from 60 miles away. We were quite comfortable there and got to know the two priests and deacon, all of who preached very good "Lutheran" gospel sermons, and the scripture lessons were anyway the same. Especially the junior priest fit Addie's spirit and ear. And the priests were after introductions quite happy to admit us to the altar. Even Addie learned how to posture and look like a RC at worship. The music was a major extra for reason of an organist who exceeded anything we had ever enjoyed.

In early July 2016 I had returned to MO for a week to replace the badly worn living room and hallway carpet in our already eight year old condo with an engineered oak wood floor. I picked a nice hot week but had AC, and pleased myself with finishing the job in less than the week allotted. I even took off a part of the 4th of July for a party at Philip's airport with his pilot friends and family. So it was a cleaner feeling returning to the condo in mid October. Addie was quite pleased to once again have her TV for the Winter. She was managing for the most part.

With my book basically done, I was free when returning to MO to focus available time and energy on finishing a library/study in the condo basement on the walkout side which had good light. The library floor-to-ceiling book stacks I had made for MN were happily reassembled, and once again I was relieved not to need to look for a certain book in a multitude of boxes. This time I didn't save the boxes.

Life was again quite normal with good medical care for Addie. She was even interested and comfortable to take a regular turn on the altar guild at church. She had so thoroughly enjoyed that work in Pershing and Finland. It made her feel like an angel. She was so proud of that contribution till one Sunday when her mind switched off. I was seated in our pew, eventually wondering what was keeping her in the sacristy. It was almost time for the service to begin. Was she being detained by an angel like Zechariah of old who had come to announce the conception of John the Baptist? The chairwoman of the guild was sitting just in front of me. She was also becoming concerned that Addie hadn't yet brought out the sacred vessels. I urged her to go check. No, there was no angel in the sacristy. Addie suddenly had no clue what she was to be doing. She was just standing there, totally befuddled. Such was the first bold stroke of Addie's dementia.

Mostly she was still functioning, and sort of, still is; But memory and appropriateness was slowly slipping. (She has no clear symptoms of Alzheimer.) I did still take her that February of 2017 for a week long visit with her dear adopted mother in Pershing IN, Clara Sowers. Addie much needed the chance to celebrate her friendship with this saint who had made such a difference and impression on her during my pastorate in Pershing. I returned home to come back a week later so as not to be in their way. Twice doing a round trip to Indy in one day was my happy gift to Addie.

There was no thought other than again to spend the Summer on the North Shore. We left for there after the first week of May, 2017. Almost on arrival, Addie had an emotional crisis that required hospitalization in Duluth. The circumstances and counseling received pointed us back to MO. She was too fragile to have any hope for a normal Summer in MN, and it made no sense to find care for her in Duluth, 60 miles from home and 700 miles from our Winter condo. Stage-one surely was to get back to MO and its trusted psychiatric care. Conversations with my children started them searching for possible nursing homes for

Addie. By the time we had returned to MO the latter part of June, Janet had a list of possibilities. We started with the best all around choice of a home. It was actually not far from where Janet and Mike were living in Ballwin, Meramec Bluffs [MB], a complete Lutheran Social Service facility with a full rage of accommodations to serve as needs might graduate. It's in the SW corner of the St. Louis metro area. Unfortunately there was nothing suitable near our more NW metro condo at Wentzville -- although LSS is planning one in a few years next door to our church in Lake St. Louis.

It took only one visit, during which Addie was interviewed to qualify. She charmed the social worker, and herself decided she could live there in an assisted living apartment, fortunately already available. I was intentionally quiet in the background to let it be her choice, till she had decided. I had often enough heard Addie tell me that she never wanted to live in a nursing home. Her LPN work for many years in nursing homes was a work of love, but she didn't relish a flipped relationship. We moved her in on July 12th. So she became an independent dependent in an apartment surrounded by her own things, including her TV. I was relieved to give her over to a staff including on-site 24/7 medical care.

Since what had transpired made it abundantly clear that we were then saying goodbye to MN, I nervously left Addie to manage at MB while I drove back to our home of almost 20 years to put it on the market and prepare for a permanent move to MO. Yet what a huge job this would be, and virtually all by myself. I was so proud of my sons that they quickly sized up my plight and offered to come when I was ready. We would again rent a U-Haul and they would drive it to MO.

But first, there were so many things or stuff to deal with, things that no longer fit the future but were not junk. I couldn't in good conscience throw them away. Fortunately, Silver Bay had a secondhand store that accepted donations, as did Goodwill in Two Harbors. We had split our stuff when moving to the condo two years earlier, and thereafter had no lack in either place. Now there were boundless extras. Some furnishings I moved quickly by setting them up on the edge of the highway, from with they magically disappeared, often before I looked out the window. Several times during that ordeal in August and September, Rusty and I drove back down to MO to check on Addie. She was lonesome and having trouble with personal hygiene. Assisted living was not fully successful. She had progressed somewhat beyond a simple assist; but we all had to tough it out.

Back in MN, there was so much stuff that was obviously of little value to anyone else. For this, our refuse and recycling company in Silver Bay brought an open top 20 foot dumpster. It felt good at first to throw in stuff that should have been discarded long before; Then came the stuff that made me sigh, and then the stuff that almost made me cry. By the time Karl and Philip arrived by plane and drove the U-Haul truck in from Duluth, the dumpster was more than 2/3ds full. They then saved me the emotion of myself needing to pitch in still more stuff till it was full on our departure.

Again I was having difficulty finding experienced help with the eventual loading of the truck. But first, after Karl and Philip had arrived, we needed to bring down from upstairs my heavy bedroom set. It didn't fit the stairs. It had to come back down like it had first gotten up, by block and tackle through the balcony railing. I had built the upstairs family room which overlooked the living room with a removable section of railing and a secure hook in the major beam above. My good neighbor and newly arrived sons took this dangerous work on reluctantly and nervously to get it over with, come success or tragedy. I had done it before, and my confidence silently mixed with fear, gave the assurance that I knew what we had to do.

That good neighbor of mine saved the day also with finding help to load the truck. His boss was connected to the Silver Bay football team, two of which were willing to grunt with us and earn a few $s. So the following day, October 23, 2017 we loaded. Did we sleep on the floor that night? Apparently we left the mattresses to be loaded ourselves in the morning. Philip and Karl drove away with the truck, leaving me behind to spruce up the house, no longer a home, delaying me several hours. They were waiting for me in Waterloo IA where we plugged in the freezer at our motel., Rusty and I had one room and Karl and Philip shared another.

We had a pleasant delayed breakfast at a Perkins in Cedar Rapids IA from where Karl took over driving the truck the rest of the way to Wentzville. Anna was there at the condo waiting for us, and she had again arranged for two men to unload.

.

Epilogue -- 2020

Since that final move to MO in 2017, I have been
reasonably content with life in a Wentzville MO condo.
Mine is a two bedroom home with full basement, which
I've mostly by now finished to include a study-library, a
full bathroom, large den, work room and wine cellar. It's an
individual unit on a narrow lot, where all yard work is done
for me. It was time to be free of needing to work outside
year round. I miss my gardens, and the view we enjoyed of
Lake Superior with its endless moods, particularly, walking
on the beach with Rusty. Here in MO I often see beautiful
sunsets, but no natural landscapes from my deck -- only
houses. And our night sky is barely detectable. I don't miss
the Winter snow, of which I've had my fill. MO is for me at
this stage of life about the right latitude for year round
living. Other than receiving a stint in a partially blocked
heart vein a year ago, my doctor and cardiologist smile at
my regular appointments.

Addie is now in a skilled care room at Meramec Bluffs, an
excellent facility of Lutheran Social Services. She has had
minor reverses which have reduced her to a wheelchair;
And she is increasingly forgetting what was said or has
happened a few minutes ago. However, she does remember
me and others, and she's quite rational. She had never loved
me more. Already in 2018 she was moved from her assisted
living apartment into MB's memory care unit, where she
did not do well -- it was a room at the lonely far end of the
hall, and the staff wasn't sufficiently personal. After six
months, she was moved to the skilled care unit where the
staff love her as the one bright spirit among the admittedly
mostly quiet and passive patients staring at or sleeping in
front of the TV in the common room. The staff loves her
for her natural wit and incomparable sense of humor, which
still shines brightly. God has also give her a friend. But she
still begs to come home, where her eroded abilities would
immediately undo her emotionally. I've up till recently been
able to take her out for rides and a sandwich; But that may

no longer be possible. She loves me with her whole heart, and I can now so easily reciprocate.

This past Summer of 2019 included many happy days, too many of them too hot for comfort, working in the garage on what will surely be my final grandfather clock -- #10. It was for grandson Ryan and his bride Amanda, who were married in Columbus in May, although now living in Cincinnati. I recently delivered it to their apartment, only a year late.

This biography has been an enjoyable project for the reason of being so consistently reminded of how blessed a life our Father has given me and June and Addie. And I thank you for your part in that gift.

Here now is an update on the current status of my children:

Janet has just retired as Regional VP of the central states division of Aetna Medicaid. She was responsible for Medicaid health plans and their contracts with state governments. She has been married to Mike Grant for 37 years, who works from home in financial management for the United States Air Force. They now live in Atlanta near granddaughter Allie, her husband, Jason, and my two great-grandchildren, Aidan and Caleb. My grandson, Ryan and his wife, Amanda, live in Cincinnati, OH and have just bought their first house.

Karl is doing incredible work as the Lead Designer and Vice President in an architectural firm based in Manhattan, where he also lives. He has overseen the building of several prominent federal court houses including the restoration of the one in Brooklyn which received many awards and is on the National Register of Historic Places. Goggle him and check his accomplishments. Just now he is redesigning all the public and support spaces for Carnegie Hall, including the exterior -- a project not yet fully announced.

Philip works in the military and space division for Boeing as an aeronautical design engineer. He primarily works in research and product development, and has designed aircraft on display at the Smithsonian Air & Space Museum in Washington DC and at the National Museum of the US Air Force in Dayton OH. He is happily married to Anna Maria, who works in leadership development for Ameren Electric.

Sola Deo Gloria

Post Script for this 2021 second and final edition:

Beloved Addie has on June 27, 2021 died and ascended in the fullness of faith for eternal life. Her victory over life is my abiding joy.